LIFE'S MYSTERIES UNVEILED

By

J. Todd Ferrier

THE ORDER OF THE CROSS

10 DE VERE GARDENS, KENSINGTON

LONDON, W8 5AE, ENGLAND

First published 1923

Reprinted 1943
Reprinted 1953
Reprinted 1978
Reprinted 1992
Reprinted 2004

ISBN900235 07 1

Printed in Great Britain by
The Cromwell Press, Trowbridge, Wiltshire

CONTENTS

Unto all my friends, those who stand nearest to me in the service of life, and those in distant lands, who are seeking the Realization of the Life and Ministry of the Regeneration, this little volume is dedicated.

PART
I.

Counsels by the Way.

*Concerning Lowliness : Imitatio Christi : Sincerity :
Compassion : Transfiguration : The Via Crucis :
Service : Nobility : Knighthood : Sophistry :
Jesuitism : Casuistry : The Order of the
Cross : Marriage : Girding the Loins :
The Pauline Church : The Holy
Breath : The Spiral Breath : The
Divine Life-Stream : The Sub-
Conscious Mind : The Healing
of Souls : Spiritual Diagnosis :
How the Master Healed :
Healing Ministry of
Healers to-day.*

THE FOREWORD The Teachings set forth in this small work, were mostly given to friends gathered in semi-private meetings. They are almost as they were given *viva voce*, and were transcribed by one present. This, in part, will explain to the reader the form of presentation, and the references to the same subject under different aspects.

Within their scope the Teachings embrace Mysteries of Life concerning the individual Being and the Planet. Primarily they are for those who are returning into high consciousness, and are accomplishing their Regeneration. For those are to be the vehicles of the Great Outpouring from the Heavens, as they rise once more into the various Degrees of Soul consciousness and power expressed by the terms Jesus, Christ, and the Lord.

*LOW-
LINESS.* Blessed are they who are lowly in mind and heart. Humility becometh the children of the Heavens. Pride hurts heart and mind. It veils the Soul from beholding the Vision of the Divine Love. Meekness and lowliness bear the Being on to the threshold of the Heavens. They are garments which fit the Being for the King's Presence. None who wear them shall ever be ashamed or confounded.

If ye would follow the true Path, ye must needs be ever humble. It is the raiment of those who would be Saints. Lowliness and humility are footprints made by the Soul in its journey along the way to the Jesushood and Christhood realizations.

Therefore, be ye ever lowly, ye who would embody the Divine Love and Power.

*   *   *   *

Most blessed are they whose ambitions are lowly, and whose ways are marked by gentleness. In them are no vain thoughts or unhallowed purposes. Arrogance is of Satan. It is Maya of the Heart. It is the ensnarer of the Will. It is the regnancy of pride within the Will. It is a dethroner of the Divinity in man. Eschew arrogance. It opens no door into the Heavens. By it are the windows of the Being heavily curtained and the Light shut out.

But lowliness of ambition, and true spiritual purpose, find open doors on the Path, and bring to the inner Being beautiful Light and Vision.

In all their ways of Life, and in all their judgments of and upon others, the children who would find the Great Secret and know the Divine Mystery, must be beautiful.

The heavenly traveller will be noble in lowliness.

7

Blessed are they who are Christ's at His coming. They shall enter into the Kingdom of the Heavens to reign with Him.

The sojourner who is seeking that Holy City whose founder and fashioner is God, will be an imitator of Jesus Christ. For Jesus Christ is the way unto that Holy City.

But the Imitatio Christi has profound significance for the sojourner. The one who sets out to become a citizen of the Holy City, has to find something more than a mere reflection of Citizenship. Imitation is not Reality. It is a shadow which may deceive.

Do not imitate. It is theatrical and leads to unnaturalness. It limits the individuality in spiritual expression, and hinders progress in the Divine Way. It garments the life with artificiality, and gives it an atmosphere of unreality.

The pilgrim to the Celestial City will not confound such imitation with the Imitatio Christi. For this latter is nothing less than the embodiment of the Christ Love, Life and Light. To imitate Christ is to have the Jesus Christ states and attributes.

Imitate no man or woman. Be yourself. Be true to the individuated Divinity within you. To be so will help you to be true in all your ways.

But always seek to imitate the way of Christ. Imitatio Christi is a likeness, not a reflection. The likeness is of the same substance, having the like attributes. It is an embodiment.

Such Imitatio Christi will bring the pilgrim into the Holy City, and make of him or her a noble citizen. It will adorn such in the garments of compassion and pity, goodness and truth, thanksgiving and praise.

Sojourner in the way, ever seek to embody God alone, in the blessed states of life named Jesus, Christ and the Lord.

8

SINCERITY. Blessed are they who follow the Path unto the finding of Truth, and walk in its radiance.

Let sincerity be expressed in all you think, say and do, ye who would bear the Cross of self-denial and self-sacrifice unto the finding of the Life Eternal.

Never say those things ye mean not. Let your words and actions convey what is in your heart; and never by word or deed lead others to believe of you that which is not in your heart.

Let Truth find itself mirrored in all you think, and speak, and do. Though you may at times find it necessary to keep the veil undrawn which hides the Sanctuary of your Being from the vulgar gaze, or from the curious, or the Jesuit, never descend to kaleidoscope the Truth. Where you may not answer or reveal, be silent. Wisdom often testifies in silence.

The children of the Kingdom of the Heavens speak only Truth to one another.

The traveller to the Holy City may not infrequently find the conditions of travel such that silence will be golden. But sincerity can shine through the traveller, even amid the silence.

Blessed are the compassionate, and those whose heart is full of sweet understanding. They reveal the way of Angelic Love.

Mock no one's sorrow, and say not that it should not have been. Rather try to be full of the understanding of each soul's travail out of the Night into the Day.

Be compassionate even though you must needs be silent through being unable to comprehend. The Angels of God in the Heavens, and on the earth, follow with tender love the Soul's travail through the Path in which the burden is borne, to the Goal when joy cometh.

Before Soul-sorrow ever be reverent. Where ye cannot understand either the cause or the nature of the sorrow, let reverent and tender love be manifested. Your compassion will comfort. And if ye should be able to comprehend the mystery of such travail, your love in its reverent tenderness will be as balm.

In this way ye may even bring the cup of joy to the sorrowing.

Sit not in judgment upon others, for the Lord of Love is Judge, and in His judgment there are no mistakes. Many judge, but few understand. Many blame because they understand not. Many are full of blame. They live in an atmosphere of criticism. Often their own states are formulated in their vision, and reflected through their mind.

Do not blame. If ye understood more the cause of the marred visage in Souls, the voice of blame would give place to the voice of compassion.

Blessed are they who walk in white before the Lord of Love. Having discovered the mote in their own eye, and removed it, they cause their love to beam upon those whom others would condemn.

10

Let Love distinguish you. To be the child of Divine Love, both in its realization and manifestation, is more to be desired than earthly inheritance and power. For love enriches the life. Love exalts the vision. Love ennobles purpose. The regnancy of Love is assured.

If ye love, ye will not fail in the way. If ye truly love ye will give Love. If ye give Love, many will rise up to call you blessed.

Love begets. It is ever creative. The offspring of Love are manifest in blessed ministries.

Therefore, love ye one another. To rule by Love those who are within our circle, is a greater thing, and more to be desired, than to rule a Kingdom of the Earth.

To love our neighbour as ourself is surely a Divine Ambition. It is the selfless way. Seek ye unto the finding of it.

Let the Good of Love, and the Truth of Love, ever be expressed in all your ways. For the Good of Love is its healing power, and the Truth of Love is its Radiance.

If ye love Souls, it will not be necessary to tell them so. Love is its own manifestor.

Where you have not yet acquired the power to give Love, do not profess it. Never say to any one that you love them, when you have not found a place for them in your heart. But pray for the Love to become within you, and then will Love look out from the windows of your Being, and its beams will fall upon Souls.

*TRANS-
FIGURATION.* If Love be regnant within the Sanctuary, it shall be well with you. For Love transforms and transfigures the whole Being. To be transformed is for every attribute to know the Divine Healing, and the power of equipoise which that Healing bringeth. To be transfigured, is for every attribute to be glorified, and be a perfect reflector of the Glory of the Radiant One.

When the Life finds this state of beautiful Atoneness, or the perfect Unity of all the members of the Soul's Household, and realizes perfect Atonement in the Divine, then the whole Being becomes transfigured. The attributes reflect the Divine Glory, because they are in fashion like the Divine, and in the likeness of God the Sublime Mystery.

Transformation of all the Attributes is through the purification and transmutation of all the substances. Just as the substance of a rose tree out of which the leaves are formed, must undergo refinement and transmutation ere it can manifest as the exquisite delicate petal; so must the substance of the Being become purer, more refined, and then be transmuted, ere the whole Being can know the glory of transfiguration.

The way to the Realization is the Path of obedience. It is not easy. It is much easier to say, "Thy Will be done," than to permit that Will to find its perfect fulfilment within us and through us. Obedience is willinghood to obey the Inner Vision, to listen to and follow the guidance of the Divine Voice whithersoever it leadeth, and to any ministry unto which it calleth.

To be willing that the Divine Purpose should be accomplished within us, is the Royal Road. It is the realization of this state that makes perfect transformation possible, and the crowning of Life with Transfiguration.

12

To the Heavenly Vision be ye ever obedient, ye who would know the glory of Life transformed, and find your way to that radiant state of Realization whose resultant is Transfiguration.

*   *   *   *

THE WAY OF THE CROSS. The way of purity is the Via Crucis of Self-denial. It is good to chasten desire and purify the feeling. Through the Gateway to the Goal means the treading of the Path of Endeavour. To attain the Goal, the Divine Cross must be embraced. The reward cometh only to those who pass through those Portals whose path leadeth unto the purified Life.

To purify is to make clean. "Cleanse Thou me from secret faults." To make clean is to follow the beautiful way in all things. That which is true is beautiful. Truth cleanseth the Mind from error, and the Heart from falsity.

Purify Desire until it be purely Soulic. Let it always be Soulic, even upon the outer planes.

Purify Feeling. Let the sense be always pure and spiritual in its manifestation. Govern the feelings from the plane of the Soul. Ever let your Emotion be currented from the inner realm.

Purify the Touch. Let it be Etheric. Transmute ordinary desire to touch and handle into spiritual quality then your touch will be Divine.

The Soul's Attributes are thus made pure; and their purification equips them for service.

*THE WAY
OF
SERVICE.* In Service give of yourself. Purification leads to a true understanding of the purpose of Life. Towards the realization of Life's true purpose, Service is a *sine qua non*. There is no attainment without Service. There is no true enrichment apart from giving. He who giveth most is most enriched. He who giveth stintedly is in that measure impoverished. Our attributes are as riches. They are ours to give. By right uses they are made beautiful and strong.

Whole-heartedness in Service is a royal giving of a royal gift. Never make pretence of giving or of service. Though pretence is an unreality, yet it has miasmic influence. It ensnares and hurts thought and feeling. The real thing is ever a thing of beauty, whether it be on the inner realm of realization, or on the outer world of manifestation. Reality in Service needs no proclamation. Let there be emblazoned on all your service, as upon a sacred shield, that holy insignia of Divine Love, which is its own manifestor, and requireth not to be proclaimed. Be silent regarding your own ministry, however great it may be in its reach, or manifold in its results: let love testify of it.

A Life fully consecrated, is rich. It possesses the most precious spikenard of Love. Than Love given in true Service, there is no unguent more precious. Its fragrance filleth the whole Life. The scene of Life's ministry is aromatic with the Balm of Gilead. In that Balm there is healing; in such ministry the Divine Physician maketh manifest His power.

To think Divinely is to grow like the Divine. To think noble thoughts and embody them, is to attain to true nobility. To be a Noble of the Kingdom of the Heavens, is a far higher degree in Life than to be simply accounted noble on the Earth. The children of the Kingdom are all noble-born. They are the ancient Nobles of the land of Israel. They were and they are the children of Grace. Grace is of the nature of Love. It is the graciousness of Love. To think and desire in Love, is to realize Grace. To be full of Grace is to be the living expression of the graciousness of Love. "Grace is a charming sound." Its vibrations are not hurtful. These are always beautiful and make for harmony. There are no dark thoughts in Grace. No hurtful images are thrown upon the screen of its vision. Its comprehension knows nothing of the errors begotten of spiritual stigmatism. Its correlation is true upon all the planes.

Its power to correlate is great, and it correctly understands and interprets. It beholds the mirage by which so many are deceived, and the cause of the illusions it can heal. The true only doth it seek, and of it doth it speak; and its healing power can change the miraging mists and transmute their elements.

To be a child of Grace, is indeed to be a Son of God.

*KNIGHTS
OF THE
TEMPLE.* The Sons of God are Knights of the Temple. They stand upon the threshold of the Vision of the Presence. They make their sacrifice unto the Most High One. Upon their banner is to be found the insignia of the Cross. They are cross bearers for the sake of the Kingdom of the Heavens. The Via Crucis for them is that of Sacrifice. All that is of the earth is left for the attainment of the full crown of Life. Their way is not only a path of self-denial; it is one of self-sacrifice. They give of the power they have acquired. They forsake all ambitions upon these outer planes that they may minister in holy things.

Forsake all, and follow on to the attainment of this Divine Sonship, ye children of the Light who once beheld the Beauty of the Lord within His Temple. To find the state of full Knighthood, ye must forsake all earthly relationships, and account nothing of personal value. The love in its ministry must not only be purified, it must be weaned from finding its full expression in and through the personal, and liberated from bondage to any one or any element.

This does not imply that Duty to all who should have your service will become less sacred to you. Redemption from the personal does not mean neglect of the personal ministries. Indeed, unto a Knight of the Temple, all such ministries become more and more sacred. Do not confound negation with transcension. Many imagine that they have attained to be a pillar in the House of God, when they have acquired the power of negativing all personal feeling. To negative is but the first step of the Cross. It is the attainment of self-denial through a process of denial of relationships which are most beautiful in the redeemed state. Let not such an inversion of the Truth deceive you. To forsake

16

all things for the Kingdom, is to transcend the state wherein all personal relationships and things are accounted as essential to your Life. To transcend them is not to deny them. Nor is it to negative beautiful feeling and love-desire for them, nor repudiate their claims. To transcend them is to forsake the state of bondage to them. It is to live above and beyond the realm of their claim and manifestation, whilst also having the power to serve within the kingdom of their claims, and give of yourself unto them in ministry.

Knighthood in the Temple of God is attained through Sacrifice. Give of yourself. Make sacrifice unto the Lord of Love. Transcend the lower in finding the higher, and know the secret of how to stoop to serve in the lower, through dwelling in the consciousness of the higher.

*   *   *   *

AVOID SOPHISTRY. Let not sophistry captivate your mind, and engage and dominate your thought. Sophistry is as "Will-o'-the-Wisp." It attracts and deceives. The children of the Kingdom are not to imitate the way of the wise of this world. The Sons of the Light must seek only the true Wisdom of God, and let that Wisdom be manifested.

Doubtless the Sophist considers the way he goeth to be that of the path of Divine Wisdom. But the way of sophistry is mostly that of deception. It is begotten of mind subtilties in which Truth is played with or prevaricated.

Never make use of words and sayings for the purpose of misleading the thoughts of others. Do not affirm anything to be of the Divine Wisdom on one plane, when it is manifestly a contradiction of that Wisdom upon another plane. For, though the manifestation of Truth be different upon the various Kingdoms, spheres and planes, yet Wisdom never ceaseth to be the Truth. It never contradicteth or belieth itself.

17

If that which is most sacred must needs be veiled from the unredeemed and curious mind, let the terms in which it is stated, veil it. But neither the terms nor the manner of their use must invert the Truth. That which is true upon the innermost realm, is also true upon the outermost. Truth is ever beautiful; and all true beauty expresses Truth. The harmonies of the outer realm are the echoes of those of the innermost. But discord has no correspondence in the inner realm, and is foreign to an unfallen world. Yet to deny its manifestations upon the outer planes of this world, because it has no inner correspondence, is mere sophistry. It is contrary to experience. The world is full of discordant elements upon the outer spheres. Truth makes them manifest. They are the resultants of failure on the part of man to recognise and follow the Truth. To say such inharmonious states do not exist, and that the discordant conditions begotten of them, never happen, because on the true spiritual realms there are no such states and conditions, is surely to prevaricate.

Children of the Kingdom, be ever true in your vision, and in your interpretation of it. If you see truly, you will see things as they are as well as they should be. Let the Wisdom of God ever guide you.

*　　　*　　　*　　　*

*ESCHEW
JESUITISM.* In close association with Sophistry we find Jesuitism—a subtle spirit that seeks to mislead and deceive unto betrayal. That spirit must be put away by those who would rise into the realm of true realization. The Jesuits have very clever mentalities. They have the worldly wisdom of religious diplomats. They set out to defeat and to win: to defeat anyone who crosses their path, and in this way find the goal they seek. The Jesuit is always

dangerous. Through the finest subtilty he will betray you into unveiling what you would hold most sacred.

Jesuitism is usually associated with the Roman Catholic Communities. But its practice may be found elsewhere. Other religious communities are not free from its insidious influences. Indeed, it may be found amongst circles outside of all ecclesiastical organization. We have even found the most subtle Jesuitism where Jesuitism, as practised by the Roman Catholic Community, is most condemned.

Let the Child of the Kingdom eschew everything that savours of such methods and practices. Never lend yourself to the unlovely attitude of mind and heart that seeks to betray others into committing themselves, that you may use what they say for your own ends. The Child of the Kingdom must be noble. He should strive always to be like the Great Master, the Lord of Love. He must be ever true and beautiful in his attitude unto others. To love one's neighbour as one's self is a great accomplishment, and it is one of the distinguishing qualities of the children of the Kingdom. Subtilty must not be confounded with Divine Wisdom. Wisdom in speech and action does not imply subtle betrayal of our neighbour.

Children of the Great Love, ye belong to the Society of *Jesus*. But the Heavens through the Messengers, do not train Souls to be beguilers and betrayers. The Heavens teach Souls to be guileless in all things.

"Behold! an Israelite, indeed, in whom is no guile," is what the Heavens would testify of you. And it is infinitely more preferable, and unspeakably more precious, than to be accounted a Jesuit of high degree.

Unto such Israelites are the Heavens open !

19

BEWARE OF CASUISTRY. There is another order of mental dominance to be eschewed by the children of the Kingdom. It is more than pride of earthly wisdom and vanity of mind; and it surpasses in its hurtfulness even the subtilties of the Jesuit. Its real name will be unfamiliar to many; but its sin will be recognised by all. It is what is known as Casuistry.

A Casuist is one who is subtle, and who loves to dominate the conscience of the people. He not only sits in the seat of judgment, like an earthly judge to adjudicate, but he also seeks to rule over the most sacred judgment of the Being. He aims at subjugation. He occupies a place of power, for he seeks such to be the instrument of his ambition. It is his aim to be Vicegerent to the Soul, and to be the Regent within the Soul's Kingdom, having all regnancy and power. He may be in Holy Orders, high in religious oligarchy, the pawn or knight or bishop of an ecclesiastical hierarchy, or even its head. Or he may be a teacher or helper of lower degree. The office may claim the Sacred Name as its authority, and make all its judgments issue as from the Divine. For this is done by the ecclesiastical and religious Casuists. They bring the Being into bondage, and fill the mind with fear. They exercise power over the mind, and dictate to the conscience what it must believe, receive and do. Today, as during the middle ages and the age of the Inquisition, it goes hand in hand with Sophistry and Jesuitism.

There are many most subtle forms of this ungodly and arrogant spirit abroad today. And they may be found in high places. By their fruits they may be known. They reveal themselves in the different degrees of mental dominance. Wheresoever men and women seek to reign over the conscience, the judgment, and the choice of others, there you behold casuistry.

There is no fear in Love; perfect Love casteth out fear.

There is no false desire to reign over others, in true Love: perfect Love gives perfect freedom in conscience, judgment and choice.

There is no bondage where Love is regnant: perfect Love reigns within others, through making the Son of God within them their true Vicegerent.

Where Divine Love reigns, the Regent over the Being is the Indwelling most Blessed Paraclete.

Where true Love obtains in the Helper, Teacher, Priest, Hierarch, in the Heavens or on the Earth, there is no desire to sit in judgment, or dictate, or even prescribe limitation of action; for perfect Love understands Divinely.

Lovers of the Via Crucis will understand that each bears the cross for himself and herself, and that true Love alone will help each one along the journey.

The Children who would find the Kingdom, will perceive that the way of Casuistry is the opposite to that of the Via Crucis, and eschew it.

The Sons of the Kingdom give in all their ministry, sweet counsel without casuistry, the Light of Wisdom in which no shadow of dictation may be witnessed, but only the Radiance begotten of that glorious Presence who giveth unto each true seeker, the most blessed Liberty of the Children of God.

21

The Order of the Cross.

What it is, what it stands for, and the ministry for which it has come into manifestation again.

Let it be understood at once, it is non-ecclesiastical in an outward sense, though it is divinely ecclesiastical in a soulic sense. It is never to be regarded as a new church in an outward way, but the expression of the living church of God in spiritual and even divine realization and ministry. It is not even to be thought of as institutional; for religious institutions, ecclesiastical and non-ecclesiastical, are abundant. The Order of the Cross, in an earthly sense, is not institutional, though in a mystic sense it is most gloriously so.

*　　　*　　　*　　　*

What is the Order of the Cross? It is an informal fellowship, here or elsewhere, for purposes of spiritual culture alone, and sweet ministry to Souls. It has no object in mere existence as a community or institution. It has but one purpose only, namely, the calling back of the children of the Kingdom into the high consciousness from which they went out; and, through them, restoring that ministry which once they rendered to this world. Many beautiful ministries have been rendered through institutional religion. Many noble Souls have passed through the ecclesiastical venues. We have all done it in our history since the Manifestation days; and all of you to whom this word is specially addressed, did it before those days in other lands through other formula and symbol and expression. And in the history of Christian worship and doctrine ye have also borne your part in other days, as well as some part in these days. There have been many beautiful ministries in the Church. Had not the saints passed through it, the Church never could have persisted. Had not the saints held sacred with holy reverence those things they felt to be most inward, in the degree in which they were able to apprehend them amid such darkness, the Church could never have obtained the footing it has done, and continued through the ages.

Let us, therefore, not forget that much beautiful ministry has been rendered through the Institutional Religious Houses; and that some of the saints of God have passed that way, though most of them have been burden-bearers, travailing amid the desert land, finding their passage obstructed as a pathway is obstructed through a wilderness, struggling with difficulties to find the full splendour of the day, ever seeking but never finding, ever yearning for the realization, but not able to come at it because of the conditions which obtained.

*   *   *   *

The Order of the Cross is an informal Fellowship; but it is a fellowship which is most real. There is no bondage, except the sweet bondage of following Jesus Christ—the Life of beautiful love, compassion and pity; and the Light, the radiant Light of His Christ who is given unto us, and is within us. Any outward form of fellowship which we may have, is but to give some faint tangible expression to the individual members, of things which are most inward, and in their real nature are to be regarded as inward and not outward. For the Order of the Cross stands for a ministry, and is the sign of the arising of Israel, the coming again of the Holy Paraclete, the real Parousia or coming of the Lord, the manifestation as the first fruits of the Avatâr, the Divine overshadowing of this world, made possible again through the Oblation, and the arising of God's Avatâras, or those who are illumined from the Lord to bear witness for Him of His love, of that love in its majestic ministry and its sublime stooping to meet the needs of all His children. It stands as the symbol and herald of those things which have been sought for, symbolizing that now they can be found. Its ministry is one of interpretation. It interprets the Soul's own travail and the mystery of its Being, through the understanding which the Heavens give of that travail and that history; for in the Heavens alone is its travail understood and its history known.

*   *   *   *

The Order of the Cross is but a vehicle through which that Name which is above every name, may again be understood. No formal membership to it could bring the understanding of that Name. (There are many of the Order who are not formal members yet). To understand the Divine Name in its mystery, is to understand the mystery of God in us.

The Order calls once more to Self-denial and Self-sacrifice, and even to Self-abandonment or Renunciation.

It calls to Self-denial in the chastening of the desires of the vehicles.

It calls to Self-sacrifice. It ennobles the Soul by calling forth all that is most noble within it, and to give itself in sweet ministry for the healing, the comforting, the enlightening, the upliftment of others.

It calls to Self-abandonment all those who have found the path of Self-denial and Self-sacrifice, that they may do just what the Divine would have them do in all things; to be willing to have their lot cast in lowly state or great state, though the great ones are always in lowly state, and great only in their ministry. For it is a great thing to minister to one Soul. It is worth while coming into this world to live, to travail, to bear burdens, in order to bring one Soul back to the bosom of that Love, to the threshold of that

Vision, to the consciousness of that Love that never fails, and that heals unto the uttermost the whole Being. For one human Being is more than all the world that is beneath it; and it is worth living to bear one back in our bosom to the Father-Mother. How much more then is it worth living as His servant to minister to the few and bear them back?

The Order of the Cross stands calling aloud to Israel. For all Israel shall hear its voice and at last shall respond. For the Souls who comprised Israel were the children of the Cross. They were the children who were the cross-bearers in this world. Have we not seen them many times, the embodiments of the Divine Cross in ministry to Souls?

The symbol which we hold sacred, is not to be held as the symbol of a masonic lodge. It is the symbol of a Divine Order. For that symbol of the Cross with its three steps, and its white ray, and its sevenfold colour, is the symbol of the Luminous Presence with us. For these things which we speak unto you are not from any man. They are not begotten in the schools of any system. They have not their origin in any earthly philosophies, nor may they give place to any such philosophies or teachings. From the inner realms they come. To the inner realms they belong. Of the inner realms speak they. Of the very Being of the Soul and of the Father-Mother do they speak. It is of that One whom we know that we do speak. It is of those things which we have seen and handled through countless ages, that we unveil unto you. It is the mystery of the Love which we have known, and do know, that Love that has never failed. It is of the mystery of that Love in its seeking in these latter ages, in the Manifestation, and since those days through all the travail of the Oblation, that we

26

declare unto you the hidden things. It is of your own origin, your own history, your relation to that Love, the ministry you once rendered upon this world for that Love, we have spoken, and do speak, and must yet speak more fully unto you.

Unto that end does the Order of the Cross have reason for manifestation on these planes. It is the return of the children of the Order of the Cross. It is the re-gathering of Israel—though not so to be named. It is the finding and calling forth and encouraging to the full arising of all the Christhood of the ancient days; not to be called Christs, but to manifest Christ. For the Christ is One and indivisible, the Eternal and Ever Most Blessed One. Yet He is within each one, each individual Soul; within every Being, the Son of God made manifest.

Most holy and blessed are His ways who hath called us in these latter days! Oh most glorious is that Love that found the way by which the children could be recovered and brought back into the consciousness of His Holy One within them! We adore that Love. We bow our whole Being before that One alone in whose Presence we would ever stand, whose glory we would ever shed abroad.

Children of the Cross, know ye whence ye are? Once more we would remind you. Oh Children of the House of Israel, know ye whence ye came? Once more we would remind you. Children of the heavenly Jerusalem, of the holy city of Zion, know ye unto what end ye are called again? We would again recall to you.

The symbol of the Cross stands as a sign of the Presence, and a symbol of the ministry of that Presence. The way to the consciousness of the Presence is by the Three Steps. The expression of the ministry of that Presence is through the glory shed. The White Light is that Light which never faileth, though men have veiled it through their traditions, and by their lifeless shibboleths, and in their dead language which has lost all its power of expression. It is the Light which never fails in illumining the Being, the Light of Love transcendent—that Love which is the Principle of our very life, the Love that is calling us. That White Light is the ray of God. It is in you.

But when the White Light is to break itself in order to reveal itself, it must have media. So every Soul becomes a prism or medium through which it can refract its glory and disperse its radiance, revealing its beauty, and manifesting its transcendent power. That White Light is the Love of God, God Himself who is Love. There is no light, no such Light as we have spoken of, without Love. The Light is but the radiance of the Love. And where that Light does not obtain, all the light possessed is but the illumination of candles and lamps lit by earthly knowledges—the wisdom of this world, naught else. But when that glorious Love radiates within our Being, and our Being is a prism through which it refracts its glory, it gives the red ray, or the orange ray, or the yellow ray, or the green ray, or the blue ray, or the indigo-purple ray, or the heliotrope ray—Love in manifestation through all of them.

For the Red Ray is Love in Life. It gives the joy of life, filling the world with purity, and the joy of purity, like the joy of children on whom rests no burden of conscious wrong, when they are full of real gladness, as all the children were at one time in this world. The red ray of glorious Love giveth joy to the whole world.

The Orange Ray of heavenly counsel, the counsel of Love in its wisdom, breaketh the Wisdom to Souls, breaketh it to their minds that they may receive and taste and see how gracious the Lord of our Being is.

The Yellow Ray—Love in its glorious adoration—is the inward prayer, the upward movement of the Being for realization that it may be a divine power, or a channel of it, to pour forth that Power upon the world—thus to give to the Being the Divine Tone, and bring it back to seek unto the finding of that One whose Love is so beautiful, and full of joy, so full of counsel and heavenly wisdom, so full of adoration when it filleth the Soul.

And the Green Ray, the Love outflowing in its glorious compassion and pity, full of power unto healing, touching the sorrows, the wounds, the bruises of life, and healing them through its compassion; touching even the creatures, seeking to defend them against the wrongs inflicted upon them by the wrong ways of men and women which still obtain in the world.

And the Azure, the Blue that is inexpressibly transcendent; the Love which, like a sapphire, pours its glory in its reflective power upon the world. That Ray in its splendid devotion of Love in ministry through the mind, healing through its purified thought, and its sweet and beautiful devotion, the distracted minds of the children of men.

And then that Indigo-purple whose very depth speaks of the mystery of God in His Righteousness. That Ray speaks of Yahweh, the transcendent Mystery of all Being and of our Being, pouring itself through His children, making them stand upright, and be strong and beautiful in righteousness, walking as His children, bearing His image, adorned with the garments of His righteousness.

And then the Heliotrope, that indefinable delicate colour, that Ray which speaks of the very Presence, not in the depth of its majesty, as the indigo-purple, but in its nearness, and

29

that which is about to be realized; and of the reverence, the Awe of the Holy One, the Awe which His Presence ever gives, full of that Peace this world cannot give nor take away when once it is held as a realization; that hallowed Breath which the Presence gives unto each one who stands in the Sanctuary before Him.

Such is the ministry to which the Order of the Cross calls.

Love that gives Life with Joy.

Love that is illumined with the Counsel of Heaven.

Love that teaches Adoration as the great power for the ascension of the Soul.

Love that knows no limitation in its Compassion, nor even in its Pity.

Love that gives itself in service with the Devotion only the Heavens can understand, because it is of the Heavens.

Love that reveals the Mystery of the Divine Nature, the Mystery that is within the Being of each one to make the whole life upright, called the Righteousness of God.

Love that brings the whole Being into the consciousness of the nearness of that Presence, aye, into the very Presence itself, filling it with the holiest Awe, making its whole Sanctuary full of the Breath of the Great Peace.

It is to bring these things that this ministry is restored. It is to bring these things to you, with the meaning of all that has been given to you of late days, that ye may understand the Love and the Wisdom of our Father-Mother, and that ye may know whence ye came, what ye are, whither ye are going, and of what nature is the ministry He would have you render.

How great He accounts us all in our lowly estate! Even the least of His children are great to Him. Beloved ones of the Father-Mother are ye! Be ye, therefore, healers of

His suffering children through the power of His Love in you. Give to them Joy, the joy of your own life, His Joy, the Joy of His blessed ones. Be ye healers through the outshining of the heavenly Wisdom. Not after the manner of this world think yourselves wise, or speak as if ye were worldly wise, or desired to be thought wise. But through the outshining of His Wisdom within you, heal the thoughts and correct the mistakes of the needy ones, and thus help His children to get back into the true paths, those paths of Truth which lead to the vision of Himself and the realization of His transcendent Love and Wisdom. And to teach, in all the teaching given to the children, true adoration, and all whom you can influence, teaching them to adore. For adoration is worship. Adoration is blessing. To teach all to bless and never to fail to bless, even those who cannot understand, aye even those who, failing to understand, would repudiate you and your blessing. Bless those even who curse you and persecute you. Bless, and never fail to bless.

That is the way of adoration in Service. The more a Soul adores the Most Blessed One, the more will it bless from Him. The more it blesses from Him, the more will it adore Him in its blessing. Let His Love, therefore, pour itself forth through you in beautiful Compassion that shuts no one out. Never shut any one out of your love. If they will not come in, you cannot compel them. But you can always let your love so flow that, if they find it, it will heal them. Never shut yourself up in any way. Though you may have to guard yourself against wrong conditions in the world, always let your love be manifest. You need not say you love. Love does not need telling, though it may be beautiful to hear of it if you were asked to express it. Love interprets itself. Its language is beyond

31

articulation through the lips. Let your compassion be beautiful unto all Souls, and your pity unto all creatures. Let the Love transmute all your service, even that which has been full of burden and pain, that you may behold how beautiful a thing it is. That Azure Ray with its wondrous depths (but of a depth that takes you up), expresses the devotion of Soul Service in sweet ministry, the devotion of the Heavens in Service. Devotion of the Being is most beautiful, not only to be devout, but to be full of Devotion; loving to serve; loving to heal; loving to help; loving to give; loving to rejoice with those who rejoice, and to bear, in the sense of sharing, the sorrow of those who sorrow.

Let your love thus interpret itself as His Righteousness, the majesty of His Wisdom in the outworking of His purpose. The depth of it! who could fathom? The vastness of it! who could measure it? Yet it may express itself through your own strength of love for Him.

And then the ministry of reverence or the Holy Awe. The Presence maketh that love flow out as reverence, till those who touch the atmosphere of your life may know the Presence is there. And though you may not have realized it in fullness, yet you will bye and bye. And those who come into your presence will share it, for they shall feel that His Presence is there. The atmosphere of His Presence will encompass you and them.

What a beautiful ministry this is. Unto this end has the Order of the Cross come back again. It is not to become a formal institution. No; only an Informal Fellowship. The moment even sacred things become institutional upon this earth, they go down into bondage. And there are always those who would put you in bondage, and the Divine Message in bondage. There can be no such bondage for our Message any more.

Children of the Cross, the Cross is in you. The Blessed Presence is with you and in you. Children of His Love, His Love is your very Being, the central and radiant point of your Life. His Love is the radiance that breaks within you; that sustains you in your sorrow; that upholds you in your travail; that fills you with a great glad hope even when the shadows have sought to steal across your threshold.

Our heart's desire and prayer is that all Israel may be saved, that all the children of the Kingdom may be found and brought back, with yourselves, into the consciousness of that Holy Glorious One, the Most Blessed Lord, your Redeemer, your Friend. Think not for one moment these things are too great for you. Who is sufficient for these things? None! Not one! Yet in Him there is power. He makes you all sufficient, even unto the perfect realization of Himself. He calleth you. He healeth you. He restoreth you. He walketh with you. He overshadoweth you. He is within you, and ye may come into the consciousness of His dwelling with you.

Ever blessed be Thy most glorious Name, Our Father-Mother! How wonderful is Thy Love! Who could gauge the measure of Thy glorious giving? Oh, our Father-Mother, how marvellous is Thy Wisdom! Who could understand the ways of Thy ministry in finding, redeeming, healing, restoring and regenerating all Thy children? Yet of Thy Holy Spirit, O Lord, know we these things; and the Mystery of Thy Presence within our sanctuary, and how Thou speakest unto us.

Questions asked and answered
at a
Healing Meeting.

Concerning
MARRIAGE.
THE OBLATION.
THE PAULINE CHURCH.

Is it well that the children of the Kingdom should marry? Marriage is a Sacrament. It should ever be so held in the thoughts of all the children. A Sacrament is a Conse-cration. The eastern and western churches were not wrong in regarding what they accounted marriage as a Sacrament, though their understanding of what it meant may not have been true, beautiful, angelic, divine. In the unfallen days it was a Sacrament to the Children of the Kingdom who came. To them it was a service, a state of consecration, a ministry. It was not a seeking for personal union. That was not sought in the merely personal sense. There was personal union, it is true; but the union had its foundations in the soulic realm. The love of the Children of the Kingdom was angelic.

All things are true and beautiful in their right uses. It is a perversion of vision to imagine there could be anything in the Divine Creation which was not true, and because true, beautiful. The perversion has arisen through the perversion of the true vision, the true understanding, the true union of souls for ministry.

Marriage is a Sacrament of Consecration. There is marriage within all the Kingdoms. But the union is for ministry. It is said that those who attain are like the angels; they neither marry nor are given in marriage. The giving in marriage, in the world sense, is not applicable at all to the state of Angelic Love. In that realm the union is spiritual. There affinity is central. It is Divine.

Union is for ministry, not for personal aims and ends. But personal choices are not wrong in themselves, if they be kept pure and beautiful, and are a fruitage of consecration. Just as the beauty of a flower is natural to the flower, and

35

should ever belong to it; so the beauty of union, even in the personal realm, should be ever present. And it should be full of joy; though the main purpose of it is not that.

*   *   *   *

In the unfallen days the Children of the Kingdom entered into union for ministry. They were not all chosen to be the vehicles of parentage. For their parentage was solely that they might be the vehicles through whom should come into manifestation again, those of the Children of the Kingdom who had to descend for ministry. Some of them became such vehicles.

Marriage of the soul is absolutely beautiful and pure. In such union, the two are one in the innermost, though not necessarily being what is understood counter-partal. In the Divine Realm, all have both the negative and the positive, the centripetal and centrifugal powers; and the negative, being the manifest side in one, and the positive in another, can bring them into perfect union for manifestation, so that the two become as one. That still can obtain right through all the planes of the Being, and make a marriage be consummated from the innermost realm to the outermost realm. And the consummation or oneness of the Beings is manifest in purpose, in their ministry, and in the service appointed unto them.

Marriage is therefore most beautiful when it is true. Perfect union is the joint purpose of two Beings consecrating themselves for blessed ministry. We are not unfamiliar with much teaching which opposes this attitude of mind, or this vision, for it is not merely an attitude of mind with us, but a knowledge of what obtained, and what will have to obtain for many ages in this world in order that the children who have been redeemed, and must needs return for ministry, may be able to find the right conditions to get the

36

Jesus impulse in the very vehicles begotten and generated through the parents. Only through pure parents can redeemed vehicles be given. The Children of the Kingdom who come after this age will come in Jesus state, not having to attain it as you have had to struggle to attain. And they can only find that state on the outer planes prepared for them through parents who are absolutely pure in themselves, pure in their intention, in their purpose, in their vehicles, even to their bodies.

*   *   *   *

Though this further word may seem a side-light to you, it is full of meaning. In the sacred Scriptures you must oft times have been impressed by the fact that angels usually have appeared in twos. This is significant. In the Divine Realm the centrifugal and centripetal are in perfect union. Through all the realms, they are in perfect state. In every Being who has realized the Divine, they are in perfect oneness. Where that Being has to give for ministry, according to the nature of the ministry appointed, that one can be in the centrifugal or the centripetal state. Where the two have to be manifest on the angelic world, and thence downward, you have each embodied very specially for manifestation in the two.

It is thus that the Divine Idea of marriage is to be understood. It is in this way that a divine marriage is expressed. The Children of the Kingdom must not seek marriage as an end in life, nor even for personal comforts and personal choice; though, as we said, those should be accompaniments. They must seek marriage for real union of Being, for some divine service in which the two are one, and to which they are appointed, because together they would accomplish more than they could individually. Or, they might be appointed for the ministry of parenthood, one of the most sacred ministries, notwithstanding all that that philosophy we refer to may affirm to the contrary.

Here we would say to you that, in the attaining of the state of Christhood, absolute aloneness and consecration of all the powers become necessary. In seeking the attainment of Christhood, a Being has to consecrate even the powers of the body. It was out of this thought, known by the Children of the Kingdom, that Monasticism arose. For the origin of Monasticism was beautiful, though the development was oft-times tragic. In life's ordinary experience it is not necessary to be celibate, but it is necessary to be absolutely pure. And in seeking the high state of Christhood realization, even celibacy becomes a necessity. Even that does not mean that there must not be union; though until the attainment of the celibate state, the Soul may not seek the outer union. For it must needs transcend the state in which there is the sense of the need of marriage. But when the state is found and realized, then the Being has power to lay down the Life, and to take it up again at will.

* * * *

The Three Visions of Jacob, illustrate the degrees of the soul's arising to that state. In his dream he saw the angels. In his vision he became conscious of their environment. And then he wrestled with the Divine Power. He wrestled with the divine power, or, the divine power wrestled with him, in the travail of his Being upward to the Realization. And then, it is said, that power touched him in the hollow of his thigh, and it was shrunken from that day.

This latter statement is a most lamentable interpretation of a Divine Mystery! It was the Divine Presence in him who touched the Life Forces, and gave him power to indraw them. That is what shrunken means. They were updrawn,

38

indrawn, and transmuted. This experience gave the soul power over the elements—power to lay down the Life if so desired, and power to take it up again; power to give in ministry even the Life-forces, and henceforth always having power to withhold those forces, or gather them up and transmute them.

The path to Christhood must needs be followed. The power of transmutation has to be acquired. That was the meaning in principle, of the Monastic Idea. It was for purification. Yet not alone for purification. For there is purity when the desire to be pure is present. With the desire essaying to be pure, all the Being must be yearning to be pure. But Monasticism had also this end in view, namely, to attain the power by which the forces are transmuted, and turned into Divine Power in the Being.

This will help you to understand many things. It is possible to be in Jesushood and Spiritual Christhood, and yet to be in union on all the planes. On the path to Christhood the individual soul has to learn how to attain. To attain is not only to attain the Realization which comes in Jesushood and Spiritual Christhood; it is to attain the power over the whole Being. The attributes must be fully trained and their labours fully accomplished, so that they can be commanded to go here, or go there, to come hither, to serve in this way or in that way. And even the Life-stream of the Life-forces share in that victory and obedience when commanded to flow inward, giving power for magnetic outpouring; or commanded to give for procreation, for the generation of forms for the Children of the Kingdom—who are to come.

This will give you an idea of the sacredness of union in the Children of the Kingdom, what a Sacrament marriage

39

was to them, and how each had the power to lay down Life itself in the form of the Life-forces, whilst always retaining the power to take them up again. And this ministry was in response to no mere earthly desire, no common fallen soul passion, but was the Divine Passion of the Being laid on the altar for blessed ministry.

The Children of the Kingdom should seek union only with those who are of the Kingdom, and consecrate all their powers unto the Kingdom of God, for manifestation of the Life of the Kingdom, in the ministry of the Kingdom, and the manifestation which that Kingdom has to make through them, whether in the ministry of interpretation, or in the ministry of healing, or in the ministry of beautiful parent-hood. And we would here say, notwithstanding all that has of late been written and spoken to the contrary, that there is nothing more beautiful than motherhood and fatherhood when it is from the innermost realms, a consecration for the divine service. It is one of the most sacred ministries. The degradation of the Idea in the wrong uses of the powers and the relationships, is that which brought so much disaster, and brings great disaster still, upon the distraught world. But everything is beautiful in the Divine Realm. There is no power or function that is not most Sacred. Even in the childhood manifestations from that Realm, all things are ever most beautiful. And, moreover, as souls rise in their consciousness, every new realm they enter, they enter it as a little child. And there is generation upon all the Realms, though not after the nature of its process on the outermost.

Could you interpret to us something of the mystery lying behind the symbolism in the allegory of the Feet Washing, as for instance, "He girt His loins with a towel?"

It is not easy to interpret that saying, though the former question will enable us to say something concerning it. The question is one which touches the very heart of the mystery of the burden-bearing of the Oblation. The Towel is an article used for the wiping and drying of the body. "He laid aside His garments," you read in the allegory. That meant the laying aside of the garments of the Christhood attributes. "And girt His loins with a towel." That signifies, He took upon Himself, because it was so appointed unto Him, the badge of a bondservant.

The bondservant is one who is in servitude or bondage to the body. The very cause of His agony in every life, was the consciousness that He was a bondservant. From that bondage He could not be freed, until all that was appointed for each life had been accomplished: then He was liberated, and rose above the servitude. To gird the loins is the symbol of putting the Reins, or the Life-force power into bondage. But in His case, the purpose was that of the Towel. It was the wiping or the blotting out of conditions.

It is impossible to unveil a ministry so sacred, and a history so tragic, as is embodied in that statement. But, we would say this, that the greater part of the Oblation had to be accomplished by means of the uses of the Life-forces. And therein lies the meaning of His descending into the hell states; not necessarily going into the homes where hell reigned, but into the states in Himself where the fires of hell burned. He passed through Gehenna, the Valley of the Fires. Most people think that that fire of Gehenna was

41

that which burned in the valley of Jehoshaphat outside of Jerusalem, where all the refuse of the city was burned. But Gehenna was that Valley, or low-lying state, in which the very passions of men and women burned and consumed them; and in the path of the Oblation, He had to pass down into those fires. Gehinnom was the valley of lamentation, dark and fearful, where all consciousness of the Glory and Divine Life seemed lost. It was the darkness begotten of the states in Gehenna. He went into it.

You will see the meaning of the girding of the loins with a towel to wipe the feet of the disciples after they were cleansed. He had to wipe the feet of all the children, by wiping away the effects of the tragedy of this world. So constituted was He in every body which He had to enter into and function through, sometimes as a man, sometimes as a woman, that the body was highly magnetic. Its elements were, in a comparative sense, fluidic. So great was the magnetic attraction of it, and the power that was reigning in Him and operating through Him, that, even whilst by the very state He was clouded in His lower consciousness, He attracted the evil things that had been formulated. These were the evil forms which afflicted the children. They fastened on them and, like vampires, drained them of their magnetism, whilst making them repeat the very passions through their vehicles by means of which these terrible forms had been generated. When He passed along the *via crucis* to deal with the forms which had been apportioned to be blotted out in each of the forty lives, He too was oppressed. Being so magnetic, He attracted them. But He was so constituted that He held them, absorbed their elements, drew them into His body and, in the Life-stream, transmuted them.

42

In the process He was made to feel exactly as the children felt. He was made to desire exactly what they desired. Oft-times he had actually to do what they had done in the generation of these awful forms. It was then that "He was made like unto His brethren, even the least," in the lowliness of the estate into which He had to enter for the purpose of the healing of the conditions.

*   *   *   *

Now, though we may not unveil to you all that it meant, yet you may understand this, that it was done through attracting the images, then absorbing them, and then transmuting their elements, eliminating the elements again after they were changed; and that it was accomplished in many of the lives through the Life-forces. It was that which gave Him sorrow unspeakable.

But there were other lives in which He had to deal with the occult powers, where His pains, suffering and agony were also unspeakable. In every life, after the work apportioned to that life had been accomplished, He rose. And as it was said of Jacob, so of Him may it be said; He was again touched, and once more attained the power of indrawing, of ceasing to be the bondservant. For throughout the ages He retained the power to lay down His life again if it were necessary, and the power to take it up again: this power He received from the Father-Mother. But during the years in which He had to be as a bondservant, He had not that power. He had only the power of giving. So He had to give unto the uttermost. Yet at the end of each life He had the power to take up His life again.

In this way was the healing done. The Towel represented the badge of His bondservice. The basin represented the Bowl, or Cup of His own life into which, from the Sacred Chalice, it is said, the water was poured for the washing.

Oh ye who have struggled to attain, and still struggle to be all you want to be, know this, that He passed through all the states of travail, being girt with a Towel, or the garment of the bondservant. His very coming to Simon Peter in the allegory, was the symbol in allegory of His approach to the western world in the latter days of the Oblation. For in that world Simon Peter reigns: on the one hand ecclesiastically through the church that claims to have the Chair of Peter; on the other hand, religiously through those churches which are of the Mind. For all these need cleansing that their vision may be true and their ways beautiful. For His last incarnations were chiefly in the western world, right from the medieval period until He appeared when the Oblation was to be fully accomplished.

We are ourselves on the threshold of the day that has dawned as a result of His passing through Gehinnom, or the Valley of Darkness, and Gehenna the pestilential Fires where the evil things were consumed and the dark things put away. And the day has broken in which no child need any longer be a bondservant, but a free man, healed, re-deemed, restored, raised up, crowned with the dignity of his manhood and her womanhood, true childhood to the Father-Mother.

*   *   *   *

Now whether we have answered this question to make it clear enough for you, it is difficult for us to say. We see the vision, we see the history, we see the tragedy, and more. And though so much has had to be veiled, we would indeed rejoice if sufficient had been stated to make it clear to you what the tragedy of the travail was.

Might we know more of the history in these days, and in other days, of the Pauline Church?

The Master did not found a Church; nor did His beloved friends found any Church. His friends had fellowships which might be spoken of as intimate Brotherhoods. The community at Jerusalem—the Fellowship—received into its circle those who were not really ready to come in; and through these not having true understanding of the Teachings, dissensions arose.

*   *   *   *

Paul appeared on the scene. He did not know the Master. He knew nothing of His Teachings except from hearsay. But he came to the Brethren, saying that he had had a vision of Him.

It was quite possible for him to have a vision, and hear a voice within himself. But it was also possible for the Astral World to deceive him; for it was not then purified. The Oblation had only begun. He was, as he himself said, an Hebrew of the Hebrews, a Jew of the Jews, trained in rabbinical law, scholarly, eloquent, understanding the Greek thought also, and sitting at the feet of Gamaliel.

He sought interviews with the Brethren. It is said that he and Barnabas went up to Jerusalem to discuss with the Brethren the question of whether the new converts should eat, or refrain from eating, meats offered to idols. That is an astral mirage. He went to Jerusalem to discuss the doctrine of the Redemption. And whilst there he was told by those who had heard the Oblation unveiled, so far as it then could be unveiled, from the lips of the Master Himself, of what nature it was, and how it was to be borne as a Sin-Offering. The very manuscripts containing the

45

Teachings were shown to Paul. That by Matthew was not used, as it did not contain the deeper Teachings, with rare exceptions. But the Logia written by a disciple named John, contained the Sayings on the Oblation, the allegories in which it was embodied, set forth, illustrated and yet veiled. And from such sections as suited him, Paul took portions. These are to be found in the Pauline epistles. *They are those wonderful mystical sayings which are projected into his theses*, and oft-times found to be quite foreign to the thesis begun by him, and a turn given to them not infrequently most personal. For Paul is the most personal being in all the Bible. Everything he does, and everything he says, gathers around the " I."

There was nothing of that characteristic in the Master, nor in His intimate ones. The person that is the vehicle of Divine Revelation is a little child. And it is the Lord alone who speaks within the Being, and through the Being, of one who is sent. And the one sent, speaks not of himself or of herself.

Paul founded the churches. Historical Christianity dates its development from Paul.

Is it not extraordinary that the western world can worship the Master, think of the disciples as Saints, and yet follow one who did not know the Master? Accept as the highest Authority one who is said to have been born out of due time? Take as the true presentation, the sayings of one who did not hear the profound unveilings amid the sorrow of the Gethsemane?

He created communities everywhere, and they rose up as Churches. To-day the western world is flooded with them. Many were gathered in to the new communities who were beautiful. Many were gathered in who understood nothing of the beautiful Teachings. *The Pauline Church was*

46

founded to defeat the vision of the Manifestation. But let it be understood that that was not Paul's intention. But it was the intention of the enemies of the vision. He was used as the vehicle by these astral occult powers. They preceded the Master, and they followed Him. They worked even whilst the Manifestation was proceeding. They made of the Oblation a burden so intensified for Him by the conditions which they generated, that His sorrows were multiplied in manifold measure. So terrible were the conditions resulting from their operations that, but for the Divine Love in its wonderful ministry to Him, He could never have returned, and would have had to be gathered up into the Divine Bosom until such time as another Manifestation could be given.

We would not now follow the comparison of what was done then, with the Pauline church to-day. There is not time, and we would fain this evening be relieved of un- veiling that. But we would say this. That Church has ever been filled with the spirit of Sophistry, Jesuitism and Casuistry, in all its branches; that it has played with Divine Secrets; that it has sought to discover and unveil the secrets of others which are open alone to the Divine World; that it has sat in judgment as Judge of Truth; that it has sat in judgment upon the souls of men and women, without understanding their spiritual state or the nature of the Being; that it has sought to make them captive to itself, to bring them into bondage on the outer planes, through formula and ritual; on the mental planes through the idea of authority exercised by Pope, Archbishop, Synod, Pres- bytery or Congregation; in the emotional planes through the fear of judgment; or in the Divine Realm of the Being, through bringing down the adoring love of the Innermost

47

to centre upon and express itself in the things that are only shadows of the great and most Blessed Realities.

When that one whose loins were girt with a Towel (mystically understood as set forth in the allegory), returned and found that which had been done, and beheld how it was making the fruitage of the travail difficult to gather, and making the Travail of the Oblation find itself still as if it were incomplete, judge ye with me of what His sorrow was.

For you, let the Oblation which has been accomplished, be as a sweet savour unto your thought, your feeling, and your love. Have this consciousness within you, that it was borne for the healing of the world, and, in many respects, for the healing of yourselves. And be ye healed. Let the shadows of Gehinnom flee away, since the new day has broken, and the glory of the Lord is being unveiled. And let the recrudescence by way of adumbration of the fires known as Gehenna, be all healed, the desires purified, the hurt to the desires mollified, the powers made strong and beautiful again, and the hurt to them perfectly healed. For the Great Love who has healed the Mind of the Planet through the Oblation, and is healing all His children within the Planet's Household, healeth you in your Desire-body, in your Mental-body, in your Emotional body, to fill each of them with the glory of His Presence, and to make manifest His glory right through all your Being, even through the body of the outer manifestation.

Unto this end, be ye in union with your Lord. Let your union be a true Marriage. If so, all else will be directed from Him. Be His Apostles, the Interpreters in life of the Mystery of His Love and His Wisdom. Be His Church, His true Ecclesia. That Church is informulate without, though of Divine Fashion within; informulate and unlike the institutions on the outer planes which pass for this

Ecclesia, yet a glorious Divine Reflection within. And in the union of all souls, His own Body, as it has been called, the corporate expression of Himself, be ye of His Church. Express the real Ecclesia in your Fellowship. Seek not to be a church of mere ritual, or mental affirmations, or emotional display, but one founded upon the Love Eternal and Glorious, whose regnality reveals the Divine Love and Wisdom in all its ways, and is the living embodiment of the Eternal and Ever Most Blessed One.

Ye are of the Church of God, to be living stones, vibrating, scintillating, reflecting, refracting, embodying His glory, which is the Radiance of Love in its most splendid realization within, and magnificent outpouring.

We have led you far, perhaps not whither ye would fain have gone. Yet we have led you to the place where you may see with the illumined understanding, the Divine Mysteries of Marriage, of the Oblation, and of the true Ecclesia of God.

Would you teach us concerning the nature of

(1)   The Holy Breath.

(2)   The Spiral Breath.

(3)   The Divine Life-Stream.

THE HOLY   The Holy Breath or Spirit, as it is rendered in
BREATH.   the New Testament, or Holy Ghost or Comforter
as it is also translated, is what is called the Paraclete. There
are Angelic Breaths. These are like zephyrs wafted on to
and within the planes of the Being. They come to exhila-
rate and sweeten, to stimulate and to exalt, to comfort and
to encourage. But the Breaths of the Angelic World are
not to be confounded with the Hagiou Pneuma. This is
the term used for Holy Spirit in the Greek New Testament.
It is also rendered Paraclete, or expressed by the word.

The Paraclete is the Holy Pneuma who was to come to
the disciples in such fulness that they would remember
all things. But though He was to come to the disciples
as the result of the going away of the Master, and the work
to be accomplished through that going away, yet it was
clearly stated that the Paraclete was within each of them.
It is, therefore, though rendered Holy Breath and Holy
Spirit, the Holy Ghost. It is the Holy Ghaist or Guest, the
One within who enables the Being to remember. It is
the Being's Higher Self in touch with the Inner World.
It is the Divine Reflection within the Being, the Divine
Embodiment which makes the Being Son of God, child of
the Father-Mother, capable of ascending into the high
state of Son of God. The coming of that Hagiou Pneuma is
the becoming of the Divine Presence within the consciousness. It is the coming of the Being into the consciousness that the Presence is there, and that the Paraclete is the

Remembrancer, the Divine Reflection by embodiment of the Father-Mother within the Sanctuary of the Being.

The motion of the Holy Breath, is the motion by which remembrance comes. He will tell you of all things, recalling them to your remembrance, whatsoever things have been known by you, spoken unto you, received by you, and held in your divine sub-conscious memory. The awakening of that hidden consciousness is the unveiling of the vision, of the power of realization within the Being, so that that one can behold passing before the soul-retina, in dioramic fashion, all the past.

The Holy Breath or Holy Ghost is, therefore, to be understood as the Paraclete who is Remembrancer, and who is also Advocate. The very word is rendered Advocate in the first epistle of John, which is supposed to have been written by John the disciple—"We have an Advocate with the Father": it is the same word. The Remembrancer is the Defender or the Advocate. Our Advocate is the God who is in us through the Remembrancer.

THE SPIRAL BREATH. This world is built up in most mysterious fashion. At the heart of it there is the Mystery of the Spiral. The human life is in many respects a replica of that mystery, for the individuated Being is built on the principle of the spiral.

A spiral may be represented as a winding staircase. The Spiral Breath which gives life to all things, is the Spiritual Life-stream. It applies to the planet and to the individual. You can understand the atmospheric breaths. Just now you feel them in the equinoctial winds that are blowing, owing to the magnetic disturbance of the planet as it is passing through the stream of divine magnetism known as the Divine Ecliptic, during this vernal equinox.

There is motion in the atmosphere in its upper layers, and also its lower reaches. The winds are as breaths. They are set in motion as the result of magnetic action. But apart from, and in addition to, these, there is the Spiral Flow at the heart of the planet. That is not so easy to illustrate, or to unveil. But you may understand something of it through your own experience. For the Spiral Breath is in each one. There is an ascension of life from the planes that we speak of as the lower and outer, as the Life-stream of Divine Magnetism moves inward and upward, even until it reaches the innermost and highest. The motion of all the planes is the outcome of the Magnetic Flow of the Spiral Breath. Without it there could be no Life. It itself is the result of divine magnetic action; and its ultimate expression is found in the life-stream of the body which acts, in a sense, like a spiral, going out from a centre, from the sacred vessel we speak of physiologically as the heart. In its centrifugal action it disperses the life-stream, the blood which flows through the body. And the stream returns again in its centripetal motion to the centre, changed in some respects it is true because of the oxidization which has taken place through inhalation.

But the breathing itself is the result of the action of the Spiral Breath in the body. The life-stream, the blood, flowing through the body, is the result of the cardiac action. Yet the secret is not physiological. For that which is taking place in the body is but the expression in the outer vehicle of that which is taking place in all the vehicles. And the motion is right from the centre of the Being where the Holy Breath operates through the action of the Spiral Breath, from the innermost to the outermost.

If you want to be exhilarated, you must breathe correctly. If you desire to feel that you are rising even atmospherically through making the body more etherial, you must learn how to breathe from the Solar Plexus. The Solar Plexus is the bellows in the body. Very few people breathe correctly. Most people imagine that when they breathe, they have simply to fill the lungs. But to breathe truly is to fill the whole body. The body becomes affected right to the very toes and the finger tips, when you breathe correctly.

The Spiral Breath in the individual has its expression thus in the vehicle we call the body. The real Life of the body, is from the inner bodies.

The super-physical body is the desire body. It contains those elements which give the outer body its desires. The super-physical body is acted upon from the mental body. It is the mental body that gives it tone, that imparts to it true power of action.

The mental body has its life-stream (it is magnetic also), even as the desire body has, and the desire body transmits its feeling into what is called the physical body, the body of outer manifestation.

The mental body is quickened, exhilarated, strengthened and uplifted, guarded and enriched from the emotional body which is like a fine atmospheric stream set flowing by the spiral action, the stream that comes through to affect the bodies outside of itself.

But that body has for its life-stream the very Spiral Breath itself, the Magnetic Flow from the top of the Spiral or the Innermost of the Being. And as that Being desires, feels, thinks, aspires and yearns, the Spiral Stream or Breath is intensified in its motion.

This belongs to each individual. It is a Divine Life-stream. The full motion of the Spiral Breath is the result of breathing, inbreathing, inspiring, aspiring, expiring, to breathe out, to give forth of the power of that which is inspired and gained by the aspiring. Everyone must breathe correctly, otherwise the Spiral Breath has not full play.

It will thus be noted that the body should have true action; the super-physical or astral body, true beautiful desire; the mental body, beautiful thought; the emotional body, sweet feeling, divine feeling, in order that the Spiral Breath may flow truly through them all: the outgoing the propulsion, and the returning the impulsion. The outgoing is the power manifested; the indrawing is for renewal. The outgoing is for ministry; the indrawing is to gather the power for more ministry.

This mystery is at the heart of the planet. It is at the centre of our Being. For as is the Macrocosm, so is the Microcosm. We are of the Mystery of the Universe. And the symbol of the Spiral has a divine significance, representing as it does, the outflow and the inflow of the Breath which is at the Heart of the Divine Mystery. The Spiral is even found in the sacred staff of Hermes, which, usually, in an occult sense, is presented as the intertwining of two serpents on his staff. But the serpentine forms ought not to be there at all, as serpents. They are the streams, the outgoing and the returning, of the Spiral Breath, the Streams of the Divine Love and Wisdom expressed in the vehicles as life, power, beauty; beauty in form, beauty of feeling, beauty of desire, beauty of thought, beauty of the very breath of our life.

How important it is to understand Life's Spiral, and that we are built upon the principle of it in the Divine Mystery! To apprehend the significance of the Spiral Breath that flows down through us, and up through us in two-fold motion around the Divine Centre! Nor can the Hagiou Pneuma, or Holy Breath called the Paraclete, be

54

realized beyond the proportion in which the soul realizes the motion of the Spiral Breath through all its planes. For the Holy Pneuma is the Divine Presence at the centre of the Being, from whom the very Spiral Breath flows. The realization of that One is the crown of the motion of the Spiral Breath within us, in perfect harmony and in fulness of expression, flowing down through us for enrichment, and out through us in ministry, and returning again full of praise and thanksgiving, rejoicing and blessing.

*   *   *   *

THE DIVINE LIFE-STREAM. The third part of the question relates to the divine life-stream, but *the* Divine Life-stream is the Magnetic Divine Life-stream. The Spiral Breath is a Stream that flows out from the equatorial region of the solar body. The Sun, as we have said elsewhere, is not what he appears to be. He is a glorious spiritual and even divine body. He is the very sum of the hierarchy of the Divine World of this system. He is, in his glory, the auric splendour of all the Beings who dwell in Sol, that is, in the solar body. The things with which material science deals relate not to that body, but to the envelope which is an atmosphere and atmospheria around the sun—the atmospheria relating to the outer magnetic display, and the atmosphere to what is known as the photosphere, which is composed of glorious elements of a high celestial order, in a state of accommodation for ministry to this world, and the other members of this system. From that Divine World there flows out a Stream of the most glorious magnetic nature. That Stream is of the very substance of the Divine World in a state of elemental condition (using the word in a most inward sense). It is reduced to a living magnetic Stream that can reach forth and touch this earth and other worlds, and all the children unto whom the Sun directly ministers. In that Stream this world once moved. All the members of this system moved within it. That Divine Stream is the quickener of all life upon this world and all the worlds of the system. Without it there could not be any manifestation of life, there could be no realization of Being. A world of a planetary order right outside of it, or souls of a human order never touching it, would pass away. Though this world does not now move within that Stream, and has not done so for long, long ages, indeed, not since the great Descent, or Fall as it has been called, was fully accomplished, yet twice a year it passes through it at the Vernal and the Autumnal Equinoxes. Its play upon the planet in the Vernal Equinox, is direct upon this hemisphere; and in the Autumnal Equinox direct upon the other hemisphere. The result is that we have Spring in this hemisphere through the Vernal Equinox taking place; and in the other hemisphere, during our winter, through the Autumnal Equinox.

That Life-stream is one full of the most glorious nourishing power. It is altogether spiritual, though we have to speak of it as magnetic. It is exhilarating, stimulating, disintegrating, unifying, redeeming, regenerating. Nature becomes, so to speak, conscious of its influx. Though men and women are unconscious of its influence, they are often disturbed by it. Oft-times you may hear people say, "I am never so well in the Spring," or "I am never so well at the fall," that is, in the Autumn. It is the effect of the Magnetic Stream upon them. The planet moves through it twice a year; it takes it about a week to accomplish this motion. As it nears the Stream it becomes disturbed magnetically for quite a week or more, and during that time its motion is accelerated, so that it is quicker than at any other time of the year, except the corresponding week in

56

September. For the Magnetic Stream has qualities in it which pass into all the planes of the planet, right to the heart of it. And it receives its renewed propulsion, not at the perihelion or aphelion, when it is nearest the Sun or furthest away, but during the Equinoxes. It is sent on its journey for six months more, receiving power of motion through being revivified. All its life is quickened into manifestation, and even its children are nourished spiritually. And it is oft-times in the proportion that they can receive and drink in of that Breath, that they are disturbed in their vehicles. But if they be equilibrated in all their planes, they can drink in great measure, and be exhilarated, uplifted and enriched. The vision brought to them at that period may be most glorious in realization of The Inner Mystery.

That Divine Life-stream flows into all life. The children of the Kingdom know something of it. It has always had to be in a state of accommodation for the planets' offspring. But the children of the Kingdom can bathe in its glory, for they may in very deed be spoken of as the children of the Sun, those who can share in the auric outflow of ineffable splendour poured forth from the Sun.

This Divine Life-stream touches the children of the Kingdom to-day. Although the planet only passes through it twice a year, the Soul can rise into it in state. The Planet-soul is enriched by it twice a year. Yea, more; for, from the great Sun spots, as they are called, there are poured out elements of the quality of that Life-stream, into the planet. The Planet-soul is nourished from it. The Children of the Kingdom can rise into it through rising in state; but the planet, owing to the condition of its outer planes, cannot move in it continuously. With its outer planes as they are, supposing it were to be so placed as to move constantly in the Stream, the planes would be broken.

57

They would be changed. That change will be accomplished some day ere many ages have passed. But not with the disastrous effects that would result to-day. For the redemption is now proceeding, and the elements will be so changed that they will be able to endure the vibrations. And likewise will the planet's children. For they will be in a redeemed state.

*   *   *   *

Behold the mystery lying behind the question! That Life-stream is the begetter of all the streams in us; not as it flows in a celestial sense merely, but in its very nature. Its correspondence is in us, or we could not receive it and endure it. Its correspondence is in the Spiral Breath in the innermost realm, so that we are able to receive of that Stream into the Spiral Breath, and by filling it, the Stream passes right through us.

What a glorious mystery our little life is! Little it is in comparison with the vastness of the universe, yet how vast even a Life in its littleness is, when it can apprehend within itself that which is of the most ever blessed ministry of the Mystery of Being? It is filled with the Mystery of God.

There is no true motion of the Spiral Breath unless it be the motion produced from the power of that Divine World Life-stream. It is the Life-stream of the Son of God. For the Sun is the embodiment, philosophically expressed, of the Logos; mystically expressed, of the Eternal Mystery of Adonai. He is, therefore, the consensus of all the consciousness and realization of power and glory of the heavenly hierarchy of this system. The Human Soul has its correspondence. Through it the Stream touches the Being, and the Spiral Breath is set in motion in its outgoing and in its incoming. And, as the Being rises

through this divine action upon the Spiral Breath, so
Hagiou-Pneuma becomes realized—the consciousness of
the Presence within.

*   *   *   *

Would you help us to understand what is meant by the
term the Sub-conscious Mind?

THE SUB-CONSCIOUS MIND. The Sub-conscious Mind is the mind in a
state in which it has no present conscious
recognition. There is but one real mind. It is
what has been termed the Higher Mind. That soul-power
can receive of the intelligence of God. This latter is named
the Divine Mind.

The lower mind and the sub-conscious mind, express
two states of that Higher Mind. The lower mind is the
vehicle through which the Mind correlates on the objective
world and planes of manifestation; the sub-conscious mind
is that state of the Mind in which it has no recognition or
memory for the time being of past events.

We will illustrate this by memory. The innermost
memory is of the Soul. But the Mind is the vehicle through
which correlation takes place, even in the intermediary
planes as well as the innermost planes. Years ago events
happened in your life. Years pass and the events are
forgotten by you. They are as if they never had been,
though they may have left their mark upon your
visage, and their shadow upon your threshold. But, if so,
the shadow has been forgotten, and the mark upon the
visage has also apparently passed from the memory. Bye
and bye, years after, perhaps many years after, events
happen, and like a flash the Mind remembers the events of
long, long ago. The shadow is there because it was not
transmuted and healed; the marring of the visage is still
there, for even if it has been healed, and the shadow has

been chased away, still the memory remembers that there was a shadow and there was a marring. The events were in a sub-conscious state in the Mind, but they had not been blotted out. It only required something to touch that chamber of the Mind where the memory was shut up, and open the door, and bring forth again the things forgotten.

That was a sub-conscious memory, not forgotten, but not brought into action in the memory; not remembered at the time, yet remembered by the Inner Being. And it only required an event of such a nature to touch the part, and throw the whole of the doors of the past open, and the Being looked back to those years, and through the events once more. The Mind gathers from day to day. It receives impressions; it gathers knowledges. It is influenced by desire; it is affected by environment.

It is thus that, in sleep, the Higher Mind can be in action, whilst the lower vehicle of it is quiescent. The lower mind rests; the vehicle sleeps. There is, so to speak, a resting from consciousness. Sleep is the consciousness withdrawn from the outer vehicle, though it may be operative in the inner. For the Being who has been fully awakened never sleeps. The Soul is always awake. The sudden awakening out of sleep, is the sudden entrance of the Mind into conscious volition within the vehicles. During sleep, the Mind that has gathered much in the way may be full of activity. During a semi-sleep, the vehicle itself may not be in a state of quiescence, with the result that there is a subconscious action or process going on.

This will help you to understand some experiences that may come to you. This law operates through all the planes of consciousness until the Being can not only touch all the planes and function upon them all, but also look through them all. The Sub-conscious Mind is simply the Mind in a state in which it is not consciously remembering; but that it has a memory is most obvious to everyone. For even the things of long, long ago, can be brought back in a moment through the magnetic action of some influence or event upon the Mind.

To illustrate this yet further, as one speaking to those who would understand healing for themselves, and healing for others: the Mind receives impressions, the Heart receives influences. The influences affect the life, the impressions are deep upon the Mind. The events which made the impressions and set in motion the love, pass away. Probably at the time, deep feeling of hurt was felt within the Being; but the Being sought to heal it by simply supposing the process of overcoming to be that of negativing it. Years after, the love that seemed to be healed is again awakened, having its old consciousness of hurt, and the Mind's impressions which seemed to be blotted out are again adumbrated upon it. With what result? In what would be called the Sub-conscious Mind, there could be the awakening again of resentment, of anger, of deep feeling of hurt, the spirit of unforgiveness of which the individual had no consciousness as being present there. You will, therefore, understand how it sometimes happens that, in the lives of the children where there seem to be present for the time being, none of these states, there is suddenly awakened in them the consciousness of hurt. This means that old influences are adumbrated upon the Mind, old magnetic currents are re-quickened and made to pass through the emotion, so that those things which were supposed to be healed are found manifesting as if they were of yesterday, having been held in the treasure house of the Mind's memory unconsciously.

Subconsciousness means, that which lies beyond the

61

personal consciousness. At one time the individual was conscious of them. But that consciousness was allowed to pass away without the transmutation or healing of the conditions. So, when the like things were adumbrated again upon the Mind and the Heart, the Mind called to remembrance, and the old hurt came back. The old resentment manifested itself. The old hurt to the Mind's pride, and the sorrowful feelings within the Heart, were all reborn unto the consciousness. Yet it may be truly said that they were always there, though they were forgotten.

This will help you to understand some things in your own experiences. They come up surely in these days, and in such souls as are in this class, souls travailing to the Holy City of the Christhood state. And they come up to be healed. When the term, the Sub-conscious Mind, is used, remember that it relates to the Mind whose memory has forgotten for the time being, events of other times. And the awakening of the Sub-conscious Mind, is the bringing back into the consciousness of forgotten events, by means of similar experiences taking place.

How is it possible to diagnose spiritually? What difference would there be in the method of diagnosis used by

(1) The Master in the days of the Manifestation?
(2) The Christ-Soul functioning through the vehicles adapted for the ministry of the Oblation?
(3) A spiritual healer in these days and the days to come?

*   *   *   *

SPIRITUAL DIAGNOSIS.   How is it possible to diagnose spiritually? That is a question only experience could fully answer and interpret. It is just to understand the Being, to see into the planes of a Soul, to look into the face through which the Being looks out, and behold its sorrow, its travail, its conflict, the shadows upon the threshold. It is to have power to sense the vehicles, feel the magnetic action of the planes, and know what is wrong, and where lies the hurt. That is what true spiritual diagnosis means.

How may you do it? No one can teach you that, except by helping you upward and inward in your own realizations; inward and upward in seeking only the Divine Way. Therein it is necessary to lose the consciousness of the personal healer, and to be more and more conscious of the Higher Powers, even until you are absolutely conscious that, though you are the vehicle of the Divine World, yet you have nothing that you would claim as your own, that the Power of true Healing is of God alone.

Can one look into the face of another and read its life's story? Can you read that story truly, understand that soul, know the meaning of its travail, see the shadows upon its threshold, feel its magnetic currents, and know the planes that are in wrong polarity, unveil somewhat, as much as that one could endure, of the mystery of the Being's Life? That power is from the Divine World alone. No man or woman of himself or herself knoweth such profound secrets. Even though the Healer may have this power to read a Soul's secrets, yet the knowledge of such a history is given only from the Divine World. And there could be no teaching of such a mystery, beyond the pointing out of the way by which the realization alone can come.

*   *   *   *

DIAGNOSIS BY THE MASTER. The Master in the days of the Manifestation knew after the manner in which we have spoken. He understood the mystery of a Soul. By looking into the eyes and the face, He could behold the countenance of another. For the eyes are not only windows through which the mind looks out upon the objective world; they are the windows which correspond to those of the soul. And through these, and through the whole visage, the countenance of the Being looks out. The Master knew what was in man. Not by reading another's thought in a telepathic sense, did His knowledge come. He knew by looking into the countenance where a Soul was, what its travail had been, how it had received its hurt. He diagnosed from the centre of the Being, which is the Divine Centre. His vision was from the Divine World. He had nothing of His own in a personal, or even in a merely individual sense; though individually He knew through the Great Realization.

In healing, He sometimes touched just the very parts that were affected; and this for two reasons. There were those who were healed much more quickly through being touched, apart from any effect His touch had upon them, through aiding the direction of their thought to that part, that plexus, or those plexi. It sometimes happened that more than one plexus was out of harmony. But He also touched, because from one who is functioning on the Inner Realm, there flows the Magnetic Stream. The planet has to move in space, and can only contact that Stream at the Equinoxes. And though our vehicles have to move through space, yet the inner Being transcends all space, and touches that Stream at all times, if it functions in the Innermost Realms. Thus, that Stream passes at all times into and through that one.

In this way the touch of the Master brought healing to those who could receive it.

Never despise being touched, if you need to be touched for healing; or, if you are healing, providing you understand what it means, and if it be to direct the thought of the one you are healing, use the touch. But be in a right state when you do it. If it be to convey through you from the Divine World, be ye in the state filled from that world, so that the touch will give that which no man of himself, or any woman of herself, can ever give.

*   *   *   *

*DURING
THE
OBLATION.* How did the Christ-Soul diagnose whilst functioning through vehicles adapted for the ministry of the Oblation?

Oh, He was so veiled at times He could not understand the mystery of His own life, though through it always there flowed healing. Oft-times He did understand consciously how to deal with suffering ones; but His own sufferings were continuous. He took from men and women their infirmities, oft-times without knowing in a personal way that He had taken them. They flew to Him as to a magnet attracting elements to itself. But He was veiled

65

in order that He might not know all that was being done through Him. For, even with the veil upon Him, His Being was heavily burdened in consciousness, and His sorrow was great.

How He healed in the Oblation, we must leave now; but just in that way, like the magnet, He attracted the elements, and absorbed that which He attracted, bearing the magnetic fire and transmuting it. Then it had to be eliminated from His vehicle.[1]

*   *   *   *

HOW THE HEALER SHOULD HEAL. The Spiritual Healer in these days, and the days that are coming fast upon us, is the healer who is to follow the true therapeutic methods, the one who is to understand souls, and be a real physician. And in this connection we would say to you, *Despise no venue of knowledge* concerning the human vehicles. Rather, gather all you can in the way of true knowledge; but always lift what you may gather into the realm of the spiritual, and transmute it. For the power to heal truly is not in outward knowledge at all, but in the inner realization. The power is not in the outer application, but in the Divine Potencies within the Being. For a true knowledge of the body; and the real understanding of its functions, its plexi, and all their motions, should be invaluable to the Healer. A real understanding of the constitution of the finer bodies, should likewise be of inestimable value to the Healer.

Despise therefore no avenue of learning and of true wisdom. Even the wisdom of the anatomy of the human frame, is surely from the Divine Centre of all Being. Who could have imagined a life so transcendently beautiful, even

---

[1] *See the answer to question on "Girding Himself with a towel." p. 41. Also pp 125 to 141.*

in the outer vehicle, as man is, and as woman is? Man when truly built in the majesty of his strength, and woman when truly fashioned in the grace of her form, surely represent Divine embodiments full of the sublime Breath of God, whose Life-stream is set in motion and acted upon by the finer degrees of the real Being through which the Divine Life-stream flows.

The mystery of the Being of Man is wonderful from the innermost to the outermost, and from the outermost to the innermost. And until you are able to stand in the centre and look through all, even to the outer, despise not knowledge which comes from without concerning the vehicles, if it will help you in beautiful ministry unto souls.

The true Healer who is coming is the one who will understand from within. And through such understanding, attained through great Realization, have the power to transmute the knowledge acquired of the outer vehicle in its functions, and of the finer vehicles and their functions, and apply the knowledge, so that the spiritual healer will be a fully equipped Healer, a Divine Healer.

Divine Science is a knowledge of all things. It is not an affirmation, but a knowledge. Divine Science is to know divinely from the innermost to the outermost, and to apply the knowledge through all the planes of the Being for sweet and gracious ministry.

As Healers ye will heal in proportion as ye realize the Divine. You may help on the outer plane, even as the medical faculty help on the outer plane, in so far as they know. For they oft-times alleviate pain. They often help souls in the outer vehicle. Though most often do they help them through their own sweet love and trust. And there are others who help souls in other ways. But real healing is from within. It comes from the very centre. It can only

67

be acquired through the acquisition of power found in God, and the acquisition of that power will never be related to the individual, to the personal equation. The acquisition of that power will not bring mere personal elation, nor pride, nor a high consciousness of that power.

Oh, it is utter vanity, aye, it is folly, to imagine that any man or any woman has real Divine Power apart from the Indwelling of the Divine. And the more the Divine dwells within us, the more shall we be as little children growing in power from Him, but growing surely in lowliness: growing in power for ministry, but surely growing in the praise of Him from whom all power comes: growing in the power of blessing souls, but ever blessing Him who blesses all and upbraideth not, and who doth use us as his vessels to pour out His Blessing.

Ye will heal, beloved friends, truly heal, not simply suspend physical trouble or astral trouble or mental trouble, but truly heal, in the measure in which ye realize the glorious Indwelling of God.

Let the Holy Paraclete give the Holy Breath, and let His coming heal the sub-conscious Mind of every hurt it ever had, so that when something awakens the memory of the hurt, there will be no soreness, no pain, no resentment; there will be nothing but just the impression that such a history did come, but has left no hurt behind it. That is healing. That is perfect health.

God in His Love doth so heal His children.

Be ye healed! And in life be as His healed and His Healers. From Him, bless all unto healing.

PART
II.

Some Familiar Terms
Examined and Defined.

The Mystery of Love : The Mystery of Life:
The Mystery of Light : The Mind : The Mystery
of the Soul : Spirit and Substance : Our
Divine Principle : The Mystery of God :
The Sacred Elohim : The Mortal : The
Immortals : The Kenosis of a Soul :
Inherent Properties of Matter :
Materialization : What is True
Science? : What is Truth? : The
True Knowledge : The Divine
Omniscience : The Mystery of
Evil : The Nature of Sin :
Three Great Mysteries—The
Redemption, The Atonement,
and The Sin-Offering :
The Mystery of Sorrow :
Jesus, Christ, and
the Lord.

In the sacred gnosis there are three key words: Love, Life, Light: they are a divine trinity. Of them is Being built up.

THE MYSTERY OF LOVE. In the sacred Mysteries this was expressed by the term Agapê. It was a word signifying the Divine Being as Love. And in the human Being it is the Divine Principle whose action gives individuated consciousness as a living soul, and enables that soul, when unfolded, to apprehend God the Divine Mystery, and even to comprehend that Mystery as to its nature.

Love is the magnetic pole of the Being, corresponding in the individual to the true magnetic pole of the earth, by which the soul is influenced, attracted, held and impelled in its motions. It is the centre through which the divine world acts upon the soul. As the heavenly Principle, it is the "Arche," that sacred word which is translated "beginning," but which means that Principle out of which life becomes; and it is in its nature by the law of its relation to the ever most Blessed Eternal One, the Amen, or fulness, or perfectionment of Being when fully unfolded.

Love is, therefore, the Divine Mystery in the individual life. From it a soul has motion, consciousness, volition, will in the sense of choice; the Divine attributes in miniature. It is thus a soul grows likest God when its love-principle is acted upon, held, directed, intensified in its motion towards divine things from the divine world. For God is Love, and they in whom Love becomes the mighty divine force of Being, in that measure embody, realize and manifest God the Divine Mystery, they themselves rising up into marvellous degrees of comprehension of all that that Mystery implies.

THE MYSTERY OF LIFE. The magnetic state known as Love produces Life. The ancient beautiful Greek term Zōē we use to denote that Life which is begotten of the Love. It means Being as distinguished from existence, which latter would be expressed by the word Bios. Life is thus the expression of the Agapê or Divine Love. It is Life related in its attributes to the harmonies of the angelic, and even the divine worlds. In such Life there is made concrete, whether it be on the more substantial outer planes, or in the more etheric inner planes, the meaning of the Mystery of God in us. In such Life the way of Love is always divine in its manifestations; indeed, the manifestations comprise the expression of the Life resulting from the magnetic energy or power of the Love. Divine Life, therefore, in its manifestations is beautifully concrete, ever harmonious, rhythmic in its motion, most beautifully substantial in the manifestation of its Being, but ever spiritual whether its manifestations be in the inner planes or on the outer planes. God is Love. God is as the love-principle, the Mystery within us. In Him is Life, that is, Being, for Love is Life: and the Life is the Light within.

THE MYSTERY OF LIGHT. What is Light? The Light that is begotten of the Life which has been begotten of Love, is a radiance: it is the radiance within a soul. Light is the effect of magnetic action; it is a manifestation of magnetic power. The light that travels from the sun to this earth comes not in light streamers, as many suppose, but in magnetic rays which are invisible, and have no objective presentation to the human vision until they reach the earth's magnetic plane, falling upon which they are turned to light within its atmosphere; and that light is reflected and refracted by the conditions of the magnetic plane and the earth's atmosphere; so that the light we receive is conditioned by the state in which the atmosphere and the magnetic plane, in which the atmosphere is, happen to be at the time. The light is the effect of the sun's magnetic rays upon the earth's substances.

Herein we have an illustration of what the Divine Light is within a soul. It is the radiance of the Life, or Being, when the love-principle is in action, and especially when acted upon from the divine world. The Light is the effect of the divine magnetism upon the heavenly Principle of the soul's Being. The degree of the radiance within a soul, therefore, depends upon the degree in which its magnetic pole is affected from the Divine world, and the state in which the reflecting substances spoken of as the mind, are to be found. The Divine Light within the sanctuary of a soul is begotten from the Radiant Presence there who is the Lord of Being, the soul's sun, in proportion as the soul's love-principle is affected from Him and the mind capable of receiving His transmitted glory. Thus the outpouring of the auric glory of a soul is dependent upon its realization of the glorious Presence within; and the realization of that Presence is dependent upon the soul's status as to its love-principle and reflective substances. For it can only radiate in the measure in which it receives power from the realization of that Presence. Thus the Light within a soul is ever and always the glory of the Lord; but the realization of that glory, and its manifestations in auric power, are dependent upon the soul.

Thus we have the Divine Trinity expressed—the mystery of the Father-Mother and the Holy Guest called Ghost, within the soul's system, the creative Love, the fashioned Being, and the auric Light or radiant manifestation.

73

THE MIND. "There is but one Mind." "There is nothing great but Mind." There is oft-times a confusion as to the meaning of Mind. It is frequently used as a synonym of Intelligence. It is thus applied to the Divine. God is Supreme Intelligence. But here we mean that God is Wisdom. Understanding, Light, Love, Power, Omniscience, Omnipotence, Omnipresence are all gathered up into Divine Intelligence. It is difficult to postulate of God that He is simply Mind. God is not a mind in the human sense, any more than He is a soul in the human sense, or a spirit in the human sense. God is Being. Infinite Being knows all things, realizes all things. All things are the expression of the Love and the Wisdom of that Infinite Being. In that sense God is Mind, and Soul, and Spirit; and all mind and soul and spirit manifested in individuated states of consciousness, are of Him, from Him, and should ever be for Him.

Now when we come to speak of man as mind we do not mean Divine Intelligence. We mean that man is mind, or, to state it more correctly, has mind, and is able to reflect through that mind the Divine Intelligence. For the mind of man in his spiritual system, is as a moon in the celestial system. It has the powers of Divine Substance in itself to enable it to reflect the Divine Intelligence. But it is only a reflector. It can receive the light of that Intelligence and reflect its glory. In itself the mind has no light, all its light being the reflected glory of the Flame of the Divine Spirit within the sanctuary or soul. The mind, therefore, is a Divine Organ with a special function, whose service is twofold. Firstly, to receive the light of the Divine Flame and reflect its glory back into the sanctuary, like a speculum receiving the glory of the sun and reflecting it back; and secondly, the mind having received that glory is able to move outward and permit the light with which it is illumined from the Divine, to be reflected into the world. The Divine Intelligence realized through the Divine Principle in a human soul, must never be confounded with an office which is meant to reflect that Intelligence, breaking it up and dispersing it in the wisdom given as knowledge to the world.

Concerning the human estate it may be said that there are two minds. There are what has been termed the immortal mind and the mortal mind. If the mind itself be but as a moon fulfilling the office of reflector within and without, then what is known as immortal mind relates to the Divine Principle of Being in man, and not to mind as such. And what is spoken of as mortal mind is simply the lower vehicle by which the mind called the immortal mind manifests upon the outer planes the intelligence it has received in the inner planes. Mortal mind simply relates to the vehicle whose fashion changes in every life that is generated, passing away with each life as its service closes, to be re-fashioned in the next generation or incarnation as a suitable vehicle for the expression of the Divine Intelligence as that is reflected through and from the higher mind. Thus we would express the Divine Mind as the Eternal and Infinite Intelligence Whose Being is found embodied in every human soul, and reflected through the mind of all His children.

THE MYSTERY   What is a human Soul? The human Ego is
OF THE SOUL.   of the mystery of God. It is individuated
from God. It partakes of His nature, being built up of His
very Substance. In the heavenly Principle of its Being, it may
be stated that God is in Being; but being an individuation, it
is as the dewdrop to the ocean, composed of like elements, but
a little miniature of the Infinite and Eternal. It is built up in
its consciousness through the process of manifold ages,
having within itself the power of growth through which
it unfolds from more to more in the fulness of its
consciousness until it is able to reflect that same glory which
the infinite ocean reflects, even as the dewdrop reflects the
sun as truly as does the great sea. The consciousness of a
human Soul when it is in high divine estate, is the outcome
of a thousand great ages, during the passing of which the
process of unfolding, enlarging, deepening and exalting of
the entire Being has been proceeding. To see a human Soul
in its inception, and when it has grown into the high
consciousness which enables it to realize the Presence of the
Ever Most Blessed within itself, is to understand something
of the majesty and lowliness of the infinite Love and
Wisdom of the Father-Mother. In such a vision it is as if one
looked upon a star of the most distant magnitude, which to
the vision would appear but as a dim light in the far
distance, but ever coming nearer and nearer and still nearer
until the great reality of its Being was manifest as a centre of
most glorious power, light and love—like a star becoming to
the vision an immense sun full of the power of warmth, light
and life-giving radiations.

A human Soul is the most glorious of Sanctuaries, more
beautiful than the most chaste and noble of earthly houses,
built up of such substances as the pure divine waters found

in perfect gems, and interpenetrated by the Sacred Flame
of the Eternal Spirit whose Presence energizes all the
substances and makes them living, so that man is verily a
living Soul. The Being within that Sanctuary, the Ego as
we have expressed it, is none other than the Divine in the
heavenly Principle out of which the Soul's Sanctuary
becomes. The Soul is both sanctuary and ego, the sanctuary
being the fashion of the ego. And the consciousness of the
ego is the Divine Spirit in the heavenly Principle, through
the power of whose Presence what is known as polarization
takes place.

It will thus be seen that a human Soul is more than
anything that can be expressed by Mind. Potentially the
Divine Intelligence is in it to be gradually unveiled as the
Sanctuary of its Being is fashioned from more to more as
the expression of the manifold Divine. And in order that it
may not only know through that Intelligence the Divine
Presence within its Sanctuary in great degree of realization,
but also be able to reflect that Intelligence even as a moon
reflects the glory of the sun, the Soul has had given to it for
office a mind to act as a manifestor by reflecting and
interpreting the Divine Intelligence.

*SPIRIT
AND
SUBSTANCE.*
"God is Spirit and they who worship Him must worship Him truly in Spirit." God is not a Spirit. Men and women have thought of Him after that manner. God is not a person nor an individual, but Eternal Being. Spirit is transcendent Being. It is the ultimate of all things. It is the essence out from which all things become. The Spirit, or Essence of Being, is at once the base and the apex of all things. Within itself all things are contained. It is the Sacred Flame that illumines, the Sacred Power that quickens, the Holy Love that fashions, the fragrant Breath that makes glorious all things.

Substance, Divine Substance that is, is the Spirit's feminine mode, Its Self condensed (though this word is utterly inadequate to express what is meant) for purposes of manifestation. God is Spirit and Substance; and all consciousness in the realm of manifestation is the outcome of the polarization of Substance in Spirit.

Of those two glorious elements is the true man composed. He is of the Substance of God, and is quickened, fashioned, and illumined by the Spirit. To worship God as Spirit is to worship Him in Being, that is, within the Sanctuary through realizing Him. For true worship could only be full and perfect in the realm of realization.

The Divine Principle is in every Soul. It is the heavenly Arche out of which all things become. That Principle is not something apart from ourselves, but is the centre of our Being. It is the Mystery of God in us. From it is fashioned our magnetic pole by which we are attracted to and held from the Divine Kingdom. Even as the magnetic pole of the planet is a divine mystery, so is the magnetic pole of every man and woman. It is from that Divine Principle in us that all true things become—beautiful love manifested, the radiant Life realized, and the most blessed service rendered. It is through that heavenly Principle the divine world speaks to us and we hear that world's message. It is through the operation of that magnetic pole, love divine in its manifestation becomes possible. It is through the operations of that Principle as it is acted upon from the divine world, that life in us grows from childhood to maturity and patriarchal love and wisdom. It is through the intensification of the consciousness contained in that heavenly Principle that we are able to ascend in our state from glory to glory, rising from Kingdom to Kingdom, until the great mystery of the Being of God fills the whole of our Being, and we know God through realizing Him as the Father-Mother—centrifugal and centripetal modes of manifestation and realization. It is, therefore, through the culture of our true self that Life becomes, that the Rose of Sharon blooms within us—the Christ-love. It is through the heavenly Principle we thus commune face to face with the Father-Mother, Lord of all Being, ever glorious, ever most blessed.

This Divine Principle is the love-principle divinely understood, and is begotten in us from the Divine Substance and Divine Spirit of which our Being is built up.

79

The Mystery of God is one by which every human Soul is impressed, before which all awakened Souls stand in awe, and after which many seek that they may solve the mystery and know God. In every language almost the word which signifies God implies the Eternal Good. We speak of God as the Eternal Love, the Eternal Light, the Eternal Life; but all are gathered up into the idea affirmed in the term God. God is Good. Good there is a quality. It is not a principle, but the quality of a principle. God is Good because God is the Eternal Love, Eternal Light, Eternal Life. Goodness is of the very nature of perfect Love, and of the Light begotten of Love, and of the Life manifested from Love. In the ancient Hebrew language Jehovah implied the Divine Principle. Yahweh was the Eternal and Ever Most Blessed One. All sublime qualities are in God as Jehovah. All sublime qualities manifest in the realm of Being, of worlds, of Life are from Him. Good in man is of the quality of the Good that He is. Love in man is of the quality of the Eternal Love. Yahweh creates children, and these partake of His qualities that He may be reflected gloriously through them.

The mystery of God is the most sublime. The transcendency of God above all manifest creation is beyond speech. So is His Immanence in the children whom He creates. The majesty of the mystery of the Being of God is nowhere more transcendently expressed than in the lowly state of a human Soul wherein the Divine Immanence is not only potential and latent, but sublimely realized.

The mystery of God is the mystery of the Divine Substance and the Sacred Flame called the Spirit. He is no person. He is no individual. God is not expressed, nor

80

indeed can He be expressed, by any terms we could command, nor any signs we could give, nor any symbol we
could fashion. God is He and She and It : that is, God is
Fatherhood-Motherhood in all Spirit and Substance; the
creative, the formulative, the fashioning, the transforming,
the transfiguring and perfecting power inherent in all Being,
and realized for glorious manifestation in the realm we
speak of as Divine. It is thus a human Soul, through the
Divine realm within it, knows the Mystery and expresses it
in all the Divine attributes which are begotten and built up,
glorified and manifested from and through and by the
Eternal Love, the Eternal Light, the Eternal Life, contained
within the sacred casket of the Heavenly Principle which is
God in the Soul.

Thus is Yahweh known. Thus is Jehovah revealed. Thus
is the Divine Mystery unveiled to Souls.

In the ancient Hebrew scriptures the sacred term Elohim occurs. In theological writings it is oft-times dealt with as having the identical meaning of Jehovah, but used by a different school of thought. Consequently, great controversies have been waged between what was called the Yahvistic and the Elohistic story of creation. The use of these two terms has led many to believe that different writers wrote the different accounts. But that need not have been so, even though both terms were used. In the original story both terms were used. Yahweh is the most sacred mystery of the Divine Being, Elohim are the Seven Spirits of God. Yahweh is the Eternal Principle in the Mystery; Elohim are the seven modes of the manifestation of that Mystery. Yahweh is the Ever Most Blessed One; Jehovah is that most glorious Being revealed. Elohim form the spectrum of His revealing on the Divine Kingdom. Each Elohe has a fashioning ministry. Each Elohe operates upon the plane appointed for its manifestation. Each Elohe is a glorious degree of the Divine Principle. Each embodies one of the great sevenfold creative forces flowing out from the Heavenly Principle. Even as on the outer planes the white ray passed through the crystal reveals the spectrum, each colour of which is prismatic, yet all from the one white ray; or as in music there are the seven tones, the five semi-tones being but the blenders, and the seven tones representing the seven prismatic colours, for each tone when voiced produces the corresponding colour. It is thus all colour is gathered up into the one ray, and all tone is the expression of the one Heavenly Principle, the tones and the colours being the expression of Divine creative qualities. Thus Yahweh, manifested as Jehovah through His Elohim, is expressed upon the sevenfold realm of creative manifestation.

82

Now when it is said in the sacred record that God said, DEFINI-TIONS. "Come let us make man after our image" and that "God created man, in the image of God fashioned He him, male and female created He them," it is Elohim that are used. For the Father-Mother, through His Elohim, or Seven Sacred Spirits, the sevenfold expression of Himself as the Divine Mystery in Principle, created, generated, fashioned, unfolded, through the operations of Elohim, that which He named a Living Soul. The process of the creating, generating, fashioning, and unfolding is the process of the operative Presence in Substance and Spirit of the different Elohe upon each of the seven planes. It is thus a human Soul is constituted Divine; made of the substance of God; fashioned from that Holy Mystery to bear it in Principle within itself; fashioned in all the attributes of Being into the image of God to reflect His likeness; unfolded through the Divine outworking, bringing to the Soul the consciousness in some degree of Yahweh.

It is thus that every Soul has its own tincture, all Souls being of one of the Seven Sacred Tinctures represented by Elohim. The perfect spectrum on the outer planes represents the sacred Tinctures on the inner planes. These Sacred Seven are Elohim, God revealed and manifested; creative and generative; operative in fashioning, in transfiguring, and in perfecting all Souls.

Herein does the mystery of Elohim deepen. Upon every Kingdom are the Elohim expressed. That which obtains in the Divine Kingdom where are the sacred Tinctures, the seven glorious Tones, the transcendent Spirits, the sevenfold Divine mystery Amens, finds manifestation on the other Kingdoms, the Celestial, the Angelic, and the Human. And even beneath the Human Kingdom does the Mystery penetrate, revealing itself in the rhythms of nature, and the colours in nature, and the mystery of colour and magnetic power in gems. So that the Divine Mystery of Elohim is revealed even to the outermost Kingdom of an unfallen world. Nay, so greatly is this mystery expressed in a human Soul, that it has its own sacred Tincture, the embodiment of one of the Elohim, which gives to it that sacred tone by which it can ever be found on the Divine Realm, on the Celestial Realm, on the Angelic Realm and even in the realm of the Human estate. For every Soul responds to the tone corresponding to the sacred tincture within it. And every Soul is moved, healed and illumined from the plane upon which its Elohe manifests.

And yet the mystery deepens still more. For, though every Soul is fashioned by Elohim out of the sacred Tincture of an Elohe and ever retains that tincture and its corresponding tone, yet it is so fashioned that it grows from degree to degree of consciousness, and plane to plane of manifestation, and Kingdom to Kingdom of realization, until its fashioning is so perfect that, whilst still retaining its own sacred tincture and tone, it can respond to and express and reveal all the other tinctures and tones. For on the Divine Kingdom it embodies Elohim, and can express through realization the Seven Spirits of God.

Thus Elohim express the glory of Jehovah, and interpret the sublime mystery of Yahweh.

The word mortal is oft-times used very loosely. It is postulated of the mind and body, and all outward things. It is thus associated with change and decay, and what is named death. But in the Divine Realm, though there is neither decay nor death, but life everlasting, yet there is change. On the Angelic world the phenomena are embodiments of glorious thoughts and desires, purposes and ministries, but their fashions change with the change of the ministries and purposes, desires and thoughts. Yet are they not mortal in the sense in which that term is used on earth. It is said in sacred story that that which is mortal cannot inherit immortality. That statement is perfectly true. Yet the things which have mortal fashion can be transmuted and know that glory which is associated with the Immortal Life.

The true meaning of the word mortal has relation to the Soul's growth. In the process of spiritual evolution, divine unfoldment and realization, the Soul, even in an unfallen world, at first is in the state of a mortal. By this we mean, that as the Soul's life grows and deepens and enlarges and ascends until it reaches the immortal state, it must needs come and go upon the outer planes, and the intermediary planes, learning from experience the wisdom and love of the Father-Mother. In the Soul's history many lives are thus lived upon the outer planes of the world of which it is a member. And when the day comes in which its experience has so enriched it that it is able to rise into the greater consciousness of the Presence of the Father-Mother, it attains to that status spoken of as the Immortal Life. It will thus be seen that the mortals upon this world were the Earth's children who had not yet attained to that high consciousness of Being implied in immortality.

*THE
IMMORTALS.* That which is immortal is that which transcends mortality. In other words, it is of the Abiding Life, Spiritual Being. In every human Soul there is the Immortal Life in principle, and that always abides. Its changing fashion is from state to state, from glory to glory through the deepening of the consciousness. The mortal aspect related to what has been termed the lower manas or the outward personal equation. A Soul became immortal through its ascension into high consciousness, but the ascension was accomplished, and is ever so accomplished, by the transmutation of the very substances of the Being, the clothing of the attributes with divine power, the realization of the Overshadowing Presence, leading to that deeper and yet more transcendent realization of the indwelling of God.

Now the Immortals were those who had risen out of the limitations of the Mortal, and who had ascended into that consciousness associated with immortality. They knew the qualities of Divine Life in realization. They knew the Divine Love in its Mystery through realization. They knew the Divine Wisdom as the Eternal Truth of the Being and the majesty of God the Father-Mother. Many of these Souls had attained to Divine Consciousness, and many to what is known as Celestial Consciousness. They were those who knew God; and they are those who now know that Divine Mystery. They formed for this world a community of Souls sent to minister, to interpret that Immortal Life which they knew; to unveil its hidden mysteries as the children, the mortals, could receive; to break upon the mind of the mortals the glory of the Divine Wisdom as these were able to receive of that glory. Even though they had to take to themselves bodily form, and be born into this world

to serve through human vehicles which seemed to partake
of the nature of the mortal, yet were they ever Immortal in
their consciousness, in their attributes, in their power, and,
in unfallen days, in their realization. Through all the ages
they were ever Immortal in all their service. They did not
require to return life after life for growth, for unfoldment,
leading towards realization. When they returned it was for
ministry, and that alone. Thus the Mortals and the
Immortals were children of the one great family of the
Father-Mother, but belonging to different folds and in
different states of consciousness, the elder, the Immortals,
ministering to the younger, the Mortals, to aid them on the
path towards the glorious realization of that Life which is
immortal, eternal and most glorious.

THE KENOSIS
OF A SOUL.
This term is met with in Christian writings. It is specially dealt with in Christology. There it is applied specially to the Master. By it is meant self-limitation, or the descent of a great soul to lower degrees of consciousness for manifestation. It is thus related to the Master as one who descended from a state of high divinity, which to many appears as Deific, in order to become man for the purpose of the Manifestation. In this sense it is a laying down of life.

Has any Soul this power of self-limitation? For that which can be postulated of one in high estate, such as the Master is believed to have been in, can surely be postulated of every Soul. And this is true; for it is inherent in the Divine properties out of which that Life becomes which is named Human Soul, that when it has reached a certain degree of realization, it should have the power of self-limitation for purposes of ministry. In this sense it acquires the power to lay down its life and to take it up again, having received this power through the realization of the Father-Mother within itself. And it has this power to descend without bringing permanent hurt to itself, without any loss to the real Being, without any limitation to that Being in the innermost realm, knowing only that limitation which is the corollary of descent for manifestation upon planes less inward and where the Divine consciousness cannot be operative in perfect fulness. But such an one can pass inward from that realm of outer manifestation, where the Divine consciousness cannot be fully operative, to that realm where all limitation is transcended in the sublime realization of the Overshadowing and Indwelling Presence.

The ancient Christhood known under the different terms of The Sons of God, The Children of Israel, The True Community of Zion, the members of which form the Elect

People, The Holy Nation, The Royal Kingdom of Mediating
Souls in High Priesthood, also known as The True Illuminati,
had this power of self-limitation in varying degrees. They
were in high Christhood. They were the Illumined Ones
who knew the Father-Mother in differing degrees of consciousness. They were sent to this world to minister. In
order to enable them to do so, limitation had to be imposed.
It was such limitation in their consciousness as the conditions
of their ministry necessitated. Though they realized always
the Presence in unfallen days, yet, for the perfect realization,
they had to ascend into the Divine Kingdom within them.
The Kenosis, therefore, relates not to the innermost realm,
but to the realm of the manifestation for service.

Herein is the beauty and glory of the transcendent Love
of the Father-Mother revealed. That Love, through His
illumined ones, can descend, imposing self-limitation for
purposes of sublime ministry. It has been thus with all the
redeemers who have visited this world in its distraught
conditions; with all the messengers; so that for the realization they had to ascend from time to time to the Divine
Kingdom, for only there could the perfect realization and
illumination take place. And in a very special sense was it
thus with that one known in the western world as the Master
Jesus. For the limitation, or self-limitation, imposed for the
Manifestation was in degree not to be compared with that
self-limitation which became so necessary for the ministry
of the Oblation. In this latter the Kenosis brought with it
the burden of sorrow, pain and anguish unspeakable.

Yet to go down for ministry, whether by Him or by those
accounted His brethren, is one of the most Divine ministries,
testifying always to that Love that never slumbers, that
never wearies, that never fails, and that knows no limitation
in its giving.

89

What is matter? True Substance is interpenetrated by the Eternal Spirit. It is ever responsive to the quickening and fashioning power
of that Spirit, according to the plane of its manifestation.
Whither the Spirit draws, it follows. In everything that is
full of the magnetism of the Spirit there is responsiveness;
there is true motion. A world unfallen in its substances is
perfect in all its motions, upon all its Kingdoms, within
all its planes and through all its zones. In no part is there
failure. In no Kingdom is there present that which makes
for discord and disharmony. In such a world all its
substances are perfect, even those which are most opaque
and belong to the outermost realm of its manifestation.
Such a world from its centre to its circumference, from
its heavenly Principle and magnetic pole to its outermost
body of manifestation, is a world where true Substance and
Spirit prevail.

A materialized world is not of that order. A materialized
world is a world whose substances have been changed.
Matter is not the ultimate of spiritual substance in creation,
but is the spiritual substances in a perverted state. The
result of this perversion is wrong combinations of substances,
resulting in opposing magnetic currents, which again give
as a resultant, conflict amongst the elements, misdirection in
many aspects of manifested life. Matter is, therefore, a
combination of elements whose polarity is wrong, and this
prevents the materialized substances from responding truly
to the law of their attraction upon the Kingdom and plane
and zone of their manifestation. Matter may, therefore, be
defined as spiritual substance in false state, unable to
respond truly to the law of the Spirit, and which has to be
redeemed back to its original state by processes mysterious
to the mind. Hence many of the phenomena manifest on

these planes in this fallen world which men and women speak of as meteorological, seismic and volcanic, all of which are the direct outcome of the fallen state of this world. But they are also the testimonies to the operation of the Eternal Spirit in the process of redeeming back the planes of the planet to their original glorious status. Concerning this latter we shall have more to say elsewhere.

MATERIALIZATION. By this is meant the bringing down of things which belong to the inner planes of Being into the world of concrete forms and symbols; and the application of truths relating to the divine world within the Soul to have reference only to outward and material things. For instance, to materialize the idea of God is to make the materialized conditions the embodiment of Him. To materialize the inner doctrine of man's Being as a living Soul is to reduce him to be a mere physical and mental entity and manifestation. To materialize the divine Son of God, who is in every Soul potentially and latently, is to make of Christ a mere man rather than the divine state of consciousness within the Soul, to which all souls are to attain, and to which some have already attained.

But materialization must not be confounded with manifestation on the more outward planes. The artist in whom divine idea is begotten may seek to bring forth that idea and express it in some beautiful concrete form, that those who cannot yet attain to the realm of divine ideas may behold the beauty expressed in form, as in sculpture; in form and colour, as in fine art; in rhythm and harmony and depth and breadth and height of expression, as in music. In this case the divine ideas, though made concrete, are not materialized. They are expressed as through symbol, making use of the substance and colour and tone available

91

on the plane of manifestation. If the sculptor's form, and the fine artist's form and colour, and the musician's rhythm and harmony had no ultimate divine meaning, no spiritual lesson to teach, no uplifting influence to send forth, no prophetic message to declare, then they would be materializations of divine ideas in which the divine idea would be lost in the more outward concrete expression. The true manifest world is thus not a materialization of divine purpose and vision and creative energy and glorious Being, but the sculptor's embodiment, and the artist's expression, and the musician's combination of harmony, all of which do express most beautifully the All-Presence of the Father-Mother in His world of beautiful manifestation. But this world, as it is at present in its outer planes, is a materialized world—a world in which the divine idea was changed, the divine planetary motions altered, the magnetic streams misdirected and confused, the elements brought down from a state of beautiful responsiveness to one wherein they lost the power to respond to the Divine Laws, and thus were bereft of the power to express the divine purpose.

WHAT IS TRUE SCIENCE? The term is used to express formulated knowledge concerning the manifest world or the Stellar Systems; also doctrines relating to the constitution of man physically and mentally. And is also applied to psychology, though that term in such science rarely relates to Being. Material science is built up from observation of the world's phenomena in its different Kingdoms, and through such knowledge as may be gained from the chemistric analysis of its elements. But science is—to know. Is the world known by mere observation? Can its mystery be understood through the tabulation of its phenomena? Does any department of

92

material science apprehend truly the mystery at the heart
of the world so as to know it and be able, through that
knowledge, to correlate all its manifest phenomena? Or,
does science as it deals with man, whether as a physiological
or as a mental embodiment, know truly what man is in
himself, what the mystery is that lies at the heart of that
man who is able to think and to feel and to manifest through
his body? Does science as expressed in astronomy, geology,
physics, chemistry, physiography, botany and physiology,
know the world in its mystery, or man the lesser mystery,
but just as real? Does mental science grasp the mystery
through its mental analysis, its observed phenomena, its
psycho-analysis, as it has come to be called in these days?

All paths to knowledge are beautiful if beautifully
pursued; and they are helpful to minds groping after the
secrets lying at the heart of the world and humanity. But
the science which comes from observation and the tabulation of phenomena, must not be confounded with that true
science or knowledge begotten within the mystery of a
Soul's Being when *it knows*. Material science and mental
science, and even what may be designated in these latter
days as spiritual science, is but the endeavour to discover
along the outer planes and the mental planes the great secret
which lies within neither, but far, far beyond them, though
finding expression through them in manifold degrees and
states and conditions of manifestation. All outward science
is, therefore, comparative; and it is only true science when
it is illumined from that realm where all things are truly and
fully known.

Material science in every department has had to change
its outlook and its postulates from time to time as new
discoveries have come to hand, showing that material science
did not know, and does not know, as such. Of its application

to man the same may be said. And the like is true of all mental science. Even in the later development of spiritual science, as it has been called, there is an obvious lack of true understanding begotten of real Knowledge of the Divine Mystery at the heart of the universe hidden in this travailing world, and in the travail of all Souls upon it.

Divine Science is divine knowledge. Divine knowledge is divine realization. Divine realization is to know the great and glorious mystery of the Being of the Father-Mother. To know that Mystery is to understand the mystery of manifest Being expressed in the glorious suns or divine realms where angels minister. To know that Mystery in its manifestations is to know what this once most beautiful world was and what it became, and how it became what it is to-day in its manifestations. It is to understand the reason for the groaning or travail of this world with its imprisoned races and its fallen planes. It is to understand the Divine world, not only in its transcendent Being and glorious manifestations, but to understand the nature and ministry of the Love that obtains in that world, and which has been manifested to this world amid its travail. It is to understand how the perfect Father-Mother, being realized in all His children in the Divine world, through them can know and understand the tragedy of a world like this, hear its groaning, feel its sorrow, and carry it in the bosom of His Love unto perfect healing by means of His redeemers, mediators, seers, prophets, healers and teachers. Thus, true science is divine knowledge begotten of divine realization in the Being. And in the measure of that realization is the power of the redeemer, the mediator, the seer, the prophet, the healer. True Christian Science is thus the knowledge of the Divine Mystery through the realization of Christ in us.

94

What is Truth? It is an old question. Many ask it, but few find the answer. Knowledge concerning ing different departments of nature and life may be true; but they are not the Truth. In speaking, as well as in thinking and feeling, and also in action, one should ever be true. To be otherwise is to deny Truth. Yet these are but qualities of the effect of Truth upon the mind, and the heart, and the inner Being. The Truth is not a quality, although it has qualities. It is not an attribute, though it has attributes. The Truth is comprised in the term the Divine Love and Wisdom. So Truth is known as Love and Wisdom realized; and all else could be but radiations and adumbrations and effects in manifestation of that Love and that Wisdom. A Soul in Truth is not simply and only a Soul seeking for Truth, and striving to be true in its seeking; it is one whose seeking has brought the beautiful realization in which the Soul understands. As God is Love and Wisdom, so is God Truth. He is the meaning of all things as He is the sum of all things; and only in Him, through Him, from Him can a Soul be filled with Truth.

When Truth has to be broken upon the mind plane the Soul moves in its ministry from the realm of realization to that of reflection, where the Wisdom as true Knowledge has to be broken, refracted and reflected. And when that Truth or Holy Wisdom has to be manifested on yet more outward realms of thought, the refraction and dispersion causing reflection makes the knowledge upon the mind appear to have special relation to the phenomenal world, planetary and personal.

Herein is the meaning of another expression, "and the Truth shall make you free." For to know the Divine

Wisdom through realization, is to have the power to transcend in understanding all lower realms. Thus the Soul is free from the limitations belonging to those realms. It has the power to rise into that consciousness wherein it may know all things. And through such realization of Truth, or the Divine Love and Wisdom, a Soul becomes freed from the bondage which obtains now upon all the outer planes of this world. To know Divine Truth by realization is to know liberation from bondage, from captivity in its manifold degrees, and to possess that perfect liberty which is the heritage of all who are truly children of God.

Now Truth may be spoken of, or it may be set forth in the language of symbols, or speech, or signs; but these must not be confounded with the Truth. They only speak of it. Truth broken upon the higher mind gives glorious light to that mind, fills it with knowledge of the Love and the Wisdom of the Father-Mother, as these can be cognized and correlated in the realms of manifestation, but they must not be confounded with *the* Truth. *The* Truth to be known must be realized. All the higher mind knowledges are but reflected light, even when beautifully true, of that glory of the Love and the Wisdom of the Father-Mother, we name Truth.

The word is generally used to indicate knowledge about a thing. It is thus applied to information about events, historical data, scientific facts. And, as applied to these realms, this is a right use. But to have the true knowledge of the meaning of historical events and the material facts of science, means something more than gathering information from without, or even tabulating the phenomena observable in nature and life. Knowledge is the light begotten of knowing. To know is to understand all the relations and correlations, seen and unseen, in the historical facts and material data of phenomena tabulated by science. To know is to understand not only the outer relationship of things or apparent relationships, but also to understand the inner relationships and correlationships of all the facts and data observable in scientific research. Knowledge, therefore, is comparative according to the plane and the degree of manifestation, unless the understanding be illumined so that the inner relationship of things is understood and the knowledge concerning them perfect. Otherwise, knowledge as such may be compared to a beautiful mirror broken and scattered, its thousand pieces reflecting in the most fragmentary way the objects presented to them.

Thus knowledge is of the Divine Omniscience; and a man or a woman only possesses that knowledge to the extent in which they are able to rise into the realm of that transcendent and most glorious power. Here knowledge is Divine. It is not of man, though it is reflected into man. It is of no person, though it can be reflected from the Divine realm of man's Being even through his personal mind. Knowledge is of God; and we truly know only in proportion as we know the Divine Mystery.

THE DIVINE OMNISCIENCE. Does God know all things? If so, then He must know all things which transpire upon the intermediary and outer planes of this world. And if He be cognisant of all such things, and we recognise that many of them are evil and disastrous, then God must know the evil and disastrous things as well as the infinite good.

The question raises a problem which confronts the mind of many, one which causes great perplexity and oft-times doubt and fear. It is a question not easily answered by the human mind, nor even easily answered to the human mind by any who may truly know. For at the heart of it there is a great and glorious mystery, the unveiling of which, in fulness, is impossible to any mind, and which certainly could not be unveiled fully to the mind ruled by the spirit of this world. There are those who have sought to get rid of the mystery of the Divine Omniscience embracing the consciousness of evil, by the sweeping affirmation that God, being the Eternal Good in Himself, cannot possibly know anything that is other than of the nature of that Eternal Good; and that hence He cannot know the evil and disastrous things which have obtained a footing and have prevailed in these outer planes.

Thus the Eternal and Ever Most Blessed One, who is at once the Absolute and the Source of all Being, and also the fulness of all Being, is presented as One so transcendent in His glorious nature, so exalted in His reigning state, that He is divorced from His world as known to most men and women, that world full of great activity mixed up with evil elements in the elemental kingdom, evil conditions in the human kingdom, inharmonious states within men and women as well as in the elemental kingdoms, resulting oft-times in disastrous things both for the planet and its children. If God be so exalted above His children,

creatures, world, then how is the world to be healed? And
how are the creatures to be purified and the children
redeemed? How are all the evil states to be blotted out and
the wrong conditions changed? And how is the
Righteousness of the Truth of God to be made manifest?

If such be the relation of the Eternal and Infinite Love
to this distraught earth and all its human freight, then
verily the lot of man is utterly hopeless, and the redemption
of the world with all its fallen elements is a hopeless
dream; for none can redeem but God, the Eternal Good.
Nothing can redeem but Love. Nothing can transform and
refashion, transfigure and transmute, but that Love whose
power is Divine alchemy wheresoever and whensoever and
whatsoever it toucheth.

It is a sad misconception of the nature of the Eternal
Love and Light and Life that separates Him from His
children thus, and from His world, even though it be in a
fallen state. The misconception arises through a misunderstanding of the nature of God, of the ministry of the Divine
world, and of the power to know even those things which
do not appertain to one's own consciousness, and which
have no part whatsoever in one's own Being. It is a sad
misunderstanding of the relation sustained by all the children
of the Father-Mother to Him and His relation to them, to
dream for one brief moment that He knoweth not all things
associated with them, not only upon the innermost planes,
but upon all the planes, even to that plane of the outermost
manifestation where the evil and the tragedy of the evil
have found a place. Hosts of things happen on the outer
planes without having a corresponding happening in the
inner realms. Things do happen in the inner realms,
though the word happen is altogether inadequate to express
what is meant. But even in the Divine Kingdom, constant

changes are taking place in the orders of ministry, in manifestations, and from the very centre or inner realm of that World, down through the Celestial Kingdom and the Angelic Kingdom, the like changes are taking place always as the ministries require them. There are phenomena manifest in the Angelic World, in the Celestial World, and even upon the magnetic plane of the Divine World. The Divine World is not in a state of quiescence. The more interior the more intense is the polar action. There is eternal motion even as there is Eternal Life, eternal service, eternal consciousness which is begotten of the action of the Eternal Life within the Being. In a perfect world, such as this planet once was, the phenomena expressed on the intermediary and outer planes of manifestation are the concrete adumbrations of the phenomena of the Angelic World, even as those phenomena are the expression or repetition upon the Angelic Kingdom, of the phenomena of the Celestial and Divine Worlds.

The things which we account of a wrong order upon these outer planes, arising out of the wrong states and conditions, do not happen in the Inner Realms. But they do happen on the outer planes. Here we have rain and hail and frost and snow; we have calm days and stormy days; we have the seasons; we have leaden skies and days of brilliant sunshine. We have wonderful vegetable growth, true manifestations of a divine order in thought forms and radiant colour and rhythmic action. We have the planet's motion proceeding daily on its axis and its orbital movement round the Sun. We have tremendous forces playing within the planet in its intermediary planes, as well as the manifestations caused by those forces upon the outer planes called whirlwinds, tidal waves, earthquakes and widespread seismic action in manifold ways, and also of volcanic action.

100

Is this planet a mere dream with all its elements and its conditions and its motions rotary and orbital? Are its day and night, its seasons and its year, and its great cycles of travail, only part of a dream? To see the planet's history through countless ages; to know what that history once was in glory, in purity, in sweet manifestation and in the joy of the children, is to know that this world is no vain dream, but that it is a world that once was glorious indeed in its unfallen days, with beautiful radiant children upon its planes. To see this world after it became changed, and even pass from its unfallen state to the great changes which took place, and to witness the great burden-bearing of its travail through tremendous cycles of ages, during which disaster after disaster befell it and all its children, when even manifest life was impossible upon its outer planes, when all its children were plunged into a state where spiritual darkness reigned; to hear the groaning, the sighing, the sorrowing, the anguishing of the Planet-Soul as it bore the burden of its mistake in travail; to see the glorious Divine ministry to this world, the sublime burden-bearing of the Divine World in ministry to it and its children; to witness the supreme efforts of the Divine Kingdom to bring back this fallen Judah, or world of Souls, to that true spiritual status in which it and all its children once were and to restore Jerusalem, the one time Holy City, to its pristine Glory, is to know verily that things do happen, that things have happened, and that the manifest world of life upon this planet is no mere or vain dream, nor the part of a dream, but the resultant of that most awful spiritual mist, or Maya, or illusion, which overtook the children of this world through the changes wrought in the elemental kingdoms, and brought the whole Soul-system down.

That the Divine World knew what was happening we do

know. That the history of this world in its travail, is written within itself, we also know. That the Book of Life which the Angel is said to open in the Divine Presence, or the Lamb of God to unseal, is the Soul's own history written within it; this also we know. And likewise, that that Soul history with all its tragedies, as well as the planetary history with its tragedies, are open to the Divine World, and that the Soul who can function there can know the world's travail in its history, and even the travail of the individual Soul upon its planes. And if that be possible to one who is in himself or herself but an individuation of the sublime Mystery of Being, an embodiment and reflector of the glorious Love and Light and Life of the Eternal and Ever Most Blessed Father-Mother, then verily that One whom we so name Father-Mother, unto whom all Souls are gathered and who in His consciousness is greater than the sum of all the consciousness of all the children of His Love who are able to function upon the Divine Realm, could not do other than know the history of this world and of all Souls upon it.

Omniscience means all knowledge, so that nothing can happen even in the sense of a dream, without it being known. God is not a person in any human sense. The Father-Mother is not an individual like a human Soul. He is not an individuation of anything to be confined within the limitations of that which is individuation. He is the Eternal and Ever Most Blessed One, Indivisible, the sum of all Being, out from whose Bosom all Being becomes; unto whose Bosom all Being returns in its consciousness; within whose Bosom in the consciousness of the Eternal Love the Soul finds its Nirvana, or eternal repose called rest, but which means absolute equipoise in Him.

The Lord of all Being is the sum of all Being; and through

the Being of each Soul He knoweth its history upon every
plane, even upon the realm of the outer manifestation. And
it is this glorious relationship between Creator and the
created, between the Eternal Love in the Father-Mother
and the child begotten, named Son of God in the human
Soul, that enables the Divine World to understand all that
happens in this world; to send forth ministries needful for
the conditions; to provide illumined messengers and send
them on even to the outer planes to bear anew the glorious
message of a Love that has never failed, that never fails,
that falters not, that hesitates not, that withholds not, a
Love whose divine alchemy is at last accomplishing the
redemption of this planet and all its children, the healing
of all its woundings and the hurt imposed upon the children,
the restoration of its fallen planes and the harmonizing of
its magnetic currents, the purification of its fallen elements
and the restoration to the true realm of their manifestation
and operation; the healing of the mind of the planet through
the changing of all its magnetic conditions; the transforming
of the wrong states of life and forms of administration, into
beautiful forms begotten of yet more beautiful states; the
transfiguring of life itself, making it once more truly beautiful
with Angelic sweetness begotten of unfallen desire and
radiant with the Radiance of Love, clothing those who are
able to rise so far in the beautiful garments which once were
the Soul's heritage, and filling such not only with the hope
of once more attaining unto the realization of the Blessed
and Most Holy Presence, but imparting power unto such
who have the vision to rise up into the high life of the Sons
of God.

The coming forth of messengers was no mere arising of
men and women as the outcome of some passing, though
deep, influence upon them begotten of the needs of their

103

fellow men and the love that was within them. The true messengers have ever spoken in the name of the Lord. They have spoken as those who have not only known Him, but who have come forth from His Presence. Their messages have had no negative side to them, all negation begotten of their message being the result of the triumph of the power of the Life and Light and the Love in the message. They have come forth from that Presence whose Name and whose Nature and whose Ministry is Eternal Love, and their message has been of that Love. All the negativing or destroying influences proceeding from that message have been nothing more than the changing processes begotten of the redeeming, transforming and transmuting power of the Eternal Love. The real messengers knew what they spake; for it is ever such with those whom the Lord Himself doth send. There is no doubt. There is no uncertainty. There is no speculation in their consciousness concerning the message He hath given them. The things they have had to speak of were known to them, understood by them, beheld in their vision, realized in the divine realm within them. Thus were they and their message ever distinguished from those who came from lower realms with ministries for the children. And these messengers came forth from the Father-Mother with the consciousness of all the Father-Mother desired for His children, because the Father-Mother knew what this world needed, and what it does need, and sent His servants with His own message of Love, and the Radiance of His Love, and the Life in which His Love finds embodiment.

A messenger from the Divine Realm knows the history of this planet in its unfallen days and in its fallen states. That messenger has all his visions in the Divine Realm. He hears, he sees, he realizes there of the Word of Life.

So greatly is this so, that the outer life he has to live is as
a dream, for he is disconnected from the life of the outer
planes; yet he knows what life upon the outer planes is.
He understands the life of the children upon these outer
planes. He knows their sorrows and their burdens; their
passions and their desires; their limitations and their
yearnings. He sees their travail to rise above the conditions
by which they are environed and out of the states amid
which they find themselves. And He knows all these things,
though they are quite apart from him. They do not make
up any degree of the sum of his consciousness. They are,
as it were, extraneous to him. Yet he is conscious of them
all. Aye, there is a sense in which he even bears the burden
of the consciousness of these things. For, being divine in
his love, he feels for all the children and even yearns over
them that they may be healed, redeemed, truly comforted
and strengthened, truly transformed until they may be
transfigured, clothed again in the sweet purity of true
childhood, and radiant once more with the Light of the
Presence within them.

*Thus, a Soul in the Divine World can know those things
which are not of himself or herself. Thus, the Eternal Love
can know all things, even those things which are the inversion
of His Love, the perversion of His Love, and the subversion
of His Love. And it is through such consciousness, such
glorious Omniscience, that that Love can lean down and
tremendously stoop, to meet the needs of His suffering
and sorrowing children, unto the redeeming, and healing
and restoration of them all.*

How glorious indeed a thing it is to know that the Divine
Omniscience embraces in the Divine Consciousness even
the knowledge of the Soul in its travail, and can hear and

answer its prayer and, leaning down, touch it, and give it power to rise out of its state and its environment into the blessed consciousness of His Overshadowing and even most blessed Indwelling Radiant Presence.

Is there such a thing as men and women name evil in this world? If there is, what is it? How may we know it and define it? And if it has come to have a place in the life of this world, how came it to have that place? And if it has become part of this world's history, how is it to be healed?

These are questions asked by many. And various are the answers given. There are those who deny the presence of evil in this world, and who say that it exists only in the mind of men and women as an erroneous belief.

That evil is the result of error cannot be gainsaid; but that it is something more than erroneous belief can be easily demonstrated. No such thing as evil can have a place in the Divine Realm of Being; but that does not prevent it from having a place in the outer realms of manifestation. There the planes of the Planet are out of harmony. Indeed, they are broken and confused, and fail to respond to the Divine Law. As a result, wrong conditions obtain, and many evil states arise. That evil has no Being, or the power of eternal good, is perfectly true; for evil is not a Principle: it is an effect of the inversion of Principle, and the outcome of false states. To deny that there is any such thing as evil in this world would not change the conditions. In all ages there have been many men and women who have believed that everything in the world was right and good. Yet through the countless ages evil manifestations have prevailed. If false states exist, then evil has a place; and the only way to blot it out is to change the states.

In endeavouring to explain the presence of evil in this world, there are those who affirm that it is the result of limitation. And there is a sense in which this may be said to be true. But evil is not to be related to that necessary limitation imposed upon all Souls by the Divine Father-Mother in harmony with the laws of spiritual evolution. Such a definition of evil would imply that the Divine Love, in states of great limitation, had ceased to be perfectly good, because of the limitations; for in the proportion that evil is present good is absent. For evil is the antithesis of good, even as darkness is of the light. There is no substantiality in darkness, it obtains simply where no light shines, and is an effect of the absence of light. But there need not be any evil found amid the darkness. Even light which dispels the darkness has no substantiality in itself. It is also only an effect of that which is substantial, namely, the Sun's magnetic action upon the superfine substances of the Planet contained within the magnetic plane. Yet, though light be only an effect of magnetic action, and in itself is insubstantial, it has most substantial results. For light is a life-giver, nourisher and adorner. Darkness leads to limitation and impoverishment, but light leaves behind it beautiful results.

In a similar way is evil present in certain wrong states which have arisen through the absence of good. All things fashioned by the Divine Love, in their original state, are good. The quality of the created things from the Divine Love is of the Eternal Good. Evil is the negation of that Good. Is it possible to have such negation? Yes. Water flowing from a pure fountain is pure. But if the water in its action passes through a channel containing impurities, though the fountain remains absolutely pure, yet the water will partake of the impurities. It is still water from the pure fountain, but the mixing of foreign elements with it has made it impure. And though it can always be healed by the process of purification and separation, and brought back to its original purity, yet it remaineth impure, full of evil elements, until that separation and purification be effected. To deny that the water, because the fountain whence it flowed was absolutely pure, had partaken of impurity as it flowed through the polluted channel, does not alter the fact of its impure state, nor effect its true healing. Mere negation is worthless. It is even worse than useless, for it leads to many disasters. You can only truly negative the power of anything evil, by positive action. You can only rightly change the conditions by the process of separation, purification and transmutation.

If, after this manner, we look at the Divine Mystery in the Human Soul, which Mystery we speak of as God who is the Water of Life, we may see how it is possible for the Fountain of all Being to be absolutely pure, and yet the Water of Life which flows from Him to become of a mixed order in its manifestation, through meeting with foreign elements in the various channels through which it has to flow. And should it be contended that there are no polluted channels for the River of Life to flow through, since God is in all things and all things are contained in Him: and since He is the Eternal Good, all things contained in Him must also be good, so that evil can have no place whatever, then we must eliminate Error also, since error does not contain what is good, and leads to falsity and wrong. For if God be in man as the Eternal Good always in the Absolute sense, so that Soul is God, then the whole man must be not only of God, and in God, and God be in Him; but he must be the perfect manifestation of God always; and in the relative he must be as perfect as in the Absolute. But if error does exist in the mind of the race, and great healing has to be effected because of that error, then the relative state does contain that which we have to designate evil—*i.e.*, wrong states and wrong conditions within man and around him.

109

And no fallacious reasoning can obliterate the fact. If error exists in the thoughts of men and women, and the effects of it upon the relative consciousness have been so calamitous that great healing is necessary, then it is mere sophistry to affirm that there is no evil in this world.

What is required is a true understanding of how error came into this world, and how it can be permanently healed. And in doing this, also to reveal how it cannot be related to the Divine Love, the Absolute Good, but nevertheless can be related to the relative life of humanity. For to understand this is to understand the Mystery of this world's mistaken dream. Even where the presence of evil in the world is most denied, it is recognised that a change came over the original man; that the effect was even as a mist upon the landscape, and that the present life of humanity is even as a dream. There are those who believe that that change produced by Maya—the Mist of Illusion—was the necessary corollary to the inheritance of good in Soul-evolution, believing that the Soul could know good only through also experiencing its opposite, evil, and in like manner know light through passing down into deep Soul darkness. Nay, by those who accept this doctrine of contrasts as absolutely necessary to Soul growth, it is even believed that to realize love the knowledge of hate is essential. Such philosophy also makes everything right, so that evil is only apparent, and therefore part of the dream of the Soul during its evolution.

Yet all recognise, whatever be their theories, that the world is full of tragedy. They may deny that evil is found in the conditions of the world, except in the form of Error or wrong beliefs; they may accept the doctrine of Maya as a necessary accompaniment of Soul evolution; or they may, as some do, affirm that evil is present in Matter,

110

coming indeed very near the Truth, but failing to reach it through a misconception of what Matter is; or they may reject all these theories and claims, and believe in the old-fashioned way of "a fall"; but all do in some degree recognise and lament the tragedies which are interwoven with the drama of human experience. In the higher races there is a deep consciousness that this world was once in a higher spiritual state than it is now.

And this is true. This world was once perfect in all its Kingdoms. Its seven planes were magnetically equilibrated, so that they responded to the Law of Divine Attraction. All was in beautiful harmony. Order reigned. The elements were all in true magnetic spiritual states. The children begotten and generated upon the planes were true spiritual offspring of a spiritual world.

But a great change took place. At first this change was only planetary; but by and bye all the offspring of the Planet were involved. The perfect elements became strangely affected. Where harmony had prevailed confusion arose. The elements became wrongly mixed and produced wrong states. Out of these, false conditions arose and the children were influenced to their hurt. States of experience and forms of existence came to have part in the drama of life, and these produced manifold tragedies. Even the eldest of the race suffered through the changing of the elemental spheres. The very Heavens of the Planet were brought down in their state; the middle Kingdom became so changed that the channels of Divine communication to the race were affected. That glorious River of Life—the Divine Magnetic Stream—which once flowed uninterruptedly to this world, and met with no alloy in its way through the channels, found all the channels affected, so that in its motion through those channels it gathered of

111

their alloy. And there were times when it could not flow, so obstructed was its path.

And as it was with the various Kingdoms and planes of the Planet, so did it become with the children upon her planes. Souls came to know Evil in this sense that they were plunged into conditions which were all wrong, the outworking of whose influences resulted in the children experiencing the antithesis of good, and coming to know the bitterness of that which we designate evil—wrong states in the elements, with resulting wrong conditions in the life. In body and mind and heart did they suffer, as these terms represent desires and feelings, ambitions, emotions and affections.

Evil is the inversion of Good. Error is the perversion of Truth, therefore error is evil. Wrong is the subversion of Right; wrong is error and is also evil. To deny that evil states have a place in the economy of this world's life, whilst error and the wrong begotten of it obtain, and in many ways prevail, is to falsify what is obvious to everyone in whom the Light dwells. To deny that evil has any power in itself apart from wrong states in the elements and individuals, is to affirm a great truth; for there is no evil power, as such, corresponding to the Divine Power. In ancient days Ahriman was only a name given to a state of intense darkness arising out of wrong conditions. Ormudz was the Eternal Light, the Infinite Good, the Divine Principle. On the Divine Kingdom macrocosmic and microcosmic, there is no evil; no wrong conditions could obtain there. But upon the outer Kingdoms of the Planet, and the lower planes of human consciousness, it is otherwise. There wrong conditions do prevail, and states which are evil find manifestation. It is there Ahriman reigns in the darkness, the fear, the disease begotten of wrong desire, falsity, impurity, pride, envy, jealousy and hate.

Now, the evil which these represent can only be overthrown by a cessation of the influences that invert the good, pervert the truth, and subvert the right. And to heal the influences is to change the states and conditions, elemental and human, out of which they are generated. In healing evil, always affirm the Divine Power of Good. Merely to deny the evil does not establish the good. Evil may be denied without God being affirmed. To deny that evil has any place in the life of this world is simply to ignore wrong, hurtful things, and the hurt given by them; and this must not be confounded with the denial that evil has any power of its own. Those who would truly heal evil must be ever true. Sophistry, Jesuitism or Casuistry should ever be avoided. Even on the outer planes, Truth must be regnant. For evil cannot be overthrown by statements that are not true. Truth in the Absolute surely must become the truth of the relative. Things do happen on the outer planes which are not of the inner realms, for the realm of Being and that of existence are not the same. The realm of existence is the manifest world; the realm of Being is the world of glorious Divine Realization. This is true of Planet and human Soul. And until the world is redeemed, the events upon the realm of manifestation, except through the redeemed, will not be in true harmony with the realm of Divine Realization. But when the world is healed the events of the outer will be in harmony with the purpose of the inner. Then only will evil cease.

"Forgive us our sins." This prayer rises from the hearts of all men and women who have devout moments. By the truly lowly and pure of heart it is often uttered. It finds a place in that prayer of the elect, known as the Lord's Prayer. By the One who was the vehicle of the blessed manifestation, the forgiveness of sin was taught. He, therefore, recognised sin as a sad state of experience in this world. To Him there never was a doubt of its presence in human experience. He saw its revealings and beheld its results. To the stricken one He could say, "Go, for thou art healed; but sin no more." To those whose heart was empty of true love and compassion, and whose judgment was unjust, He could say, "Let the one who is without sin cast the stone." To the truly lowly and sorrowing ones whose consciousness of sin filled them with deep regret and grief, He could say, "Thy sin is forgiven thee: enter now into Peace."

But there are those who deny that sin has any place in human life, or that there is any need for forgiveness. There is, therefore, no need to pray for forgiveness. There is nothing to forgive if there be no sin.

In this way is the Teaching of the true Messengers controverted and annulled. But much more is done. The very purpose of the blessed manifestation is made fruitless. More tragic still is the thought that the divine purpose in the Oblation or Sin-offering was a great mistake, and that all the agony, sorrow and pain endured by the one who was the vehicle of the Oblation as well as the manifestation, were needless and useless.

If there be no such thing as Sin, then the heart of humanity must always have been right. And all must be well. Even everything that seems most wrong must be right, and wrong

114

have no place. For people to complain that wrong has been done to them would have to be accounted a mistaken view of the supposed wrongdoer's action.

But all such affirmations concerning the non-reality of evil and sin, are illusions. By their own conduct in the relative, men and women contradict what they affirm. In certain states of experience they do not hesitate to go to Civil Law to have tangible or imaginary wrongs against them condemned and righted. They seem to be ignorant of the fact that no one who knows the Divine Love in nature and operation, and who seeks to embody Christ in life, could dream of calling upon the Civil Authorities to judge between them and others. There is but one Law for those who be in that Divine State of Love: it is the Law of Love, God's Law. And it is a Law that teaches the Saints not even to seek what they might justly call their own. There are no civil courts in the Heavens; and for the Saint there should be none on earth. Love is the Law, and Compassion is the Court. The very actions of those who deny the presence of evil and sin show that their affirmations are a mirage of facts, and an inversion of what is true. There are many wrong beliefs in this world and surely this is one of the most dangerous. It is quite true to say that if we can heal wrong beliefs, sin will be healed. But, as we shall unveil presently, to heal wrong beliefs is to do something more than change false ideas or opinions. It goes more deeply into Life than that. It affects the Desire nature, which needs to be healed. It touches the Will, the power of choice, whose direction in most men and women is wrong. It enters into the realm of the Heart, for the emotions require to be purified and ennobled, so that the manifestation of Love will be beautiful. And its magnetic current must enter the Mind to purify it of its vanity, enmity, pride,

115

love of power and dominion and all false ambition, so that it may be lowly in its attitude and meek in its spirit. For the true healing of wrong beliefs or error is the enhancing of the whole Being, from the realm of the Absolute or Divine Innermost, to the outer realm or the Relative.

How few there are who seem to rightly understand the nature of Sin. In the general judgment of the theological schools and religious communities, there are many things classed as Sinful which do not partake of its nature. And, in strange contradiction, many things are considered by these schools and institutions to be right, just and good, which do partake of the nature of Sin. There are many things legalized by both State and Church which are not only of a sinful order, but lead to most disastrous sinful experiences. Sin is in the Will. It is often used as a synonym for evil and wrong. But evil may exist without Sin. Wrong may be done which is not sin. Even transgression may be made and no sin come into the heart. Many do wrong unwittingly. Some choose to do wrong when thrown into the lion's den of temptation, and are tried beyond their endurance. And these mistakes may bring forth sorrow. But they must not be confounded with what is more terrible in nature and results. For Sin is done where the Will chooses deliberately to do an unholy thing to the hurt of all that is most beautiful within that one's self, or to the injury of another, knowing that it will hurt. It is a deliberated choice of wicked conduct for the purpose of accomplishing something which that one desires.

But for the presence of Sin in life's experience in this world, the healing of all its false beliefs and wrong states would have been accomplished long ages ago. For, speaking generally, it is much easier to heal effects, than to effect the healing of the Will. The rulers of this world have chosen

116

to go their own way in lording it over God's heritage. This has been manifest in the realms monarchical, social, intellectual and religious. By their way the very evil conditions have been aggravated, more intensely evil states generated, iniquities multiplied, and the people and even the creatures, thrown into hells of pain and anguish. And as a resultant, the natural corollary of such wickedness, sin has increased its ravages and hell enlarged its borders.

To forgive sin and its results is to heal the Life. The forgiveness of sin is the healing of mind, heart and will. And this is more than changing beliefs. You may change beliefs without healing wrong desire. You may turn the mind from its outlook on life, and thus help it to apprehend something of the true vision; but to accomplish healing, the true vision must not only be apprehended, it must be made concrete in life. The forgiveness of sin is the healing of Desire and the redemption of the Will.

The healing of Sin was the supreme purpose of the Oblation. The Planetary Karma accumulated upon the realm now spoken of as the Astral-Occult had to be transmuted. That Karma was built up by the children of this world during the period known as the Sodomic ages when the most awful forms of wickedness prevailed. The middle Kingdom was filled by the most grotesque wicked images which these children had fashioned upon the super-elemental world when they went down into the states named Sodom and Gomorrah. And, through writing this history upon the middle Kingdom, they shut the very heavens to all but those children of the Kingdom who were of the ancient Christhood. These latter were able to transcend the elemental world until this latter became so denizened with the terrible evil forms, that they also became affected, and found it most difficult to rise into spiritual altitudes. The human races were unable to work off that Karma. The handwritings of their deeds were too great for them to blot out. So it had to be accomplished by a Redeemer. This was the burden of the Oblation, the process of the Sin-offering, the service that had to be rendered to make Redemption possible and the Atonement a reality. To blot out that Karma by bearing its effects was the great work of the Master. From the state of the Manifestation He passed to take up the burden of travail necessary to the blotting out of that Karmic burden, and the bringing of healing to the mind of this Planet. And through the sorrowful travail which covered all the ages since the Blessed Manifestation until these latter days in which the Oblation has been completed, the permanent healing of the children of this world is now made possible. The Forgiveness of Sin is accomplished. The effects of the sins of the race have been borne unto the transmutation of them, and now all Souls may be redeemed from sinful desire and healed of all the hurt imposed by sin, and enter into the blessed experience of the true and full "Forgiveness of Sin." That which the Church has professed to give through its priests with sad and disastrous failure, the true Healers sent forth from God have the power to make manifest. All sin can be healed. But it is not healed or forgiven by repeating a Divine Fiat. Forgiveness means the restoration of the Soul's powers to true polarity and equilibrium. It is the healing of the mind in its attitude and thought, the heart in its desire and love, and the will in its choice. Forgiveness brings the whole Being of man to the threshold of the Blessed Presence where the Sanctuary becomes filled with the Divine Radiance whose magnetic stream flows from the centre to the circumference, from the Ego or Divine Principle, to the outermost planes.

How few there are who rightly apprehend what true healing means, even amongst those who believe in spiritual healing. And even amongst these latter have we met with a strange lack of the true understanding of the nature of the forgiveness of sin. Aye, even amongst those who affirm that there has been no true healing given since the days of the Manifestation until these latter days, we have found an astonishing irreverence towards, and a palpable lack of perception concerning, Divine Things. They seem quite unaware of this fact, that whatever mistake was made in the presentation of the work of the Master by those who came after Him, the chief reason why true healing became a lost knowledge was the lack of power to deal with the conditions which prevailed. Nor could that power come, except to the very few, even of those Souls who were once of the Ancient Christhood, until the Oblation was fully accomplished. The Christian Healing Centres which claim to be the vehicles for the interpretation of true healing, and with some show of reason for the claim, could never have arisen with this healing mission, but for the Oblation. For they are the rehabilitation of the ancient Therapeutic Societies. And yet by a strange contradictory attitude of mind, which in itself is the sure testimony to the limitations of the ministry of such centres, the Leaders and Teachers are ignorant of the nature and work of the Oblation, and even deny that it took place.

Well might the Master say, "When the Son of Man cometh again shall faith be found upon the Earth?" For faith is Divine Understanding. It is the power to perceive heavenly secrets. But those therapeutic communities fail to truly perceive and understand the Divine ministry to this world. The full meaning of the Master's saying to Simon Peter has yet to come home to their understanding, "If I

119

wash not thy feet, thou canst have no true part in my mission." For true forgiveness of sin means the purification of the mind, and the heart, and the body. It inspires true compassion and pity, even to the creatures. The forgiveness of sin embraces the healing of all that is wrong in eating and drinking, as well as in thinking and feeling. It takes in the whole man and woman. It signifies true lowliness of mind, the majesty of love in its beautiful humility. It is not consonant with the following of earthly traditions in the service of life, nor with the seeking for earthly enrichment. To seek power to turn dust into gold is idolatry. It is a high form of the worship of Mammon. To be able to operate upon material things occultly, so as to bring them to one's feet, is of the very nature of that occultism which has wrought many disasters upon this distraught world.

What have the true Messengers to say to it all? In earthly estate they were always poor. Nor did they seek for earthly enrichment. They came enriched from the Divine Kingdom with the treasures of the Divine Love and Wisdom. They had no power to use for the conversion into gain of the elements of the Earth. On the outer planes they were, and always had to be, as little children; though they were as giants in spiritual heritage. The perfect Praise of God filled them. They were ever reverent, always lowly, without ostentation, though full of heavenly understanding and power.

The healing of sin which they would recognise would be full-rounded, clothing the Healers and the healed ones in the garments of Love Divine.

And such was the healing of sin given by the Master.

In the sacred writings there are many references to a profound Mystery spoken of as the
Sin-offering, sometimes as the Atonement, and
more generally as the Redemption. Great Libraries are
filled with volumes which have this Mystery as their theses.
But though the Redemption, the Atonement and the
Sin-offering are written of as being of the one Mystery, they
are not the same; and their relation to one another is purely
accidental.

*   *   *   *

THE REDEMPTION.   The Redemption relates to the purification
and healing of Humanity. It is usually inter-
preted to mean that by the death of the Master there was
something accomplished for humanity which had as its
resultant the Forgiveness of Sin. For He is believed to have
wrought out Salvation for the race, delivering all Souls
from the just judgments of the Divine Righteousness by
satisfying something in the Divine Nature, thus reconciling
the race to God. The basis of the doctrine of the Redemption that is so greatly emphasized is this, and it is summed
up in the often quoted words, "Believe on the Lord Jesus
Christ, and thou shalt be saved." As it affects humanity the
Redemption is, therefore, only efficacious when the
Messenger is believed in.

But the true Redemption is something much more substantial than anything acquired by mere belief in any
Messenger. It is a belief in the true doctrine of Life as
propounded by the Messenger, and the reduction of that
belief into concrete form. The Redemption is the process
of redeeming back the entire Being to a state of purity,
goodness and love. It is no hypothetical redemption
accomplished by any process of intellectual or metaphysical
reasoning, but that which is most practical. It relates to

121

all the desires, feelings, affections, judgments and ambitions of life. It purifies the body of every wrong desire and the mind of every ignoble thought and false ambition. It changes the heart's love and devotion in their expression, bringing them to be both impersonal and selfless. It exalts the will in its choice, until it chooses the path that leads to the most exalted Life and becomes beautiful in its willinghood that only the Divine Will should be wrought out in the Life. For the Redemption is the healing of all the attributes of man. It is the process of the Forgiveness of Sin.

And its relation to the Sin-offering is only incidental. If the human race had retraced its steps ere the last great descent took place which carried humanity once more below the Human Kingdom, there would not have been any need for the tragic sorrow by which the Karmic Burden of this world had to be blotted out. For the Redemption could have been accomplished without it. But the conditions had become too great against Humanity. The Karma written was overwhelming. To change the conditions which were so inimical to spiritual growth, and make the Redemption possible, the burden of the Sin-offering was borne. And now, as the fruit of that tragic burden-bearing the Redemption is not only possible, but it is actually taking place. It may be witnessed proceeding in and through all the enlightened, purifying movements which have for their objective the advancement and upliftment of Humanity. Purity in diet, humaneness towards all the creatures, compassion for all who have known misfortune, justice for the oppressed, truer and nobler thoughts concerning social questions, more reverence for womanhood and parenthood, greater desire to reach out unto the realization of loftier manhood and womanhood, and so to live and to serve for the blessing of all. These are a few of the outer signs of the coming of the Redemption.

And there are many other manifestations of a more inward nature. The religious life and outlook of men and women are changing. They are seeking for the spiritual. The truly Mystic questions are finding more earnest disciples. Many are finding true healing in body and mind and heart. The claims of the Unseen Realm are receiving more sincere attention; and to many that realm is becoming the most real world of all. And there are those who now know the full meaning of the Redemption, and who have found even the Divine World of Being.

The Redemption has relation to Life: it is Divine Healing. And they who have entered into the glorious meaning of it are the Redeemed.

*   *   *   *

THE ATONEMENT. The Redemption is the prophecy of the Atonement: for the Soul it is the herald of its becoming. Because the Atonement is a realization by the individual, and is not, as has been supposed, a mysterious work wrought on man's behalf apart from his own purpose and spiritual growth. It is attained by a Divine satisfaction; but it is the satisfaction of fulfilling the Divine Law of his growth, and not merely the satisfying of Divine Justice and Righteousness outside of himself, and by another.

The Atonement is believed by the Religious Schools of the West to have been something accomplished by the Master during the Roman Crucifixion. It is believed that in His death He made a sacrifice for humanity, and in doing so atoned to Divine Justice for humanity's sin, and that thus He satisfied the Divine Righteousness so that man could be accounted as righteous.

If the Pauline Epistle to the Romans had never been received as an inspired work by the early Church raised by the Paulites in the name of the Master, it is certain that no such view of the work of the Master could ever have obtained a hold upon the dimmed vision of its leaders and teachers. It was over this very interpretation of the doctrine of the Atonement that the early Brotherhood and Paul entered into conflict. That the Church founded to embody the Christhood revealed through the Master should have chosen to follow the interpretations of the profound Mystery given by one who did not know the Master, nor those innermost Teachings unveiled by the Master only to His most intimate friends, is another remarkable testimony to the evil influences which were at work seeking to destroy the Message He gave by casting over the vision such a glamour of the Pauline personality as to make of the latter an inspired Messenger, and of his interpretations of the Mystery, a Divine Mandate. Thus was the true vision miraged, the truth inverted and materialized. For the Pauline view of the Atonement is nothing more than a recrudescence of the fearful Jewish sacrificial system, with the venue changed from the creature to the human victim.

Atonement is Reconciliation. It means, to be at one. Had evil and sin never entered into the fabric of this world's history, and the system had remained unfallen, Atonement would still have been necessary. For its necessity in the human experience, it is not dependent upon evil and sin: apart from these states all Souls must be atoned. For it is the true corollary of the postulation of man as a Spiritual Being. It is the bearing forward of all his attributes into a condition of perfect At-one-ment with the Divine purpose as manifested in the true Laws of Being. It is the Reconciliation or harmonizing of all his attributes, the

124

equilibrating of all the planes of his life upon the different Kingdoms as he rises from glorious state to yet more glorious state. And the most perfect degree of At-one-ment, what is known in the East as the Nirvanic state, is the full fruition of spiritual growth. It is perfect oneness with the Lord of all Being, and the abiding consciousness of the Overshadowing and Indwelling Presence.

The entrance of evil conditions into this world has made the realization most difficult for all but the elect few. Nay, even many of these latter have found it the most painful path imaginable owing to the fallen elemental states. But that most desirable state of life and consciousness, when the Soul is one with the Lord, may now be entered upon by all who yearn for its becoming, and who follow the true path of its attainment. For that has been wrought out by the Divine Love and Wisdom upon the Elemental Kingdom known as the Astral realm, by which it is now possible for Souls to know the Atonement.

*   *   *   *

THE SIN-OFFERING. The Sin-offering is that profound Mystery which we speak of as the Oblation. Its relation to the Redemption and the Atonement is very intimate, though only incidental. The Atonement is inherent in the very constitution of man as the corollary of the true evolution of his spiritual consciousness; whilst the Redemption is only incidental, being necessitated through the coming of evil and sin into the human experience, and has to do with the purification of life upon the fallen planes of this world and the human Soul. But the Sin-offering stands out from these as something so profound in its nature that it is said even the Angels desired to look into the Mystery. Certainly none could look into it and fail to be filled with wonder and awe. For by means of it the Middle Kingdom of this world was redeemed, its circuli purified and made habitable once more for the children of this world when they pass from these planes from one generation (or life) to another. So the Redemption is now in process of becoming very real unto many; for through the healing of the Astral or Middle Kingdom, Souls are now able to rise out of evil states and conditions and find the way of purity and goodness.

But how few are yet sufficiently awake in their spiritual nature to enable them to enter into any degree of enlightened understanding of all that the Oblation meant for the Master. How few even of those who are able to hear in these days of its profound Mystery could imagine how great the work was which had to be accomplished, and how tragic was the Burden that had to be borne. How very few there are, even of the elect ones, who could endure the unveiling of that tragic history, even though, like the Angels, they might desire to look into it. And yet, only they could apprehend in any degree the nature of the Burden of the Oblation. For they were members of the Ancient Christhood Community, dwellers upon the Heavens, ministrants for God, and sent to this world to aid its children in their spiritual evolution. They should have the prescience to penetrate deeply into the Divine Mystery, and to understand the significance of it. They alone of all Souls in this world could appreciate all that is meant by the descent of the Master from high Christhood to the lowly, fallen states of the children of this world. It was in this sense that He laid aside His glory that He might be able to descend into the states of conscious experience necessary for the fulfilment of the Divine Will in the execution of the work by which the Middle Kingdom was purified. And these elect ones could with some degree of sympathetic understanding, enter into the great sorrow entailed in such a sacrifice; for when they were sent into this world for ministry, a certain degree of limitation had to be imposed to enable them to minister unto those who were but as little children compared to themselves, and their limitations became more accentuated during long ages of misery amid evil conditions, though they yearned continually for liberation from such bondage as the conditions brought unto them. Throughout the long ages they have longed for the return of the Presence in blessed fulness of realization. Therefore they should be able to realize deeply what it must have meant for the Master to descend from high Christhood wherein the consciousness of the Blessed One was ever His inheritance, both in the Overshadowing and the Indwelling, to states of consciousness which involved the loss of that glorious realization. For it made Him feel like a Soul lost amid the wilderness of this world, though He sought by day and night for the return of that most Holy One to His Sanctuary. For the dwelling in this lowly state was essential. Only in this way could He accomplish the great work of purification by the process of attraction, absorption and transmutation.

The Oblation is the Sin-offering in which, with rare exceptions, all the Churches of the West have believed. Though it involved death to the Master, it was not the supposed dissolution on the Roman Cross, but that spiritual death which pursued Him all through the burden-bearing. It was the dying of Jesus, and the crucifixion of His Christhood, and the pain of it was infinitely more poignant than any physical suffering, and the anguish it brought was unspeakable. For the burden of the Sin-offering was beyond description, so terrible was it. So very real was it that it stands out in strange contrast to the hypothetical burden-bearing associated with the belief held by the

127

Church. It was indeed a sacrifice worthy of a God; a burden-bearing which only the Divine could accomplish; a work that the Divine Love and Wisdom alone could have projected and borne and effected. For, though the Master was the vehicle through which it had to be borne, it must ever be related to the Divine Love and Wisdom. Apart from the upholding, guarding and sustaining power of that Love, the Master could not have fulfilled the Divine purpose. To have endured the terrible strain and awful anguish alone, would have been impossible.

It is not easy to describe that Burden. Indeed there are parts of it which would baffle description. The half could never be told even of those things that may be spoken of; the sadness of it all, that it was necessary; the tragedy of it, that it had to be of such a nature; the Anguish of it, that even the Temple's veil was rent; the pain and sorrow of it that the Sun of the glorious Radiant Presence had to be eclipsed in every one of His forty lives. For the Oblation made it necessary for the Master to descend into evil conditions and pass through states of experience which were absolutely at variance with all His high purpose and holy desires. Only in this way could He attract unto Himself the evil magnetic images which infested the Astral and Occult Kingdoms for many long ages. They had their origin in the Sodomic times. They were fluidic and magnetic, having been built up out of the fallen elements of the magnetic plane. Consequently they were terrible in their magnetic power over the bodies and minds of the children of this world. Begotten of the low desires and passions which obtained and prevailed amongst the younger members of the race, these awful magnetic forms made them repeat the very deeds which brought about the disastrous conditions. And thus history repeated itself through long

128

ages, perpetuating the sadness and sorrow begotten of the awful horrors.

It was the destruction of those terrible images that formed the burden of the Oblation. As they were fluidic and magnetic they could be obliterated only by a process of attraction, absorption, transmutation and elimination. To attract them, the Master had to vehicle through bodies whose magnetic constitution could draw those forms. They approached Him as they did the children of this world, and made Him feel as they felt. But whereas the children of this world had no power to resist the terrible influences of these forms and went down before them, He held them, absorbed them into His own body, passed through the experience of the low desires they set up in the body and lower mind, and in doing so transmuted them. And then He had to pass off the elements, thus freeing Himself from their effects. And thus were they destroyed and the circuli of the Astral and Occult Kingdoms were redeemed.

But the process took all the ages that have intervened since the days of the Blessed Manifestation until now. That which is supposed to have been accomplished within the limited space of three earth-days, took no fewer than three great cycles of the Naros, three prophetic days, inter-Solar-Lunar-Earth cycles, each covering over six hundred years. Those were the days during which the Master descended into the hells. For He laboured amid the hell-states. Those were the days during which He was buried, and the beautiful Christhood with Him. For, though the Western World believed that He arose from the dead and ascended into the Heavens, and it has professed to worship Him as humanity's High Priest who pleaded for the race before the Father, yet He has been as dead to that world, for it has not known Him, nor His glorious message, nor

129

even understood Jesushood and lived the life, let alone apprehended the meaning of a Divine Christhood. Those were the days of the great temptation in the wilderness, when He was face to face with the wild beasts of elemental passions, when He had to fast from the Divine Love and Wisdom which had been at all times His Soul's meat and drink, and be tempted of the devil or spirit of negation to change the passional elements into means whereby to satisfy His hunger. For thus was He tempted and tried like His Brethren, being in fashion like unto them: and this for forty times or lives. Those were the days of the great loneliness, when He sat by the well of Jacob in the City of Sychar full of a weariness none could understand, sorrowful even unto the laying down of His burden of travail and find real rest.

The Sin-offering was the blotting out of the fruits of the sin of low passion: the Oblation was the giving of Himself for the accomplishment of this mighty work for the race. Of Himself He made an offering or oblation that He might bear this world's burden for it and carry away the effects of its sin. And now it is accomplished; and, as a first fruit, the Redemption has truly begun. For the Day of Salvation for the world is at hand. It shall now know the joyful sound of the glad tidings of Divine Healing. And the hour for the Elect ones has also come; and the Atonement for them is at their very door.

What is sorrow? In the human experience it is common to all Souls, and especially is it so to those who feel deeply and aspire greatly. So much is it a part of the human drama that it is not strange that it has come to be looked upon as a part of the necessary experience in the Soul's travail. It manifests itself upon every plane of the consciousness. We see it on the outer realms expressed through the consciousness of personal loss in earthly relationships, or in material things. We see it operating upon the mind plane, for the mind becomes overburdened with the sense of loss, and suffers. We witness its manifestation on the plane of the emotions, where the love principle in its personal revealings and associations becomes conscious of personal and even individual loss. Upon the plane of the higher mind whose office it is to receive the Light from the inner realms and reflect it upon the outer, we may behold sorrow manifesting itself in disappointment through a consciousness of failure. It even touches the faculty of faith, as it is sometimes called—the power of the intuition to discern heavenly secrets—when the Being becomes conscious of a loss of that power, and yearns unutterably to regain that power that it may again understand divinely. By the very few it may be seen operating in the very innermost realm, where it becomes grief, the Being yearning for a realization it once inherited, and grieving that through limitation upon some of the other planes of its consciousness, it is unable to enter into that realization, even in part in some cases, in others with a greater degree of fulness. And we may see that grief also manifested towards Souls as a Redeemer alone can manifest it; for it is the Divine Grief begotten of the travail of the Divine Love within the Being in the office of redemption, healing, restoration and

131

transformation. For there is such a thing as Divine Grief experienced by those who are His appointed servants, His messengers, His redeemers in this world as it is constituted today.

*   *   *   *

Though sorrow is common to the lot of humanity because of the conditions which obtain in this world, yet there is no experience through which the Soul passes, less understood as to its nature and even its ministry. There are those who deny that there should be any sorrow in this world even as life is now constituted. They affirm that there is no cause for sorrow, but only reason for joy. They would have all Souls forget their sorrow, transcend it, and be filled with gladness and rejoicing.

This is truly beautiful both in its purpose and the realization, if that purpose could accomplish the realization in the true way. For the children of this world do not desire to sorrow, unless they be in an excessively morbid state. Indeed, most men and women seek to flee from sorrow, or, rather, from the memory which sorrow brings, and drown the consciousness of that experience amid the intoxicating things of sensuous delights in some form or other. Men and women do not want sorrow for themselves, though by their thoughtless words and actions they may bring sorrow to others. They would banish sorrow from their own hearts and the threshold of their homes, if they could; and this would be beautiful, providing it could be done in the true way. But to deny there is such a thing as sorrow, even Divine Sorrow, is not the true way to heal the sorrow of this world. To affirm that there is no need for sorrow, and yet leave the world in the very throes of the conditions out of which sorrow is begotten, is not the way to heal the world of its malady.

Sorrow is begotten oft-times of great limitation in the individual, limitation of vision, of understanding, of love. It is oft-times the child of conscious loss or bitter disappointment. It may be the outcome of conscious injustice administered by others in their thoughts and their words and their deeds. It may be just the pain of the whole spiritual Being expressing itself as the outcome of the flagellations imposed by even its own intimate friends. It is quite true that a Soul may rise above all these states in its consciousness, when earthly losses and disappointments and limitations and even the flagellation of the oppressors are all as nothing unto it, so that no sorrow would be within that one begotten of the loss or limitation or pain imposed; yet that one with clear vision beholding the thoughts, the deeds, the states of injustice, could be filled with the sorrow of a great grief. In that one's own self there would be no sorrow begotten of any state within; yet the very purity, the beauty, the goodness, the tenderness, the love, the transcendent vision begotten of the radiance of the love, would make that one the more conscious of the lovelessness, the darkness, the unrighteousness, the injustice, the false judgments, the harshness, the lack of sweet, tender feeling, even to the filling of that one with great grief that such states could be within any of the children of the Father-Mother.

This is Divine Sorrow. It is this that is meant when grief is spoken of in relation to the Divine Realm. For God the Ever Most Glorious Being is no stoical spectator looking out upon a world filled with disasters. He is not apart from His children as expressed in worlds, nor His children as expressed in the individual units of Souls. He is not an observer. He is the Being at the heart of all Being, whence all existence of Being operating in the realms of manifestation derives its sustenance. He is one with all His worlds. He is one with all His children, though transcendent in Himself in nature, in purity, in goodness, in love. Far removed from the ordinary concepts of life in His Being, yet manifesting unto His children, He knows them unto the full understanding of all their needs, and provides ministry for them.

Thus in all their sorrow there is a consciousness of it in the Divine Realm, whether it be begotten of earthly loss or disappointment, or limitation, or failure to reach the heights the Soul glints in its vision, or because of the injustice in judgment, or the unrighteousness of the burden to be borne, or flagellations filling the Being with pain unspeakable.

It is in this way alone that that astonishing expression which has come to be associated with the Master known as Jesus Christ, can be fully understood. He has been called "the Man of Sorrows" and one well acquainted with grief. He is thought of as beautiful, as one who was in a state of purity begotten of true vision and sweetly balanced mind and heart and life. With Him, Love supremely is associated and revealed as broken in His compassion unto Souls, and His pity unto the weak and defenceless ones, even the creatures. It is believed of Him that He realized in great measure the sublime mystery of the Being of God, and that He dwelt ever in the consciousness of the Overshadowing and Indwelling of that Glorious Presence. Many there are who think He attained to that most wonderful realization in the life described as the days of the manifestation. Many there are who believe that He had attained to that state long ages before He came in the days of the Manifestation. But whether it be the one view or the other, the result is the same. He knew God the Father-Mother. In most intimate fellowship did He abide with the Father-Mother.

134

He was never alone, though in this world He knew the unspeakable aloneness of a Soul whom none could fully understand even in those days. He could speak in intimate ways of the Father-Mother; yet it was an intimacy that was ever reverent and beautiful, and full of sublime adoration. In Him, when speaking of that Holiest of Beings, there was no flippancy. There never was an approach to irreverence. There was no lack of conscious recognition of His own nothingness, and the sublimity of the fulness given unto Him from the Father-Mother.

Now it is naturally said by many in these days, as in other days, that He could not have been "the Man of Sorrows," because He had those realizations which bring to the Being the supremest joy. There are many who feel it is a misnomer to give Him such a title as "the Man of Sorrows," well acquainted with grief. Surely if any one should have had joy, He should. There are not wanting those who even try to turn that cryptic exclamation uttered in the midst of His anguish in the Gethsemane, which, in the narratives is presented as having been spoken on the Roman Cross—"Eli, Eli, Lama Sa Bach Thani," into an exclamation of joy proclaiming how God had glorified Him. The confusion which has arisen out of the narrative associated with Him in the New Testament is beyond defining, so great has it been, and so tragic also have been its results.

In the biographical sketches the real life is not beheld, nor is the ministry portrayed there, such as He gave. As the manifestor of the Father-Mother, and the interpreter of the meaning of the life realized and expressed in the states Jesus Christ, the Lord, He had supreme joy. His joy was of God. The Angelic World was the atmosphere in which He thought and felt, desired and served. Its joy He knew. Even that higher joy begotten of perfect oneness

135

in the Father-Mother was His. He was no "Man of Sorrows" in the early days of the Manifestation; though He did grieve over the many things which He witnessed in His dearest ones, and saw manifested through them. He sought ever to bring joy to others and to help them to the realm where joy abounded, to lift them up that their joy might find fulfilment through Soul fulness. From their hearts He banished sorrow, in so far as they were able to receive from Him. And it was His supreme desire that their days should be crowned with gladness and their lives with joy.

As the manifestor, He was not the "Man of Sorrows"; and He did speak of the joy of God as few could. It was only in the latter days of His ministry that the shadows fell which made Him a man of sorrow. That was when He beheld opening out before Him a vista of all the states of consciousness which would have to be entered into in that other part of His ministry associated with burden-bearing for this world. That burden-bearing has to be expressed in the term *The Oblation*, commonly called by the churches *The Sin-Offering*. It was then that the first stage of that profound experience expressed in the terms "The Man of Sorrows" well acquainted with grief, was entered into, and it was then that He spake the Logia which related to the Oblation, and which are so burdened with coming sorrow for Him. It was in the lives of the Oblation that He became the real "Man of Sorrows" well acquainted with grief. For in the lives of the Oblation He had to descend into states of consciousness which brought upon Him such great limitation that, whilst His whole Being was crying out for the majesty of that Love He knew so well in the perfect state, to express itself through Him in the perfect realization, He had to be as a bond-servant,

136

as one bound by the limitations of the states into which He had to enter, in order that He might accomplish the will of the Father-Mother and blot out those conditions which they represented.

For forty lives did this path of travail continue, even through all the era known as the Christian, until these days in which we ourselves are manifesting. Upon Him He bore the burden of the world, in this sense, that He took upon Himself this world's karmic burden which had been fashioned by its children long ages ago when they denizened the circuli of the planet's heavens with grotesque and evil forms, the children of their own creating through sensual thoughts, desires and ways. He carried up into each life a portion of this burden, treading the winepress alone, staining His beautiful Christly garments with His own Life-stream as He shed it for the blotting out of those awful forms. In every life He cried out for the living God, for He always longed to realize divinely; but His path took Him down into those states for conscious manifest experience in which even the least of the children dwelt. He went even down into those states where what are called the devils, the evil elemental spirits, had their habitation. And it was in this burden-bearing travail that He was "the Man of Sorrows" well acquainted with grief. He yearned for the divine fulness, but had to be in limitation where it could not be realized. He cried out for the Father-Mother in conscious experience; but He had to be in the valleys deep down where so glorious a Radiance could not be entered into, nor even beheld. He had to pass along "the via dolorosa" in every life, and through all the days of each life. He knew betrayals continually. Flagellations were familiar experiences even from the hands of His friends. Crucifixions He had in abundance. The aloneness of His

travail was unutterable. THOSE WHO AFFIRM THAT THE ONE
KNOWN AS THE MASTER WAS NO "MAN OF SORROW," NEVER
KNEW HIM IN THOSE LATTER DAYS OF THE MANIFESTATION;
NOR COULD THEY UNDERSTAND THE MYSTERY OF HIS TRAVAIL.

This aspect of sorrow we have introduced to illustrate
what is meant by Divine Grief revealed as sorrow. For
all His sorrow was begotten of the conditions in which He
was placed, and the limitations imposed by the states He
had to enter into. It was intensified also by all the losses
that seemed to pour upon Him from within Himself as
well as from without, loss of His own powers and of friends.
And what shall we say of all the bitterness of misunderstanding, misrepresentation, repudiation and crucifixion?
He sorrowed because He had to be what He became in
order to help this world in her travail, and make possible
the redemption of all her children, aye, even the arising of
the children who were of the Kingdom of the Heavens in
their consciousness. He was filled with grief, Divine Grief.
It was the Divine Grief expressed through Him in such
burden-bearing.

This world may seek joy; and we would that it found
true joy. This world may rejoice; and she shall rejoice
bye and bye most beautifully. Many of her children may
look upon this unveiling with astonishment that such a
thing could be, and repudiate it, and drown the echoes of
the anguish amid the shouts of their own joy. Even many
of the children of the Kingdom may wonder why He
sorrowed so. They may wonder how it came to pass in
the Days of the Return, He should have appeared as one
whose visage was marred with sorrow more than that of
the sons of men. But who could understand fully the
nature of that sorrow? All the denial of it by those who
could not understand, did not, and could not alter the fact

that He was a "Man of Sorrows" well acquainted with grief, every grief, every sorrow with which this world has become acquainted, only much more fully; for He knew the Divine Grief over this world.

All this we have written to illustrate the reality of sorrow in this world through its wrong conditions and states and limitations; and the reality of grief in the Divine Realm over this world's states and conditions; and the reality of that grief embodied in the one sent to carry away the karmic burden of the world, in order to make the healing of the nations and all the races possible. In this instance, sorrow is the revealer of the Divine Drama for the healing of the tragedy of this world. The ministry of sorrow in so far as it may be revealed in relation to that "Man of Sorrows," was ministry for the healing of all the children. And in this world, sorrow itself has even a ministry. It is to teach the children to rise up out of the limitations of the con-sciousness of personal things; not to forget them or fail in beautiful ministry on the plane of their manifestation, but to rise up out of the bondage in which personal things hold the thoughts, desires and affections.

Sorrow is a sweet ministrant in that it keeps alive and tender the emotions in a world whose influences would tend to dry the stream of the emotion with its beautiful feeling, and render love inoperative. But in that very ministry, it teaches the Being to arise and seek those realms where all things outward find a new interpretation, all things personal have their true relationship unveiled, and also all their abiding relationships, and to find in that realm healing for all sorrow in the consciousness of the Great Love and the Light of His Wisdom.

Merely to negative sorrow as a state does not heal Souls; but to negative the states which give birth to sorrow, and transmute the elements of those states, is to lift the Being into the realm of new power, new vision and blessed realization. It is to heal the Soul of its sorrow. To deny is not to change, though by negation elemental powers can be overwhelmed. Yet merely to negative elemental states does not change the elements and bring them back into states of purity. But to transmute them to a higher realm, does. God Himself transmuteth our sorrow. And the very elements which produce the sorrow, after transmutation, give joy.

Oh, ye who have known sorrow, and think your sorrow beyond all sorrow, know this, that the Divine Sorrow expressed through "the Man of Sorrows," doth gather up your sorrow into itself, and transmute its elements, to fill you henceforth with joy.

Oh, ye who have not passed through the deeper valleys to know the aloneness of being without God after having walked with Him in realization, and who think that only joy should obtain in everyone at once, and even be manifest through such as have travailed for this world's healing— know ye this, that the Redeemers of God, sent forth for the healing of this world, have ever been men and women of sorrow, expressing through their sorrow the Divine Grief as they bore their burden for the healing of this world. And also understand this, that He who has been acclaimed by the churches "the Man of Sorrows," did know such sorrow in His travail as no human tongue could express, nor mind understand, nor even the heart conceive. And also understand this, that, if that one sorrowed greatly in the days of the Return, it was the grief in Him of the Great Love for the children, and the vision of all that had been met with in the way, culminating in the bitter sorrow

140

occasioned by those whom He had ever loved, but who, even in the days of His Return, did not understand Him, nor understand one another. They could not endure with Him in His sorrow. In the midst of it, they once more fled from Him. For them He had agonized, yet they knew it not. For them He travailed, but they accounted that as naught.

Yet His sorrow was never meant to cloud or lessen in any way the joy of all the children of the Kingdom, and such of the children of this world who were able to receive of the Divine Gladness. His whole ministry in the Oblation, as in the Manifestation, was unto this end, that, through the divine healing, joy might fill this world and all its children; and that the joy unspeakably glorious might fill all His beloved friends who were once with Him in the Kingdom of the Father-Mother.

JESUS CHRIST   These three terms were applied to the Master
THE LORD.   when the gospel stories were written and
the epistolary letters sent to the Churches. Throughout the
centuries which have passed since the days of the Manifestation, that One sent forth from the Father-Mother to
manifest Him has been named and worshipped as Jesus
Christ the Lord. That a great mistake was made is self-
evident. Those who wrote the New Testament records
became betrayers of one of the most beautiful and most
sacred divine manifestations. That the Master was both
Daysman and Redeemer, is true. He was essentially the
vehicle of the Divine Mystery—the Lord of all Being, for
the manifestation once more of the transcendent Love of the
Father-Mother; and to recover and show forth the only true
path by which the human Soul could travel if it would reach
in high degree that sublimest of realizations known as the
Christ-consciousness.

The Lord is never a man. Nor is Christ any man. In all
the children of the Father-Mother lies latent potential
Christhood, and even that realization known as oneness
with the Father-Mother, or perfect at-one-ment. The names
given to The Master have other than personal signification,
and can only be understood mystically.

*   *   *   *

JESUS. This is a state of consciousness made manifest
in the Way of Life. It touches the glorious love-principle,
and reveals that love in sweetness, in gentleness, in tenderness, in noble thought, in beautiful desire, in lowly service.
It begets compassion for all living things, and manifests it
unto all Souls. It radiates pity, and throws its beautiful
mantle over all who are needing help—the weak, the defenceless, the helpless, the dumb, the blind, the deaf, the maimed,

the poor, the oppressed, the misunderstood, the misrepresented, the outcast, and even the creatures.

The Western world does not understand Jesushood. Through misunderstanding it, the schools have always misinterpreted it. Through misinterpretation on the part of the schools, the Church has misrepresented the meaning of the state. Jesus is a redeemer. But He redeems through a life that is redeemed. Jesushood is the life redeemed. He is the desire purified; the love-principle made beautiful till it seeketh not its own; the attributes healed, strengthened, made serviceable, and consecrated to service. Jesushood is the Life of the Divine Love in manifestation through His beautiful children. In this sense the Master was Jesus. But the name He was known by was other than Jesus. He was a centre acting as the apex of a triangle through which the divine glory of love was broken, reflected, manifested. What was done through Him even unto His personal life, was impersonal in its nature. And it is to be accomplished through all those whom He was sent to find, namely, the elect ones, those who could understand such a life, rise into it and become the vehicles of this aspect of Divine manifestation and redemption. For Jesus is ever a redeemer. And all Souls who are in Jesushood are, by their very state, and through all their ministry, redeemers.

*   *   *   *

CHRIST. This is a state of Being. The Eternal Christ is the Lord of Glory, and is no man. But in every individuation of Eternal Being, there is the Divine Principle, and that Divine Principle is Christ. Christ in you is the glorious hope; by which is meant, that the Divine Christ Principle is the prophecy of the very highest realization for the Being. Because of that Christ Principle the Being can become one with Christ, and know the exalted state of the Son of God, which is a state of most blessed consciousness.

In this sense the Master was Christ. He was not The Christ in the Absolute, but in that high state of Christhood which enabled Him to be one in and with the Absolute. He never claimed to be Christ any more than He claimed to be Jesus. But He knew He was in the states represented by both names, as was evidenced in the Teachings which He gave. Christ is the Radiance or Eternal Light of the Eternal Love. Christhood is the state in which that Love irradiates and fills the Being, and pours itself through the ministry and the life expressed by the term Jesus.

Christhood, therefore, is a glorious state unto which all Souls are called. It is the ultimate of their creation. For the elect ones, or elder children of the Kingdom, it is the transcendent realization possible unto them in this age. The Master's chief mission in the days of the Manifestation, known as that of Jesus Christ the Lord, was to find those Souls and recall them out of the conditions into which they had gone down through beautiful ministry to the children of this world who dwelt amidst the gross darkness, and help them back into that glorious degree of radiance from the Divine Presence.

The theological schools of all the churches have built their theories concerning the Master upon wrong premises, and have turned into a personal equation that which is absolutely soulic and divine. The result has been that the Western World, through all its religious institutions, has followed after an inverted picture, and has never been able to see the real image meant to be represented. It has followed, or thought it has followed, one who was the vehicle of the glorious unveiling of the meaning of Jesus Christ;

144

but it has missed His meaning. It has missed the beautiful
vision He gave. It has adored the man. Whilst doing this
it has utterly failed to find the Holy Grail or Cup of Divine
Life unto which He in His ministry called all Souls. The
result has been that the sins of the Western world have not
been blotted out. Nor has that world's mind been healed,
nor the life saved through the healing. Today, after more
than eighteen centuries of the so-called Christian belief
and worship, its redemption has now to begin. For the
healing of the nations of the world is the great work to be
accomplished in this age, and that healing must proceed
till Jesus come. That means, till the world is made beautiful
in all its ways, in its ministries, in its loves, and in all its
ambitions.

The churches should be the vehicles of this redemption;
but they must first be themselves healed through being
purified. They have yet to learn the meaning of compassion
and pity, true self-denial, true self-sacrifice, beautiful
purity, beautiful consecration to the Divine; for their feet
must needs be washed. The way of their going has still
to be made beautiful. When they are, then the Light of
Christ may find a true vehicle for its manifestation through
their altars and ministries. In that day they will guide the
peoples to the real living fountains where cleansing and
healing for all sin can be found. And they will then be in
true apostolic succession, with all their outer phylacteries,
beliefs, traditions, rituals, ceremonials, transmuted and
illumined from the radiance of the Christ-Light upon the
altar of Being. For an apostle is one who is sent, having
acquired the power through discipleship to be the vehicle
of divine ministry; and there is no other apostolic succession. The Holy Apostolate of God are those Souls who

145

are full of the power of His Love and the radiance of that
Love, those whom He endows and sends forth as channels
of divine ministry to Souls.

*   *   *   *

THE LORD. The Lord is never a person. Nor is He to be
regarded as an individual in the human sense. He is Perfect
Being, and the manifestation in the Divine World of that most
glorious and most holy mystery we name the Father-Mother.
He is that Presence who filleth the sanctuaries of the Divine
Heavens, and the Angelic Heavens, as an atmosphere and a
radiance transcendent and ineffable. And He is also that
Presence who filleth the sanctuary of the human being with
that transcendent glory, when that one can rise to know Him
through the estates of Jesushood and Christhood. He giveth
the atmosphere within the sanctuary. He Himself maketh
the radiance that is the Light of Christ within. He Himself
magnetically doth affect the love-principle until it is, in its
response, even as His own Love, and maketh manifest in
Jesushood. The Lord Himself dwelleth between the
Cherubim where He unveileth His glory unto His child, as
that one rises in consciousness into perfect oneness with
Himself.

Therefore, as Jesushood is the crown of the beautiful
Life, and Christhood is the radiant crown of Jesushood, so
the Lord consciousness is the crown of the Christ Light.

The Master was in that state in which He knew the Lord,
being one in that Presence. It was thus He knew the
Father-Mother. His relationship was most intimate, most
sacred. But though intimate in the sense that He had the
living consciousness of that Holy Presence ever within Him,
when He spake of the Father-Mother it was in terms and
tones the most reverent. For He was ever conscious that

all He was of beauty and truth, all He had acquired of
inward light and transcendent realization, all the power of
the glory of the Kingdom of the Father-Mother that was
broken through Him, were from and of the Father-Mother,
and must ever be for Him alone. He, therefore, though in
the high state of the Lord consciousness, never could have
allowed His beautiful friends to speak of Him as the Lord
Christ Jesus. He was in His own consciousness, and always
in His address to His friends, ever the lowly servant of the
Father-Mother.

Even as He Himself realized that sublimest consciousness, the indwelling of the Father-Mother, so did He call
His most intimate and most beloved ones to seek that high
estate; for it was to be their inheritance again.

PART
III.

Initiations of the Soul.

*Through the Path of Occultism to the Mystic
Vision : The Mystery of the Son of God :
The Soul's Divine Inheritance : The
Realm of the Prophet—The Call to
Separateness : Within the Sanctuary :
The Training of the Twelve, or
the Soul's Attributes : Priest-
hood after the Order of Mel-
chisedek; the Urim and
Thummim : The Shekinah,
or the Office of
Cherubim and
Seraphim.*

Through the Path of Occultism to the
Mystic Vision.

*OCCULTISM
AND
MYSTICISM.*
It is oft-times thought that there is no point of reconciliation between what is known as Occultism and what is termed Mysticism. The occultist thinks the mystic is a vain dreamer, not dreaming in vain as far as he himself is concerned, but a dreamer of dreams and a seer of visions for himself alone, and that the language in which he seeks to clothe them is a language which is to most readers and thinkers, an unknown tongue. The occultist thinks that occultism is the true path of knowledge, and that the knowledge derived along that path is the true knowledge by which life may be enlightened and guided; and that only along that Path may occult power be attained and manifested.

Now, the words themselves belong to different realms of thought, and that which they signify belongs to different Kingdoms, and the knowledge derived by the path of each, is related to different planes of consciousness. But these things are not necessarily contradictory.

An occultist is one who is supposed to seek for hidden knowledge and the acquisition of hidden powers. A mystic is one who is supposed to dream of God, and seek to abide in that dream, realizing that dream within his own Being, but in a realm where none may come who have not also dreamed and seen as the mystic has. Occultism is of the Mind. Mysticism is of the Soul. Knowledges which have to be acquired must belong to the mind, for it is the mind which acquires; but knowledges which are of the Soul, are not acquired. They are realized. Hence they are *known.* That is, they are the fruit of experience. Knowledges that are acquired are knowledges about events, mysteries, powers. Knowledges which are realized are known, and become part of the Being. The Occultist travels through the world of reflection to gather upon the intermediary planes such story of the Soul, of the Planet, of the world's history, as may still be gathered there. The Mystic transcends those planes. He seeks the bosom of God. In the bosom of God alone are all things known. In that bosom, there is found the mystery of the consciousness of that Indwelling. That which the Occultist strives after through the mind, is seen and known by the Mystic. The one transcends the other. The one can interpret the other. The higher understands the lower; but the lower cannot interpret the higher. It does not *know*. It only knows *about* the things.

Now, the path of occultism is the path of mind education. Occultism obtained in the unfallen days. True, it was not as it is to-day; but it was the path of acquisition through the mind in a pure, beautiful way. For the children of this world were educated into the great mysteries by the children of the Kingdom who came to be their teachers. They were educated along the path of the mind. An illustration is at hand, though bringing the mental processes down on to the objective plane. In the true occultism which was taught by the children of the Kingdom, mysticism was present; for all the Teaching given was spiritual, though it had to be taught upon the plane of the mind. The true nature of the flowers was taught. Their inherent properties were revealed. The meaning of the great mystery of their creation, in so far as it could be received, and of the Principle of Life that operated, and the substances out of which they were built up, was unveiled. The children of the Kingdom were the Mystics who knew. So they were able to interpret. But when the Wisdom was broken upon the mind, it became occult knowledge—that is, the Mysteries as unveiled along the path of the mind. For the children did not yet know through realization. They had to grow into that high state, and be taught the way through occult knowledge.

Realization is the outcome of ages of spiritual growth. Intuition is the store-house wherein all the Soul's history is gathered up into it as knowledge. It is there hidden until its door is opened or veil lifted. When opened, it becomes intuition to the Soul. *The Soul knows. It perceives.* First it discerns. Then it perceives. And through the growth of discernment and perception, it understands more and more fully, until at last it knows. It knows only in part at first; but goes on to know in greater degree, from more to more, until at last it knows all things from the Divine bosom. That is, it at last dwells in the consciousness of the Great Mystery, the Father-Mother, and knows all things.

Occultism, therefore, is not a new thing. It is a new name to an old process. The children of men were educated through the mind, not as the mind is trained to-day, but more beautifully. For the flowers, the whole vegetable Kingdom, existed not simply to adorn the earth, though in the economy, the spiritual economy of the earth, the flowers played a great part. The trees played a great part. They play a great part today.

Now, along the occult planes these things were taught. All knowledge was gathered from the outer manifest world, but the interpretation was through the intermediary planes. Souls were thus taught to seek to learn, to seek to know about things, and by this process to grow up from one degree of consciousness to more, and into the state in which they would come to understand, and then pass into the Path of the great Realization.

Occultism is, therefore, a Path. In the unfallen days it was a pure path. In the fallen ages it has not often been a pure path, for not infrequently occult powers have been sought for wrong uses. Occultism is a path by which is acquired knowledge of how to control the elements. And where the Soul is not in true polarity, and that knowledge is acquired, the wrong use can be made of the powers. Remember that many have been the tragedies and great the catastrophes which have been wrought upon this distraught world, through the wrong use of occultism or the powers of the mind.

But in the unfallen days the process was beautiful. The children rose on stepping stones, "from their dead selves to higher things;" but they rose from lesser degrees of consciousness to the greater degrees of the consciousness through knowledge of the Mysteries imparted to them in the interpretations of the things that were all about them, manifest in the vegetable Kingdom, and manifest to them in the creature Kingdom also. For these were interpreted too, and the meaning of them manifested right up and on to the human Kingdom. As they grew up they were able to receive more and more. But just before what is known as the Fall, or the great descent of this planet took place, the eldest children of this world were so advanced that they were able to receive those inner mystery teachings which could never be known occultly, but only mystically. Occult knowledge of God is knowledge about Him, not knowledge of Him. Mystic knowledge of God is knowledge of Him. It is the realization. None can ascend unto the Heavens but through the Son of God who is in them. The Son of God is not an occultist. He is never an occultist. He is the Soul's Divine Principle which is ever mystical and makes of the Soul a true Mystic. It is that power within the Being that makes it dream: dream of the realization before it comes: dream, and seek the Vision of the dream, before the realization of the Vision of the dream becomes.

Mysticism in its fulness, that is, in its innermost realm, is the beautiful ultimate to which the Soul is ever moving,

155

when it is seeking, when it is adoring, when it is loving, when it is serving. Mysticism is that endeavour to realize the Mystery—that Mystery which cannot be known through the mind. Occultly you can only know *about* the things which are only *known* through the Realization. Occultism is on the plane of the mind, and the mind is a reflector. Mysticism is the Kingdom of the Soul. The Soul is the Sanctuary wherein the Radiance is present.

Now in the unfallen days the path to the higher was through the lower. You see it was a true path, and beautiful. The children grew. When the Father-Mother fashioned His children He fashioned them in Principle. How beautiful that is! When the Father-Mother fashions a rose He fashions it in Principle; but, for the manifestation it has to grow from the Principle. It has to gather to itself the elements which will enable it to manifest. The Divine Principle in it, in order to manifest, has to have the elements that come from the world of manifestation. It has to have the stimulation of that Principle from that world which is Divine. The rose must have certain rays from the sun to enable it to transmute the elements, and gather them up to help it to give manifestation.

Likewise in a human Soul, the Father-Mother fashions through the Divine Principle of it, the Being called the Son of God, His Son in you. But there must be the elements. The Principle gathers up the elements. It gathers to itself the knowledges found along the path called the occult world, through the manifestation in the objective world interpreted by those who know; first of all interpreted in the language which is as the alphabet of the greater language; at first in the simple terms, and then in the greater terms, going deeper into the mystery, and the Soul the while gathering up all the elements, all the knowledges, and transmuting them. And in the process, the intuition also gathers up into itself as into a store-house against that day when the Heavens will enable it to open its store-house and bring forth from it that which will enable it at last to realize the very Presence within itself. The end of creation, the fashioning of our Being, is thus a perfect mysticism.

KNOWING   Now the path to it is ever the path of purity,
THE   of beautiful love, of true joy, of true rejoicing
MYSTERY.   in beautiful service. There is no other way.
Heaven works miracles for us, but it works them within us.
In no other way. It works them within us and thus accomplishes the growth of our life. For one who had never seen a rose unfold, to watch it issuing from the twig, not quite sure whether it was a new leaf coming, or something more, it would come as a mystery, a wonderful mysterious thing to see that tiny shoot getting larger and larger and yet larger, and firmer and still firmer, till it would seem as if it could not be opened without hurt to the flower; and then when it enlarged, to witness it gradually opening of its own accord, and revealing what is so beautiful, a glory no man can imitate, no man can reproduce, a beauty of its own, and poured forth from the heart of it a fragrance no one would ever have dreamt was there. For though you smell the trunk of this rose-tree, or the branch or the leaves, though many of them have beautiful fragrance about them, yet the fragrance of the rose would be quite distinct, all its own. And that fragrance it pours forth. There is the mystery.

So in a Soul. It unfolds. God works the miracle through the Heavenly Principle within, through the gathering together of the elements, and the transmutation of them. Through the stimulation and the energizing from the Divine

World of the Life-principle, and the action of that world upon the pole of our Being, Life unfolds. In the process it is like coming up through the occult kingdom. In the occult kingdom all is cold. It is not often you get mentality that is warm and radiant. If you do, it is reflected radiance and warmth. Remember the warmth is not in the mentality. The mental world is a cold world. And if Love does not make it warm, and if Love does not reflect its glory into the radiance which the mind may have, then all is cold. There is no potency of Divine Heat to energize. There is no warmth to comfort. There is no power to lift the Being. None! The dynamics of occultism without the dynamics of mysticism cannot elevate a Soul. They cannot bring that Soul into the consciousness of the Father-Mother. That is why intellectualism is a cold thing. That is why a heart overflowing with love is a beautiful and Divine thing. It may be beautiful for the mental mountain climber to walk over the glaciers. He or she doubtless loves the exhilaration of it. But it is more beautiful to bask in the radiance of that Love where there is no danger of great and permanent hurt; where there are no hazards to the very Being itself; and to ascend those mountains where the radiance streams ineffably, and the glory is ever transcendent within the Sanctuary, and the Soul knows even as it is known, and the Being looks out upon a world with all its history written upon it, and *knows*.

Now you will note this, that in every one there are the two modes, the occult and the mystic. Every Soul passes first through the occult and then through the mystic. Some occultists have spoken of the mystic as a younger brother, and occultism as the elder brother. But occultism is of the mind, and it is the mind that is the younger brother. Mysticism is of the Soul, therefore the Being is the elder. The mind is an office of the Being, and therefore could not be the elder. There could be no office until the Being *became*. The mind is an office, and it has a function. Its power enables it to function upon the occult plane of the Planet. It is an office through the exercise of which a Soul acquires. In its function it is to reflect. It is a power for ministry, and it has to learn to serve. But the mystic is the Soul who has scaled the heights of all occultism and reason, and ascended into the consciousness of the Father-Mother. There are a host of books written about him and his mysticism which are most misleading. Many things are written about mystics and mystical things by those who are not mystics at all. For true Mysticism is not a groping after the Mystery. It is the consciousness of the Eternal World within, and the attainment of it by the Being. So that the Mystic is indeed the elder, though he never thinks of himself in that way at all. The nearer a Soul is to the Divine, the less that Soul thinks of itself in any personal way whatever. No message from that inner world ever comes as the message of that Soul. It could not. The Mystic would know it could not be. He would know it was, and speak of it as, the message of God. So that you will understand, that no one from that Kingdom speaks of the message as being his or hers. The personal I has no place. It could not be. That Soul could not so think. For there the Soul knows absolutely that it is the Father-Mother within. The Being realizes that all its powers, those named Soul potencies, the mystic attainments, and those called mind powers, occult potencies and attainments, are His alone, and that the Soul has nothing of its own worth the holding—absolutely nothing!

Children of the Kingdom! Mystic Souls! Souls seeking to find true mysticism; the two modes are within you, and though at times you have to go through the mind processes in the return to the consciousness of the innermost

159

things, ye are ever to regard yourselves as mystic Souls—
Souls seeking the Mystery, the Realization. And it will
come. As truly as the rose comes into full bloom, given the
conditions, so truly will that fulness come to you. As truly
as the rose-tree will bear to the utmost of its strength and
its powers, and its opportunities, if you give it the conditions,
so will your Being bear unto the utmost of your powers, in
glorious consciousness, the realization of the great Mystery,
the Father-Mother within you, that mystery named the Son
of God. This is the end for which ye were begotten of God;
for which ye are re-fashioned of God; for which ye have
been making your travail through the ages back again into
the Kingdom of the consciousness of Him. This is the end,
that ye may know the mystery transcending all the mental
states; not casting these latter away, oh no! but keeping
them pure and beautiful, and transcending them, these
states remaining with you to be used when it is necessary.
For the mind has not only one function in its office. It is also
a reflector. But the Being is to realize. It is the mystic in
you who knows. And if you find it difficult sometimes to
bring it through, it is not because it cannot be brought
through by you; it is not because it is not realized. The
most inward things are the most difficult to bring through.
But given the conditions, so much can be brought through.
On the plane of the mind you may write and speak much.
In the language of occultism ye may speak and write. In
the realm of the Soul that is less easy, but it can be done.
The mystic things can be and are brought through. They
can be and are presented and broken upon the plane of the
mind. *But they never lose their spiritual power.*

Note this difference between purely occult things and
true mystic things. When the occult things are broken on
the plane of the mind, they are still cold. And though they

may be as knowledge unto you, they will not move you. But if things from the Divine Kingdom are broken upon the plane of the mind, they will move you; for they retain their inherent divine power. It is thus that a message from the innermost realm is vibrant with the power of God. A message from realms which are not divine, is lacking in that most essential potency. In this, mysticism does transcend occultism. And the Soul who knows through realization, is the one who indeed is elder brother. The Soul is ever elder brother to the mind. The elder brother is the vehicle through which the Divine can pour forth from the innermost realm those glorious potencies which vibrate upon and through the whole Being of the children. And such things from the inner world bring their own conditions. They generate their own atmosphere. They change the atmospheric elements of the mind until they are in tune with the Holy Breath. And such things are not of the man or the messenger, however beautiful. They are of God, the Father-Mother. *"Try the spirits whether they be of God."* Test the things that are given you, and ye will know whether they vibrate with the very potencies that make your whole Being radiant with Love; whether they comfort, heal, uplift, restore, and make you attuned, not simply in the body, or in the mind, but in all the Being. Ye may know that those things correspond to the very centre of your own Being, that realm where the Divine Mystery is in Principle; and that if they have had to be broken unto the mind, it is that they may be distributed through all your Being, and that the magnetic influx and outflow will be commensurate with your power to realize.

Children of the Father-Mother, in these days there is a recrudescence of the ancient dark occultism, as well as pure and beautiful occultism. Differentiate between them.

Whilst there are those who must needs pass along the plane of occult philosophies and occult ministries, seek ye for yourselves as the first and highest thing, the true mystic vision, and the mystic state. You will not be hurt there. But in the other path you will be hurt unless you be guarded; unless you know how to guard, or some one can guard you who knows. There are many movements afoot which would allure the children of the Kingdom away from the path by which alone they can come at the sublime Divine Vision. Try, ever try, the spirits whether they be of God, the Divine Mystery; whether they be of the mystic state, the Kingdom of the Soul; and seek ye alone unto the realization of the Son of God in you. No hurt can come to you then. Only the glorious, beautiful, Divine Realization is found there.

The path of your travail in your return, is a path full of sorrow; and it was through the astral occult powers that ye were all made to suffer, and are still made to suffer unto this day. That is, it was through the impure occultism. The mystic realm never hurt you; it could not. As children of that realm you find your home there. You are happiest in aspiration. Your fullest joy is found in beautiful looking within and upwards, seeking more and more the sweet realization of the Presence. The consciousness of the Presence around you to be felt as the sweet breaths of the flowers from heaven is your desire. The consciousness of the Presence overshadowing you, recognised as the glorious light within the azure of your Being with its radiant sun, is the goal of your endeavour. The consciousness of that Presence within you which is the ultimate, is the Realization of the Father-Mother in your consciousness; knowing yourself to be not only the child of the Father-Mother but to be in that state known as Son of God, the crown of the mystic quest. For it is the mystic who seeks the Holy Grail —not on the outer planes to find a cup; not on the intellectual planes to find powers of the mind only; but on the inner planes of the Being to find that Holy Grail or Cup of perfect Realization, even the Presence of the Lord God within the Sanctuary. For the Presence of the Father-Mother within the Sanctuary, is as Son of God who is the Sacred Cup of Being to us; the Chalice most holy; the Wine that makes us one with the Divine Mystery.

How much ye have grown towards this state, ye yourselves could not tell. But we could tell you. To see your growth thither is beautiful. And we would not have the flowers which are growing out from you in manifestation of your love, hurt; nor the atmosphere the Father-Mother enspheres you in for your growth, injured; nor the blessed yearning of your inmost Being for His becoming within you, repressed and wounded. We pray that ye may have beautiful conditions for thought and aspiration; Angelic atmosphere for worship; and redeemed conditions for service; in which to just grow and unfold more and more beautifully up into that mystic vision which the Father-Mother hath given unto you once more to manifest the Christ within you, through the Jesus Christ life, the Jesus Christ love, the Jesus Christ radiance of love, the Jesus Christ ministry of love. In your homes, out of your homes, in the school, in the world of business as well as in the Sanctuary of adoration and praise, even to manifest Jesus Christ.

Be therefore of good heart. He who is with you, even the Holy One of the Father-Mother, and who is within you as Son of God, is great of heart, and ye shall know even as ye are known, mystic Souls in whom the glory of the Father-Mother becomes. And the consciousness of His Presence is your abiding inheritance, to go out from it no more. For it is the day of the return when Zion shall sorrow no more, because she will go out no more. The Soul will abide forever in conscious Christhood.

The Mystery of the Son of God.

THE MYSTERY OF THE SON OF GOD. The Mystery of Life is the Mystery of the Son of God in us. The end of creation is the realization of that Divine Mystery. The creation in the Principle, begetting and fashioning of human Souls, is unto this glorious consummation, that the Eternal Mystery may find individuated embodiment in each one, each Soul differing from the other, even as the millions of stars in the heavenly galaxy differ one from another in their state and ministry and manifestation, though all built up out of the glorious substances of the Infinite Mystery. Who is this Son of God of whom tradition speaks through all religions? He is Adonai. In the macrocosmic world He is the glorious manifest Presence of the Eternal God; in the microcosmic world of human Souls the Divine Principle which contains within itself in miniature the attributes of the Eternal One. By creation and generation all Souls are children of God. In them is the Son of God potentially expressed and latently present. They are always God's children, meant to become Sons of God in state. That state is the realization of their Divine childhood in which the Son of God becomes a realization within them and a manifestation through them. This attainment is the overcoming of life. It is the overcoming of the world elemental, astral, mental and affectional in the merely personal sense, and the triumphant arising of the Being through the various stages of Soul evolution which might be designated the occult path into the realm of the angelic or truly mystical experience, and still onward and upward, acquiring more, giving more, realizing more, until even the threshold of the Divine Realm is touched and the Soul stands upon its altitude, realizing the glorious nature of the Life begotten within it, until it knows itself to be one with the glorious Presence known as Son of God.

This is the meaning of the mis-translated passage in the

epistle of John "Who is he that overcometh the world? Even he who believeth unto the becoming within him of the holy estates of Jesus Christ." For the overcoming of the world is the attainment by the Soul of that conscious and most blessed realization of the Mystery of the Son of God within its Sanctuary.

The end of Soul creation ultimates in the sublime realization of the Son of God; but the path to it is through countless ages. The creation, begetting, fashioning and perfecting of a human Soul is something transcendently greater, something infinitely vaster, something unspeakably more profound, than the mere appearing upon these outer planes of children begotten, born into manifestation, growing up in their form within a few years into manhood and womanhood, carrying burdens physical, mental, emotional and spiritual for a few passing decades, until what is misnamed old age comes on, and they pass away again. All such experience is as the meteor in the sky appearing suddenly to go out, its bright exhalation lasting but a brief moment; or, like the planetary round year by year along its orbit as it moves round the centre of its life, the sun, in each round knowing the experience of rejuvenation, re-manifestation, and then the passing away of all the manifested things.

The history of a Soul, from its creation to the consummation of its Being in conscious realization in which it knows itself a child of the Father-Mother, and then reaches up to that higher altitude of consciousness when the Son of God is realized within it, covers thousands of great cycles, during which the Being has appeared manifold times in the realm of manifestation, passing through generation after generation, gathering into itself of the glorious elements born unto it from the Angelic World, growing richer, ever more beautiful in its unfolding, writing its own history as its attributes grow

167

in their power, and reflect through them something of the Mystery of Being itself.

The Soul began its journey in the Vegetable Kingdom, but not as a vegetable. The Vegetable Kingdom is one whose substances are semi-fluidic, though they can be and are condensed, not only into concrete form, but even into solid elements. That kingdom is the most spiritual still of the fallen elemental kingdoms. In the unfallen days everything within it was absolutely perfect in form, in colour, in rhythm. That kingdom was fashioned as a training ground for the new created beings. It was as a living kindergarten where the children were spiritually educated. All the plants, those in lowly state and those in great state, were spiritual embodiments. The tree itself was a symbol of life, both spiritually and in phenomenal expression. The flowering plants embodied pure angelic thoughts and thus became concrete reflections in the phenomenal world of the glorious experiences, thoughts, joys, forms and radiance in the angelic world. The fruits, in unfallen days, were all perfect. The fruits are the quintessence of the life expressed in the plants, and in their substances are beautifully spiritual. They are manifold, and were then manifold in their kinds, each order representing degrees of spiritual attainment. It is thus that the eldest Souls in purified states of consciousness and life seek to build up their bodies on these outer planes through the elements derived from the pure and higher fruits.

Though there is consciousness in the Vegetable Kingdom it is in a diffused state. A nebulous consciousness must not be confounded with a polarized consciousness in which there is conscious centrifugal and centripetal manifestation. There is consciousness through all the spiritual substances out of which the Vegetable Kingdom is built up. There

168

is latent consciousness in all true spiritual elements. There is in the ether. But that consciousness never becomes self-directing until it is polarized and individuated. In the lives of the trees and plants there is distinct individuation; but it is a directed growth, the outcome of a beautiful ministry from the outer or lower angelic planes. There are super elemental spirits, as they are designated, or reflections of the wonderful growth in the Vegetable Kingdom. There are elemental ministrants sent forth to direct and guide so that the Vegetable Kingdom may be, that is, in its unfallen states, a true expression of the wonderful, spiritual manifest world of form and colour and rhythm. For all the sweet and beautiful plants, and noble trees, and the exquisite flowers in their manifold forms, have their full meaning upon the angelic planes where they may be beheld in most glorious order, form, colour, rhythm.

It was into such a world the Soul was ushered. The like elements were within itself in a state of polarization, only it had more elements than are manifest in the realm known as the Vegetable Kingdom. Those great and glorious elements, so wonderful still in their purity, out of which all the pure gems are formed, are found in some degree in all Souls, giving to each Soul the power to receive and to reflect the glories of the Angelic World, and even the Divine Kingdom. Still more; for the mystery deepens. Within the Soul there is an element, which, in recent years, material science has discovered in this planet, and named it radium, an element most mysterious, most valuable, most precious, most glorious in its power, giving to the Soul the inherent power of radiation. It contains in its elements, in part, the great mystery of the auric display around a human life.

With such elements it began its journey as a very little child functioning in that kingdom where it could learn the law of harmony and form and colour and sweet ministry, the phenomenal expressions arresting the consciousness drawing the attributes into service, thus calling forth the Divine Mystery latent in that child Being. For the first process of culture was through the phenomenal world, and this took place, and still takes place, upon all the kingdoms. For the phenomenal realm or realm of reflection, is that wherein the Soul is first educated. Through the objective the subjective is awakened, quickened, cultivated, deepened, enlarged and exalted. Thus the process of realization goes on continuously from more to more, until a human Soul passes up on to what is known as the Human Kingdom, which, in the unfallen days, was none other than the realm where the Angelic life was first expressed in such childhood. The children on the Human Kingdom had the Angelic form, because the human form is Angelic when it is in an unfallen state.

From its very inception the Soul had thus hidden within it the Mystery of the Son of God. It had within itself in miniature the very elements of the Eternal Mystery, even as the dewdrop contains within itself the same elements as the great fountain and even the mighty ocean. And because of this expression of the Eternal Mystery in the microcosm, man can grow from more to more, reflecting as he grows some degree of the Radiance of the Eternal Presence. He has the power to rise from kingdom to kingdom, and from plane to plane within each kingdom, and from state to state within each kingdom and plane, becoming crowned with the Angelic glory, as a star shining in the heavenly galaxy of the Celestial Christhood, and, though it seem a tremendous height to climb to and well nigh impossible, he may ascend on to the threshold of the Divine Kingdom as a Son of God in state, and reign in ministry from that realm for God. In this most glorious attainment

170

he knows the Father-Mother. He is ever in the bosom of the Father-Mother. The Son of God in him is realized so that he is verily "very God of very God" in his substance and his state, the express likeness of the Father-Mother, the image of His transcendent glory. In him ten thousands of thousands of ages are gathered up. He is hoary with the glorious Wisdom of the Father-Mother, the Soul's old age being the realization of that glorious Love and Wisdom in stupendous fulness. In him the Godhead finds embodiment in his realization as the crown of his travail and service through the countless ages. Into his Soul are gathered up and epitomized all the treasures of God.

Every Soul upon the Human Kingdom has travailed through countless ages. Every Soul upon that kingdom has come up from such childhood as we have described. For, though this world in its human freight carries the burden of unspeakably more than its own children, having upon its planes the children of beautiful Luna and two other systems, as well as those children of the ancient Christhood who came to this world from another system to minister to it, yet all Souls who have reached the Human Kingdom, and those who have transcended it long ages ago, but are functioning upon it for purposes of ministry in this world, have come up from lowly estate as children of the Father-Mother, knowing the lowliest degrees, though ultimately crowned with the very highest degrees of consciousness. And there is not a life, however fallen it may seem, that is still functioning upon the true Human Kingdom, in which ten thousand ages of wonderful history and travail may not be found. The grandeur of a human Soul, who knoweth it, but the Lord of all Being who fashioned it? The majesty of a human Soul, who comprehendeth it? None but they who have passed into that high consciousness in which the

Father-Mother is realized within the Being as Son of God.

Oh! the Wisdom and the Love of the Father-Mother, how glorious they are! Even the most fallen one is still child of the Infinite Mystery begotten in Love and in Wisdom smitten and brought down by the misfortunes imposed through the fallen elemental, astral and occult conditions which have obtained and prevailed. So that in even the most fallen there is the Mystery. If the gem can be brought up out of the false conditions amid which it has been buried, its elements and its facets be all purified and a true setting given to it, that gem of the human Soul may still come to reflect most gloriously the Radiance ineffable of the Eternal Mystery of the Eternal Love and Light and Life—even the Father-Mother. For, even in that Soul the Son of God can and must become manifest in order that the Soul's true evolution may be enriched with the gift of Eternal Life, which is to know God, and crowned with that Crown of Life which passeth not away, which is the abiding consciousness of the Eternal Mystery understood and known.

Such is the Mystery of the Son of God in every Soul.

Such is the mysterious grandeur of the Temple of your own Being.

The Soul's Divine Inheritance.

LIFE'S
MYSTERIES
UNVEILED.

*OUR
INHERITANCE
IN GOD.*

There is not in all creation, of substance and element, which had not its beginning in the Great Mystery.

We name that Mystery God.

If we use terms, we should understand something of the meaning of the terms themselves.

If we make postulates, we should understand that which is postulated.

It is not a mistake to seek to define that which is definable, for through definition apprehension is illumined. To float in a great sea of non-polarized consciousness, is the way not to find definition or conscious realization of the Presence of the Eternal Mystery.

There is consciousness present in all the elements.

There is consciousness in a diffuse state through all manifested life in the Vegetable Kingdom.

But when the Divine Mystery essays to manifest itself upon higher realms, that which is in a diffuse state is gathered together like a mysterious nebula in the Celestial Heavens, and polarized in its centre, so that individuated consciousness becomes, whether in a great world, or a smaller world, or in man.

That we came out of the Eternal Mystery, we know. That our consciousness is the upgathered diffuse consciousness of manifold elements, we also know. That the creation of our life was a creation by the glorious Divine World, we apprehend and realize; and likewise, that the consciousness in us is from, and of, and for, the great and glorious Mystery we name God, the Father-Mother.

In the realms where those things are fully realized, there is no diffuseness, nor lack of definition, true apprehension, and perfect understanding. The unformulate becomes formulate. That which could not possibly be apprehended by any man of himself, is realized in the Being.

And the realization there testifies to that most glorious fact, that we are the children of the Eternal Mystery; that we have that Mystery within us; that in fashion we are the repetition in miniature of that Mystery, the reflection through embodiment of that Mystery, the glorious polarized expression in a microcosmic sense of the glorious macrocosm expressed in the terms Father-Mother.

That our inheritance is Divine we can testify. We are from God. We are of God. We are manifestations for God, embodying His Life, reflecting His Attributes, blooming on the Tree of Life as the flowers of the Divine World, expressing the exquisite beauty of form, revealing the transcendent radiance of Himself in miniature, and shedding the fragrance of His Life of Love which He has given to us, as the consciousness of Himself deepens within us, and finds expression through our attributes and manifestation through our lives. To have such an inheritance is surely to crown the human unit with Divine Dignity, and to clothe the human life with the Attributes of the Son of God.

We would show in this unfoldment that such an Inheritance is illustrated in the Creation Story. For, though that story has undergone great changes at the hands of editors in different ages, it still contains the wonderful gem of the mystery—or we should rather say, the gem reflecting the radiance of the mystery—of man's beginning, man's creation; man's manifestation as the child of the Eternal Love.

And here we would say in a word or two, that to attain to and dwell in the consciousness of the Absolute, does not rob the individuated Being of the vision, and the consciousness of definition, form, correlation, harmony, manifold degrees in Estate, Worlds, Kingdoms and Beings, but

175

that all are, according to the plane of the revealing, in perfect harmony with that high consciousness in which a Soul knows itself dwelling in the Absolute, one with the Lord of Being.

For, in the glorious world of the Divine Mystery, things are formulate, and formulated, and manifested, and are most exquisitely beautiful, transcending all human imagination, though they are impersonal in the earthly sense.

Now, in that sweet story of the creation of the child of the Eternal Love, notwithstanding the false trappings that have come to adorn it, we have a presentation of the wonderful Mystery of God in man.

Adam and Eve represent most wonderful things. They are not the names of a man and a woman, or a race of men and women, but of the whole created Being of the race. Adam is translated red earth or dust, showing how the materializing power can delude the mind and mirage the truth. For the word does not mean dust, nor red earth, but substance, the Red Substance.

And you will note this where the mystery is unveiled, God said, "Come let us make man." Jehovah speaks and Elohim act. Jehovah is the Eternal Mystery; Elohim the sevenfold manifest powers of Jehovah operating. For, though the term Elohim has been rendered in relation to the Eternal Father-Mother Mystery as synonym of Jehovah, there is this difference, that the one represents the Eternal Mystery in Principle, and the other represents the sevenfold operation of that Principle in creation. By those who do not understand the inner things, the two terms are used as correspondences representing different ages of writers, and therefore different creation stories.

Now, it is said God fashioned man out of the dust. Is

man a child of dust? A creation out of matter? Oh no! he is of the Red Ray and the Red Substance. The Red Substance represents the Divine Substance in the seventh degree of manifestation. Every race represents one of the Elohe. There are seven great races; and all others are sub-races or branches. In the beginning man came up from the outer circle to work inward to the innermost. The Red Substance is the Divine Substance in the realm of manifestation upon the seventh plane.

Thus man has Celestial Being in his very Substance, Divine Nature in his very fashion. God, through His Elohim, fashioned man from the Red Substance, the glorious substance of the Eternal Father-Mother Mystery, beginning on the outer and working inward. So that man is in his substance of the nature of God. He is of Elohim, for all Elohim operate; and each Elohe works for the perfection of the Being of man. Elohim represent the seven Spirits of God, the seven glorious Divine Creative Agencies, the seven great Degrees of Realization, the seven Amens or Consummations of attainment upon the seven degrees. They represent the seven Thunders or reverberations or realizations, of the sevenfold Divine Mystery within. Man begins in the Heavenly Arche, the Divine Principle within him, and works unto the Amen; and then through the Amen to the sevenfold Amen or perfect consummation of conscious realization of Elohim.

Now, in the beautiful story it is reported that Adam was first begotten and afterwards Eve was fashioned. But it is said that Eve was in man from the beginning, and that she was taken out of him, or brought forth into manifestation. Man was fashioned from the glorious Substance of Elohim to bear the image of God in the sevenfold fulness of Elohim. Then a deep sleep was passed over him, or caused to fall

177

upon him (so it is reported), and during that sleep Eve was begotten and fashioned.

Those who can see will discern that it is a monogram of the beginning of man. His consciousness is a glorious divine consciousness from the beginning, but working up through manifold degrees of realization. He is seen at first working as one in a dream, one in a trance state, one who has not yet come to the awakened vision. And in that state Eve is brought forth from him, fashioned into the most exquisite manifestation.

But what is Eve? A woman? Aye, and more than a woman. Yet not in a personal sense. She is the woman in man. Generically, she is the woman in everyone, the Divine Feminine in the race. The Divine Masculine power operates. It is the centrifugal. It goes forth to create. The Divine Feminine is the centripetal. It operates to fashion the created, and make manifest.

Eve is from a term modified from Yahweh, a Hebrew word meaning God. Yahweh is from Jehovah, and represents the feminine or Motherhood in the Eternal Mystery. Eve is said to have been the Mother of all living. Yet it was in no earthly sense, though it may have a beautiful earthly association too. Yevah or Yahweh, realized in the Being, becomes the mother or begetter of all things in the consciousness. The revealing, the understanding, the correlating of all the Mystery, is through Yevah, when the consciousness of Yahweh is attained.

The Creation story may thus be seen to be one revealing the very Divinity of Man, the glorious character of the inheritance which is his; showing that, from the very first, in that substance spoken of as the Red Substance, there is present in latent form, and in great potentiality, the very Mystery of God expressed in the Divine Fatherhood-

Motherhood. And thus it is unveiled that Adam is the Substance, and that Yevah (Eve) is the Realization. Adam is the life begun, moving up through the circuit of the Divine World represented by Elohim: Yevah (Eve) is the Realization—the realization of Yahweh when the Soul knows in perfect fulness.

The Creation story is, therefore, one of the most mystical embodiments in all the records. It is a story which, when seen in its true form, shows the Divine Estate of this world, the glorious Spiritual Orders which were upon it, which were inherent in its very substances, and which are expressed even in the fruits of the earth. It is a story unveiling man's appearing, the order of his creation, and the manner in which his dominion is attained. For his dominion is not that expressed in the oppression of the creatures. For, in those days to which we think back, there were no evil creatures at all, nor wrong forms, nor anything that lacked in beauty. His dominion over all the kingdoms beneath him was through coming into the consciousness of spiritual power amid the deep sleep. For during that sleep, he passed through those kingdoms, and rose above them until he came to that state of consciousness in which he could stand upon his feet as a man with the consciousness of the Presence of Yahweh. The expression, *deep sleep* covers the whole evolution of man as a spiritual Being and a Divine manifestation, from the inception of his Life to the perfect Realization when man walked with God. Then man heard the Voice of God. Then man understood Eden and the Tree of Life in the midst of it. Then man had within his Eden the River of Life in its fourfold dimensions, flowing through those dimensions full of living waters. Then man was unfallen.

But the story as a picture of Human Soul Creation is more than simply the story of the creation of the human race upon this world. For even the Christ-souls through whom that story came, because the eldest of them knew the Mystery, came into fashion in like manner upon another system, growing up as little children into the splendour of childhood before the Father-Mother, until they knew Yahweh, the glorious Presence within them. In this way the story becomes a monogram of the Soul's creation, whether the Soul is a child in this world or a child in some other world. For it is thus that individuated Being becomes, and passes upward into the great Realization. Our Inheritance is one that is so full of majesty, that the consciousness of it should drive from every heart's threshold, all fear, all shadow, all complaining, all doubt, all distrust; and it should heal all sorrow. So vast is the Inheritance, that the Soul, through the use of it, finds its riches increasing from day to day, from age to age, from æon to æon.

Here we have a vision of the sublime mysteries of how God has given to us an Inheritance incorruptible, undefiled and that passeth not away.

Here we may see how He, through His Christ, His Eternal Son in us, doth elevate us to the heavenly places; for the consciousness of such heavenly things comes through His Christ in us.

Here we may see the real value of a Soul. By placing in juxtaposition that saying attributed to the Master concerning the real value of a Soul—"What shall it profit a man if he gain the whole world and lose his Soul? Or, what shall one give in exchange for his Soul?" we may come to understand just what he meant. To possess all the world is to have the cosmic power in a material and mental sense, all the riches the earth-spirit can lay at our feet. Though the world spirit, the Zeit-geist of the age, could lay all the wealth and power of all the realms at our feet, the possession of these would be trivial compared to the possession of that Inheritance which is of the Father-Mother in us. For that Inheritance is a consciousness by which the Soul can transcend all the lower and intermediary spheres, and look out upon this world, interpreting all things. It is an Inheritance which gives the power to soar to other worlds, at last understanding them all in their correlation, aye, in their Mystery, knowing all that is meant by the newly re-promulgated doctrine of Relativity. It is an Inheritance that gives to the Being the Divine right to rise to the Divine World and comprehend the Mystery at the heart of all Being, your own Being, of God in you, of Elohim, of God's sevenfold Spirit, of the Sardius Stone glowing with the Eternal Fire, of the Red Flame, of the Red Substance out of which Life became through the operation of the Eternal Mystery.

To know God, that is glorious!

To know the Father-Mother by realization, that is transcendentally greater than all else!

To know our inheritance, our inheritance as His own gift, the gift of the Mystery of His Being expressed in His own attributes in miniature in us, that is surely the most glorious child-consciousness that any Soul could desire!

What care we for all else? Only in so far as all else may be used unto the glorious ministry for Him, is it of intrinsic value to us.

What value shall we attach to anything in this world, except only wherein it may be of value unto us towards the great Realization, and for the beautiful blessed ministry for Him?

What else live we for, or desire to live for? Naught! For this alone is Life worth living—to know Yahweh in the gloriousness of His Love and the splendour of His Wisdom. That is Life. That is Love. That is the end or purpose to seek.

Seek ye unto it, and doubt no more. Belittle yourselves no more, but think of your Divine Childhood.

And we would say unto you, ever be lowly. In the Divine Kingdom, in the highest of the Heavenly Hierarchies, the spirit of lowliness is beautiful in its manifestation. It could not be otherwise.

But whilst being ever lowly in heart, and in mind, and in spirit or purpose of Life, revere the majesty of God in you. Adore the splendour of the Life unto which He has called you; aye, which He has given you. Walk uprightly as children whose countenances are to radiate that glory. Let the Fire of His Love pour itself through you in Radiance, as ye walk with this great consciousness, I am His child, Adam-Yevah. Adam—of His glorious Substance and His glorious Spirit, and His wonderful Presence giving you the consciousness of Himself. Yevah—the Mother, the Cause of all things becoming in you, knowing all things, apprehending at last all things, realizing all things, even that which has been named the Absolute One.

Of your sorrow be healed by this consciousness. Out of your tribulations arise. Let your limitations be transcended, those limitations which have come as the result of your travail.

He encompasseth you. He overshadoweth you. In the Garden of your Being He walketh with you. There His Voice shall yet again speak within you.

Ever blessed be His Name! Unto Him be the glory and the power of His Kingdom in us for evermore!

The Realm of the Prophet

A.

By the Brook Cherith,

or

The Divine Call to Separateness.

When a Soul is called into high office by the Divine Love, it is also called into a state of *Separateness.* The prophetic office is one requiring in the Being, separateness from the world. For the true Prophetic Office is one of Illumination, full of vision, leading on to the sublimest realizations. It is that Office wherein the Elohim speak to the Soul, and through that one, to the children of the Father-Mother.

States of high Soul consciousness cannot be attained by any other means than those of separation upon all the planes of the Being, from the ordinary life of the world. In true prophetic ministry the Being must transcend all the lower planes of consciousness, not failing in any respect to use them as servants in the Lord's ministry, but rising above them all into the realm where manifestation is known through realization.

Separateness is Consecration. It does not mean mere aloofness from those who have to be served. It does not signify standing by them and ministering to them with any consciousness of being superior to them. All such comparisons are absent from the true prophet. The Being so called thinks only of God, the Eternal Love, Light and Life. In the Inner Realm there is no room for personal equations, except in the sense of ministry unto persons; nor is there any room for individualism, except in the sense of recognising each individual as an individuation of the sublime mystery of Being. The prophet, in the Realization, transcends all such things. In himself he is scarcely a person whilst in a state of realization. Amid the realization, when the consciousness of the Presence is intense, even the individualism of the prophet is swallowed up in the glorious consciousness as it is enriched from the Ever Most Blessed One. Consecration is separateness. It is withdrawal from the outer things. It is that *aloneness* by which the Soul can be filled in its consciousness, even whilst in the midst of men and women, until it even seemeth to be as a stranger and pilgrim in an unknown land. In that state it is nourished, enriched and illumined of God. In that hour of separateness its Vocation comes to it; for that high office can be given to it from God alone.

*　　　*　　　*　　　*

Illustrative of this there is a remarkable instance given in the Old Testament. It is associated with the prophet Elijah, though it really concerned the prophet Elisha. In the story of the prophet Elisha there is great confusion in the Jewish scriptures. Some of the miracles and experiences attributed to Elijah, are, with certain modifications, practically repeated in the case of Elisha. It is remarkable that in these latter days when the old scriptures have been passing through the fires of separation in searching criticism, eminent scholars should have come to the conclusion that there is no historical evidence to be trusted concerning the appearing in prophetic office of Elijah.

Herein is confirmed the glorious mystic truth, which no higher criticism could ever reveal, that Elijah was a Divine Name associated with a special manifestation of the Eternal Love unto the prophet Elisha, and through him, to his people, the children of Israel. The very term applied to the prophet contains the divine meaning of the manifestation. It is that of Eli-Jah—the Lord of Righteousness. The Righteousness of God is the Divine Love manifested in its Majesty. It is Eli-Jah who appears upon Horeb unto the prophet. It is Eli-Jah who appears to him in a chariot of fire. It is the mantle of Eli-Jah that is cast over him whilst in spiritual ministries, he is ploughing the land. It is the mantle of Eli-Jah for which the prophet cries out in order that his prophetic office may be sealed with power from on high. It is Eli-Jah who calls the prophet to the Brook Cherith, to come Eastward and dwell by the side of the Brook. It is Eli-Jah who provides for him, commanding the Divine Bread to be meted out for his needs, nourishing him through the ministering Spirit. And it is Eli-Jah who also sends him unto the little city of Zarephath, to make manifest there the power of the Most High One.

In the story it is said that the prophet was to drink of its waters, and that ravens had been commanded to feed him in the morning and the evening with bread and flesh. How easy it is, when hidden meanings are not understood, and when the vision is dense and the desires impure, for those who translate sacred writings to misrepresent the writer's meaning. The Jewish scriptures have undergone many such changes at the hands of scribes.

In this incident the result is most manifest. There is a representation of divine action towards a prophet of the Lord who was called unto the most sacred office, which is utterly at variance with the truth. For the Ever Most Blessed Love and Wisdom is represented as providing for a prophet's temporal needs with bread and flesh, the flesh of creatures. The incident has been accounted a remarkable miracle that ravens should have understood to bring bread and flesh in the morning and in the evening unto the prophet, and for many days. And the miracle is accepted as an evidence of the divine sanction unto His beautiful children to take flesh as a necessary and right article of food.

The hand of a betrayer is most obvious in such a mis-representation. The Divine Love and Wisdom never did, and never could, recommend the children to eat the flesh of lesser children of His creation. The Divine Love and Wisdom ever calls man upward, still upward, yet still

186

upward; never downward towards a form of living that is not only gross in its nature, but is a violation of the fundamental principle of the Mystery of Being.

This wonderful incident is rich in mystic lore. It is the unveiling of what takes place within a Soul who is called apart. It is the revelation of a state through which all Souls must pass in their way unto the perfect realization, and of how the prophetic office within a Soul is prepared for ministry.

Cherith means separateness. The Brook, or stream of Cherith, is the Truth that brings about this separateness or consecration. Of the waters of consecration had the prophet to drink for many days, even until the waters were all used up, like the first wine in the allegory of the Marriage in Cana of Galilee. Whilst by those waters separated from the outer activities, dwelling in the realms of immediate intimate fellowship with the Eternal World, learning the divine way, the divine will, the divine purpose to be expressed through the prophetic vocation, the prophet was nourished on the bread which is the Bread of Life, or Flesh of the Son of God, the which, unless a Soul partakes of, it can have no Life Eternal within itself. That Bread is the Heavenly Manna. That Flesh is the Sacred Substance, even the Divine Substance given unto the Being. We live by the Life in us of the Son of God, the Lord of Being, the Lord of Love, Eli-Jah. And the ministrants of heaven sent forth by the Divine Love and Wisdom provide for us, as for Elisha, that Bread which is the Flesh or Substance of the Son of God.

The statement concerning the ravens is a perversion. It was a dove who ministered, with which, in some old writ, the raven is confounded. The dove is the Holy One named the Eternal Flame, the Spirit, the Holy Spirit of the Lord.

187

When a Soul dwells by the Brook Cherith, drinking of its waters of separateness and consecration, looking Eastward unto the land whence it came, realizing how once more to become an inhabitant of Gilead (the Divine Kingdom in its healing ministry), the Most Blessed Spirit cherishes that one, enriches that one, nourishes that one upon the Heavenly Bread which is the flesh or substance of the Son of God. It is a time of great realization.

When the Soul has drunk unto fulness, and eaten unto that fulness necessary for the ministry, it is sent forth into the city of Zarephath in the heart of the Zidonian country or state, there to minister in making manifest the power of the Love and Wisdom of the Eternal One. For the city of Zarephath represents the Workshop, or state wherein Divine Alchemy is revealed, where the base metals of life are transmuted into the pure Gold of Being; and where the Zidonians (the Fishers) may be truly ministered unto whilst they are fishing, or seeking for the Divine Mystery of Being to understand what it means.

It was there, according to the record, the prophet had to go after his dwelling by the Brook. It was there he was to meet a woman unto whom was to be made manifest the wonderful Love and Wisdom of the Father-Mother. It was there that astonishing miracle was to be accomplished wherein the little barrel of meal should never grow less, nor the small cruse of oil fail in its supply.

For who is this woman of Zarephath, this dweller amid the Zidonians, who is lonely, and who is conscious that her barrel of meal will soon be exhausted, and her cruse of oil fail to supply her need? She is the Intuition struggling amid great impoverishment to remain alive, unable of itself to transmute the baser things into the gold of higher

things; unable to find amid all its fishing the true interpretation of the Divine Mystery of Love; unable to main-
tain itself amid the drought and the famine of spiritual
inspiration and knowledge, and in need of the coming of
the Man of God, the illumined Soul in prophetic office
representing the Love and the Wisdom of God, as the
Eternal One manifesting His power in and through him.

It is the Intuition whose meal, or material with which
to make Living Bread, is running short; and whose oil or
spiritual power for making the Bread, giving the truth
cohesiveness, adhesiveness and enrichment, is filling the
Soul with the consciousness of failure.

It is the Intuition that becomes conscious it has nothing
to give away, no bread to offer, no enrichment to lay before
another.

It is the Intuition that perceives and recognises the
prophetic office, the Man of God, but finds it difficult to act
fully upon that perception, owing to the doubts that arise
within the mind.

It is the Intuition that at last perceives the need for having
its meal and its oil touched by the Man of God, the one sent,
the one who comes with a message from the Eternal Love.

*   *   *   *

The woman makes her cake and shares it with the
prophet, that cake which she believed would be the last
she would ever make, for there was no more meal nor
any oil left. Yet the barrel of meal was mysteriously
replenished, and the cruse of oil as mysteriously filled day
by day as the cakes were baked and partaken of. The hungry
Soul, the impoverished Soul, the fearful Soul, recognising
the Divine Love and Wisdom and responding to the call
of that Love, giving all that it has, though it seems so little,

189

has performed within it the great miracle. The spiritual bread is provided. It is multiplied. It never grows less. According to the daily need, so is its provision. The oil fails not, for where love is given, love cannot die or fail.

The sign of the coming of the Blessed Presence through the ministry of His prophet is made manifest in the spiritual miracle wrought on behalf of the Soul within its Intuition. Once more is it nourished. Once more is it enriched. Once more does its land of Zidon become a state of great discovery; for the blessed Mysteries are entered into as realizations. Once more does its little city of Zarephath become a state of consciousness wherein the divine alchemy is made manifest. Once more is it nourished and enriched, preserved, upheld, uplifted, illumined, gathered up out of the land so stricken with spiritual drought and famine, into a land where famine is unknown, into a state where the Soul's meal never grows less, and where its oil fails not. For the meal is the living Truth, and the oil is the Eternal Love. Love gives cohesion to Truth. Love correlates Truth. Love enriches the knowledge of Truth. Love transmutes the knowledge of Truth into glorious power. Love faileth not. When a Soul maketh a cake for Eli-Jah, giving Him of its best, giving unto Him of all that it has, even all that it possesses, it knows no more any impoverishment. The state of Zidon brings forth great revealings. The city of Zarephath has marvellous manifestations of the Immanence of God. For the Soul enters into the consciousness of great and holy things, and gains the power of divine alchemy by which it can appropriate them, transmute them, and become enriched through them.

Such is the ministry of provision made for the spiritual needs of the Father-Mother's children when He sendeth forth His prophet to make Him manifest in His Love and Wisdom. And such is the prophetic office, that that one must at no time seek anything for himself or herself, no material interest, no personal enrichment, no earthly glory, no self-aggrandisement, but only the supreme glory of the Lord. For himself the prophet can ask nothing. When he asks a cake to be first made and given to him, as in the story it is recorded, it is not to be thought of in any personal sense, nor even in an individual way. For, in any earthly loss, in any outer impoverishment, if he be a true prophet, he will also be a burden-bearer, and share the burden for the children who suffer. For the Lord alone must he ever ask that the cake made of the meal and the oil of the Being, be offered first. By the Brook Cherith a Soul learns that in itself it is nothing, though of glorious fashion from His hand; that of itself it can do nothing, though it can be a vehicle for Him of most glorious manifestations; that from itself it has no message vibrant with that power that giveth Life and Light and Healing, though through His Indwelling, grace and the power of grace which is Love, can flow from that one.

*　　*　　*　　*

Unto you who would be the servants of the Most High One, Healers, Redeemers, Interpreters of His Wisdom, Revealers of His Love, Manifestors of His glory, know ye this, that of yourselves ye are nothing, and that only in Him, and through Him, and from Him, have ye power. Give glory unto Him alone. Let the widow's cake be given to Him. And if ye would enter into the consciousness of the glorious power bestowed through the giving of Eli-Jah unto you to dwell within you, the Lord of Being in the majesty of His Love, then unto you He calleth that ye may go Eastward and dwell by the Brook Cherith, drinking of its waters, being nourished from His Holy Spirit upon that Bread which is the Body of the Lord and the flesh or substance of the Son of God.

Only thus are prophets made.

Only thus is Eli-Jah known.

There alone is the Soul fully called and fully equipped for so high a vocation.

There alone is the Being prepared for the vision of the chariot of the Fire of His Presence, and to receive that blessing and be endued with that power which the coming of the mantle signifies, even the power of Eli-Jah.

The Realm of the Prophet.

B.

Within the Sanctuary.

WITHIN
THE
SANCTUARY. This unveiling is the complement to that entitled "The Brook Cherith." In the latter there took place the separation of the prophet from the outer life; his preparation by the Brook Cherith, of whose waters he drank; his nourishment upon the Bread of Heaven, which is the Body of the Lord, or the Flesh of the Son of God; his equipment to go down to the city of Zarephath where transmutation took place, and where, within that workshop, or centre of Soul activity, he was nourished on the meal that never wasted and the oil which never failed, the Wisdom and Love of the Father-Mother in daily provision amid the impoverished conditions of a famine-stricken world. All of which things are the preparation for the Soul who is to be called to a yet more inward ministry.

Of the call to that most inward prophetic office we have a most beautiful illustration in the opening words of the book of Isaiah, as set forth in the Logia of the Vision.

It is an embodiment of what takes place within the Being of one who is called to the highest office. It is an echo of that transcendent drama which took place in the Divine Heavens when the Oblation was projected.

By the Brook Cherith there were blessed experiences amid the loneliness; but the vision that accompanies the glorious Realization did not come there. It does not come there. Though great things are done for the Being who is called, whilst dwelling by the Brook Cherith, the transcendent vision is not there. That is a realization which comes only when the Being is in the Innermost Sanctuary.

It is said that the prophet Isaiah went up to the temple, and as he stood upon its threshold, all outer manifestations became strangely changed; all outer services were transmuted; all conditions begotten of intermediary powers of thought and desire and purpose were left, and that the

194

Being stood alone within the Sanctuary. There the prophet beheld unveiling to his vision the most transcendent and most glorious Presence. That Presence he recognised to be the Lord of the Heavenly Hosts, the King of all the Kings or Christs. The Radiance of that Presence filled all his Being. He himself appeared to be the Temple with the Presence overshadowing its high altar. Amid the radiance he beheld with the Presence, forms described as Seraphim, and these proclaimed, in language unutterable, the glory of that One whose Being was the mystery of their Being and of his own Being. They cried in antiphonal song, "Holy, holy, holy is the Lord of the Heavenly Hosts! The Heavens are full of His glory; and the fulness of all the earth is from His glory."

Here we have a vision of the very innermost of our Being. There is no temple reared upon the earth planes so glorious as the Temple of man's Soul. It is the dwelling place of the Presence. And when a Soul gets there in conscious realization, all else is forgotten. All is transcended, except certain elements of the consciousness which may need healing.

When a Being is called to high office, that one must be prepared through Separation, through learning the power of Transmutation, through acquiring the attribute by which Ascension is accomplished, to enter into the Most Holy Place. For it is there the highest prophetic office, even that of the Redeemer, is given. It is there the Being sees— which seeing is a realization so profound, so exalted, so vast, that description is impossible. It is in the Presence alone the vocation is given to the prophet. Prophets are made in the Divine Realm. They are made in the Divine way alone, and cannot be made in schools where learning is given, whether occult or religious, even though the teaching be concerning the Mysteries. The prophet is the Man of God. He is God's Man. He is a Divine Man, having reached the realm where divinity is beheld, and seen, and known, in sublime realization.

*   *   *   *

Before passing from this aspect of the Call of the Prophet, we would here say a word that may be helpful to some who may read these things. It is concerning *form.*

It is affirmed that God is formless. It is not easy to think of the Great Mystery known as the Father-Mother, as being without form. The human mind naturally reduces its thought into some concrete form. When the Soul realizes, it is known that the Divine Mystery is formless in the human, mental concept of that term, and yet never without real form. For all true and beautiful form is the expression of the Divine Thought, the Divine Purpose, the Elohistic activities.

This is true in the innermost planes, and through all the planes to the outermost. Form is an accommodation. It is used in different ways upon the different kingdoms. The same truth expressed upon the seven different planes, would have a different form corresponding to the plane of its expression. The divine manifestation is in harmony upon the different kingdoms with those kingdoms themselves, and even differs upon each of the seven planes within each of the kingdoms.

Thus, when the Being is realizing the Presence, as described in the prophet's call, the very highest and most glorious form is assumed. Cherubim and Seraphim carry up the human form even on to the Divine Kingdom. Yet so changed is it that it is manifestly more than a human form.

The Seraphim had each six wings. With twain they covered their faces in adoration. With twain they covered their feet, expressive of unspeakable lowliness. And with twain they did fly, expressive of the power of motion through the Divine Realm. To express to a human Soul, to the individuated Being, the mystery of the power that is within it, what could be more beautiful than the form of the Cherubim and Seraphim? Where that vision is, there is beautiful lowliness of mind and heart. Where that vision is, there is unfailing reverence and most glorious adoration. Where that vision is, there is the consciousness of power to soar, the power derived from the Presence, the flight of the Spirit. Where that vision is, the King—the Lord of Being—is the most glorious of all form of expression, at once that which is highest in man, and that which is the very centre of the gloriously balanced universe, the macrocosmic cross, clothed in such a radiance that no Soul could behold it unless it had been by the Brook Cherith, nourished there and prepared in Zarephath. For the vision of the glorious Presence is in form transcendent and eternal, in such form as cannot be expressed in language giving definition after the manner of human concepts, in form that is so glorious that it is the upgathered forms of all beautiful manifestation, into one sublime and adorable embodiment.

The prophet is said to have stood upon the threshold of the Temple looking at this most marvellous vision, and to have been overwhelmed by the grandeur of it, the sublime purity of it, its radiant, ineffable glory. It made him conscious that even he who had been by the Brook Cherith, and fed by Eli-Jah on the Bread which was the Flesh of the Son of God, and refreshed by the waters of the Brook, and who had learnt how the Divine Presence transmuteth all things, and doth give His ministrants power unto transmutation in service, felt, nevertheless, as if there were lacking something in himself of purity, of lowliness, of love.

For he had an overwhelming sense of his need which only the Divine Presence could meet. And it is written of him that he cried out, "Woe is me, for I am undone; for I am a man of unclean lips who dwells amongst a people of unclean lips, for mine eyes have seen the King, the Lord of Hosts."

But this rendering is not in harmony with the state of a prophet Soul standing upon the threshold of that Presence. It must needs, therefore, be differently translated.

"The Holy Awe of His Presence filleth me.

I am as one overwhelmed, so great is the Glory of His Presence.

I am but a man; my lips are unworthy to utter His praise.

Who am I that He should call me into this vision, whose service is amongst the people who are still unhealed?

Who am I that mine eyes should look upon the Lord, the King of all the Kings, and the Lord of all?"

*   *   *   *

Now, in the Vision there came to him one of the Seraphim with the Glowing Stone. It had been in the Sacred Fire upon the Altar. The glowing stone is called a live coal. It was nothing earthly. It was nothing that could be symbolized by any earthly, material thing. It was that most precious gift which is at once the foundation stone, and the corner stone, and the copestone or completion of the Temple of man's Being as fashioned by the Eternal Love.

It is the Glowing Stone of the Mystery of Being expressed in the living flame of a Love that never dies, whose light is never extinguished, whose purity maketh clean where it toucheth, and maketh whole all Being through its ministry.

It is the White Stone given to him who overcometh ; given first in the Angelic World as " the Crown of Life, " and then in the celestial state or consciousness of divine childhood, as the Bright and Morning Star, and then in the innermost realm as the consciousness of the Eternal Lord of Love, named Son of God, the Christ of God, the realization of that Being whose Flesh the prophet ate by the Brook Cherith.

The Being overwhelmed by the grandeur of the Presence, is lifted up and made strong in that Love, and by that Love, for ministry.

The Being who feels utterly undone when face to face with that sublimest Mystery, is enriched and strengthened, and exalted and crowned, for the sublime ministry of that Love.

The Being who, having attained to so great an estate as to be able to stand upon the threshold of the innermost sanctuary and behold the transfiguration of its own Life into the Temple of the Lord, and to witness the dramatic unveiling of Cherubim and Seraphim, and the Presence high and lifted up, the Overshadowing Cloud upon the Sanctuary, and to hear the very Divine Heavens crying out in worship and adoration, feeling the while an overwhelming sense of his own littleness, his limitations, his very impurity that he falls down as one overwhelmed, is, nevertheless, raised up, lifted up, comforted, healed, strengthened to be a ministrant even unto the people described as unhealed, as of unclean lips, whose praise was not yet perfected.

*   *   *   *

Such is the call of a Prophet-Soul through the Realm of Separateness unto that of Transmutation and Manifestation.

The Training of the Twelve,
setting forth the qualities
and powers of the
Soul's Attributes.

THE TRAINING OF THE TWELVE It is said that the Master chose twelve from amongst the more general company of followers to be His intimate friends, His chief disciples; and these are always said to have been named apostles.

The mystic and most glorious ministry set forth in the doctrine of the Training of the Twelve, has relation to the Divine in the human Soul. It is a mystical picture, now all mixed up and overlaid by traditional story, of the divine training of a Soul's attributes.

Seen from the inner realm, it is a picture full of beautiful and radiant purpose. It is a picture with twelve aspects, each one independent of the other, yet all so intimately related that they are necessary for the perfect embodiment. Just as the terms Jesus Christ the Lord related to states of beautiful life, sublime vision, and most glorious consciousness, so the training of the twelve related to the purification, transformation and transfiguration of the Soul's attributes. Those attributes were signified in the chief terms used— John, James, Peter, Andrew, Philip, Thomas, Bartholomew, James of Alphæus, Matthew Thaddeus, Jude, Simon Zelotes and Nathanael.

These twelve form a Round Table. They make a circle. They correspond to the Twelve Houses astrologically, understood in their mystic sense; to the Twelve Zodiacal Signs understood in their celestial sense.

The circle begins in and issues from the Divine Principle, the Agapê, the Eternal Love; manifesting as the Eternal Life, Zōē; radiating as the Eternal Light Phōs; serving as the Celestial Sign of the Cross; reflecting as the Star in the firmament, the glory of the Radiant Presence; having the power to descend from the Celestial into the next Kingdom of manifestation.

201

The Eternal Love, Life and Light, are represented in the initiate terms which are translated John, James and Peter.

The power of Celestial cross-bearing, the sign of that ministry with the power to reflect the glory of the Radiance of the Eternal World, and the power to descend to the next Kingdom for manifestation, are represented in Andrew, Philip and Thomas Didymus.

Bartholomew begins the next trio of spiritual manifestation. He is the Angelic side of Thomas Didymus. In James of Alphaeus there is the Eternal Life Principle manifested in the Angelic Human. The Angelic Human is full also of enquiry, for Alphaeus is Cleophas. And there is Matthew Thaddeus who represents again that quality begotten of Angelic emotion.

Jude, the beautiful Love expressed in the individual personal relationship, commences the outer trio; for the individual expression lives when the outer vehicle is laid aside, just as the Being persists and serves, feels, thinks, desires, aspires, rises, ascends, though the coat that has been worn, or the garment to cover all the vehicles which has been in use, is laid aside.

Then there is Simon, who was Canaanite, and also Zelotes (such are the terms applied, and these represent a fallen state of the attribute). Simon is the vehicle of the mind's vision in correlating upon the outer planes. But that power is always an attribute. It is the power by which the Being correlates in the Kingdom of the outer manifestation.

And Nathanael, the guilelessness of the Love in the individual and personal realm, beautiful, pure and gentle, and able to descend without hurt.

*   *   *   *

Such is the end of this marvellous outgoing of the Being, the Soul's circle beginning in the Divine Centre, and taking the whole compass in the circumference of Life. These are tentative statements of which more bye and bye. Let us look at them in their Divine Trinity upon each Kingdom; see them in their correspondence upon each Kingdom to each other; and behold how beautiful they are in their nature and manifestation, and how wonderfully interpretive when truly correlated.

*   *   *   *

JOHN   The Eternal Love is the Divine Principle within us.
JAMES   It is the Mystery of God in our Being; and as Divine
PETER   Love, becomes not only Principle, but is an attribute.

From the Principle, all the attributes proceed. But within in the Principle, all the attributes are also contained. They cannot be divorced from the centre. They are part of the Being. But their manifestation is upon different Kingdoms, and in different degrees according to the varying stages of realization.

The Eternal Mystery is in each one, in the child as well as in the aged man or woman. The Divine Love is in each one. The Mystery is alike in the Soul that has seen unspeakable cycles of ages, and the Soul greatly younger, though it too must have known thousands of generations.

From that Divine Centre, Love becomes the great power. All the other attributes are great and glorious only in the proportion in which the central Principle is revealed through them and interpreted by them. Our attributes are beautiful in the proportion in which the Divine Centre affects them. Love is the foundation of all Being. It is the transcendent fulness of all realization. There is naught so great in altitude, nor so profound in depth of mystery, nor so all-encompassing in the vastness of its comprehending and all-embracing power, as the Eternal Love that is in us.

The disciple John, therefore, represents that Principle. It is he who is said to have leaned upon the bosom of his Lord. It is Love that dwells in the bosom of God. The individual Soul dwells there, realizes there, leans there, rests there, is nourished there, through the Johannine power at the centre of that Soul's Being.

James, in the English form, is the name that is given as the translation of the term that signifies the Life-Principle. It is said that the Master called John and James, and named them the sons of Boanerges, Thunder, the Bi-unal Divine Radiating Power. It is from Love all illumination comes. It is from Love all power is manifested. Love is the Fire, and Love is the Power that enables a Soul at last to hear the Inner Divine Voice, and to interpret that Voice, to realize who that Voice is. James represents the Life. He is the Life-Principle realizing itself. He is one of the sons of Thunder. He is one of the sons of the Fire of God, the Eternal Mystery in the individual system representing the Fatherhood—Motherhood Principles.

The Radiance of the Love and Life, is Peter. He is the Light, with the power of discernment in the innermost realm. He is not the intuition, for the intuition may discern approximately without correct divination. It may sense without being able to proclaim or interpret. But the divine power represented by the Petrine faculty, or attribute, is that power which is contained in the Life-Principle through the Love-Principle, and by which it is possible to make the glorious display on the Celestial Realm of the auric splendour of the Being. He is the diviner of the Mystery of the Love within, and is the Light of that Love, the Light of the Life.

Thus you have a most wonderful manifestation of the Divine Mystery in man himself, in the three innermost attributes. They are the three disciples who can realize the Transfiguration in sublimest fulness, and look upon it with open vision. They are the three who can witness that sorrow which is said to have taken place in the Gethsemane, though they slept awhile. It is said, indeed, that they slept for very weariness. And it is also recorded that on the Mount of Transfiguration they slept, and that what they saw, they witnessed in trance. They represent that mysterious trinity of power by which a Soul is able to descend even into the Gethsemane of unspeakable sorrow and burden-bearing, in the midst of which they are liable to sleep, to lose the true vision of the meaning of the sorrow.

This divine trinity is in each one. There is the Love, which is also the Life and the Light. You are here because these are within you. They express the Divine Mystery in you. The Holy Trinity in you, even the Fatherhood-Motherhood of God in the glory of His Son, find their expression through these three attributes, of the Love-Principle, the Life-Principle and the Light-Principle. For, whilst there is one Divine Principle in the Being, building up the Being, manifesting from the Being, there proceed from that Principle the attributes in the innermost realm of the Divine Presence,—the Love, the Life, and the Light.

*   *   *   *

Now, you may find these wonderful Mysteries in yourself. How beautiful to think of it! We are like God. We are of God. We are very God in miniature. We are meant to live for Him. Indeed, we do when we live truly. Then we live to embody Him, to realize Him, to express Him. And that is the meaning of our life. A Soul is filled with the glory of the Heavens the more it seeks to embody Him.

Never judge a human Soul and think that one of these three is lacking. They are in each one. And they can be found. They can be called forth. Oft-times they seem as if they slept. They may appear as if still very latent powers, and as if it would take ages to bring them into manifestation. Yet know that they are present.

If you had never seen the electric light, nor heard of it, nor seen any of the plant by which it is generated, and you had been taken into a generating station and shown the plant, it would have conveyed nothing to you except that the engines represented some wonderful combination of mechanical power and engineering genius. But if the silent motors were set in motion, the dynamos made to function, then presently, all around wherever the necessary plant was laid and bulbs provided, you would behold the effect of the setting in motion of the hidden motive power and the operation of the dynamos.

So is it with the human Soul. When the great dynamo in the Love-Principle is set in motion, there is Life, as the outcome of the motion, and there comes Light as the realization. The Light is the auric display, the Celestial Radiance of Love's motion.

Thus much have we spoken unto you of the Mystery of the Divine Kingdom within you that you may recognise that that Kingdom is in each one, with its Holy Trinity, or attributes, and to ever remember that though you may not be able to discern the motion of the Great Dynamo we speak of as the Divine Mystery in the Love-Principle, yet, that it can be set in motion, that there may be motion; that, though you cannot see the radiance, there is radiance, though it is not intense, and that the day will come, a day that can be hastened, when, through motion, Life can be exalted into and ensphered by the very Radiance of God.

*   *   *   *

Now look at the next Kingdom and its Trinity of Power.

ANDREW There are Andrew and Philip and Thomas
PHILIP Didymus. Andrew is the Celestial Cross; Philip
THOMAS is the Radiance of the higher Mind; Thomas
Didymus is the power of that Mind in its twin nature to
receive the Radiance, and to descend to the next Kingdom
for manifestation.

Andrew is the cross-bearer, for Love is ever the burden-
carrier. The Innermost Divine bears the cross. Thus you
have the Celestial correspondence to the Divine.

In Philip you have the correspondence to the Petrine
faculty, as the Mind receiving the Radiance and reflecting
it. For Philip represents the Celestial Mind in its office of
Evangelist, reflecting the Glory.

And Thomas Didymus represents the Celestial Mind in
its Celestial Life, and its power to descend for ministry.
From the Divine Kingdom all power is given. From the
very heart, or centre, of our Being, when realization is great,
power is given to all the attributes to enter into the Kingdom.
They can realize themselves. It is thus in the Celestial
World, in the Celestial state. There is Andrew, Simon
Peter's brother—the Light giving the Soul the consciousness
of what its ministry is to be, to bear the cross. Philip, who
was of the city of Andrew and Peter, Bethsaida, carrying
the knowledge of the Great Love in the Mind, and reflecting
it to a Nathanael, saying Come ! we have found Him whom
we have been seeking for, even that one who dwelleth in
Nazareth. And Nathanael saith, Can such a thing, such
a state, come out of Nazareth ? Come and see, bearing
within the consciousness of the mind, that it is true. For
Nathanael represents that beautiful Love which is often
realized on the outer planes in Souls who have not yet
awakened to the great realization in the inner planes, but
who nevertheless seek the manifestation of what is guileless

and pure and beautiful in their personal and individual life, and who could never dream that out of such a state as they themselves are in, there could come forth Christ.

The Higher Mind, the Celestial Mind, can say to such a life, Come and see! It is not simply with a knowledge that is only a reflection, but with a knowledge which is begotten of realization, that the Mind, Philip, can minister. In hieroglyph the white horse is his symbol. The word Philip comes from the Greek word that means a horse. In its mystical sense it is the Intelligence; and the rider upon the white horse, upon whose vesture is written the Word of God, is the Logos in the Being, the Adonai in the Sanctuary riding upon the power of a purified Mind.

Thomas Didymus is called the twin. On the higher side the vision is radiant. On the lower side the vision is under limitation. The Celestial reflects the Divine World; the Angelic World reflects only the Celestial World; and this world in its pure state, reflects only the Angelic World. Here we have the meaning of the twin. When the attribute is looking in the lower world, it sees not from the innermost.

The attribute has also to do with the Will in the Mind of Philip. The Will is in the Divine Principle. But its realm of manifestation on the Celestial World is through Thomas Didymus.

Once more you see these attributes are in you. You have the correspondence. There is the cross-bearer in you. In the Celestial World, the divine cross-bearer is the Andrew spirit, the heart that loves to bear the burden of others, the love that never falters to take up another's sorrow. That love bears the Divine Cross. It never says, Oh Cross, thou art too heavy for me! Though that love may say, I could not bear thee but for the Love that bears me up!

which would be beautiful and absolutely true.

You also have the Mind that reflects the radiance of that Love that loves to bear the cross, and can say to the sufferer, Come and see; to the seeker, Ye shall find; to the one who is fearful lest living the beautiful life should not lead to that glorious state, the life represented by Nazareth and the Nazarene, can and will bring you to Christ.

Then surely ye have in you the willinghood to find Christ in beautiful realization, and the willinghood to express Christ in the Angelic World or state of the beautiful Jesus love! How wonderful is that attribute of Will in us, which finds its manifestation upon the Celestial and Angelic realms of our Being! The realm of the Mind catches the rays from the Divine World. The realm of the Will has to choose the way of manifestation through service as well as through living. And these are also within you. Each one has these glorious attributes of the Sons of God.

*   *   *   *

BARTHOLOMEW   Then there are the correspondences on the
ALPHAEUS   next Kingdom. There is Bartholomew, the
MATTHEW   Angelic side of Didymus. He is the reflector of Angelic love, the interpreter of the Angelic song, the sweet singer of the praise of the beautiful love.

Then comes James the Less. He is the Life-Principle, not in the innermost in realization, but in the realm of beautiful outward ministry. The same Life, less only in the degree of the intensity of its realization and manifestation. He is brother of the Lord also, in this sense, that it is the correspondence on the Angelic realm of the very Innermost Life, the glorious Life-Principle of the Divine. We have the three glorious powers which we have spoken of as Celestial, reflected in the attributes which are of the Angelic World through Bartholomew, James the Less, and

Matthew Thaddeus: the Mind that can forsake all to follow; the Mind that can be the scribe, and a power for writing in the very deeds of life the sweet story of the Jesus Christ life, and make concrete the Jesus manifestation.

*   *   *   *

JUDE
ZELOTES
NATHANAEL
And then there is Jude, and Simon, and Nathanael—the attributes of gentleness, pure thought, guileless spirit. These show forth the Heart weaned from the world whilst serving in it, filled with Compassion and Pity; the Mind redeemed from the state of the Canaanite, and from zeal after worldly life; and the sweet Spirit, ever diffident yet guileless, seeking the beautiful, and responding to it when it comes along[1].

*   *   *   *

Now the Training of the Twelve is the training of these twelve attributes in one's innermost Being from the Divine, by the Divine, for the Divine. Disciples all they must be, each one learning the power to realize and manifest. They are Apostles in the making. Each one by very nature is meant to be apostolic, to be in apostolic succession from the very innermost, outward. These are divine attributes made apostolic, which have to interpret Life through manifestation. These are the twelve powers of the Being acquiring Knighthood through learning and serving, realizing the overcoming Life, knowing the Great Realization, and thus becoming the Twelve Holy Ones of the Lord, who interpret Him, who reveal Him, who manifest Him from the Divine Kingdom, from the realm of the Realization, through the Thought proceeding from the innermost of our Being, through the Angelic Love ministry of our thoughts, desires and emotions, and through the personal equation in compassion and

[1]For a fuller explanation of these attributes, see page 390.

beautiful consecration for ministry, and in the guilelessness of our spirit.

These are all within you, and in great measure cultured. They are all yours that ye may manifest the Mystery of God. They are all yours, for ye are Christ's and Christ is God's. And God is within you. His Christ is within you. The Round Table is there with its White Stone. The Table of Sacramental Bread and Wine is there with its Sacred Cup. The Table of the Soul's Oblation is there also with its Divine Chalice.

The four courts of the Temple are within you. The Innermost most Holy Place; the Holy Place; the Middle court of priestly sacrifice and ministry; and the outer court of the daily oblation. Even the court of the Gentiles is present in the vehicles through which ministries are rendered which are spoken of as the ordinary ministries of life, daily personal living, acting and serving.

These realms are within you: the Divine; the Celestial; the Angelic; and the outer or common court.

Thus the twelve powers are yours, as these are represented in John, James and Peter; Andrew, Philip and Thomas; Bartholomew, James the Less, and Thaddeus; Jude, Simon and Nathanael.

What a galaxy of attributes! What a zodiac of the Soul! What Houses of splendour in their enrichment from the Divine Love!

In the Innermost, there is Love Transcendent! Life in the sublimest Mystery! Light that is ineffable, inapproachable yet apprehendable!

On the Celestial Realm, Love bearing its cross! Love reflecting the cross in its thought for others! Love with its power to descend yet further, and willing to descend as well as to rise!

211

In the Angelic Kingdom, Love as a sweet angelic Breath! Love as a beautiful angelic Life! Love as a blessed personal ministry! Love in the life, in the thought, in the personal service! Love as compassion and pity, shutting none out and forgetting none, but encompassing all! Love in the Desire, changing the Canaanite into one redeemed and full of devotion; turning the earthly zeal into the heavenly zeal and consecration! Love crowned with the sweet guilelessness that never betrays by word or feeling or thought! Love whose subtlety is the Heavenly Wisdom, whose manifestation is in the clarity of the Divine Radiance, the guileless love.

What more may we say to you of the vastness of the Temple of God which ye are! Of the inexpressible splendour of His Temple! Of that Glory of His Indwelling which must needs be approached through realization.

*   *   *   *

Oh, Love most blessed and most adorable, Thy children bow before the Mystery of the Being Thou hast given to them from out Thy glorious Being! And we would adore Thee in every attribute; through every power, in every Kingdom of our Being; upon all the spheres of each part of our Being; in all the houses of experience; through all the qualities with which Thou hast enriched us!

Oh Love Majestic and Eternal, that Thou shouldest have condescended to have fashioned us so like Thyself!

Fill us with the Holy Awe which Thy Presence giveth!

Divine Priesthood

after the

Order of Melchisedek.

DIVINE   Priesthood is mediatorial.

PRIESTHOOD.   It is an office filled by the Being, to mediate for the Divine unto His children.

It is a ministry essentially spiritual, whose garments express the insignia of God, and whose power of officiation is derived directly from the Divine Presence.

It is a state of conscious realization of the glorious Overshadowing, the Cloud upon the Sanctuary.

It is a state in which the Being is able to stand upon the threshold where the Presence unveils, to minister before that Presence and for that Presence.

It is a realization so transcendent that the Being dwelleth, so to speak, in the consciousness of that Presence at all times, looking upon the Manifestation of the Divine Mystery, receiving from the heart of that Mystery ever-deepening unveilings, and having power for ministry transmitted from the Presence to go forth mediating of the Mystery itself, and all for which it stands, that the children of men may have brought to them the Atmosphere and the Radiance of the Mystery of the Glorious One who dwelleth within the Sanctuary.

In such a Priesthood all the powers are consecrate. In such a Priesthood the Being has but one will, even the willinghood to do the Will of the Father-Mother. In such ministry the Being has but one authority, that which bears the image of the Father-Mother, the impress of the Lord of Love.

Priesthood after the Order of Melchisedek, is Divine. It has no earthly father, no earthly mother, no earthly begetting, no earthly authority, no earthly insignia to give it authority. The signet of the ring upon the finger of that Priesthood, is that of the Divine Marriage of the Soul in its Oneness with the Lord. It knows no beginning of days

214

nor end of years in any earthly sense. It is not formulated from without, nor governed by planetary motion in the outer realms. It is a Soul realization, for it is of the Divine Mystery. That Priesthood after the Order of Melchisedek has a beginning, is true; but it is in the Heavenly Arche, the glorious Divine Principle of Being itself. And the beginning is in the realization, when all the powers of the Being are gathered up into that state of most glorious polarity in consciousness wherein the Father-Mother is known. It has no end of days or years. It is a Priesthood that is eternal in its nature, exalted above all time and place, though it may be laid down if the Being be appointed to some other ministry for other worlds, other children, other service. But when once realized, even as it knows no beginning so it knows no ending, for the Being has always power, if commanded, to come on to that threshold of mediatorial revealings for the children, to take up the office again.

There is the office of the Prophet, and the Seer, and the Priest. The Prophet apprehends, and thus knows. The Seer beholds, sees and knows, through realization. The Priest is Prophet and Seer crowned with the most inward divine ministry. That is the state of a Priest after the Order of Melchisedek. For the Prophet and the Seer and the Priest are three great orders. They are three Degrees in the soul's Ascension. They are three Manifestations in the soul's ministry. They are three offices through which the Divine Mystery becometh unveiled.

The Prophet who is Prophet indeed, is also Priest; but not yet after the Order of Melchisedek in realization. For the Prophet is mediator, mediating the knowledges between the Divine World and the realm of the mind.

The Prophet is a man of God and a woman of God, one

215

who has realized great degree of the Christhood estate and, therefore, mediator, according to that degree of the Divine Love and Wisdom, unto the children whom the Prophet is called upon to teach.

*   *   *   *

The Seer is a Priest. He is of the realm of the Sanctuary, where, through the Veil, Cherubim and Seraphim are beheld in their ministry, and also the Overshadowing Glory of the Lord upon the Sanctuary. The Seer is not simply one who beholds clairvoyantly upon the Occult Kingdom, or in the Astral Realms, looking upon reflex images, or signs and symbols thrown upon those Realms from higher degrees of heavenly ministry. The Seer is one who transcends all these, having the power to look upon those Realms when necessary for ministry, but whose real ministry is to look within the Veils, and even to behold within the Sanctuary. He is a man of God; she is a woman of God; prophetic in power for interpretation of the Vision, the Seer having the power to behold the Vision also through the realization.

The Priest is within the Veil of the Innermost, when the Priesthood is after the Order of Melchisedek. The consciousness there is one with that Being's Lord. The Being is ever conscious that it is but an individuation of the glorious Mystery, yet there realizing that Mystery in such fulness that it becomes one in consciousness, seeing as if with illimitable vision, hearing with powers transcending all earthliness, realizing beyond all that could be realized beneath such a state, of the glorious Mysteries, and being endued with power from the Holy Presence, clad in the garments of High Priesthood from on High, can go wheresoever sent by the Divine Love for ministry.

Now it is in this sense that the High Priesthood of that one known as the Master, is to be understood. He was named a Priest within the Holy Place. It was said of Him, as spoken in sacred story, "Thou art a Priest this day after the Order of Melchisedek." By that it is to be understood that He was appointed unto the office of Divine Mediator.

Mediation is through the Seership and Prophetic offices, hence the Manifestation. There were manifold manifestations of that Priesthood long before the days known as those of the Manifestation. There were manifestations upon other Realms unto the children of the Kingdom of the Heavens. There were manifestations given to the children of Israel long ages before even the Priesthood, expressed in the Manifestation days, was thought of.

To give utterance to such thoughts might raise doubt in some minds, and would certainly raise doubt and opposition in many minds within the orthodox communities, and indeed in many of those that are otherwise considered. For it might be said that if the Father-Mother be Omniscient, then all things He knoweth must have no past, present, nor future; that there is only with Him an Eternal Now. If that be so, then the whole universe becomes a machine, and all that we account wrong must be a part of the outworking of that Divine Omniscience.

Such a misconception of Divine Omniscience arises from the misconception of the nature of the Eternal Mystery, and through thinking of God anthropomorphically. Those who have Realized, do not think of God after the manner of a person like the human. The Divine World is ever thinking; but not after the human fashion. It is ever projecting, creating, fashioning and ministering through that which is created, bringing into manifestation great and glorious worlds and systems. But the process of bringing them into manifestation takes thousands of ages, as we have to calculate. Though there is no time in the Divine Realm, there is time in the Realms of manifestation where there is motion and regulation. And there must ever be time where there is such regulation through motion. Yet even there, time is comparative, being circumscribed and expressed by the motion of the world and the system. So Omniscience has past, present, and future within its vision. And new realms come within that vision.

*   *   *   *

Now, the Priesthood of Melchisedek is the Priesthood of the regnancy of Righteousness, as the word signifies in its first meaning. And then, the regnancy of Peace, which is its second meaning. There is no true priesthood that is not begotten in and emanated from the Mystery of the Divine Love. And though a Priesthood of the Soul in its ministry may not be so fully rounded as that which is expressed as the Priesthood after the Order of Melchisedek; yet, if it be begotten of Love, it is of that Order, though it has not yet come to the full realization. And if priesthood be of any other order, it is without power to bring Divine Healing. It is without power to bring the Divine Presence. It is without power to Absolve Sin. For any healing that is other than that begotten of Love, is of a passing order. It can only be temporary. All souls must come back to the Divine Love to be healed.

The Priesthood of God is the Priesthood of Melchisedek. He is the King of Righteousness. His Priesthood is the Majesty of His Love in its glorious ministry, from the very Innermost and the most exalted states, down to the lowliest expressions.

And if the Divine Majesty can go down from that exalted state to express itself in lowly ministry, where may His children find themselves, if not there, growing from lowliest states through manifold degrees, until they reach the Prophetic Office, and then have the garment of Seership, and then the richly embroidered raiment bearing the insignia of the Priesthood after the Order of Melchisedek?

*　　　*　　　*　　　*

If ye have imagined that the Divine Majesty of the Eternal Mystery keeps Him, Her, It (for all are included), even the Father-Mother, in that state of Absolutism such as a Deist would believe in, that there can be no stooping, no lowly manifestation, no passing through the Kingdoms, and all the Realms, and all the Planes, for testimony to the great Reality, then ye have misconceived the nature of God the Father-Mother, and misread the meaning of the Divine Mystery. For that Love which is regnant Righteousness, is majestic in its stooping. And it stoops through all its children who have reached the state of Priesthood after the Order of Melchisedek, and the Seers, and the Prophets, and the true manifestors of Jesushood, and the true interpreters of His Love expressed on the Human Kingdom. He doth ever make manifest His glorious Presence.

Unto whom would you liken Him, the Most High One?

He is the Sum of all Being, and no man.

He is the expression of all Being, and is not circumscribed by all the intellectual concepts of Him which have dominated the minds of men and women.

He filleth all the Heavens. The Heavens are filled with systems most glorious, many of them far, far more glorious than this system of which our world is a member, on which we are denizens. And through all those Realms the Mystery of Being reveals itself. The Glory of the Father-Mother manifests itself, From great world to little world; from system most glorious in its majesty to the system of quite lowly estate, like our own, He doth reveal Himself, and through them doth manifest Himself.

Nay more! All the concentrated embodiments of Being revealed in those worlds and systems have their heavenly Hierarchies. These are Divine, Celestial, Angelic. And through every member of the Hierarchies, is the majesty of the Love made manifest. The very story of Angels visiting the earth is one of beautiful condescension and lowly ministry. It is not to be supposed that the Angels would dream of thinking of their ministry as an act of condescension. Love never feels that it condescends. It is not conscious of any such state. Love just goes where it is sent. It descends to the state to which it is sent. Love comes as on the Flight of the Spirit, just to the very place where it is appointed to minister. Even as the Majesty of that Love is revealed through all the glorious ministry of the Heavens, and in the lowly Realms, so is it manifested through His children upon this world. When a Being loves divinely, that Love is regnant within it. It knows nought else. It is a vessel of Love. And according as it is moved from the Divine Realm to pour out, so does it give in ministry. And through all the degrees of Being, the Divine Mystery comes down, even to the most lowly. And in the Divine Realm, the most lowly is equally beautiful with the most high. All that is true is beautiful. All that is beautiful is from the Realm whence all beauty proceedeth.

*   *   *   *

Were it not for such a ministry no child could reach the high estate of being a Priest after the Order of Melchisedek. But for such a ministry, how could ye yourselves return into the consciousness of that Love? Without the ministry of that Love in its majestic stooping, how could ye ever come back again into the realm of perfect Peace, amid a world whose vibrations are all against that transcendent realization?

The end of all soul-evolution is the Realization of Divine Childhood to the Father-Mother. That ye once attained.

The end of your Regeneration is to get back into that high state wherein the Office of the Prophet shall be yours again, the realization of being the child of the Father-Mother. The Priesthood of the Prophet is that of childhood to the Father-Mother, and the interpreting of that childhood to those in the lower degrees of consciousness and understanding and experience. In your Regeneration, Seership comes back again. The prophetic mantle is also one that bears you within the Veil to glorious vision.

The Seership of the Soul is not to be confounded with clairvoyance on the lower realms. It is the clairvoyance of the Being, wherein the Divine Mystery is beheld beyond the Veil. The Being stands upon the threshold where minister Cherubim and Seraphim; where the Radiant Cloud abides between the Cherubim; where the Altar of the Soul's Oblation is found, and where the great Sacrifice is made. And, passing within those gates or veils into the Innermost Sanctuary whose Altar the Seer beholdeth, and moving, filled with the most awe-inspiring conscious reverence, towards that Altar, and lying down upon it, so to speak, there is the offering up of one's whole Being. To be one in our Being with our Lord, even as in our Substance and our Spirit we are one in Him—that is the chiefest desire of the Being in real priesthood. And surely to give our very substance, and the Spirit He hath enriched us with, for sublimest service, is our supreme desire.

The supreme act of a Soul who becomes in such a day, the day of its Ascension into that state of high Priesthood

221

after the Order of Melchisedek, is the laying down of its Life. All else gathers around that sublimest act, and emanates from it. From that day the Being is no more merely individual, but is ever so much one with the Divine World, that whatsoever that World seeks from it in ministry is at once gladly rendered as the most sacred service.

The Great High Priest after the Order of Melchisedek, is the Lord of Love, who is at once King of Righteousness— Love in its Majesty; and King of Salem—Love in its glorious Peace-giving, Love that healeth all things, Love whose vibrations never disturb to hurt, whose outflow bears the healing of God even for the elements, Love so marvellous in its magnetic power, that those things which are not ready to be healed, flee from it.

Oh, child of the Great Love, thou art called to be a Priest after the Order of Melchisedek, a mediator of Love in its Divine Majesty, and in the glory of the Peace it sheds.

*   *   *   *

O Most Ever Blessed Father-Mother, most glorious art Thou! Thou dost shed Thy Glory not only through the worlds of Thy creating, but through all the Being of Thy lesser children. Them Thou hast made great in estate, even unto the knowing of Thee through Thy Holy One within them.

We would adore Thee. Within the Sanctuary we would bow adoringly before Thee. In Thy Presence all the long shadows flee away; our hurt becomes healed; all our sorrow finds the branch of healing; and life's cup knows the fulness of joy.

We adore Thee! May we indeed be true Priests for Thee, mediating Thy Love in lowly mind and heart and spirit, shedding wheresoe'er we go, the breath of Thy Great and Holy Peace.

We would indeed embody Thee; reflect Thee; express Thee in Thy glorious Love, and in Thy sublime giving unto Thy children. In all our ways we would adore Thee. In all our service we would express the praise of Thee.

Unto this end constrain us to Thy Bosom, and enrich us from Thy Love.

The Urim and the Thummim,
Being of the Mystery of
God in us.

These terms express the Mystery of God in us. They are unfamiliar, though to the reader of the Old Testament they may be recalled as spoken of in connection with the Aaronic Priesthood. In the description of that Priesthood said to have been borne by Aaron, the Urim and the Thummim are named as being parts of a remarkable Breastplate which he wore. That garment was called the Ephod. In the centre of it there was what was termed the Breastplate containing the twelve precious stones, upon each of which was engraven one of the names of the House of Israel. When Aaron entered the Most Holy Place he had to put the Breastplate on, and then the Urim and the Thummim. These latter are represented as being parts of a linen garment which were drawn over the precious stones when he entered the Most Holy Place.

Religious history, in all ages since this fallen world began and all the conditions of life became changed, has undergone many strange phases. These have often been hurtful, and, in some instances, quite disastrous. The religious history has been one of rites and ceremonies, outward sacrifices greatly acclaimed as the things desired by the Most Ever Blessed One. The Inner Things have been veiled. The vast history of the human Being has been lost amid rabbinical law or overlaid with material wares. The history of the Soul's true growth has been veiled in language none could understand, or hidden away like a treasure hidden in a cabinet whose door is locked, and whose key is lost.

Religion is in the Spirit. It is the Spirit. All religion must have relation to life, and the life expressed must have relation to God; for religion is of the Spirit, is from the Spirit, is for the Spirit, is the Spirit of God in us seeking expression. This is what has been lost at the very heart of all religious manifestations, all ecclesiastical expressions, all

225

endeavour to set forth with elaborate wares the meaning of the profound Mystery of Being

In this way the vision of God became veiled to the Soul. In this way the true knowledge of the Soul's own nature was lost. In this way religion was transferred from the inner realm of Being to the outer realms where its manifestation found its fulness in rites, in ceremonies, sometimes in labyrinthine doctrine, priestly ministries, and material sacrificial acts. The language of symbolism ceased to have living meanings.

*   *   *   *

The whole story of religious interpretation is one of sad and terrible materialization. It speaks in a dead language. The true meaning of the Temple of God which is ever within, was lost amid the priestly occultism of outward temple ministries. The sacrifice of the ox and the heifer, the ram and the goats, the lamb and the turtle dove, which were offered by Jewish priests, have relation to spiritual quantities and qualities of Being. The ox and the heifer represent the consecration of the male and female powers or attributes of the body. The two goats speak of the lower will and the higher will—the will that operates in the world objective, and the will in which divine choices are made or rejected. The ram sacrificed represents the Soul's divine power of sacrifice as in giving the Life for healing. The lamb speaks of that Love which knows no measure in its giving, spotless, without blemish, the Lamb of God, the very Mystery of God in us, the Divine Love who is ever on the throne with the Lord. Where the Lord reigns, Love reigns. Where the Lamb of God is triumphant, the Lord is regnant. The turtle dove is the symbol of the Spirit whose consecration in the sacrificial sense, is the giving up even of one's spirit in sublime self surrender for ministry for

226

God and the Soul. The priesthood referred to is an inward priesthood, the officiating thoughts, powers, desires expressed in sweet ministries. The Aaronic Priesthood is of the Presence within. Aaron, *the Aaron*, is no man, but the Son of God within. His Priesthood is after the order of Melchisedek, without father, without mother, without beginning of days or end of years, the Eternal Principle within the Being manifesting through mediation for God. The Great High Priest wearing our nature, is the Son of God within us. Our nature is from Him. It is of Him. It is to be for Him. The ministry of the Priesthood was and ever is within.

This does not mean that there need be no religious rites, as they are called. Many are helped through many avenues. All avenues which truly help souls should be beautiful. And if they be beautiful, are aids along the path. But the Priesthood, the Sacrifice, the Sanctuary, the Presence—these are within. And there is no more beautiful testimony to the great reality of all this, than the Urim and the Thummim. The High Priest with the Ephod represents that which is ever borne upon the bosom of the Eternal One. And all that is in the Eternal and Ever Most Blessed One, is reflected into us, to be re-embodied in us. The Ephod with the sacred Breastplate containing the Twelve Precious Stones, symbolizes the Divine Encompassing Presence, the enfolding of God, the ensphering of the Soul from God, the encompassing He gives to His children. The Breastplate is the insignia of His Indwelling, the sign of the Mystery of His Being in us. For the names of the tribes of Israel are the names of the Divine Attributes. And those attributes are reflected through us as they find embodiment in us. They are ours to be manifested gloriously; and in their glorious manifestation, to reflect the very splendour of the Mystery.

The Twelve Precious Stones are graded, seven transparent

and five opaque. The opaque stones represent the precious substances which, when understood, become a veil unto the Soul, not to hide from it the Divine Presence, but upon different planes to protect the Mystery within.

The seven transparent stones represent in their very colours as well as in the names they bear, the glorious divine substances which are built up into the Being. These contain within themselves the radiance of the seven tinctures of Elohim, and have the power to reflect the Radiance of the Presence, and even to refract its Light, to break it up and reveal the splendour of the ever deepening Mystery of Being.

The five opaque stones represent the qualities of the attributes whose action is upon the more outward planes. But though more outward, these are beautiful like alabaster or marble or jacinth or agate, or jasper, as that term is now understood.

The seven precious stones, with their transparency, their luminosity, their magnetic inherent power of attraction and repulsion, speak of those divine attributes through which, upon the seven planes of consciousness, the glory of God is to be manifested and interpreted, and, after having been realized, perfectly revealed.

And over all of them are the Urim and the Thummim, without which they could have no radiance, no perfection-ment of Being, no fulness of expression, no divine revealing and manifestation. For the Urim is the Radiance, as the word means, from which all the attributes derive their iridescence and their radiating power. The Urim is the glorious, magnetic, central power acting upon the magnetic pole of the attributes. It is the magnetic centre of the Being which acts upon and through the attributes, generating light in them, making that which is latent, living, that which is inherent, to become manifest, that which seems to be light without giving radiance, as in the gems, to be a power to send forth light, to make the jewel flash, and each facet of each attribute reflect the radiance of the sacred tinctures.

And the Thummim is the perfect expression of the Mystery of Being revealed in those twelve precious attributes. When these are clothed with the divine majesty of Love, they acknowledge the Mystery of the Father-Mother as all and in all. And they give to the Being a consciousness of the Overshadowing of that Mystery, and the power to rejoice in that consciousness, and in the sublime blessing His Presence giveth. The Thummim represents that which is quickened and perfected. That which quickens is the perfect Life, the perfect Love, the perfect Radiant Presence within the Being.

*   *   *   *

All these are within. All power is from within. You may clothe the body beautifully; you may garment it, adapting the clothing to the temperature of the atmosphere; but howsoever it be adorned, though the adornment may change the outer manifestation or appearance, it does not change the substance of the body, nor vitalize the substance. All vitalization must be from within, even that vitalization which comes unto the outer vehicle of man. All power in the vehicle is from within. As truly has it to be said, that all spiritual power is from within. It cometh through realization. And the divine power of a Soul is according to its realization. The divine splendour in a Soul, and manifested through a Soul, is in the measure of its realization. None can speak of the Divine Mystery except through realization. Men and women may speak about the things they have read or heard of concerning that Mystery. But the Mystery can be spoken of only through having come to know it within. For that great reality within each one, must be realized by those who would know God.

What a glorious mystery of Being there is within you, children of the Father-Mother! How full of Divine Wealth is that inheritance He hath put at the very centre of your Being! It is thus ye are of Him. It is thus ye may know Him. It is thus ye may acquire the power to fully manifest Him. To manifest Him in fulness is to have the Breastplate Stones scintillating as living stones, and radiating the glory of His Love. There is no other way to know Him. Who shall ascend unto the Heavens to bring Him down? What philosophies can ever take you into the realm of the realization? Only through His Love in you can ye ascend. Only through that Love can ye come to the realization. Only through the realization is He known. And He is known. He can be known. And He may be known by you. He is to be known thus by you. *The summit of the hill of vision is the Realization.*

Behold, what an order of sequential growth there was presented in that symbolic mediatorial ministry, though it was overlaid and materialized beyond all recognition! Offer your body with its attributes for sacrifice unto the Most High. Offer your mind and your will with their attributes, and all their powers, unto the Ever Blessed One, for ministry. Offer your love-principle in its power to manifest, to bear burdens, as a sacrifice unto the Great Love for such ministry as He may appoint. Offer your Innermost Being without reserve, withholding naught from service in that ministry. Offer your very Being for the Divine Service, even unto the giving up of Life itself. And in the doing of this, there shall come unto you that vision which is realization; that vision which is no mere reflection cast upon the mind, but is the splendour of His Day within you. It is a vision that becomes such a realization that *henceforth you know that Presence who walks amid the Golden Candlesticks,* who bears upon His bosom the Ephod of the righteousness of the glorious Love, the Eternal Love in the majesty of its power in ministry. You will be conscious of that Presence upon whose very heart is engraven every attribute of the Eternal One and who reflects into your Being each attribute that these may find embodiment, and be perfected through the realization within you. For it is that same Divine Presence who bears the names of the House of Israel, the qualities of Issa-Ra-El, to give them in fulness unto you; that Presence who is the expression of Urim and Thummim, the glorious Divine Principle and Overshadowing One, the quickening, life-giving, perfecting power, touching all your attributes from the innermost to the outermost, until they become most radiant and reflect the glory of His Love. For the glory of the Lord is the glory of His Love, the radiance of His Love revealed, interpreted, manifested through your attributes in life, from the innermost to the outermost, from the outermost to the innermost.

As Children of the Kingdom of the Heavens, behold ye once more the nature of your Life. Know henceforth the quality of the Mystery hidden at the very Soul or centre of your Being. Realize the meaning of God in you, of Christ in you. Understand the meaning of the power within you to know God, to realize His Christ, to manifest Christ, to know the Lord as the Overshadowing and Indwelling Mystery, who is ever present, and nevermore to be unconscious of that Overshadowing and Indwelling. Behold the Mystery of your Being in its reality. And if your mind should be attracted to look at the little things because they seem to you for the time being the greatest things of the objective planes, hold sacred the memory of the grandeur of your Being, of its greatness, even unto infinite vastness. For all things are possible, all things that are beautiful, lowly, true, radiant, begotten of Love, His Mystery of Love in you. Let the consciousness of this Mystery operate from the very centre of your Being down through all your planes. Learn how to look from the centre of your Being through the different degrees of consciousness. If you have not yet got there, look always from the very innermost part that you can reach; and if it only be the middle court, yet from the middle court always do everything in the outer service. Let the Divine Light illumine everything. And though all things can only be understood from the innermost, yet His Light, broken upon the mind and reflected through it, will change the very outlook and meaning of the vision on the outer planes of experience. If you be only as yet in the middle court, the court of aspiration, the court of the altar of incense, yet from that court you may enter the next where the Presence is. Through lowliness of spirit; through humbleness of mind and sweetness of heart; through gentleness; through beautiful love in its strength; through loving-kindness, the beautiful deed as well as the beautiful thought and the beautiful desire; through compassion, giving healing thought, healing feeling, desire, deed in sweet ministry wheresoever needed; through wonderful pity, spreading the wings of your love for defence that the helpless, the weak, the suffering, the struggling, all who are needing to be sheltered by your love, be defended in their name and their fame and their ministry and their love in every way; through singleness of purpose, purity of heart, lowliness of concept and ambition, and the giving of one's self in love, the Innermost is reached.

Through love alone, for love's sake, do ye enter that Holy Place to come at the vision which is realization. But the glory is broken all along the path; for the Mystery is in you, and the Light streameth from the centre. And the path is in you from the centre to the circumference, the path you are following and looking out upon, as ye seek the Divine within you. At all times, ere ye turn to outer service, seek the within. Pray the Divine Presence to lead you, to guide you, to overshadow you, to inspire you, to illumine you, to touch what you have to touch with the rod of magic love that maketh evil flee, and which transmuteth base things into gold.

*   *   *   *

The Urim and the Thummim are within you. They represent the Mystery of the Father-Mother.

The Urim is the power of His glory in its irradiation.

The Thummim is the perfection or consummation of Being in you.

The Urim is the glorious Arche, or Divine Mystery out of which your Being becomes manifest.

The Thummim is the Amen in whose glorious fulness ye have the consummation of your consciousness.

The Urim and the Thummim thus speak of the two-fold glorious Mystery unto the realization of which ye are called, to be His manifestors through such realization. Unto the interpretation of these sacred verities surely ye are called, to be the revealers of the Mystery of God. Through your attributes to be reflectors of His glory, even from glorious state to glorious state in the ever varying degrees in which Souls can receive of His Love as the Mystery is broken through your attributes and embodied in you. And though you feel, as you say you do, in your ministry, quite unequal of yourselves to bring to the very threshold of life the great reality of Being so as to make it unmistakable to others, yet remember that God is in you, that He is in the Sanctuary as your Power. And bear in sacred remembrance that His children are on these planes for Him, not for themselves but for Him, and that they are the inheritors of His promise, the inheritors of His Christ to be the embodiments of the Christhood, the revealers of His Wisdom, the interpreters in manifestation of His transcendent, never failing, all healing, redeeming and perfecting Love.

The Divine Mystery for all will thus become unveiled. Those things which seemed to be but symbols for them, will live again, if you realize them unto manifestation and interpretation. The Urim and the Thummim are to be brought by you, up out of the darkness of the long night of the Soul amid which they have been lost, into the splendour of that day that knows no setting. And Souls will behold, and see, and learn, even unto knowing the glorious Mystery of His Love and His Wisdom, His real Fatherhood-Mother -hood, His Indwelling in their Sanctuary, and Overshadowing Radiant Cloud to illumine and guide them.

The Shekinah

or

The Ministry of

Cherubim and Seraphim.

*THE
SHEKINAH.*

The Mystery of God the Father-Mother is expressed within us in the Shekinah, and the ministry of what is named the office of Cherubim and Seraphim.

The Shekinah is the Ark of His Testimony and Covenant.

His Testimony is the eternal manifestation of His own glorious Being within the Principle of our Being. That Mystery is meant to testify of the Glory of His Presence and His handiwork in the Mystery of our Being with its divine attributes, and in the manifestation of those attributes in ministry truly sublime.

His Covenant in man is His Law eternal and unchangeable, the realization of which can alone bring to any individuated Being, rest, perfect repose, complete and glorious realization, power for manifestations of an order wholly spiritual, celestial, and divine.

His Covenant with man is not a mere promise that He makes to His children, as men make promises to one another; His Covenant is the Mystery of His own Being as the eternal embodiment of the Law of Being, even of His Being in us.

The Shekinah is, therefore, the fashion of our Being in the Innermost. There is the Testimony of the Lord, the Ark of His Testimony, the Divine Principle of our Being. And the Ark of His Covenant is the testimony of His Indwelling Spirit, the Ark being the symbol of the Spirit.

Out from that centre floweth all your true feeling. From that fountain which He hath filled in your own individuated Being, flow your true emotions, the magnetic streams of your love, and the Divine Life-stream, as that latter is set in motion through His Overshadowing. From that centre all power worthy of the name proceeds, whether it be the power that is revealed through the mind in its concepts, in its reflections, in its powers for ministry; or through the emotions in their wonderful feelings expressed in their passion for ministry, or through the body in all its attributes of desire and strength for ministry. All real power comes from within. And all power that is not begotten there, is but seeming power; and is of that which will not abide the day of His appearing—which means that everything becomes changed in the measure in which He appears in us, manifests through us, is realized by us.

The Shekinah, therefore, is the most sacred of formulated thoughts. The Ark of His Testimony signifies that we are of Him and of His Covenant, that the Laws of His Love and Wisdom are our heritage, and that we may come to know them all through knowing Him. In the measure in which we know them we come to know Him more fully, more deeply even, until we apprehend the full significance of the Mystery, and comprehend in great measure all that it means.

* * * *

Connected with the Shekinah are His servants the Cherubim and the Seraphim. The Cherubim, in the symbol of the sacred Ark, overshadowed it; and in the Mysteries they were described as Overshadowing and facing each other whilst looking upon the Ark, upon the upper portion of which was the Altar of Oblation called the Mercy Seat. The Mercy Seat is the altar of the perfect healing given by Love. For Mercy is Love's compassion, full of sweet understanding, whose quality is ever Divine, containing within itself the power of the sacrificer to heal the very Being, through his or her sacrifice; and to heal the very Being of those who have been wounded in the way.

The first thought therefore associated with the Cherubim, is that of the Overshadowing Presence. They are of the innermost Sanctuary. "Oh Thou who dwellest between the Cherubim, make Thyself manifest unto us." Thus cries the Being of those who know. In the old form of the Mysteries it was represented that the Divine Presence would commune with the Being from between the Cherubim. It was there the High Priest stood alone, looking between the Cherubim on the great day of Atonement. Thus it is portrayed in Jewish story. But it was a wonderful inner mystery brought down into the outer sacrificial system; a mystery of the Divine Presence realized by the Being in that high state of Priesthood which is after the Order of Melchisedek, as the Soul, making its oblation, looked whither that Presence alone could be beheld, whence alone the Radiance of that Presence could pour itself forth, where the Being stood face to face with the Holy One.

*   *   *   *

That Presence is a glorious reality. It is no dream of the imagination. In that Presence you are in the Absolute. But the Absolute there is not undifferentiated. The Absolute there is not nebulous. It is a great polarized reality. When you dwell in the Presence of the Absolute, you do not dwell in the presence of that which is informulate, though the Eternal Mystery has ever to be regarded as informulate, that He may not be thought of after the manner of a man, or any form, or any likeness in the heavens above or the earth beneath. For He is all form that is true and beautiful and perfect. And according to the status and the order of the Being, is the formulation of that vision within the Sanctuary wherein that Informulate One becomes the manifest Father-Mother. You may dream of nebulous conditions, and live in nebulous thought; but if you get

238

within the Sanctuary, and there stand before the Over- shadowing Cherubim, there will be nothing nebulous to you, but instead, a most glorious formulate reality which you could not express in any language or any sign you might call to your command and your use. There is nothing so wonderful as that Vision. There is nothing more tangible than that Great Reality. There is nought that is sublimer than the Realization of that One Who radiates between the Cherubim, and unveils His Glory there. For He doth make it manifest unto Benjamin—the Intuition; unto Ephraim—the Understanding, and the Mind in its office of a reflecting ministry; and even unto Manasseh, both on the east side of Jordan and on the west—the intermediary attributes, and the outermost attributes. The power of the Glory of the Lord Presence is thus made manifest within the Sanctuary of our Being.

*   *   *   *

Now, those Cherubim which represent the Overshadowing of His Presence are differentiated in ministry, as Guardians, and also as those who minister from before the Altar inwardly. The Cherubim attributes within us are those divine qualities which enable us to seek for the realization of the Presence. For it is through the recognition of the Ark of The Testimony and The Covenant, and the Divine Overshadowing, that the Vision is come at. The way into the Holiest is by the path of Seraphim and Cherubim, the ministries which those most sacred attributes signified in the ancient symbology of the Mysteries, and ever signify within the Sanctuary of your Being. It is set forth early in the old scriptures, how the Cherubim guard the way. And no one can get to the Tree of Life except by means of the Cherubim, the Guardians of the Innermost Portals.

*   *   *   *

It is said in the story of Eden that when man had gone down in the great Descent, he was driven forth from Eden. That meant that he went out from the Edenic state, losing the consciousness of the Indwelling Presence—going out into a strange land, with face towards the setting sun. For the Garden of Eden was eastward. In going out he was going westward. Whilst his face was westward, the Cherubim guarded the way lest man should return in a state unfitted to touch the Tree of Life, and should seek to get back to the centre where he was once a dweller, a communer with God. For the Tree of Life itself has to be guarded. It is the secret of the Divine Mystery. And it is guarded unto this day, that no one from outside the state represented by the Garden of Eden, may approach the Tree of Life, the Divine Mystery, to the understanding of it by the eating of its fruit. No one can understand the Mystery of Life from without. It can only come from within. No one can find the Within where The Tree of Life is to be found, except through the portals guarded by the Cherubim. The Being must acquire the right to the Tree of Life.

* * * *

The Cherubim are the ministrants of the innermost Sanctuary before the Divine, for the Divine, unto the Divine. They are represented in the soul's motion when it seeks, not only the sacrifice of the daily offering called the Altar of Burnt Offering, when it would offer as an oblation its body, and its outer attributes for service; nor when it seeks the Altar of Incense, the Altar of Aspiration for the mind state, for devotion in ministry (all of which things are absolutely necessary, but they are but stages, initiations on the way): it is not even when the soul would touch the Table of the Shew-Bread which none but the priests might eat, and make its sacramental vow unto the Lord, for that

240

is only another part of the way: but it is when the Being, having traversed those paths, finds the Veil drawn, and it enters into the Most Holy Place where the Ark of the Covenant is found, and the Ark of the Testimony abides, and the Cherubim minister.

* * * *

The Cherubim of God Overshadow the Being; the Cherubim of the Soul minister before God. They are the priests in the innermost ministry—the innermost Love, Life, Light; the innermost desire, vision, power; the innermost knowledge, which is perception perfected through transmutation in realization. The Cherubim minister before the Divine, inwardly, gathering up the very powers of the Being, laying them on the Altar of Oblation, the Mercy Seat, the altar of perfect healing. They minister of perfect healing for the Being.

There are those who do not think the Being needs any healing; that it is never hurt; and that it is only in the outer body and the mind where healing is needed. It is sad to reflect upon such a statement. But the statement is a shadow. It is a shadow that would darken the great Reality. The Being does need healing. Is your deepest passion of Being for God, merely of your body, or of your mind, or even of your emotion? Or, is it of your Being? And what will heal it? Nought, nought, will heal it but the Realization. You may suspend the pain of it through affirmations; but you do not heal it in making the affirmations. No; the Being can be healed only from the Altar of the Soul's Oblation, through the ministry of Cherubim and Seraphim during the Soul's outpouring on that Altar. And in the measure in which the Soul's outpouring is upon that Altar, is it healed.

241

Beautiful are the children of the Father-Mother, who seek unto the Shekinah, the Mystery of His Presence within the Soul, the Ark of His Testimony and His Covenant, the formulation of the Divine Mystery of His own Being, and the perpetual proclamation, through manifestation, of the Eternal Life with which He has endowed the Being. The very yearning of your own Being is the resultant of the operation of His Cherubim within you. They guard the way to the consciousness of Him, until the other courts are passed through. They hold the Flaming Sword that turneth every way, the Spiral Flame of the Spirit which none may approach unto until that hour comes in which they too may enter in to the glory of the vision, the transcendency of the experience, the ecstasy of the Atonement— the At-one-ment in consciousness with the Divine. And the preparation for it all is through the ministry of His Seraphim.

*   *   *   *

His Seraphim bring into the life, beautiful healing. "Then flew one of the Seraphim"—not a Cherub, not one of the Cherubim, but one of the Seraphim—"unto me, having in his hand a glowing stone which he had taken with the tongs from off the altar. With it he touched my lips and said, Lo this hath touched thee." He touched my power of soul expression.

It was the mystery solvent of the Divine Love, the healing given from the Divine Touch. "This hath touched thee." The Divine Love comes from the Altar of the very innermost. The Seraphim bring it. They are the ministrants in the outward, as the Cherubim are the ministrants in the inward. The Cherubim belong to the inward motion of the Being in its flight in adoration; the Seraphim belong

to the outward motion of the Being in its flight in ministry.
The Seraphim go outward in their Service. But they move
inward in their praise of the Holy One. And from their
praise they proceed again in ministry for that Blessed One,
unto His children. They are the attributes that minister
from the inner Court, proceeding through the Being, outwardly; bringing forth the Power and the Glory of the
Kingdom from the innermost realm, bearing these outward
through the courts of the Being, and through the attributes
of the Being, unto the most blessed service. Whilst the
Cherubim flight is upward, ever upward, ever inward to
the Presence of the Most High; realizing, and still more
fully realizing, the transcendent glory of the Mystery of
Being: in the inward motion, approaching the Sanctuary
from the without, the Seraphim lead the Being upward
and onward. In the Divine ministry of the Christhood
souls, their ministry is from the Within where Cherubim
stand; and outward through the vehicles into manifestation,
making formulate that which has been in realization, and
that which has been formulate in the realization. And
though it is impossible to formulate such glorious things
in sign or speech, yet the Seraphim can bring it through into
formulated presentation, even as the Glowing Stone—the
Stone of the Fire or Energy of Love; or as the Shew-Bread—
the Bread of the Wisdom broken as the children are able
to receive it; or as the sweet Incense—the prayers of the
children arising.

This ministry is yours. Cherubim and Seraphim are
in you. The Soul is a vast world, and not to be measured
by the stature and apparent capacity of its vehicle of manifestation on the outer planes. So vast is the Being of Man
in its power for apprehension and comprehension, ascension

243

as well as descension for ministry, that the Mystery of all things is miniatured within it. All the worlds find response to their magnetic touch within the Being. The Divine Kingdom is expressed within it, unto it and through it. There is no height the Being cannot climb, providing it be radiant and full in its love, beautiful in heart and mind. All implied in the Vision of the Ark, the Mystery of the Shekinah, the Overshadowing Cloud of Radiance, the Glory manifest between the Cherubim, the Seraphic ministry of Seraphic Song and Blessing—is found expressed within the Being.

And the Being has the power of expansion through its attributes unto the perfect realization of all these glorious elements of the Divine Mystery, the Father-Mother within.

*   *   *   *

Behold, what manner of love the Father-Mother hath bestowed upon us, that we should be called His children! That we should be named, in our fashion, after the Divine Mystery! Beloved ones of the Father-Mother. Now are ye His children. And though the manner or nature of the Mystery of your having become His children, is not yet fully unveiled to you, yet know ye this, that, when He shall appear (have become realized) within you, ye shall be in fashion like unto Him, and ye shall know Him as He is.

Look at the capacity of the Soul therein indicated! Look at the vastness of its life, at the power of its apprehension, at the circumference of its comprehension, into the depth of the mystery of its Being! And, seeing such a vision of yourselves, make inquiry why ye should fear? Why ye should doubt? Why ye should be any longer weakened in the way? Why ye should remain as pilgrims and strangers to Him—which means, to the Mystery of His Life in you?

244

Why should the shadows lie athwart your threshold, even to the outer courts? Why should the shadows fall upon the mind, like those which we should call penumbra—dark thoughts? Why, oh why, should ye stand outside the gates of Eden, sorrowing, with your face turned westward where all things seem to have their setting, when by looking eastward, all the darkness of the night would flee away, and the breaking of the dawn would be beheld? Why fail to see through the portals the Cherubim awaiting you again, and the ministry from out those portals of the Seraphim of God bearing for you the Glowing Stone which giveth perfect healing? Why fear aught this troubled world imposes upon you, when with steadfastness of purpose, and holy song, ye may pass through the portals, the Sacred Flame illuming you as you go, energizing you for greater ministry, enriching the Flame of your own Being, and making your love glorious? Why fail to realize that Eden is the state of the Being who stands upon the threshold of the Shekinah where the Cherubim dwell; and the Sacred Fire upon the Altar, the Sacred Flame, is ever present?

*　　*　　*　　*

Ye are noble ones, who have toiled through the night amid sorrow and oppression; who know sore travail, not simply in the body, or in the mind, or in the emotion, the travail of which is hard to bear, but who know also the travail of Being in the very innermost, which is the travail of God for His children. For He could not be separate from His children. In all their afflictions He was, and is, afflicted. The Angel of His Presence went before them, and still goeth before them. He is ever for them the Pillar of Cloud by day—or the Overshadowing Radiance that illumines; and the Pillar of Fire in the night—the Sacred Flame that

245

giveth holy, holy, most wonderfully holy, life and illumination unto His children. It is the God within you who travaileth, as ye seek to realize the Great Presence again, to regain the consciousness of the Overshadowing, the realization of Oneness with Him Who is the Shekinah, and its Glory, and its Power, within you.

Let the Cherubim in you adore Him. In priestly ministry serve ye Him, bringing unto Seraphim all your powers that you can call outward, to sing the Seraphic Song, to give the Seraphic Message, to bestow the Seraphic Benediction of your thoughts and feelings and desires that you can bring outward to touch life, the life of daily ministry, and those unto whom you minister, and everyone with whom you have dealings. You need not speak of those things in language as understood by men; and yet the line of your magnetic influence through such ministry, will go out unto all the earthly parts, wheresoever your ministry has called you, testifying of the Testimony of the Lord within you, and the Sacredness of His Covenant.

Go forth, therefore, and fear nothing. Through you, sorrow will find His Joy. For trouble, His own Peace will come. And if in your ministry the cross seemeth to be beyond your bearing, He Who is ever unto us the Glorious One, doth take us and the cross into His own Bosom, and carry us there, nourishing us by His own Love, whilst we bear the cross of service for Him, and minister unto His children. Thus will ye minister before Him and from Him, even as His Cherubim and Seraphim.

PART
IV.

Initiations of the Soul.

*The Mount of Olives : Good
Friday : The Two Anoint-
ments : The Passion of the
Soul : Joseph of Arima-
thea : The Guest
Chamber.*

The Mount of Olives.

In the mind of the devout ones whose love turns reverently towards that one who was known as Jesus, the Mount of Olives has sacred associations. It lay near to Bethany and Jerusalem, and is supposed to have been the scene of many visits from the Master. But especially is it associated with that episode in which it is reported that, in an hour of great sorrow, He went up to the Mount, and, looking over the city of Jerusalem, wept over its state and uttered His great lament.

It is also associated with the profound sorrow which He is reported to have had in the Garden of Gethsemane. For there it is said He anguished unspeakably. For the Garden of Gethsemane lay at the foot of the Mount of Olives.

It is likewise associated in the minds of many, with the Ascension; for, in the Acts of the Apostles it is implied that He ascended from the Mount of Olives. It was upon the Mount of Olives the disciples are supposed to have stood when the angels appeared unto them saying "Ye men of Galilee, why stand ye here gazing up into the heavens? This same Jesus whom ye have seen depart, shall in like manner come again."

The Mount of Olives was but a small elevation outside the city of Jerusalem, though it is sometimes spoken of as a mountain. It lay on the east side of the city, like Bethany and Bethphagee. But in the prophetic writings it is spoken of as a mountain, and even as a mountain of the Lord. It is upon the Mountain of Olivet that the Lord is to stand in the day of His return. For it is recorded that in that day His feet shall stand upon Olivet, and the Mountain shall be cleft in twain through the power of His coming, and a valley shall run from the east side unto the west, dividing the Mountain, one section moving northward

250

and one section moving southward, and that through that valley the people of the Lord shall return, even between the Lord's Holy Mountains (meaning the two sections of Olivet). And in that day when the people return by that path which gives them Olivet to the north of them, and Olivet to the south of them, there shall be no more any night, but only day, even the day of the Lord unto His people. Even at eventide it shall be light; for the ever-lasting day shall have broken, and there shall be no more any night. And in that day, rivers of water shall flow, divided as the two rivers in another vision in the prophetic books, one flowing towards the inner sea, or divine centre of the Being, and the other to the outer sea, or the world of manifest life and service.

It is most evident that the Mount of Olives was not a mountain with geographical situation on the outer planes. A mountain is a high elevation, not a low hill, nor even an upper hill, but a hill of great altitude. Mystically, a moun-tain signifies elevation of Being in the consciousness; elevation of vision; the vision from the summit of varying peaks on the mountains of God. When the Lord calls Souls up to His mountains that He may pass before them unveiling the Laws of Being unto them, revealing the train of His Presence, speaking unto them from out the Cloud, He calls them into high states of spiritual and divine con-sciousness. For it is only in high states of consciousness that the Soul or Being can hear the Voice to know it, behold the Radiance and rejoice in it, and receive the radia-tions produced by the Presence. That the Mount of Olives was no geographical mound lying east of Jerusalem, we are assured. That a slight elevation lying east of Jerusalem came to be so called, is doubtless true. That the mystical teachings wherein it is named should have been associated with the little hill, is not to be wondered at when it is known that the writers of the New Testament materialized most of the teachings given by the Master, not knowing their inner mystical significance. For they understood not the terms which He used to express soulic and divine things.

The Mount of Olives is forever associated in the Soul with the coming of the Lord. It is a state of consciousness. It is one of the states through which the Being passes upon the outer circuli or planes of the Divine Kingdom, upon which and from which the Soul can look out upon the past and even see into the future. This is the meaning of the Master, in an hour of great sorrow, sitting down upon that Mount, or in that state, and looking out upon the city of Jerusalem, and sorrowing over it. Even in the terms in which the great lament of His Soul over that city is to be found in the New Testament, there are revealings as to His knowledge of that city's history. It is said that He uttered such words as these: "Oh, Jerusalem! Jerusalem! Thou that killest the prophets and stonest them which are sent unto thee. How often would I have gathered thy children together as a hen doth gather her brood under her wings, but ye would not." If that passage reveals His knowledge of the history implied in the rejection by Jerusalem of the prophets, the killing of them and the stoning of the messengers, how much more wonderful is the unveiling and how profoundly more sorrowful the lament when it is known that Jerusalem as understood by Him, did not refer simply to the Jewish centre of religious life, but to Jerusalem, the whole spiritual household of this planet. For in its unfallen days this world was a holy city, or community of Souls. It was a glorious city, for its children were all beautiful. It was a city of wonderful terraces and

252

palaces, the terraces which became broken down and the palaces which were levelled with the dust. For the palaces were the spiritual states and temporary spiritual dwelling places of the children, the many mansions or states which then obtained upon this planet. And the terraces were glorious magnetic circles or belts composed of most beautiful divine substances in a state of manifestation for creative purposes. These were the planet's planes.

When the Master sat upon Mount Olivet, or in that state of high consciousness in which He could look through all the past, and beheld Jerusalem as she had become; beheld the awful things that had happened to her beautiful planes and the sweet homes or states of the children; when He beheld the children in their attitude to one another, and how that once most beautiful home whose harmonies were echoes of the harmonies of the Angelic World, had become a house divided against itself, and how the prophetic office had been slain and the prophets silenced, and even the messengers stoned by the hard conditions of Jerusalem, driven out of the city, finding ministry almost impossible; when He beheld in the days in which the Manifestation was proceeding through Him of that Love that had never wearied nor failed, and was about to carry the burden of all the children unto the blotting of it out, the way that Love was received by those who professed great religious devotion, who in the outer religious performances strained at the gnat but swallowed the camel, the vision became so overwhelming to Him that He uttered the great lament, which readers will find in The Logia. The Mount of Olives had an association with Him in that high state of consciousness in which the whole planetary history stood out before Him and filled Him with overwhelming sorrow.

On the slopes of Olivet and at its foot, it is said, lay the Garden of Gethsemane. The olive is an oil fruit. The olive tree symbolizes the peace of the Great Love, and its fruit the oil of gladness begotten of that Love. The Mount of Olives, mystically understood, is the state in which the oil of gladness begotten of the Love is poured out for the healing of the world. The garden on the lower slopes of Olivet is called Gethsemane. Philologically it is interpreted as the oil press, the place where the oil is taken from the olive. Mystically the Garden of Gethsemane is the Garden of Sorrow, of deep Soul travail. It is there the Master is said to have sorrowed and anguished even until He sweat, as it were, great drops of blood—as if the very life-stream must needs come through the pores of His beautiful body. It is there He is said to have prayed that the cup He had to drink, might pass away. It is also there He besought that the Divine Will alone should be accomplished.

The Garden of Gethsemane was not a garden of geographical situation for the Master, but a state of overwhelming sorrow at the consciousness of all that Jerusalem had become, and all that it would mean for Him in the pouring out of the oil of the Divine Love for the healing of the sorrow of the world. Upon Olivet He beheld all He would have to pass through; all the lives He would have to live; all the states He would have to enter; all the burden in its general aspect which would oppress Him in each life. Thus Olivet became His Gethsemane.

That was the meaning of the divine sorrow that welled forth from Him at the foot of the Mount of Olives when He saw all that He would have to pass through in the accomplishment of the restoration of Jerusalem. Elsewhere we have written of the nature of this burden.

It is said that the Mount of Olives was the scene of the Ascension, and of angelic visitants to the disciples, and that it was to be the scene of the Lord's return. Now, the Lord is never a man, though He revealeth Himelf to His children and manifesteth through them. The Lord is not even an individual in the sense in which human beings are individuations of the eternal substance of Divine Being. He is a Presence in all Being, from whom all Being has proceeded and in whom all Being finds its consummation. As a Presence He is potentially in every one, for He is the centre of every individuated Being. In the system of every one there is the principle expressed in the Mountain of Olivet. Therefore, when a Soul grows, unfolds, unveils, realizes from more to more, the day of its illumination cometh when it can behold the Radiant Presence, stand upon Olivet and look into the realm of the Eternal Now. In that state the Lord stands upon Olivet. In that state He comes into the consciousness of the Being as a living Presence. Upon that high mountain the Soul becomes one in the consciousness of Him.

The children of the Kingdom of the Heavens who came forth from divine realms to minister within the city of Jerusalem, knew something of Olivet. They had all been there, though the degrees of consciousness were greater in some than in others. These children were within the city of Jerusalem when the enemy overtook it—wrong elemental states. They became involved in the great changes which overtook the city when all within its walls were led into bondage to the material powers, represented in the ancient times by Egypt and Assyria, and in later times by the Roman. For long ages did they suffer limitations whilst performing gracious ministry unto the children of Jerusalem. In the day of their return when the Lord shall stand upon

255

the Olivet within them, the mountain shall be cleft in twain. The valley, or passage, made between the heights running north and south they will behold to be the very path by which, in the return, they come back to Zion, travelling as those who have been a far journey, strangers and pilgrims in a land of great weariness unto them. For the valley will be clear to them. They will behold the path of it in the Light of the Presence, and they will see the meaning of their travail through the ages. On the northern slopes of Olivet shall be reflected all their history, for the Mount will be illumined. It is the mind in its understanding that is represented by the north. And they will there behold again those things which of old time they knew. They will see the meaning of their own travail. On the southern side of the slopes of Olivet they will feel the great breaths, the divine radiations, the magnetic coursing of their own emotion. For, whilst reflected on the north, or in their mind, they will have the knowledge given them; in the south through the high consciousness operating through their emotion, they will recover in their travail, in their deep feeling, in their burden-bearing. For the emotion is the etheric stream through which the love magnetic current passes for manifestation. In that day all things will be clear unto them. It will be for them the Day of the Lord. Now they have brighter hours and darker hours, and sometimes even the darkness of night; but then there shall be no more any night, for it shall be one day. Even in the eventime of their experience on these planes, it shall be as the light of noon-day. And out from them shall flow streams of the living waters whose wellspring is within them. One stream towards the east in adoration, in recognition, in sublime devotion, in glorious love to the Lord of their Being. Another stream will flow towards Jerusalem in the outer sea of ministry through the planes of the emotion and the mind and the body, full of beautiful healing in sweet ministry to Souls. For in that day the Lord shall reign over all their Being, the earthly parts being one with the heavenly parts. The innermost will be able to reveal perfectly through the correlated outermost. Thus the Lord shall be manifest again through them. Such will Mount Olivet be for the children of the Kingdom in their return.

Now, the day of the Return is with us. The Lord has descended upon Mount Olivet. It is the day in which it was said the Master Himself would return. That that one has returned, we know. The tragedy of the Oblation has just been fully accomplished. The oil press has been operative throughout the ages of the Christian era. The oil of His Being has been poured out. He was the vehicle of the Divine Love. It is ever the Divine Love who accomplishes all things for the children, who pours out the Oblation from the Sacred Chalice. In the day of His return, His feet were to stand upon Olivet. That is to be understood simply, that He would again pass into that state in which the Overshadowing of the Most Blessed Presence of the Lord would gather up His Being into the Cloud of the Radiance wherein all things would become clear unto Him again. Once more has He been able to look out upon the history of Jerusalem, and to unveil to the children of the Kingdom who they were and are.

But His coming again in these latter days when the glorious Presence was to return, and has returned, has been as mysterious as was His going away. As, in the going away, only His intimate ones knew Him; so in the return, none could know but those unto whom it was given from

257

the inner realms. And this is as it should be; for, even as the Lord is no man, neither is the messenger to be thought of merely as a man. For the revealings are of the Lord. He alone is the revealer. And the revealings or revelations are all from Him.

The Mount of Olives has come back again, that high mountain of the Lord, that glorious state of consciousness in which the Lord Presence fills the Being. In that state alone can the history of this world become known even to one who is sent. How sacred the Mountain of Olivet should be to the children of the Kingdom who have climbed its slopes many a time, and communed with the angels of the inner realms! In those days, they knew the Oil of Gladness begotten of a perfect love, even the Love of the Father-Mother in them. Unto all the children of the Kingdom the Lord cometh upon Mount Olivet, calling them back again into that high consciousness, according to the varying degrees in which they all once served, and from which they went out.

Children of the Kingdom, it is the day of your return through the valley running right from the west to the east of the Mount of Olives, the Mount of the mystery of your travail, now cleft in twain, giving you on the one hand the revealings which interpret; and on the other hand the profound movements of the deep sea of your Being which bring back to you again the great realization, with the meaning of all you have passed through in your travail through the ages.

In your Return into the Realization, your feet shall also stand upon Olivet; and ye shall sojourn in the Light of His Radiant Presence.

Good Friday.

The Mystery of the Veiled Cross.

GOOD   It is a day consecrated by the western world
FRIDAY.   to commemorate the Crucifixion. It is a day
during which, for some churches, there are services so
arranged that the Stations of the Cross, as they have been
called, are gone through. The day is not one that is resonant
with joyous accents. It is filled with the closing scenes of
Lent—a season commemorating the forty days' fasting
in the wilderness by the Master. Therefore, it is a day of
shadows; though it is looked forward to as one in which
to express devotion as well as sorrow, and gladness amid
the sorrow, because in the commemoration of the
Crucifixion the western world believes that it is commemorating those events through which its redemption was
accomplished.

It is difficult at any time to speak of some of the events
which then took place. Nor is it easy to unveil the deeper
significance of Good Friday. That the western world does
not understand its significance is most obvious to anyone
who can read its religious history. That the western world
has never known the meaning of the real crucifixion of
the Master, it makes manifest continually by its manner of
living. That the western religious world has yet to learn
the meaning of Good Friday, would doubtless be difficult
to impress upon that world as a whole, so wedded is it to
traditional thought and formula and belief. Yet its symbols,
in a hidden way, contain more than is known by those who
use them to express their sorrow and their devotion.

Remember this, that there are many beautiful Souls full
of real sorrow who at that season consecrate themselves, in
so far as they understand the way, to live it, and to serve in
it. And even though they walk in a path that is shadowed,
there being no clear light shining within and around them,
as we understand that light, yet such true Soul sorrow and

beautiful devotion bear their fruits, and are contributory to the enrichment of the Being.

Now, there is associated with the church's festival of Good Friday, that symbol of which we would particularly speak. It is *The Cross veiled by heavy purple veiling.* In some of the churches this is done at the beginning of Lent, the veiling of the cross upon the altar signifying the sorrow of which Lent is symbolical. For the season of Lent covers forty-two days, that is, from Ash Wednesday to the Sunday known as the Resurrection morning, Easter day, though Lent really culminates on the Friday.

Lent speaks of the Forty Days' Temptation and trial and sorrow amid the Wilderness. Now it is a remarkable thing that, as the issue out of many controversies and many changes in the duration of the period of Lent, the Church should have at last hit upon forty days, and that the High Church and the Catholic Church should have, during that period, veiled the cross. For the Forty Days' Temptation which they think was an incident in the life of the Master during the days of the Manifestation, were the Forty Times, the forty lives, the earthly risings and settings in which He was travailing, bearing the burden of this world's Karma, to blot it out. And that during that period the cross, for which He stood, was veiled. He was Himself veiled, that no one knew Him until the end of the Oblation. The veiling of the cross is significant of the hiding of it on the very altar of Being.

What a wonderful mystery the Church holds without understanding it! It holds it in symbol, but does not know what it means. Holds it in a symbol which is looked upon by many as an element of superstition, but which has a real meaning when it is unveiled, speaking as it does of the long period of tragic sorrow which obtained and prevailed through

261

the forty days of His Lenten abstinence, not from food for the body simply, but abstinence from the high consciousness of the Overshadowing Presence. How remarkable it is that the Church at the beginning of Lent should put this veil over the cross that stands upon the altar!

He went down veiled and no man saw Him any more to know Him until the Oblation was at the close of its accomplishment. Nay, more! How remarkable that the Church should put that veil over the cross, veiling that which is the very central symbol of all spiritual and Divine Being! For that symbol lies at the very heart of the universe.

Here we speak reverently of the Church in all its sections, from the Catholic to the Rationalistic. What has the Church done with the cross? Veiled it, by making it relate to the events of an outward Calvary instead of to the Soul's own history, to the very nature of the Soul itself; nay, more! to the Divine Mystery of Being. For the cross is in God. He is the Cross even in us.

The meaning of the Cross, the Macrocosmic Cross, the Luminous Cross, the Cross of the Redeemer, became veiled. Nay, more! The very Cross of the Burden-bearing became veiled. The meaning of the Oblation has never been understood.

If you had passed through the Theological Schools and read all the theories which are set forth concerning that Mystery, you would know how little assurance the Church has concerning its true meaning. And though the theories are many, yet they are all built up on four great principal theories. There is the Doctrine of Commutation, or, that He died for our sin, bearing so much burden as punishment for so much forgiveness. Then there is that known as the Rectoral theory, in which it is affirmed that the Divine Father-Mother made a great display of His righteous anger against sin, and that the Master was the subject of this display, the child who was to bear this affliction, this punishment, this expression of the Divine judgment, in order to demonstrate to the world that the Divine Love could not regard sin without chastening it. Then there is the doctrine of Identification, a beautiful doctrine mystically understood, containing great and glorious truths, just as the other two did, but without their perversions. It is a doctrine which sets forth that the Master came to identify Himself with fallen humanity, taking the burden of humanity's sin and sharing with humanity that burden, even unto the confessing of it. But how it was blotted out is not stated. Yet the underlying principle is beautiful: the doctrine of identifying Himself with His brethren, and sharing the burden of their destiny. These great doctrines were very specially taught, mostly, by Scotchmen—Dr. Crawford, the doctrine of Commutation; Dr. Wardlaw, the doctrine known as the Rectoral Display or manifestation of the Divine Justice; the Identification doctrine by Dr. Campbell, in which he made a supreme effort to get at a truer interpretation of the meaning of that wonderful Mystery expressed in the burden-bearing of the Master. And then there is the doctrine of Martyrdom, so beautifully and wonderfully illustrated in the sermons and teachings of the late Frederick Robertson, of Brighton. These are the four chief theories —the Commutation, the Rectoral, the Identification, and the Martyrdom.

But apart from these there are many other theories, and the schools are full of controversies concerning that sublime mystery. Not one of them has any assurance at all as to what it meant, though they all believe that it meant something mysterious and profound. How sad to think that the Church, which should have been the Church of the living God, should have failed to have understood the most marvellous expression of the Love of that living One who is our Father-Mother. How amazing it is that the Church should have so terribly misunderstood the ministry of the Master, and the Love of the Father-Mother, as to have set forth such theories as are contained in the doctrine of Commutation, and the Rectoral doctrine of the Righteous Display; or that of Identification, without its full understanding, or even that of Martyrdom.

All these are gathered up into the meaning of the Cross as it was borne. There was so much for so much; but not in the sense there understood. So much had to be accomplished, because so many things had to be blotted out; and every image that had to be blotted out, imposed anguish upon the One who had to accomplish it. There is, therefore, great truth in the doctrine of Commutation. But not after the manner in which the Church has believed it. Nor was it a divinely imposed burden, but one imposed by the necessities of the children's states.

There is also great truth in the Rectoral theory; for was there ever such a display of the Righteousness of the Divine Love, the Divine Love in its Majesty? For it purposed to clarify the Middle Kingdom, and make it possible for all the children of His Love to be healed; and this by a process of identification, which would reveal how the Divine Love stoops to find and save. It was such a display, in the sense of manifestation, of that Love as no human mind could ever have conceived of. It astounded the Angelic World when it was proclaimed what was to be done.

And how beautifully true the doctrine of Identification is! For the Master became one with His brethren in laying aside the Christhood, though in a degree that cannot be

264

expressed by any terms we might use in our speech. He became one with them, identified Himself with them, but unknown to them, and became even as the least of them. Though in happier days He had ministered to them through long ages, He became as the least of them, with His face veiled and His visage marred, bearing their burden; one with them, feeling as they felt, suffering as they suffered, and in such state redeeming all the time; extinguishing the very fires of hell through which they suffered, and so changing the intermediary planes that the light could break through to make the Valley of Hinnom—that terrible valley of spiritual darkness—receive again from that world whose Rays give glorious Light of understanding to the Soul.

And then in the theory of Martyrdom there was also this great truth, that the martyr is one who is sacrificed for truth. A martyr is one who lays down his life for truth. But in this theory there is no such thing as the Atonement, as it has been called; or the Sin-offering, as it has been named; or the Oblation, as we speak of it.

There is a true philosophy of the Redemption; and there is a festival in which it is celebrated; and there is a great reality lying behind these; and Good Friday speaks of that reality. Gathered up into it, are the forty days of Lent. It embodies the final crucifixion, the veiling of the Cross, the hiding of Him, and the veiling of all He spake concerning the Mystery of the Divine Love who is the central point of our Being, the Mystery of the Divine Love and Divine Wisdom in their ministry, the Divine Macrocosmic Cross whose miniature is in our Being. It was the veiling of the Divine Cross, through the veiling of all the Teachings He gave concerning it.

The Master has never been known nor understood in the western world. The significance of the estates known as

Jesus Christ the Lord, have never been truly apprehended. They have been related to Him personally. He has been known as Jesus Christ the Lord; and worshipped as Jesus Christ the Lord, and as the Lord Christ Jesus. Songs have been written about Him and sung to Him under those titles. But what does the western world know of Jesus-hood, the life of beautiful love and compassion and purity? What does the western world know of Christhood, that same love illumined with the Radiant Presence? What does the western world know of the Lord who is that Presence in every human Sanctuary, to be realized in the fulness of time when the Son of God comes to birth and to full realization within that life? The western world yet knoweth not these things.

Good Friday is the day on which Lent practically ends. It is the day of the celebration of the full crucifixion, the cumulative effect of all the crucifixions the Master passed through. Good Friday is the day whose very darkness presages the coming of glorious dawn. Good Friday is the day whose very sorrow speaks of the breaking upon the world of a joy that will die out of it no more. Good Friday is the day of sorrowful song, but whose very surges are the undertones of Angelic songs—songs of gladness, songs of rejoicing, songs of triumphant note. Good Friday speaks of the veiled cross, the Soul in darkness knowing not the mystery of its sorrow, yet heralding the coming of that day, so near at hand, known as Easter-day, when the cross becomes unveiled, and the glory of the Heavens breaks upon the world. For the cross that is veiled through Lent, and made darker still on Good Friday, is unveiled to the vision on Easter morning.

And what is Easter morning? To the western world it

266

is the day on which is commemorated the supposed resurrection of the Master; His triumph over the death of the body; His coming forth from the grave in which they laid Him, and the beginning of the period to ultimate in His ascension into the heavens. How little that world knows of what took place for the Master, and for the world on Easter day! Easter day is the day of Esther.[1] It is the Soul's day. The dawning within the Soul of the day of its healing. The resurrection of the Soul's Lord, the Lord of Being, not out of any earthly grave (though the Master came forth from the graves of matter into which He went down), not from the tomb fashioned of stone, but out of the tombs of the stony conditions within which the Soul was held captive. Easter day! It is the day when the whole Being can rise up into the consciousness of the Vision that the Lord has indeed risen within it; that the light has broken, the joy has come, the darkness has flown away, the night of the Soul's sorrow has ended, and the day has broken, heralding unto it the perfect realization. We have said to you aforetime, the very story of Esther is the story of the Soul's resurrection. Easter day is Esther's day. For Esther is the Soul deposed through the machinations of evil influences, raised again to the very Right Hand of the King of the Heavens—that is, into high and holy and blessed estate. For the story of Esther is an allegory of the Soul's own tragedy and its restoration.

Is it to be wondered at that the cross is unveiled on Easter morning? The cross in its unveiling on Easter morning speaks of the Luminous Cross, the Cross of the Presence through whom the light comes. The mere outshining in the outer life is not to be confounded with Easter day for the Soul. The mere attainment to an understanding

[1] See article on Easter for fuller unveilings, pages 359-365.

on the mental plane of what was done through the forty days of Lent in the burden-bearing, is not to be confounded with a deep realization of the meaning of the travail of the Master in the accomplishment of the Oblation by the blotting out of the graven images, and the healing of the planet's heavens, and making the way plain for the coming of the Lord through the healing of the children.

Yet, even that is but the grey dawn of Easter day. For the dawn of Easter morning becomes, when the light breaks within the Soul, and once more the Being comes back into the consciousness of that Presence out from whom it went.

Who can know what Easter morning means for one who had been in the Divine Presence continually through long ages, but whose Light, like the cross, became veiled, until it was as night when no star shone in the firmament of the thought, or the vision, and all was black? Then to awaken and hear anew the very music of the Angelic hosts; to hear again the voice of the Angel of the Lord; to behold once more the vision of the Presence of the Lord of Glory; to come forth out of the grave of matter, out of the bondage of material limitation, out of the limitations of the strictures of the mind which had to be imposed for the purpose of burden-bearing! Do you know what Easter means for that Soul, when it breaks within the Being and the glory shines once more?

*　　*　　*　　*

Easter day is a Soul's day, not a merely historical day commemorated. "Christ the Lord is risen to-day." That is the song sung on Easter. Will Christ the Lord be risen within the Churches? Is He risen within the consciousness of those who believe such things? Christ the Lord is risen within a Soul when the Day breaks for it. It is the Lord of Being bringing the Soul into the consciousness of His Presence through the holy estate of Jesus—the life of love, of compassion, of beautiful ministry; and Christhood—the life illumined from Him.

Christ within, is then no longer veiled, but revealed. For the Christ within each one of us, is the central point of our Being. And that is luminous by nature. It is ever luminous when it is acted upon from the Divine Realm. It is the miniature expression of the Luminous Cross of the Heavens. And the unveiling of that Cross is the taking away of the Night of the Soul, which lies upon it, hiding from the Soul's own vision the Blessed Presence over-shadowing it and dwelling in the very centre of its sanctuary.

*   *   *   *

Good Friday! It should be for all a time of light. It should be a day of gladness: a day of joy: a day of rejoicing: a day of great peace: a day of hallowed memories broken from a long past: a day of new consecration: a day of hallowed giving of one's self unto the service of that Love who has never failed, and who has given in such sublime fulness unto all.

Let it be a day of gladness. For the Cross is unveiled now, and the mere commemorations held by the Church without understanding them, may pass into realizations of things accomplished. The Cross is unveiled. It is Easter day, the day of triumph over all the inimical powers; the Soul's triumph by her ascension out of matter; out of materialized elements, out of restricted thought, out of cramped and hurtful conditions, out of all wrong emotions, into the splendour of the Radiance of that Presence whose Love is Life indeed.

Now wipe away all tears. Let the Heavens wipe them forever away. Worship no longer in a sanctuary whose cross is veiled, but within the Sanctuary of your Being with cross revealed, because the Lord is your Luminous Cross, your Light, the Light of your own Cross, the Light of your Being. Let the Stations of the Cross that precede the ascent to Calvary and beyond, be fully accomplished.

Good Friday heralds Easter morning, and it is Easter day now. The Lenten time is to be passed, the time of sorrow when Zion shall sorrow no more. Those who come up into Jesushood and Christhood, shall sorrow no more because of their going out, though they may continue, and indeed, must needs continue, to minister amid the sorrow of this world unto its healing. It is the day of the ransom of the Lord. The ransomed of the Lord are returning to Zion, into their heavenly state, with songs of everlasting joy within their hearts. The bells of everlasting gladness ring upon the planes of their minds. And the ransomed of the Lord shall return unto Zion with everlasting joy—the joy in which there are no false notes. That joy abides. That joy is abounding and full of gloriousness.

Such should Easter be for all who are looking for the Daybreak, though the sorrow that has had to precede it is beyond telling! Oh, the burden-bearing by which it has been brought to pass! Oh, the travail by which such an Easter could dawn upon this world! Yet of the sorrow think not too greatly; though never be forgetful of the travail of Love on your behalf. Rejoice ever that that Love has travailed for you, and that the travail is accomplished. That Love would have all Souls to be full of joy. God hath done great things whereof we are glad. Bless the Lord, ye His children. Make mention of His name in praise. Glory in Him alone, in your blessing; for He Himself it is who hath wrought such great things on your behalf. Glory in no man, nor in any woman as such: though you may bless those who bring blessing to you. That is beautiful and it is right. You may rejoice with those who bring rejoicing to your threshold. Surely that is as it should be. It is sweet and wholesome and angelic. But ever unto the Father-Mother give all the praise, for all true blessing is from Him. And no servant of His can bless except from Him; and the blessing given is just commensurate with the blessing received by that servant from Him. Adore God. Adore the Father-Mother. Live in the Light of His Splendour and the glory of His Love. Live in the consciousness that that Love never failed you, could never fail you, will never fail you. In such Thought there is perfect Healing. In such Blessing there is perfect Peace. In such Adoration there is perfect Joy. And through such Blessing and such Peace and such Joy, the perfect Realization will break upon you and within you.

The Two Anointments.

A.   *In the House of Mary.*
B.   *In the House of Simon.*

In the New Testament there is given in the third gospel record, the story of the Anointing in the house of Simon. In the fourth gospel record there is given the story of the Anointing at Bethany. The action in both narratives is dramatic and most similar. The astonishment created by both in the hearts of some present, is also profound in its meaning, and illustrative of states of consciousness. So much alike are the action and the drama in both stories, that many commentators have felt that they must have been one story presented under two aspects, and that Mary of Bethany was none other than the woman who is said to have been the sinner.

Many beautiful things have been spoken and written about both the anointments. Standing outside of the scenes of the dramas and looking at them, one seems to have special reference to the death of the Master and the home in the little village of Bethany, whilst the other appears to point to the way of the Divine Love in its healing of Souls, its forgiving power, its restoring mercy, and to the justice of the Divine judgment in separating that which is apparent from that which is real, by unveiling that which is real and unmasking that which is unreal.

The two records are one in this respect, that they are soulic, and that they are most intimately related to the Master. But one has to do with His passing away, and the giving of Himself for the Oblation; whilst the other is related to His return from the Oblation. In both He is one of the actors. But in the return, it is Himself who is in the Simon story, as the sorrowing Soul; whereas in the anointment at Bethany, the action is by Mary.

In addressing ourselves to the days of the Manifestation and the home in Nazareth, we did not bring it down to the

273

time when the home was at Bethany. Of course, we always desire that the terms Nazareth and Bethany should be understood in their mystical sense; for the real meaning contained in both Bethany and Nazareth, refers to states of the inner Being, though villages came to be so named. For the home in which the Lord loved to dwell, and which is said to have been in Bethany, is the home of the Soul when the Being is in a state of Divine Love and Wisdom represented by Bethany. There the Being can sit at the feet of the Lord, and learn from Him. There the Life can serve the Lord, and learn from Him how to be patient and beautiful even when serving on the outer planes of ministry, as well as when serving in the inner planes. The two modes of service are represented by the sisters, Mary and Martha. Mary is the contemplative or inner; Martha is the active or outer.

And in passing, we might remind you of things we have said to you in other unveilings, that it is in the outer service the mind gets most disturbed, and not in the inner. It is not in the act of adoration, of beautiful worship, of joyful responsiveness to the Voice that speaks to you, that you become perplexed and troubled. It is when you come to the intermediary and the more outward planes, and are serving there, that the mind, forgetting the inner vision and the inner Voice, and all the beautiful things spoken, wonders how it will ever get through its ministry, and in a voice expressing somewhat of impatience, you may command that some other help come to lighten your ministry. In that state, the mind would fain dominate.

The more you serve within, the better you will serve without. The more you realize the Presence, at whose feet ye would sit, the more beautiful will the service be in the intermediary and outer planes. Mary and Martha are two pictures of one life, scenes in the life-drama of everyone who seeks to serve the Great Love.

It is quite true there were most intimate friends of the Master. There were several Marys, and Marthas too. And there were homes which He visited where they loved to have His presence and His fellowship. But in touching the Records, always get to the mystical significance of the stories associated with Him, and then you will not get far wrong. Indeed you will not get wrong at all if you seek the mystical, the true Soul-meaning, the real inner vision, iridescent light, the spiritual glories such stories were meant to shed upon your life. For the glory of the Lord does not shine outside of us unless it shines within us and through us. It can shine around us from another life; but then that is not ours. If it shines around us from another, it shines around us from that other, because it shines within.

We would look at these two stories. We would have you understand something of the import of them, beyond any-thing you may yet have realized, that you may be caught up into the very atmosphere of that consecrated ministry of which they speak, imbued with the spirit which they set forth, and which penetrated those who were the chief actors. For, as we have said, these stories are soul histories, and not merely outward events.

What was that anointing at Bethany where they made a feast for Him? It was a spiritual allegory. The feasts He sought to attend were Soul-festivals, to break bread with those He loved. He had His intimate friends with whom He partook of fruits and bread, and had sweet converse. It was at such gatherings, amid blessed fellowship, the unveiling of many things took place. Of course, much that was spoken had to be hidden. Even who the friends were, and especially who Mary was, had to be veiled.

275

Has it ever occurred to you to ask yourselves this question, how it came to pass that so little is said about the home and its dwellers, if the home in Bethany were such a blessed retreat that the Master loved to go there to be ministered unto, because those dwelling in it loved Him, and ministered unto Him; and also that such an event took place there as the Anointing; and, likewise, that in the home there was one named Lazarus, who, when the Master was far away in the northern regions, fell sick and passed over, but who was raised up again, according to the story in the fourth gospel? Has it never occurred to you as seemingly strange that there should be no references to Mary and Martha, except those two incidents of the fellowship and the anointing; and that even Lazarus is only twice named—his sickening unto death, and his presence at the anointing?

There is reason why the personal equation of nearly all the intimate friends of the Master, is veiled. There is a meaning in it. But even though they are veiled, we know that, in many respects, what He sought to guard the Teachings against, crept in, until the events were made personal rather than mystical. The Anointing at Bethany thus became a beautiful outward act, a token of love by one in that home who appeared on the scene with her sister and passed away again. For you will note this remarkable fact, she is not of the Marys at the cross. You do not find her named after the twelfth chapter of the fourth gospel.

Now, who was that Mary? What was the meaning of the anointing? It was the Mary who is said to have sung the glad song of the Magnificat, though that is an old Soul song. It was Mary of Nazareth. It was Mary the mother of the Master. It was Elizabeth Mary as the mother of the Master was named. It was she who alone fully apprehended with the understanding what was to be accomplished in the

276

Oblation. And it was she who anointed Him. But she understood what she was doing. As we ourselves use symbols at times, so she used these as symbols to express all that she understood, all that she felt, all that she loved. Aye, in that sublime act she unveiled her own heart, and revealed her understanding of her own part in the drama that was to prove so tragic for Him, and also for herself, during part of the Oblation.

There were those who murmured at what she did. When people do not understand things, they are liable to murmur. They question the wisdom of an action, or the wisdom of a service that has been rendered, or that has to be rendered. Many things Mary did during the days of the Manifestation, were questioned. She hid many things in her heart. She spake many things out of her heart. And there were frequently some who questioned. Yet her actions seemed like a response to that question which was put, or is rather said to have been put, to two disciples who were brought to the Master, with the request that they might share the Kingdom with Him, one on His right hand and one on His left hand. He said that such things were not His to give. They were attainments, and were given only from the Father-Mother to those who attained. He looked upon the two who came. He knew them well and loved them much, and said unto them, "Are ye indeed able to drink of the cup of which I shall drink? And to be baptised with the baptism with which I shall be baptised?" And they said "We are able." How many were able to be baptised with the baptism with which He had to be baptised, and to drink of the cup of which He had to drink? Why! They fled! Did not all flee from Him, but Mary? Many things are not recorded. It would not do. No beautiful purpose could be served. But there are indications in the records of the veiled sayings we have uttered to you. Mary alone understood through the most intimate fellowship with Him, what He was going to do. It is represented that she anointed Him unto His burial, and thus expressed her love. What she really did was to use symbols to give expression to the deep emotion of her own Being, and to indicate just what she was going to do. For she meant to pour out from the sacred cruse of her own Life, the precious unguent of her love. It was her purpose to share with Him, in so far as she might be permitted, the burden of the Oblation. The alabaster cruse, the wonderful beautiful vessel, was the sacred Chalice of Life, full of that unguent whose fragrance ever fills the room when it is permitted to flow forth, the most precious spikenard of a love unalloyed, a love angelic, a love divinely begotten, God inspired, and absolute in its giving.

Who can understand such a love as that? None but those who have gone that way and are able to perceive the meaning.

So the anointing at Bethany was nothing less than the outpouring of the Soul-devotion acquired within the House of the Christhood. In that state of sweet, gracious ministry, there is ever the outpourings of the fruits of the Life Eternal in Love. And, in this sacred act, it was the precious spikenard of the Soul's love giving itself in ministry to share His burden, or rather, to have part in the children's burden with Him.

There were some who were appointed to be with Him in the days of the Oblation. No one was with Him all through the lives of the Oblation. In every life there were always some who accompanied Him; for conditions had to be provided. But she was with Him more than the others, and shared more deeply His burden. Those who had to accompany Him, had to do so without knowing Him. And He

Himself was unknown to them. Drawn by a strange inner world relationship to one another, those who followed Him were appointed to provide conditions for Him from time to time. It was thus that even some of them became as His enemies. He was often heavily smitten in the house of His friends; for they created conditions as enemies, and were the cause of His smiting. It was not their heart's desire to smite Him; but they had their part to play in providing the conditions by which He should be driven to do those things which were necessary for the work of healing. It was thus some of them betrayed Him unto the uttermost. Even that one who loved unto the giving of the chalice of her love, betrayed Him through her love, for the accomplishment of the work that had to be done.

The mystery of the Oblation is a mystery that could not be fully unveiled to you in all its ramifications, so contrary do many things seem in it, so contradictory to the ways of the Divine Love and Wisdom. And yet the very contradictions created out of the extremes meeting, provided just the conditions which were necessary for the accomplishment of the work to be done. Some day ye will know. And in that day ye will understand.

The anointing at Bethany speaks to you, thus, not only as a story associated with the Oblation, but as a dramatic illustration of the giving of the Soul's love. When the chalice is filled from the Divine with the most sacred unguent, the Being serves, listens to the call of the Divine, gives itself to the Divine, ministers for the Divine in any ministry unto the children. And this ministry for the Divine is expressed in giving sweet healing wherever needed, the blessing of joy to those in sorrow, the blessing of peace to those in trouble, the blessing of direction to those who are seeking the true way, and the blessing of the upliftment of love unto the children.

There are always those who grumble when Souls give themselves. So do not be dismayed. There are always those who murmur when they do not understand, especially if they think that theÿ do understand. To all who would manifest Jesus Christ we would say, where ye do not understand, murmur not. Where ye cannot fully apprehend, misjudge not. Be ever in a state of love. Let wisdom shine through your love. And know this, that in all true spiritual ministries, the Divine Love is ever overshadowing and directing. He will Himself lead you into the understanding of the things to be done, as well as the things which have had to be done.

In the New Testament story it says that "wheresoever this gospel is preached it shall be told what this woman hath done." But that is not what was spoken. The gospel is the glad tidings unto the children of the redemption. It is the glad tidings of the redemption resulting from the Oblation. It is the glad tidings of the accomplishment of the Oblation by the Divine Love. And it shall be told in relation to that ministry and that alone, that "Mary hath wrought a good work."

*   *   *   *

And now we will look at the second Anointing. And you will note that there is a remarkable similarity in the action, though the actors are not all the same. In the first instance, it is in the House of Bethany, the Home of the Christhood, the circle of those who were of the Jesus Christ community. The second act takes place in the house of Simon. But those who were at the house of Bethany—the disciples, are also present with the Master in the House of Simon. He was asked to dine there as the guest of Simon.

Now, Simon represents the mind. He represents the mind in its outward look. That is not necessarily an unredeemed state. For there was Simon, or Simeon, at the gates of the temple—a picture of the mind in its beautiful elevated feeling. There was Simon who came to be called Peter. He was the Simon of the illumined mind, who recognised the meaning of the Christ consciousness and the Christ manifestation. He was afterwards called Peter, because the word Petros represents the illumined understanding. And the Master used the plural—when He said "Upon such Petra (rocks, solid understandings, beautiful foundations) shall the Church of God be built." The Church of God is built upon all that is of the true vision, the true understanding, the life of consecration.

But when Simon is said to have been a pharisee, it means that he was given to narrow judgment, to traditional outlook. And when it is said that he was a leper, or had been a leper, it means that he had been spiritually impoverished.

To fully unveil all that was implied in that wonderful allegory, is impossible in this hour. But you may take it, first, as relating to the western world. The mind of the western world became enamoured of the historical Jesus. It is the historical Jesus who has been worshipped for ages by the mind of the western world. You will note this difference between mere mental affirmation, and true adoration and Soul realization. Where the Being loves, life is realized. There is not only the understanding of things, but there is the understanding of Life itself. Love triumphs. Love is glorious. And it is the Divine who is adored in a state of true love. Jesus becomes impersonal though individual. There is naught of the personal when the Being is lifted up in vision to the Divine Presence, and in realization

281

to the Divine estate. The mind may have concepts and hold tenaciously to them, as the western world from age to age has done, without giving Soul-adoration, without realizing divinely, without being truly consecrated. The saints have always loved divinely. They have sought divinely. But the saints are a small community. They are but scattered numbers of what was once a glorious order. They are largely scattered throughout the western world. They may be found within the house of Simon whose mentality invited the Christhood to come and dine, to make his threshold glorious with His presence.

The western world has held the Master as the Son of God in its thoughts, without understanding what that implied for Him or for the individual Being. It has believed that He died for the world, without understanding how He died, or what His death implied. That world has thought that His death meant His crucifixion on the Roman Cross. It has believed and taught that He became a Sin-Offering for the world. Its priests have preached it as the basis of all redemption; preached it as the one thing necessary to be believed. But its priests have affirmed the fact, without understanding in the least degree what the Sin-Offering was. They have proclaimed that Jesus is the only name given from the heavens to the earth, whereby Souls can be saved. But the beautiful truth underlying that saying, they have failed to apprehend, namely, that it is only through the ways of the Jesus-life that the individual can be healed, the true path found that leads back to the glory of the vision and the realization of the Presence of the Father-Mother.

The mind of the western world, as Simon, has sat in judgment within his own house. And surely it has been a house divided within itself. It has sat in judgment upon all the other religions, and upon all the other races. And the different sections have even sat in judgment upon one another. They have all claimed in their turn to be right. Though they have all groaned beneath the burden of oppression from age to age, yet whensoever a section found a measure of liberation, upon gaining power that one in turn became the oppressor. It could not be otherwise. The judgment of unenlightened mind could not reflect the Divine Love and Wisdom. The judgment of the mind that becomes pharisaical, could not possibly be right. It could not apprehend truly, let alone apprehend fully, the mystery of such an event as that described in the story of the woman who was a sinner. That story is an allegory. Through the teachings given by the Master, Christ was invited to the house of Simon. The western world with its intellectual thought centred upon great outward progress, and where religious traditions are valued beyond inward illuminations, and where ceremonial is more important than Jesushood, and where there is a remarkable lack of things essential— that world claimed Christ, and does to this day. The water pots with the water for purification are absent; the kiss of welcome to the true Christhood is withheld; the gracious anointing filleth not the understanding. Who Christ is; what Christ is; how Christ cometh; how the Oblation was accomplished; what the Oblation has meant for this world—these things are unknown to Simon. Yet into that House, Christ is asked as guest.

Look at the picture! In the anointing at Bethany Mary uses symbols to express her devotion, and the part she is going to take in the dramatic ministry that would be so tragic to Him, but which would be so full of healing to the world. In the anointing in the House of Simon, you see one stealing across the threshold of the western world, entering the very House of Simon, the house of religious beliefs and ecclesiastical traditions, full of strange sorrow, burdened with a consciousness of grief none can understand, with visage marred more than that of the Sons of Men, beholding a vision within that house and pursuing it unto the finding of it. You may remember Rossetti's picture of Maria Magdalene entering the house of Simon, where one well-known sat for the head of the Master, and is seen through a window looking out upon the approaching figure flying up the steps to cross the threshold of Simon's house. It is a mystical picture. The drawing is illustrative of that one who had borne the burden of the Oblation, in His return journey flying up, as it were, the altar steps to kneel at the feet of that once glorious vision. He beholds that one set forth in the pictures. He discerns the true vision of the Eternal Christ who is supposed to be presented in the narratives of the Gospel records. He beholds the sad travesty in the picture painted by ecclesiastical Christianity. He recognises the true vision, and knows that Christhood such as the Master knew in the days of the Manifestation, was a state in which every way of life was beautiful. But the one in Simon's House has unwashen feet. There is no trace of those conditions which accompany Jesushood. The path of life portrayed in the presentation is minus true compassion and pity. There are no waters for the cleansing of the feet provided in Simon's House. At least he does not use the waters or truths for that purpose. And that sad and lonely outcast weary one beholds this, as He steals across the threshold. He is bowed down in grief. He would show Simon the true way to the true vision. In sorrow, aye, in sore anguish, He pours out His love and devotion. The judgment of Simon upon His own character and action, is naught to him. He maketh the vision beautiful. And He doth kiss the brow of that Holy One, for He doth see how

Simon and his friends have failed to apprehend the meaning of this welcome to the Eternal Christ, and what real adoration meaneth. And He likewise recognises how far removed they are from understanding the nature of so Divine a guest, and the meaning of His Presence. For those who requested that He should become their guest, failed to provide the precious spikenard of love. The meaning of the anointment is lost upon them, even as is that of the outpouring of the precious unguent of the Soul's love from the sacred Chalice of Life.

There is a wonderful inter-relationship between the two Anointments. The one shows the Soul's love poured forth upon the Master, proclaiming its willinghood to share with Him in some measure the Burden of the Oblation; though in giving her love, Mary consecrated herself in the first instance to the Divine Love. The other anointment reveals His own passion during the days of the Return, as He finds the House of Simon and enters it, burdened with the consciousness of æonial travail, and all the history that had to be written in it; conscious of the deep-dyeing of His own garments which once were so beautiful, and of the strange contrast between His restored vision of the Divine Estate of Christhood, and the conditions which accompanied Him as the result of the travail. In the one Mary pours out, through the symbols, her Being's love to be one with Him in His travail; in the other it is His own Being that is poured forth for the world's healing through the restoration of the true vision of the Christhood and all that the travail has meant. In the one Mary adores the Love that can give unto the uttermost; in the other, the contents of the sacred Chalice are emptied at the feet of the Divine Presence for the healing of all Souls. She kissed His feet and His brow, and anointed them for His journey; He bowed before the vision in His return journey, with His Being full of anguish and His spirit utterly broken. Sorrowfully He saw and understood what had taken place in the House of Simon. In the anguish of His Soul He wept that it could ever have been so. He kissed the sore-travailed feet of the Divine Love. He kissed the noble vision of a Love that could endure all insults, yet fail not in tenderness and sweet ministry. And He poured out His whole Being once more in the precious spikenard of Love.

He could not rest until again He took on the glory of that Love to reflect it unto the children of men. He would fain bring the living Christ to the threshold of Souls, for He saw that the view Simon held was only that of an historical personage. It was an historical Jesus Christ that was invited to his House as Guest, not the glorious Lord Christ Jesus, Love, Light and Life. It was an historical personal vision without the indwelling radiant Presence. The outlook of Simon past and future was personal and historical, without a true apprehension of the meaning of Jesushood and Christhood. Amid the glamour of publicity given by those who love the phenomenal, He beheld the perversion, and saw how the schools had confounded the Eternal Christ Vision with the vehicle of that glorious manifestation.

Who may understand what such an experience meant for Him? Who may fathom the depth of His sorrow as His travail took the form of this ministry of the Anointment? Who may gauge the intensity of His Passion as He passed up the altar steps to reach the glorious Presence, regardless of those who looked on, or any harsh criticism they passed, or any cynicism they manifested? Who may measure the sorrow or touch the depth of His anguish as he washed the feet of the sacred vision, and emptied His Chalice of Love even until the very Life of Being seemed as if it would be poured forth?

Children of the Great Love, oft-times have ye asked that the inner mysteries might be unveiled to you yet more and more. To do so is not always easy. But, in so far as we may do this from time to time, it brings us joy, though oft-times sorrow because of the themes. And we would say this to you, that these events were not only chronicled long ago, and the mystery of them worked out in the Oblation so recently accomplished that we are indeed on the threshold of its passing; but the very events recorded in these apparent instances in the life of that one, have been readumbrated in these days. And they have even been gone through by those unto whom it is given to unveil these mysteries to you.

Ever listen to the voice of the Great Love. Seek always the innermost, and fear not what Simon may say. Religions of the outer, and religions that are just crowded with mentality, may serve their purpose for those who need the outer, and those who need the mental. But for the children of the Kingdom, there is the religion of the heart. It is the religion of the inner Being; the religion of the Realization; the religion of the glorious Christhood expressed in the terms Jesus, Christ, the Lord; the religion of the Eternal Love. It is the glorious vision which becomes realization in these very states. It is the religion of the anointing of that radiant One; the serving of that glorious One; the pouring out of the precious spikenard of your Being. And if ye think it be not precious enough, remember ye cannot gauge how precious it is. But He doth weigh, and measure, and gauge, as you cannot. And all the unguent of a Soul's Being in its love is precious unto Him.

Oh! Beloved ones! Anoint the Divine Vision. Anoint the Divine Love. Pour out your Being in ministry, and

287

count nothing too great a service or sacrifice. That Love has poured itself out unto you and for you. That Love would fill you unto the outpouring of itself through you. No more burials shall ye know in that tragic sense, that Soul sense, of *going down*. For you there is come the day of the glorious resurrection, the uprising, the flying up the altar steps unto the Vision. Yet not as He did with all that past in His consciousness, like one hunted through the planes of this world, and haunted with the memories of the tragedies which were His burden. For you, not these things, but joy, and yet more joy, and still more joy, the joy of the angels of God. For you it is the day of the anointing in Bethany. But it is an anointing of your own Being; your own chrism; the Christ in you. He anointeth you. He giveth unto you the chrism of His Christ. And He doeth this that ye may anoint and find the Holy Grail, the Sacred Cup, the Divine Chalice which He filleth, and maketh to overflow.

The home of Nazareth with its Nazarenes, became the home in Bethany, in the vision of the Lord. It became the Home of Sorrow in the going down of Lazarus. In these days it has once more become the Home of Light and Life and Love and Joy, in the resurrection of Lazarus; in the coming back from the burden of the Oblation into the consciousness of that One who is the Lord of Love, the Overshadowing, the Indwelling, most glorious Presence.

The Lord anointeth you. He doth anoint you to bear the chrism of His Christ within you, and to pour forth from the Sacred Cup the Love of the Christ which healeth, which restoreth, which bringeth joy, which createth peace, which proclaimeth that the Kingdom of the Heavens is come.

288

The Passion of the Soul.

THE PASSION We speak of the Passion of the Lord. That
OF THE SOUL. which the Lord of Love could experience
in glorious ministry for His children, His children may
experience in individuated degree. If there be passion in
that Lord of Love, then there is passion in all His children.

The word has come to be wrongly used, and because of
this the glory of the Divine Mystery in motion and service
has been veiled. It has been said that in the Divine Mystery
there is no such thing as passion; that in the Eternal Love
there is no such experience—as if perfectionment implied
that the Being was as an immense statue having life of
motion, but no life of feeling; having the spirit of purpose,
but none of burden-bearing.

The stoic conception of the Eternal Mystery is that of a
God who has in his very nature no such thing as we understand by passion. Yet we cannot refrain from speaking of
the Lord's Passion. To imagine for a moment that there is
no such thing in the Divine Mystery, would be equal to
imagining that the great deep, the sea, though so vast, when
it was unmoved upon its surface, had no invisible, deep,
profound motion; or that the sun in his vastness, because he
is a glorious and perfect system of and for the Divine, had
no passion of output, no passion of power for ministry.

The Absolute One is not an immovable nor an immobile
Being. The Absolute has no relation whatever to the stoic's
God. The Absolute is the Eternal Mystery of all Being into
which all Being is gathered up; and it is the Realm that all
Being, even in its individuated forms, can touch, must
touch. It is the Realm whence proceeds the Soul's passion.
Without passion there would have been no outgoing, and
there could be no return. All true, beautiful experience
within the human estate are reflections of, and in part,
embodiments of the Divine Mystery of feeling and passion.

290

And the higher a soul climbs, the more deeply it feels; and the more inward a soul moves, the greater is its passion, and the wider the horizon of its ministry. To enable you to understand this, we will look at the Soul's passion. First in its nature as to what it is; and then in its motion; and afterwards in its purpose.

* * * *

The nature of a soul's passion is contained in the Mystery of Love. Love is the Divine Principle within the Being; not a quality, but The Mystery; the Divine Arche to become in realization the Sacred Amen in individuated form. Love is a quality in its manifestation, in the degree of its revealing in ministry; but in its nature it is The Mystery itself, having within itself all the qualities of good, of the true, of the beautiful, of the harmonious, of the gentleness of God, of consecration, of blessing, of adoration, of absolute giving. And the passion of the soul in its very nature, is the desire begotten of the motion of Love within the Being.

Passion is thought of as desire. It is imagined that desire cannot be postulated of the Divine Nature, because men and women who postulate it do not understand the nature of desire, relating it to the outer vehicles of the human manifestation. Desire is intensity of feeling. It is divinity of purpose. It is the Sacred Fire in its motion, purposing and acting. And soul passion is the soul's love in motion, of which desire is begotten. Desire is only wrong when its manifestations are of an inverted or misdirected order, inverted indeed through misdirection.

The very passion of the soul is of God. It is the Divine Mystery within the Being expressed in feeling and purpose. And it can touch every vehicle, even unto the outermost the while remaining pure and beautiful according to the purpose for which it is expressing itself in ministry. The soul's passion in its nature, is its desire to realize God; that is its centripetal motion or real inwardness. Then its desire to manifest through its centrifugal motion, is its true out-going. Though both inward and outward motion, the centripetal and centrifugal, play their part, there must first be the upgathering for realization, before there can be the full outflowing. Yet there is a sense in the evolution of the human soul, in which there must be first the outflowing and then the perfect ingathering. This will become more obvious to you as we proceed.

*　　*　　*　　*

All the potentialities which form the very Springs of Life are contained in the Love-Principle of our Being. Love becomes a hidden spring. It is a spring that makes itself manifest through the uprush and outflow of its waters.

The passion of the soul contained in the Love-Principle, is like the hidden spring away up in the fastnesses of the mountain. In the Divine Estate of the Being, it is in the very innermost, in the very heights of the Being's Life. And there is no suppression of that spring without ultimate disaster. There must be that uprising and outflowing, or there cannot be Life. The waters of that Spring are almost self-contained to begin with; and the rivulet is apparently quite small. But as it expresses itself, it makes its channel. It finds wherein to flow. And as it passes down the mountain side into the valleys, that is, into the outer Realms of manifestation, it gathers on the way from the hidden mystery springs of experience. It has many small contributaries which in themselves increase on its journey, and grow larger, enlarging it, deepening its channel because the waters become mightier, widening its channel because its flow is so much greater, bearing its manifestation onward and still onward, even until it touches the Great Deep and becomes one in and with that Deep, thus returning to the Mystery in the Absolute out of which its own mystery was individuated. For the hidden springs come from somewhere, even in the Planet. And they come within the soul in like manner, out of the Mystery of the Great Deep, out of the very presence of God in us, out of the Mystery of His Arche and Amen within. The human soul's flow is towards an enrichment of life, and a manifestation of life that reveals, and demonstrates in the revealing, the glory of the Father-Mother. That Stream must flow. But for its flow, that Stream must be nourished from the Springs. And those Springs must be enriched from the Great Deep, or there can be no Waters of Life.

In the outer vision of things, the soul in its evolution seems to be working from a hidden principle, from the centre, outward. But all the time it is really in its motion only touching and gathering that it may work the more mightily inward and upward to the Divine. For the waters that flow down the mountain to the ocean return to the mountain. The springs must needs be replenished. There is no end to the mystery of our Being. In the Absolute it is not lost. There it is understood. In the Absolute the individual river or stream of soul passion is not lost. There it is unified. It becomes one with the Eternal. Even a river whose waters are swift, carries its motion for many, many miles even after it reaches the great deep. Though there seems to be no change on the surface, there is the motion of the waters beneath from the river.

And in like manner, but more truly differentiated, the Soul has ever its own motion as a Stream from the Divine. As an expression of the great Ocean of Being, it is a revealing of the Soul's passion for beauty and truth. Its passion becometh desire for the expression in Life of love most beautiful. The deeds of its passion are the garmented revealings of its Love in motion and embodiment. The action of its passion is the magnetic throbbing of the Divine Mystery through the Being.

*   *   *   *

What a mystery our Life is! We begin, seemingly, as little children, and we grow from more to more, even till we touch the Divine Estate. But we never outgrow our Source. Our channels are deepened and broadened, and the flow of our life enriched. Life becomes mightier and still mightier. But it is individuated, and never equal to the Ocean into which it flows, and out from the heart of which its waters proceed. The desire-nature as the passion of the soul, flows from the innermost through the channels, expressing as it goes the Mystery of God within us.

How marvellous a thing Love is that can so desire! How profound is that Motion that can so express itself! How great is the Mystery of God in us, when, through the expression of our passion, God who is the Mystery becomes revealed! How stupendous is that Life of Love in the Divine which could desire into manifestation such Hierarchies of Worlds and Beings! How sublime is that Love in its majestic stooping that can make of the individuated soul a perfect world, a complex beautiful system, a reflex of His own Glorious Mystery, and embodiment of the fashion of the Lord!

If ye have ever thought of the Great Mystery of Love in the Father-Mother, after the manner of the stoic, know ye this, that, in that way, the Absolute can never be touched, even though it may be affirmed; the Realm of Omniscience can never be glimpsed in its great and glorious reality, though it may be spoken of; the Omnipotence of God can never be understood from that standpoint, since God is no person, no mere individual, but the Sum of all our Being.

How wonderful is that Love in its purpose, desiring into Being such children as we are! How tremendous is the Passion of the Eternal Mystery of Love in its motion, flowing through myriad channels to make Itself manifest, making every channel glorious with its own Mystery and Motion!

*   *   *   *

This is even more obvious when we consider the purpose of the Soul's Passion. It is the outflow of the magnetic desire stream from the Love-Principle, seeking for fulness of life in the realization of God, seeking for that through many avenues, until the life realizes that experience in which the consciousness breaks upon it that the avenues through which its perfect realization can alone come to give its desire absolute satisfaction, are avenues which are from the Divine, leading unto the Divine, and that only in Him can the glorious Realization be found; and then, that the purpose of the Divine ministry unto it is for manifestation upon all the planes. The Passion of the Lord is in a soul, that by its motion it may realize the Lord; and also, that in doing so, it may realize the Mystery of Love in its giving. No one can realize the Lord without realizing the Mystery of Love in its giving. For, to realize the Lord, is to realize the perfect Love. The perfect Love desires perfectly. The perfect desire, whose passion expresses itself toward all souls, ever seeks to reveal the glory of the Lord of Love through all its individual ministry. Its ministry is from the very innermost to the outermost, every service becoming contributory to the manifestation of the divine power for the accomplishment of the glorious end of the healing, the uplifting, the redeeming, the comforting, the joy-giving, the light-bearing, the re-awakening of the Great Mystery itself within souls.

The Passion of the Divine World has been expressed in Creation. It is expressed in the Celestial Hierarchy. It is revealed in all that is beautiful in this World. It is expressed in the Mystery of our Being, and made manifest in all life, even in the lives of those who have gone furthest away. It may be seen through the visage of men and women even where most marred.

The Divine Passion has revealed itself in ministries most marvellous in their graciousness, unspeakable in their depth of feeling, and in their immeasurable encompassing. To know the Passion of the Lord is to understand how the Divine World loves and gives; how it pours out its streams of Life for the healing of this world and all its children; how it has borne in travail in its desire and purpose and ministry, through all the long ages of the tragic drama of this world. Anyone who understands the Passion of the Divine World will understand how the Oblation was possible; what it was in its very nature; how its desire was the passion of the Soul, and how it expressed the purpose of the Heavens. They will understand the real meaning of the Passion of the Lord, and know that it was the passion of no mere man, but the Divine World Passion concentrated, as it were, and filling the Soul of that one who was the vehicle of the burden-bearing.

The Passion of Love is sublime. It is Divine. Love is ever most beautiful, even in the fallen state. Love is never more beautiful than when it can give all it has to give, even if it knoweth that the giving will mean sorrow and anguish.

Would ye understand the Passion of the Lord revealed in all His beautiful ministry unto you, and unto this world? Let your Fountain be filled from Him, and let its Waters flow out as living streams full of magnetic power for blessing.

Would ye understand the Lord's Passion in the Oblation?

Realize within yourselves the Passion of Love to give to the Divine, to give for the Divine, even unto the absolute giving of all one has; not simply on the outer planes, but all one has of attributes and of powers and of consciousness. For the ultimate of the Soul's Passion is to find the Great Deep. And in finding the Great Deep of perfect Realization, the Being is one with the Divine, one in the Divine, and as one from the Divine, willing to be a little stream, even a contributary down the mountain side, contributing the same waters, full of the same Passion, the same Love, the same marvellous Life.

Real ministry does not consist in the greatness of its outwardness, but in the profundity of its inwardness. Real ministry is, in its power, commensurate with the realization of Being in the Love of the Father-Mother, and in the giving of one's self. The end of the Soul's Passion is to be as God in the world, and as His Christ in ministry; not to be thought of as a God—unhallowed thought—nor to pose as His Christ or His Christs. When the soul's passion is moved from the Divine that soul is a little child, seeking no earthly recognition for itself, but only desiring to minister in such a way that the ministry may be from the Divine, and for the Divine; and, in its giving, the actual blessing of the Divine upon the children. The end of the manifestation of the Soul's Passion is to live for God; to move for God; to embody the attributes in our fashion of the Great Lord of Love; to be like Him in our giving, the giving of ourselves; to be like Him in our blessing, forgetting ourselves, and remembering only Him in our blessing, and the dear children who seek His blessing through us, and unto whom He has sent us, that they may be helped unto the great realization of His Blessing.

The Passion of the Soul is indeed Divine Desire begotten of the motion of the two-fold Flame of the Father-Mother Principle within our Love-Principle. Its motion is from Him, for He is the centre. It proceeds from Him and returns back to Him. Our Springs are in Him. From Him we have our outflow for blessing; and the return of our blessing is unto Him. And the purpose of the desire and its motion, is just to embody Him as His children; to be as the Christs of God, those in whom is the Anointing of His Holy Spirit; to express the Glorious Love that makes everything it touches move sweetly and beautifully. Such is the sublime purpose of our Life's Passion, even to embody Him, aye, even if it be in sorest travail unto the healing of this world.

Who would wish to be other than as the Lord of Love! Who would be satisfied in their desire-nature with being other than in unison with Him, one in and for Him? Who would desire to reveal, except from Him? Who would pray that the revelation be other than Himself in the Glory of His Love and His Wisdom?

Oh, children of His fashioning, the individuated expression of the Passion of the Lord's Love, behold and see how beautiful the Mystery of Love ever is! How profound its motion always becomes! How immeasurable and all encompassing and all upholding is the purpose of that Passion in its glorious ministry unto souls! And learn ye this, that to be like Him, is to embody His Passion of Love in Life, in the motion of Life, in the service of Life. And likewise know ye this, that, when the Being is filled with Him, bearing through its channel the motion of the Passion of the Lord, the Springs are never dry, and the River grows ever fuller, and its contact with the Great Deep, or the Sublime Mystery, is perennial and Eternal.

298

The Mystery of

Joseph of Arimathea.

JOSEPH OF ARIMATHEA. In the New Testament it is said that one who was a rich man, a disciple and friend of the Master, was closely identified with the events which followed the Roman Crucifixion. Apart from his connection with the one chief incident of taking down the lacerated form of the Master from the cross and providing a resting place for it, there is no record of any friendship between the Master and Joseph of Arimathea, or of his having been associated, even in the most indirect way, with the intimate circles who were spoken of as the friends of the Master. It is true, the Master had many friends outside of the small circles which are named in the records, and to which the inner group of discipleship and the apostolate is related. Those friends were, many of them, most intimate with Him, and were disciples indeed, and veritable apostles of the Jesus Christ life and vision. As we have oft-times said to you, the groups of intimate friends, though not large, were fairly numerous. And the discipleship covered considerable ground. But the little circle which was supposed to form the innermost group of the disciples, as set forth in the Records, was a mystic circle, and had relation to the Soul's attributes, the redemption and training of which was aimed at in His intimate conversations with His friends.

Joseph of Arimathea, however, seems to stand out so emphatically in the latter part of the days of the Manifestation, as the record of that event is found in the Gospel stories, because of the singular part which seemed to be assigned to him, that of begging the body of the Master from Pilate, and providing a resting place for it.

In mystic lore, however, there is much more assigned to

Joseph of Arimathea than that one incident. For, in the story of the Holy Grail, in its mystical development, it was assigned to Joseph of Arimathea to receive the sacred Basin, or Bowl, or Cup, from the hands of the Master Himself. And he also had the sacred office of holding up that sacred vessel during the crucifixion, to receive of the life-stream which flowed from the Master's pierced side. And it is likewise recorded, that it was given to Joseph to bear the Sacred Vessel unto others, that, looking upon it, they might find the blessing of healing and peace.

Thus a most sacred office in the mystery myth was appointed unto him, that of receiving the Grail, and bearing it up for the blessing of many.

*   *   *   *

Thus far, only, may the historical aspect lead us at present. We have named it, and glimpsed it, that you might see, in some measure, that there must be a deeper significance in that history than men and women wot of; and that you may apprehend something of the mystery couched in the very name itself, and in the ministry unto which that one was said to be appointed. For, when you leave the outer to seek the inner; when the vision is no longer satisfied with the objective, but realizes that the reality is to be subjectively apprehended and understood, and seeks unto the beholding of the glorious meaning, then it is a Divine Mystery that is beheld, and not simply a historical event. A Soul Mystery is unveiled, rather than a passing event in the outer life of the Master. A great tragedy is revealed, but the outworking of it is beheld from the innermost realms. A great Divine Mystery comes before the vision; but it resolves itself into a sublime revealing of that transcendent Love Who never fails His children, and Whose ministry is unwearied and endless.

There was a Joseph at the beginning of the Manifestation who is said to have been the foster-father of the Master. There was a Joseph at its close who is said to have performed an act of great reverence and tenderness and love. There was a Joseph who was to guard Maria through whom Christ was to be manifested, and who was to take Maria with the Christ child down into Egypt, to be in hiding there until the time appointed for the return should come, when the Angel of His Presence would again command that return to be accomplished. Then at the crucifixion, Joseph appeared again to guard the outer form of the Master; in reverent love to take it and find a resting place for it; and to guard that crucified one, and find the hidden place where He would have to be laid, wherein no man had ever so lain.

As at the beginning of the Manifestation, Joseph is I-o-seph, the Divine Overshadowing One—representing a high state in the Being—taking the burden-bearer down into Egypt for the purpose of the Oblation, and, in the Return, bearing that one back again into the Nazarene state. During the long crucifixion He was present to guard the Cross-bearer, to prevent Pilate who represented the Zeitgeist or world-power, and Herod who embodied the social, astral regnancy, and Caiaphas who was high priest of the ecclesiastical, dominating, religious authority, from utterly destroying that which was so sacred.

The word I-o-seph, signifies a Divine Mystery, and a ministry issuing from it. Thus Joseph of Arimathea becomes I-o-seph, the dweller in the Heights of God, the word Arimathea meaning, The Mountains of God.

*   *   *   *

Now, in the sacred mystery of the Master's Initiations, which were not on the outer planes at all, but in the Heavens,

He was crowned Ioseph Maria. By that was meant, the high consciousness of the Overshadowing Presence within the Being, and the ministry which had to be rendered as the result of that realization. For, you will understand that even in the Innermost Realms, no one liveth unto himself. None may live unto himself or herself. All that is attained, even in the Divine World, is attained for ministry, and not simply for individual realization, joy and glory. The glorious state is a state of joy and radiance, but it is a state for manifestation. The realization of God is for the embodiment of God, in whatsoever world appointed, upon whatsoever plane the revelation has to take place.

As we have said to you elsewhere, His Divine Parentage may be expressed in the terms Ioseph Maria. But not so the earthly parentage. For Zacharias and Elizabeth Mary were His earthly parents.

And furthermore, Joseph is represented as taking that one with Maria, down into Egypt. The very Being and the manifested Life are shadowed forth in Maria and the Christ child. And the taking of that one down into Egypt expresses the gradual descent of the Being. And this latter will be shown to have been the true Descent from the Cross.

Ioseph of Arimathea is, therefore, ever to be understood as the One on the Heights, or the Mountains of God. And it is He who lets down the very Being of the Master. There is a descent from the heights into states wherein the lower faculties of consciousness are veiled. He is let down into the very pit where the miry clay obtains and darkness reigns. The allegory of Joseph and his brethren is full of significance as a symbolical story. In the Oblation it finds its full meaning. Mystically understood, the Master was sold by His Brethren. And He was let down into the pit of the hell-states, where everything obnoxious to Him had to be met with and overcome.

The true Descent from the Cross, was not the taking down of the lacerated form of the Master by Joseph of Arimathea and other supposed friends. That would not have been a Descent from the Cross in any very special sense, though it would have been a liberation from a position which imposed upon Him great anguish through His form that was so lacerated. To descend, is to descend in state. Therefore, the real Descent from the Cross, was the descent from that state of consciousness in which the Being was one with the Divine Cross, the Luminous Cross, the Macrocosmic Cross.

The Cross is in God. It is not an accursed cross, as the Calvary Cross has been named and thought of. The Cross of God is the transcendent Love that ever gives; that gives to enrich; that enriches to make glorious; that makes glorious to manifest the Radiance of the Love. It is the Cross that fashions Worlds, Systems, Hierarchies, Beings. Of it and from it, Worlds and Beings are individuated to express God. That Cross is creative, exaltative, illuminative, and always sacrificial.

The Descent from the Cross in which Joseph of Arimathea took part, was the descent of that One known as the Master, from the state of exaltation of Being wherein He dwelt within the Sanctuary of the Divine Mystery, having the consciousness of God always as an overshadowing and indwelling Presence. And the Descent was even unto the loss of that consciousness. For His Lamp had to be veiled. It was in the days that followed the Manifestation that the Descent took place. His going away from the state of Christhood was His Descent. And the Gethsemane was the shadowing forth of it upon the threshold of His vision. In

304

it He beheld the path that had to be trod, saw the states that must needs be entered into, and at times shrank from the very thought of entering them; yet desired to have no will done but that of the Father-Mother, though He confessed that the burden would be heavier than He had anticipated. It was thus He prayed as He saw what the Descent would mean:— "Oh, my Father-Mother, if it be possible, let this cup pass from me: yet if it must needs be for the healing of this world, Thy Will be done."

The real Descent will thus be recognized to have been the descent in consciousness and state, from the "vision of the glory of" the Luminous Cross, which could be beheld as Ioseph Maria, into that state of burden bearing in which the glory would all have passed, as if it had not been; yet a state in which His very soul would be crying out for a Life no man gave unto Him, for a Love no one could impart to Him, for a Realization He could not define any more in His thought, but after which He yearned unutterably, as the hart panting after the water brooks, but knowing not where the brooks were to be found.

The taking down of His poor lacerated form from the Roman Cross was a little episode in the outward history of suffering, a passing moment only, and scarcely that, in the great tragedy that found re-embodiment in forty lives, the lives running their course over eighteen hundred years.

His descent was into hell. When will the churches understand the things they profess to believe, and utter in their creed?

It was only through having been in the state of Ioseph Maria that He was permitted to descend. It was only because He had known that glory that He could yield up His spirit, to yield which meant the withdrawal of the

305

consciousness of the Sacred Flame. It was only because He had known so transcendent a Realization as that of the Father-Mother Presence, that He could sorrow in Gethsemane with the anguish of the Gods.

Who understandeth that sorrow? Not those who have not as yet touched the threshold where the glory of the Vision came unto Him.

*   *   *   *

Who could understand such a Gethsemane? Not the writers of the Records, nor even His intimate ones. Though these latter sensed much, they were not permitted to do more than glimpse all that it meant for Him. For the tragedy of their sorrow, which He saw was coming upon them, would be quite heavy enough to bear, apart from their understanding the depth of the Passion of the Lord poured forth through His Being for the healing of the world.

What He bore in that Descent, was borne in less degree of intensity by the Children of the Kingdom who came into these realms to teach the children of this world. They came as the Cross-bearers, bearing the Sacred Cross, reflecting the Luminous Cross within themselves and through themselves, having grown in fashion like the Divine Love and Wisdom. Under great limitations had they to come. But there were no shadows caused by their limitations; nor was there the sorrow begotten of wrong conditions amid which they had to minister; for then the world was unfallen. They were simply elder children sent out from Home to find, through the very teaching they had to give, the younger children, and through that teaching bear them home into the same consciousness, the same life, the realization of the same Love and glorious Wisdom. But when the world descent took place, they suffered a great descent too, for they went down from having the consciousness of the Luminous Cross always with them, into the darkness, out of which they had to be gathered from time to time and again shown the Vision and the Glory, and be strengthened that they might be able to go back again, and descend to minister unto the suffering children of Judah. Through the long ages have those children travailed through their descent, suffering, sorrowing, oft-times anguishing.

But that anguishing of the Gethsemane in the Great Descent from the Cross, was so intense, that all the others seemed almost to be gathered up into it; for He sensed the whole world's sorrow, and all the children's anguish. He sensed the very fires of hell. He felt their consuming flames. The troubled waters which had overwhelmed the lives of the children, beat upon Him. He was also conscious of the deep yearning of the Children of the Kingdom to return.

His descent was not gradual, but hurried. He hastened down into Egypt, the land of bondage, the land of the task-masters, the land of sorrow, the Goshen of spiritual darkness. He hastened into the Valley of Hinnom where no light broke, and through the Valley of Gehenna where the pestilential fires of perverted desires burned, in order that the fires might be blotted out ultimately and the darkness chased away, and the land of Egypt in the children and in the planet, come to speak the language of Canaan. For in that day, when the effects of the Oblation were to be fully accomplished, Egypt would have five cities speaking the language of Canaan; and Egypt would come to Assyria and Assyria would go down into Egypt, and together they would be ministered unto from Israel. For Egypt is the outer life—the lower manas; and Assyria is the mind life—the mental states; and Israel is the inner realm of realization. And when the mind and the cities of Egypt—the real desires and the real senses—speak the language of Canaan, then the life will be healed, redeemed, purified, exalted, crowned with the Life of the Son of God.

The Descent from the Cross was for the healing of the Planetary Mind, the Intermediary Heavens. By it was accomplished the blotting out of all that was graven, all that was impure, all that was hurtful, all that was inharmonious, upon the Middle Kingdom, in order that there might be new heavens for the earth, and that through that wonderful, mysterious process there might be made of the Heavens of the Planet, new Heavens, new states, glorious conditions through which the Lord of Love and Wisdom could again make Himself manifest.

*　　*　　*　　*

Joseph of Arimathea taking the Master down from the Cross, may now be truly understood as the letting down of the very Being of the Master for the purposes of the burden of the Oblation. It will be seen to have been a Descent from the state of Realization with and in the Divine, a Descent from the Luminous Cross Realization, to the Calvary of unutterable crucifixion; a Descent from the Cross of Glory, or the Divine Radiance, to the Cross of shame where hatreds reigned, the Cross that was to be accounted accursed.

How often that One begged Caiaphas to be gentle and merciful, and Herod to cease his mockery, and even Pilate to put away his heartless judgments, during that long descent! For Caiaphas, Herod and Pilate, embody the spirit of Institutional religion, the Social Tradition, and the callousness of the Zeitgeist, or mind of this world.

And now we are in the days of the Return, days which speak of the full accomplishment of that Descent, and of the work for which that Descent was made. We are in the day when the burden of the Cross which was changed from that of the Glory of the Heavens to that of the darkness of the Hells, from the glory of perfect Love, the Radiant Love, to that of the Cross of shame and faction, of enmity, and even of hatreds, shall again become the service and glory of the Luminous Cross. For the Oblation is accomplished. The Heavens of the Earth are re-made, renewed, restored, purified again, and the ministry upon them become most wonderfully beautiful and full of glory.

And in the return aspect of the Descent from the Cross, the Descent becomes once more an Ascent. It is a descent from the Cross of Calvary, a passing away of all that the tragedy signifies, and the ascent of the Soul into the consciousness of the Presence of that One Who is the Luminous Cross, the Lord of our Radiance, the Lord of our Being, the Lord of our Love. For He who descended, and who had first to ascend in order that He might descend, having accomplished that Descent, naturally would again ascend into the consciousness from which He went out to accomplish the purpose of the Divine Love for the children of this world. And who should take His lacerated form, as it were, down from the Cross of the Calvary where it was pierced through and through, not simply in the outer forms, but also in the visage that became marred more than that of the Sons of Men; who should take that form down from that Cross, but He Who is the Eternal Ioseph, and Who gives to a soul the state of Ioseph Maria? For only of the Lord of Love alone are we taken up from the Cross of our crucifixion, and healed, to find the Cross of the Radiant Presence, and all the glory which that Presence radiates within our Being.

*   *   *   *

And so the story, seemingly but an incident on the outer

309

planes, becomes one of Divine Mystery, full of real meaning, with real soul passion in it, with great divine purpose lying behind it, with infinite tenderness and reverence expressed through it. And, taking the myth of the Grail aspect of the story of Joseph of Arimathea, who received from the Lord the Sacred Chalice, the wonderful Chalice filled with the precious spikenard of His Love for distribution? Who received that Sacred Bowl and held it up to receive into it the very Life-stream of the Lord's Passion? It was Joseph, the Soul, who was in the state. But it was the Chalice and Basin of His very Being which were filled for the outpouring unto the healing of the world.

That same Presence is with us all, that One Who Overshadows His children, and doth fill their Cup and their Chalice; that same Presence Whose Love is the most precious of unguents, Whose Love makes sweet wherever and whenever the Chalice is opened and its fragrance comes forth; that Love which never fails to heal the wounds of our crucifixion, and even the pierced side of our soul's love in its travail. Go ye forth, therefore, feeling and realizing that Presence with you, letting you down from the Cross of Calvary to gather you up again into the Radiance of the Luminous Cross, that ye may reflect Him, embody Him, manifest Him, and be the embodiments of His Great and Holy Love and Wisdom.

Cast out all fear. For you there is no more spiritual death. There awaits you Life, Immortal and Eternal, the Life of the Immortals, the power and glory of those who have transcended the limitations of time and space, those who have risen above the elemental conditions, though they may return here for ministry; and the Life Eternal to know God, which is the Life of the Great Realization. Go forward bearing your Cross. Have on your banner the insignia of the Living God Who doth give to each one of us as we are able to receive of Him, the fulness of His Holy One. Henceforth, affirm your childhood to Him, and uprightly walk as His child, having within you the Holy Awe of His Spirit, the Fear of the Lord, and no more any shadows of earthly fear or doubt or distrust. The Lord reigneth! Let your Being be glad! Sing aloud, and give thanks, and make melody in your heart, for He cometh! He cometh in His regnancy; and in His coming, He becometh within your consciousness. Hearken not to the voice of Caiaphas that would crucify such a vision; nor to the Herodian spirit whose mockery still reverberates through the ages; nor to Pilate who knew not what truth was when he beheld and heard. In the Light of the Radiant Presence, walk and listen and hear; for the Heavens rejoice with great joy, and the earth shall yet be filled with gladness. But it is waiting for your rejoicing; and in the measure in which you rejoice in the Vision and realize the Glory, shall the earth and her children be blest.

The Guest Chamber.

The Guest Chamber is the Sanctuary of the Being where the Divine Presence in His Over-shadowing abides. It is the Sanctuary wherein the glory of the unveiled Radiance of the Ever Most Blessed One is made manifest. It is that most holy court of the individuated Being, wherein man comes to the consciousness of glorious oneness with the Ever Most Blessed Mystery, known as God the Father-Mother. It is the Chamber spoken of as the Upper Room where the Lord met with the Twelve, and where He ever meets with the Sacred Twelve. All earthly associations given to the Upper Room and the Sanctuary, are but endeavours to focus into the personal consciousness, those things which are Divine Realities. In all Divine Manifestation there is a correspondence carried through, even to the outer realm of manifestation, as in the case of the beautiful flowers in their form, their colour, their fragrance and their ministry. But the Reality is always in the Divine Kingdom. Those true earthly sanctuaries, which become veritable Guest Chambers into which the very atmosphere of the Angelic World descends, and the vibrations from the Divine World enter, are expressions in the realm of outer manifestation, of the great and most sacred verities which, to be understood, must needs be realized by the Being. No earthly house is a sanctuary, even though it be most beautifully built and set apart as such, unless the atmosphere of the Angelic Heavens pervades it, and the glorious Life-stream proceeding from the innermost world of Being, interpenetrates all its uses and its service. For unless such conditions obtain and prevail within its form, its courts, its service, its uses, its ministry, it cannot be said that such a sanctuary is a Guest Chamber where the Being is aided to pass from the without to the within to meet the Lord, and become conscious of the ensphering of the

Angelic World, and the influx from the Divine World of the glory of the Lord, as the Divine Love and the Divine Wisdom.

In perfect realization within the Guest Chamber there is manifestation upon all the planes. And such a manifestation converts even a simple room, not built ostensibly for the more outward ceremonial of religious expression, into a Guest Chamber, where the sweet Breaths of the Angels are inhaled and felt, and the Radiant Presence is beheld in great measure and beautifully realized. That which such a simple room might lack in form on the outer, would be supplied by the glorious form from the innermost.

* * * *

Many have thought that the Upper Room spoken of in sacred story, was a room selected for the purpose of fellowship between the Master and His twelve intimate friends. It is quite true to say that He met with His most beloved ones on these planes, in upper rooms, from time to time in different localities; for His ministry was much less public than is supposed, and was much more inward and seclusive than the western world has ever imagined. The messages He had to give, were given chiefly in secret. They were spoken in places far removed from the public throng, and mostly in the homes of His beloved ones.

But there is special reference to an Upper Room in Jerusalem, whither, it is said, He went to meet the Twelve on the eve of the Passover, and where, it is reported, He celebrated the Passover with the disciples. That celebration has come to be spoken of as the Supper of the Lord, the Holy Eucharist, the Holy Communion, the Most Blessed Sacrament. That Upper Room is thought of as the Guest Chamber where the last fellowship was held.

314

In the outward presentation of it, a most sacred mystery has been brought down and materialized beyond the recognition of even those who were of that Inner Group, on that evening when He took His departure from them for purposes associated with other ministry. The real Guest Chamber was the Sanctuary of the Being; their Being and His Being. The Twelve who are said to have celebrated it with Him, were not men, but His own glorious attributes. For, in that sacred hour, His beloved ones consisted of a few noble Souls, some noble men and some women (for there were beautiful and noble women in the discipleship and apostolate, even as there were men). Twelve is the number of the divine attributes which find expression in the Being of a man or a woman Soul. And when the Lord celebrated His Passover within the Guest Chamber with the Twelve, it was the celebration within the Guest Chamber, or Sanctuary, of the Being of the Master, wherein all His attributes shared in the glory that was poured forth from that Presence. For in that hour, He realized in absolute oneness with the Lord of Being, the glory of the Love and the Wisdom of the Father-Mother. It was that hour, that last hour of most transcendent realization, in which the glory of Divine Christhood was fully entered into, partaken of again, and then gradually left behind as the Soul became veiled for its passing to take up the burden of the Oblation. For it was the Passover, or passing over from the Christhood state in its gloriousness, into those states of consciousness which had to be passed through in the deep valley of Hinnom, whither He went to tread the path that lay through the pestilential fires of human passion, called Gehenna (for these had been fashioned and carried up into the planetary heavens), that He might extinguish them. The Guest Chamber for Him was flooded with the Radiant Presence. It had been through countless ages of transcendent, spiritual and divine realizations. It was the Sanctuary where the Presence abode in Him, giving the perpetual consciousness of the ensphering of the Heavens, the Overshadowing of the Inner Worlds, and the Angelic or Soul Immanence of the Mystery of the Father-Mother, a Mystery He understood. And the Celebration was His Last Supper in that state of consciousness, before descending in His state, to go where no one would recognize Him any more, until the Work given Him to do had been accomplished.

*   *   *   *

To-day is prophetic. Notwithstanding the heavy shadows which lie athwart the threshold of the world, to-day is harbinger of glorious things in their coming. It is the day of the return of the Son of Man to the Guest Chamber. The Son of Man is an old mystery term meaning Adonai, realized by man. It is the day in which the Master Himself returneth from Edom, or the Land of Forgetfulness, of shadows, of darkness in travail. It is the time when there should be unveiled to His beloved ones, His very garments, though they be still, as it were, red-dyed, as one who had been treading within a winepress. For in His travail in the land of Edom, all His garments were afflicted. In His return unto the land of Bozrah, out from which He went down into Edom, He beareth with Him the marred visage, with its veil of unutterable sorrow. It is the time of the accomplishment of the Oblation, and the full return of the Son of Man. For within His Guest Chamber the Lord Himself hath celebrated the passing over, and all the tragic travail through the Valley of Hinnom, of great spiritual darkness and loneliness unutterable, and the lives of anguish resulting from that ministry in which the consuming fires within the planetary heavens, were extinguished. It is the

316

day in which that Being once more has risen up into the consciousness of all that passed, and to know once more the blessed ministry in sweet and hallowed consciousness within the Guest Chamber, of the ensphering Heavens, the Over-shadowing Divine World, and the Immanent Presence of the Sublime Mystery of the Father-Mother.

*   *   *   *

In that day of the Return two of the beloved friends were to precede Him, and render a sweet ministry. It is said that Peter and John were to tarry upon the earth planes until He came. To tarry is to linger. It is to wait. It is to remain, in a sense, quiescent. And from the days of the Manifestation, Peter and John have tarried. They represent divine princi-ples. They are the Understanding illumined, and the Divine Love manifest. Since the days of the Manifestation, both the Divine Love and the Radiant Wisdom have verily tarried. In the western development, or religious interpretation passing for Christianity, they have both been sadly wanting. But the day has come when the Light is again breaking. And, though it be but the grey dawn of the day most glorious which is to follow, still it is the Light. The day has broken. The Eternal Love shines again. The Light of Love is no cold intellectual expression of knowledge as wisdom, but a glorious, generating, healing, purifying, uplifting, transforming, transfiguring power, making life to be once more radiant with the glory of the Lord.

These things, these glorious things, are taking place. Peter and John have once more been the heralds at the grave. It is said in the Records that these two disciples ran both together unto the sepulchre, but that John did outrun Peter. Love would have the Understanding accompany it on the way. And it should ever be so. But Love in its manifesta-tion always does outrun Peter. Love in its finding the Truth must outrun Peter: it is more vital; it is more youthful. Without Love the Lord could not be found. For, of itself, the Understanding cannot find the Lord. The mind may have reflected into it the glory of the Lord, and the understanding be illumined with that glory; but it is through Love alone that the Lord is known. It is through Love alone that the great Realization comes. It is through Love that all the powers of the Being become, at last, one in unity of purpose, of experience, of service.

*   *   *   *

These things are ever to be understood mystically. There are those who concern themselves with personal things, and they wonder to whom Peter and John refer. They associate them with individuals rather than with divine principles. Many have the Petrine faculty, for there were many Peters in the old and glorious days. Many have the Johannine love; and there were not a few Johns in Spiritual estate in the days of the Manifestation. Some of these were women. It is well, therefore, always to keep clear of the personal, so destructive have the personal interpretations of the past been to the great vision and the glorious messages which were given through the Master. And we say this, and would emphasize it, even though we know it to be beautifully true, that two whom He most dearly loved were His helpers during the years of the Return. Unto them was appointed a special ministry to Him, though here, for the present, we must draw the veil.

The Guest Chamber once more knoweth its Lord. And though the shadows of the sorrow begotten of the travail, still lie upon His raiment, yet, within the Sanctuary in the Presence of His Lord, lieth no more any shadow; for the Radiance of the Eternal Love filleth the Guest Chamber, and the Bread and Wine which are the very flesh and the

318

life-begetting stream of the Son of God, are ever upon the altar of the Being, and evermore to be anew partaken of. And, as into His travail were gathered up the very adumbrations of all the travailing of the children of the Kingdom, as well as the Karmic burden of the children of this world, so the children of the Kingdom may now understand their own travail through this world in which they have ever been as strangers since the great Descent. And with this understanding and perfect interpretation of their own burden-bearing, there may come to them that healing for which they have cried out, even the restoration of all their Being into the bosom of the Eternal Love. For there, all tears are wiped away. There, all tribulation issues in the Great Peace. There, all sorrow begotten of Soul travail, emerges in joy triumphant. And there, once more, they shall partake of the Pascal Lamb in the Supper of the Lord, even that perfect oneness in that transcendent Love called "the Lamb of God."

The Guest Chamber is the Most Holy Place, even the Sanctuary of the Being. And there the Lord of Love doth abide with those who seek His Face to behold His Glory.

PART
V.

Initiations of the Soul.

The Divine Messengers and

Their Message.

*THE
MESSENGERS
OF GOD.*

A Messenger is one sent from the Divine World bearing a special message concerning the Divine Love and Wisdom in its purpose towards this world and its children. A Messenger is, therefore, an illumined one. He or she, as the case may be, is not simply a disciple of some order of belief or of some teacher, nor a follower of any traditional or historical line of thought. Nor is that one an apostle to represent any existing order. The Messenger comes from the Divine Realms to be the express vehicle for manifestation and interpretation of the Divine purpose contained in the message.

There have been many Messengers to this world. There have been many who have been acclaimed Messengers who were apostles only, and some even only disciples. There have been not a few regarded as special Messengers whose whole message and method of interpreting it, were entirely at variance with what a true Messenger could possibly be. There are those who believe that the Divine World has sent forth Messengers of judgment, as in the case of Mahomet, to accomplish great things by means of the sword. There have been those who have regarded as Messengers some who laid the foundations of new ecclesiastical orders.

The true Messenger is always one who wields only the sword of the Spirit, that double-edged Sacred Flame which separates, but also purifies and heals. The true Messenger is no Sophist. He or she is never a Jesuit. And Casuistry would be absolutely unknown in the message and ministry of such an one. The Messenger who comes from the Divine Kingdom, *knows*. That one does not speculate in thought. There is no lack of vision. There is no hesitancy as to what is true. That Soul dwells in the innermost

324

realm, and from that realm alone ministers, though the manifestation has to be on the outer human realm. That one is but the vehicle of the Lord; for the Lord is ever His own Messenger, though He manifests, reveals and unveils within His servants, and through them, in harmony with the message which has to be proclaimed.

It is quite true that teachers are sent from the Divine World to teach upon the mental planes occult knowledges of the glorious mysteries; for knowledge of an occult or true mental nature, has to be broken for all the children. It is quite true that special teachers as interpreters arise from time to time, giving fresh impetus to the purer and nobler interpretations of the Divine Love and Wisdom broken upon the occult realm, and these teachers and interpreters are ministers of the Divine Love and Wisdom upon the intermediary planes. In a limited sense they may be thought of as Messengers, though the term should not be so used. They are teachers and apostles who have been disciples themselves upon those planes, and have learned something of the glorious Wisdom of the Father-Mother broken there. But they must not be confounded with the Messenger of the Lord in any age or at any time. When they speak, they speak as those who are versed in knowledges gathered along the occult and historical planes. But the Messenger never so speaks: his message is direct from the innermost realm. He knows the things of which he speaketh; and the unveiling of these things is dependent upon the hearing ear, and the understanding heart, and the yearning aspiring Being, of those unto whom he is sent. For the veil of the Eternal World cannot be drawn except to those who are of humble mind and lowly heart and pure desire, and are children of true love. The Eternal World can only be open, so to speak, unto those who are capable of standing upon its threshold to gaze upon its glories.

Thus the Messenger from the innermost realm, comes first to those who have the power to respond to that realm. The message spoken within that one, through that one, is not for the multitude, but for the few. The unveiling of the Divine Glory within that one, and through the message of that one, is for those whose gaze is pure, whose intention is beautiful, whose purpose is the realization of the Love Eternal. It is unto such that the Messenger comes. His message is for the few alone. It has always been so since this fallen world began. It was so before the Descent took place. The Messengers who came to this world were the Christ-Souls: teachers and interpreters and manifestors, the Sons of God, the embodiments of His Love and Wisdom to be broken as the different races upon the earth were able to receive. Unto them, the Sons of God, Messengers were sent from time to time with special ministry from the most Divine Realm.

And as it was then, so is it now. It is unto that once most glorious, ancient community of Christ-Souls, that the real Messengers are sent. Even unto this day is it true, "many are called, but few are chosen," that is, many hear about the messages which come through the true Messenger, but few are able to follow. Even in the days of the Manifestation it is recorded (which record is most true), that as the Master gave His message from the Father-Mother, some of those who even accounted themselves His brethren, went back from Him. The multitudes, said to have been charmed by His message, melted away until only the very few elect ones who were able to receive His Teachings, remained with Him. Such is ever the experience of the true Messenger. His life, or her life, is a lonely one so far as the outer and intermediary planes are concerned. He is alone, yet never alone, because the Father-Mother Presence is ever in Him. His whole Being is caught up of God, and his realizations are all in the Heavens. The life on earth is ever a burdened one. For the Messenger, through the light of the Eternal Radiance within him, sees through all the planes, even to the outermost, and cannot but be burdened with what is cognized upon the intermediary and outer planes. He must ever be nourished from the innermost realm alone, for he could not endure the vibrations of the lower planes as they are at present constituted. He must ever be encompassed from the Eternal Love or he could not persist amid the realms of manifestation as these are now constituted; for they are still far from redeemed, though much healing of late ages has come to them through the ministry expressed in the mysterious Oblation.

*   *   *   *

The Messenger carries a message from the very Presence. The Messenger has no message of his own. The Messenger ever speaks for the Divine alone. All that is personal, all that is even individual, must needs be laid aside that the message be unfettered, and be the Word of God only. Thus the Messenger has nothing of his own, though in the Great Love he has all the treasures of the Heavens poured out for him and into his Being. His message could not be other than the message of Love. It is not historical, except in a Divine sense. It is not ecclesiastical, except in that high meaning. It is not astral, though its vibrations will make the astral kingdom purer and more beautiful. It is not mental, though its radiations will equilibrate the mind, and heal it of its tribulation and its sorrow. It is not higher

327

occultism, though it will illumine the mind and make it a true reflector of the Divine Radiance. It is the message of the Eternal Love whose magnetic stream flows through all his Being, and has to be expressed as flowing through all the planes of the consciousness, healing, redeeming, restoring, equilibrating, transforming, transfiguring, giving perfect transmutation as the children rise from the outer to the inward, and to the still more inward.

*   *   *   *

Of late days a number have arisen as the Messengers: these could be named. They have had a ministry to give certain teachings, and those teachings are helping many. Some of them are mental. Some are philosophical. Some are occult. Some are angelic. But they all have their ministry, and are accomplishing much good. These are teachers and interpreters, mostly of a very high order, but they all interpret upon their own plane. And any interpretation that is not from the Innermost, is necessarily limited, seeing what is upon its own plane and the planes beneath, but not what lies above and beyond. Whereas the Messenger, through the message given to him, ministers from the most inward realm, seeing through all the planes, and interpreting the message given upon the other planes, harmonizing those passages wherein they seem to differ, understanding them all, knowing them to be fragmentary rays broken upon the various planes for the guidance and help and redemption of the children whose needs demanded such messages. In the Messenger's message, all other messages are contained, though he has not the office of breaking that message upon those planes which are occult, mental, philosophical, historical, that office being reserved for those who are sent to be interpreters upon those planes, and teachers of the Divine Love and Wisdom broken upon them.

Thus it is to be understood that though the Messenger does not speak in the language of occultism, or the philosophies, or the mental interpreters and teachers, because his vocation is to unveil the world whence all Light cometh unto the Soul, and interpret for those upon the threshold of that world, the glory of it and its mysteries, yet such an one doth verily understand fully the meaning of all these other lesser statements and unveilings and ministries. As the message given him contains all Divine Messages expressed in the realm of philosophy and occultism, historical interpretation and mental affirmation, so the Radiance within that message throws light upon all these others, and perfectly interprets them, giving each one its place.

The Messenger is but the servant of the Lord. "There was a man sent from God whose name was John. He came to bear witness of the Light. He was not in himself that Light, but he came to witness of that Light. In him was the true Light whose Radiance it is that illumineth every one rising up out of this world." In those days he witnessed for that Light which is the Radiance of that Love which is the mainspring of all Being, which, when realized, is the Eternal Life, even to know God.

That which was spoken concerning that One, His servant John, is once more to be made manifest unto all who are able and willing to receive.

For the Temple of the Living God with its sacred Ark of the Eternal Mystery, is again open, and the Voice from out the Sanctuary speaks once more.

Ever Blessed be His Glorious Name!

329

The Nature of a Christhood.

The word "Christ" is very specially associated with the Western religious expression. The Western world professes to follow Christ. It professes to preach Christ. It is well, therefore, to understand what is meant by "Christ"; for undoubtedly the thought of the Western world is vague concerning so profound a mystery.

Who was Christ, and who is Christ in the thought of the Western world to-day? The Second Person in the Godhead; the eternal Son of the Father, as the Athanasian creed expresses it, "Very God of very God," of the same substance, the same nature, the same attributes, the same powers, the same omniscience, and in a sense the same omnipotence. Though the Western world believes in the Divinity and even in the Deity of Christ, it also believes that Christ was in the form of man, and was a man. Libraries have been written on this thesis. Controversies have been waged through endless years; and those taking part have either earnestly sought to get at the solution of what was evidently a mystery, or, being too confined within the limitations of the traditional beliefs in which they were trained, they have simply affirmed without understanding, affirmed without seeking to understand, affirmed dogmatically those things which they could not explain.

In the Divine Realm there is no conflict; there could not be. In the realm of perfect understanding there is no contradiction. In that realm where all things are known, the vision is clear. Therefore all those things we have indicated are evidences of the trend of the human mind to solve a Divine Mystery. But it cannot be solved along the paths of the mind. Only through perfect realization in the inner realm of Being is the Mystery known.

Was the Lord a man in the days of the manifestation?

This is a pertinent question, to which we make answer that the Lord is never a man. The Lord, as the Presence, is in every man and every woman potentially; and in many latently; and even in the few consciously. As we have beforetimes said to you, God the Eternal Love, the Father-Mother, is in every one of His children as the Heavenly Principle called the "Arche." In the prologue to the fourth gospel, and in the prayer known as "The Lord's Prayer," when understood as it was given in those days, the heavenly Arche or Principle of our Being, and the Amen or perfect realization of the Life of Being, are given. The Lord is within our sanctuary. Were it not true that the Divine Presence is there potentially, no one could ever apprehend in the least degree the Mystery of God. No one could apprehend in great degree that mystery, unless the potential forces within them were not only latent, but unfolded in large degree. That which is one in principle, and capable of being revealed, and becometh within the Being even unto manifestation, is capable of perfect realization. And of the human soul this is to be predicated, that it is capable of perfectly realizing God. Such a realization is Christhood. It is even Divine Christhood.

Now, the soul who perfectly realizes God may be functioning on these outer planes through the form that is spoken of as man. That soul is a human soul. That is, it is a spiritual Being; but it is designated human soul only on the human kingdom. That one is a human soul even as ye are men and women; but the forces potential within that one, have unfolded into the degree in which that one is able to transcend the lower conditions, the outer planes, the intermediary planes, and rise in consciousness into that state in which *God is known*—not only knowable, but is known through realization.

Who then was the Master known as Jesus Christ and worshipped as the only-begotten one of God? He was one of the Father-Mother's children, one amongst many brethren who was sent on a special mission to this world to meet His brethren and reveal to them, that is, to re-unveil to them, the Christ-state in which they once were, that, through the recognition of it, they might pursue it unto the realization of its glorious heritage again. He was sent to this world to reveal the Father-Mother unto such of His brethren as were able to receive the revelation, to recognise it, and to pursue it unto its sublime ultimate, which was the realization of the Father-Mother within.

The eternal Son of the Father-Mother is ever Adonai. Adonai is no man, nor is He ever a man. He is, in the Grecian or Alexandrian philosophy, spoken of as the Logos; and although the term is beautiful it is comparative, and we prefer to use the old Hebrew expression *The Adonai,* meaning the substantial Being of the Eternal Mystery revealed within the soul, even the Eternal Christ.

That Christ is within every man, every woman. He is Christ in you the hope of glory, or the glorious hope of the perfect realization. He is the Christ principle, the Christ Love, the Christ Light. And the end of soul-creation is high Christhood resulting from the Christ Love Principle, which is the Divine Principle, or Arche of the Being. Whilst Christ is in everyone thus as a Principle, Christ is nevertheless no man.

The Master came, not as the Eternal Son of God, the Eternal Christ. He came to unveil that One to the vision of His brethren. That is the meaning of the expression, which seems so hurtful to many through not understanding it, that He came to find only the lost sheep of the House of Israel. That was His mission. Others would take the

333

mission beyond that. He came to find Israel, that is, the souls who were once full of the Spirit, Issa; and the Radiance of the Lord, Ra; and the consciousness of the overshadowing and indwelling reigning Presence, even the Lord of Being, El. He came to find them. He came to find the sheep or members of the Divine Fold. In finding them, He found those who could respond to the vision of God.

Now what was the meaning of His Christhood? We have seen that He was not the Eternal Christ. Though He was Jesus in the sense that He was in the Jesus state, it was His life that was Jesus. For the word itself is not to be understood personally. Though a man or woman may have names with Divine meanings given to them, yet it does not signify that they are those Divine attributes in any personal sense. The Master was called Jesus by those who wrote the gospels, and not by those who knew Him best and loved Him and the Teachings. He was Jesus in His life as the Love-manifestor. He was the manifestor of the life of Love. He was the manifestor of the Love that heals, the manifestor of a compassion that turneth none away, the manifestor of that pity which takes under the wings of its protection all hurt children and creatures. The Jesus in Him was the glorious pure beautiful Angelic Love realized. It was the manifestation on the outer planes of the Divine principle within Him. Jesus is, therefore, divine, in the sense that it is a state begotten of the Divine principle within the Soul, and cannot be otherwise begotten. It is only begotten of the Divine Love in any one.

He was also Christ in state; but not in name. He was Christ in this sense, that the Heavenly Principle within, was so affected by the Divine Pole, the Divine Presence overshadowing, that it radiated the light of the heavenly wisdom. That is Christhood.

334

In the Hebrew language, and in the Hebrew terms, it is oft-times spoken of as "the anointed" or "the anointing"—"Thou anointest my head with oil." Thou dost fill my Sanctuary with the light and radiance of Thy Spirit through thy Love. Such was the relation of the term to Him as Christ.

He is still worshipped as Lord, the Lord Christ Jesus, showing how little the people understand the term. For the word translated Lord means, the reigning Presence within. A Divine Christhood is a state in a soul who has risen in consciousness through the holy estates of Jesushood, the manifestation of the Love, into Christhood, the radiant consciousness of the Presence overshadowing, and through it into the higher consciousness of the Divine Lord Presence dwelling within it, reigning as the Lord of Being. And when a soul realizes that glorious estate, it must needs thus speak of itself—*I have nothing of my own. I know nothing of myself, or from myself.* I can do nothing of myself or from myself. The Father-Mother, He speaketh within me; the words that I speak, He speaketh within me. The works that I do, He doeth through me. For that one, though of the innermost realm, is one with His brethren. Yet, though in the form of lowly estate, He is full of the consciousness of the Absolute One. For that One is manifest within the Being in what is called the Eternal Christ, or the Presence within. The Heavenly Principle is realized in the consciousness of the Presence within.

Such was the Christhood of the Master, that it was true to say of Him He was "Very man of very man," and He was "Very God of very God." Yet in this latter respect, it is not to be thought of in the sense of Deity. Every soul is of God, but not God. Every soul is of Him, for He is the Heavenly Principle in all. Yet they are not God, though from Him; not God, yet able to realize God as the Presence encompassing, and overshadowing, and indwelling.

335

Now this will throw light upon the Master's teachings. It will throw light upon your own history. It will throw light upon the purpose for which you are here in ministry. It has been said "There is a Christ in every man." There is the possibility of a Christ in everyone, say some. We would put it differently because it more truly expresses what is meant. *There is the possibility of Christhood in everyone.* There is but one Christ, the manifest of the Father-Mother. But the Christs of God are many. Yet each one is not *the Christ.* They are Souls who have attained to Christhood. And everyone who is in Christhood is of the community of the Christs of the Father-Mother. And these are interpenetrated from the innermost to the outermost of their Being with the magnetic stream of the Eternal Christ, who is the manifest Divine Substance in the Soul.

Now the purpose for which the Master came was to find certain souls. It is quite true He said "Other sheep there are who are not of this fold," they also must be brought. But first, the sheep who are in the fold, that is, those who had reached the state of the Christ-consciousness in great degree, but had laid it aside in order to descend for purposes of ministry to those who were so far down in their estate that they could not have received from souls who were functioning in the inner world. That was the first ministry of the Manifestation Days. It was the supreme ministry of the Master to find those who had been in the Kingdom. When He first began His ministry, He began it as John the Baptist. He was John the Baptist. It is one thing to read the stories nearly eighteen centuries after they were written, but quite another thing to stand in the consciousness of the light of the inner world, and know these things. For He was John, the man sent from God, He was the baptizer, but not with earthly waters, nor in earthly rivers, but with

336

the truth of God unto purification of life and the transmutation of knowledge into heavenly wisdom and power. He
was that John who came into the wilderness of this world,
and from the wilderness led those who were able to hear
Him, into the land whither their innermost being sought to
go, even the land of the Christhood. The degrees of His
ministry were these: the Baptism; the Jesus Manifestation;
the Christ radiating the consciousness of the Father-Mother;
then the unveiling of the Oneness in the Love of all Being.
They are all so clear when you see them, though they are
veiled in the Records.

He came to call souls into these states. His teaching,
or rather the Divine Wisdom that was given through Him,
was given for the purpose of finding those souls, not only
whilst He was here on the outer planes as the Manifestor,
but of finding long afterwards, those souls who could
respond. Have you ever asked yourself this question, how
it came about that four gospels, each professing to portray
the Master and teach what He taught, and to lead men and
women whither He Himself had gone, acting like a magnetic
charm upon the mind of the people, should unto this day
still remain uncertain writings wherein the Christ vision is
veiled? And also how it is that unto this day the western
world in its consciousness, should never have touched even
the hem of the Christ garment? How has it come about
that unto this day the world that took Him, or professed
to take Him, into its home, and make a feast for Him, and
build Sanctuaries in His name, and even bow down and
worship Him, should be a world that knows not yet the
meaning of redemption? Have you ever asked yourself
how it came about, that when you have read these gospels,
certain passages have moved you strangely? Well they
might! When you have read some of the epistles, the

mystical passages, you have been moved equally strangely! Well might you be so moved, for they were spoken by Him. The form was altered later by the writers of these Records, and these wonderful things that moved you are so placed, so covered up, so overlaid, that the meaning has remained hidden to this day.

Who was Jesus Christ the Lord? The western world will tell you what we have unveiled to you as to their beliefs, that He was the Eternal Son of God and the second Person of the Trinity. There are no persons in the Trinity. Our word "person" relates to the fashion of our life upon the outer planes. The word that is translated person, is in a sense untranslatable in our tongue, for it means substance. It is the hypostasis of the Divine, that Substance which is in every soul, even in its Trinity form. For the Father-Mother is the mystery Principle of Being in its two modes, active and passive, in its double manifestation of creative, nourishing and perfecting; and those two are in every soul as the Father-Mother, the Divine One in union. And the Trinity is also in that soul; for the Divine One in union as Father-Mother, brings the soul at last into the consciousness of the Son of God. Only the Son of God can understand God; that is, only one in that state. Only the Son of God can realize God. That one has attained the state of Sonship.

Now it is unto this estate that ye are called. For the nature of the Christhood such as the Master unveiled, is potentially within each one of you, and latent in you all. Nay more, it is on the threshold of manifestation in you. But the manifestation is through Jesus. No one can find Christ but through Jesus. The Greeks are said to have come saying, "We would see Jesus." Only through finding Jesus, can Christ be realized. That is, only by finding the state of the Jesushood in the manifestation of Love, the

beautiful Love of the Father-Mother, can a soul find Christ.
So Culture it! Cultivate Love. Love is the Divine Principle
within a soul, and only through its cultivation can the Christ
in you manifest. The first degree of manifestation is
Jesushood. The path to it is through John the Baptiser.
John not only represents the Master as the Messenger, but
the Love-principle. The word John means the Beloved. In
every soul is the Christ to be manifested.

Herein is truly a great mystery. It is the mystery of your
own Being which is to be realized in beautiful fulness by
following the path of Jesus. And the wonderful symbol of
the Cross on the Christian altars throughout the length and
breadth of this land and throughout the length and breadth
of Europe, speaks of Jesushood and Christhood. For the
Cross that stands upon the altar, illustrates the mystery of
the Christhood. The western world worships a crucified
Christ. It crucified Him; and it crucified the vision. It
crucifies unto this day. It crucifies the Lord of Glory
through its mistaken conceptions of the meanings of these
Divine Names. The Cross represents the path, and there
is no other way but by the Cross. The burden-bearing
imposed lovingly by the Father-Mother, is self-denial, self-
sacrifice, self-abandonment. No soul is asked to take the
third step on the Cross and surrender itself absolutely, to
abandon itself to the Divine absolutely, until it has learnt
the path of the first step, and attained in fulness the path
of the second. For the first is Jesus, the Love purifying
the Life; and not simply that, but manifesting tenderness
and compassion and gentleness. Jesus is great. He is
great amongst men; that is, the state is great. You can
understand the hymn in its mystical meaning which is sung
in the Churches, especially at missionary services—"Jesus
shall reign where'er the sun" shines. The western world

sings it, meaning the man who was the Master. But it is the state that must be understood. When Jesus, as the Jesus-state, reigns in men and Love is triumphant, then this world will be healed. Why, God will be manifest, not only in the mystery of His Being, but in His Love. The world will be full of Love. The world was once in the Jesus state, as a planetary human system.

The purpose of the Manifestation was to find those who could manifest this very state, and rise beyond it into the Christ radiance, in order that through such manifestation they might accomplish the redemption, or the bringing back of the children to that state. Only by Love can you create Love. Only by Love can you redeem to Love. Only by Love can you heal the Love that has been crushed and wounded and oppressed. Only by Love can you create confidence, fill the soul with the great glad hope. Only by Love can you interpret the nature of the Father-Mother. It is no good preaching Love except through manifesting it, for that is the only messenger of power for the healing of the children. By healing, we do not mean healing them only of their diseases begotten of tribulation in their body and their mind, but healing them in their spiritual nature, where doubt has grown until the whole vision has become darkened, and because of the lack of Love, distrust has sprung up and the heart has felt as if there could be no God, no Father-Mother whose name was Love. This is the path that the soul is called to follow, to take the steps of the Cross, the first, then the second, and then the third. Those who have never taken the first can take it now. It is the step of self-denial for one's own good, but especially beautiful it is when done for the good of others. It leads to Jesushood, to that life of Love which is all compassion and pity, that Love which, when passing through the prism of the mind, manifests itself as compassion and beautiful pity. Compassion is on the human kingdom, and is the reign of Love; pity is that same reign translated on to the creature kingdom. If you took these three steps as the three great crosses to bear—self-denial, self-sacrifice, the giving of oneself in service, self-abandonment, or the great surrender—then would you know all that is meant by the giving up of one's whole Being to be used by the Divine Love just as He decides, as He purposes. We have to use language and speak of the Father-Mother as if He were an individual, though there is infinitely more in our thought than any terms can express. For He is no man. He is no individual. He is the I Am, the Being at the heart of the world's mystery, of all mystery, your mystery. He is Being. He calls a soul to surrender, but leads it step by step to that state in which it can give itself up absolutely to His will regardless of everything, counting not the cost, never asking what will be the result to the personal. For that would be individual and personal. When the soul gives itself to the sublime vision, makes of itself an oblation unto the Lord, it does not think along those lines. It gives absolutely. It is the most difficult, it is true, to acquire; but the Father-Mother leads us on. And the nature of a Christhood in its path is the nature of the three steps on the Cross; and the three steps on the Cross represent the three great stages or degrees represented in the terms, Jesus, Christ, and our Lord. For only by the absolute self-abandonment of itself can a soul come into the high consciousness of the perfect realization of the Father-Mother, the Absolute Being within. In the Jesus state, a soul redeems through its life. In the Christ state, it radiates whilst it redeems, that is, in the sense of healing through Love and Wisdom. In the Christ state it radiates the light of Spiritual Christhood. In the Divine

Christ state, which is the Lord-consciousness, it is one with the Lord. And its ministry is then transcendently more, for it heals the soul, or rather—for it is that we mean—the Divine Love in that one, and through that one, heals the very soul, or the innermost.

Behold what a Christhood means, and see how impersonal it becomes. In the Jesus state, the love radiates in the sense of ministry spiritually, angelically, but along the more outward planes. In the Christ state (the state of Jesushood is spiritual Christhood, but there are higher degrees of it which we have to designate as Christ), in the Christ con-sciousness, that same love ministers, but in a more inward realm, so that when it touches the outer it only touches it from the more inward realm. In the state spoken of as Divine Christhood or the Lord consciousness, that soul is the vehicle of the outpouring of the magnetic stream of the divine world, something most difficult to unveil as to its real meaning.

Now behold ye the Path of Life and also the nature of the Life unto which ye are called; how transcendent, transcending everything of the outer; but always lowly, most lowly. The saints of God are lowly. The true saints in all the ages are the lowly ones. They are of humble heart, of pure and beautiful love. Ye behold the nature of the life unto which ye are called—what Jesushood is, and how the whole world would be changed if Jesushood were known and followed; how the whole national life would be purified; how the inter-national life would be harmonized if the people all rose up and lived the things they profess; how changed everything would become. Behold the nature of the life unto which you are called, even to radiate love, His Love, to be children of love, divine love, breaking compassion which is full of healing, and not forgetting to manifest pity and defend the helpless.

342

Behold how great is the state unto which ye are called, the higher state of Christhood. The Christos is the Radiant One within, the Presence that radiates around you, the Presence that acts upon your love-principle so that it radiates, that it not only gives an atmosphere of tenderness and beauty expressed in healing compassion and defending pity and in beautiful devotion, but it is so acted upon by the divine magnetic currents that its radiations give light within the Sanctuary, increasing more and more unto the perfect day of His becoming in the Great Realization.

Behold ye now the nature of the life ye are called to. It is in you, but it has to be cultured. The life ye are called to is the manifestation, the expression, the realization of the transcendent life. It is to be as Jesus and Christ in the world, the children of Love, the children of Light, the redeemers of men, and the illuminators of souls. Although only from the Father-Mother can light come called illumination, He uses His children to awaken that state in others of His children which enables them to respond to the divine influx, and be acted upon by it until they also are radiant within. So behold, yet once more, the nature of the life unto which ye are called. Ye are called not only to live as Jesus is said to have lived, and to do the works Christ is said to have accomplished, but ye are called to be One with your Lord, called upward, still farther upward into the high consciousness in which there is no longer any shadow, in which there is no limitation, in which God is known, that state in which ye are known again of God, meaning by that, that in your consciousness ye know Him in glorious fulness.

When it was said in the Epistolary Letters that in Christ was all the fulness of the Godhead bodily, and it was applied to the Master, little did the writer imagine what an interpretation would be put upon that saying or surely it would have been differently spoken or written; for God could not be contained within any of His children, even in a Divine Christ. He is the Absolute One who filleth all things, not only all souls upon this world, but all worlds within the glorious universe. And yet it is true that a human soul can be filled unto all fulness of its capacity with the Godhead, in so far as it can transcend everything that may be spoken of as limitation. There is no limitation there, except in this sense, that no soul is God any more than the dewdrop is the ocean, though both reflect the same splendour of a glorious sun at noontide. The soul can realize God in perfect fulness and know the mystery of Being, know it in the sense of understanding that mystery.

Oh! see ye unto what a Life ye are called, and the nature of it, the beauty of it, the glory of it, the transcendent power of it, the unspeakable wealth of it, the riches of the Wisdom and the Love of it from the Father-Mother! Aye more, as we have written elsewhere, the whole creation of this world, of the created things in this world, travaileth in pain, awaiting that healing which can alone come through the manifestation of the Sons of God. In proportion as souls rise into Divine Sonship, or true childhood to the Father-Mother, shall the world be healed. Who is to interpret the Father-Mother? Not the schools of the present day, who do not know Him. They only know the theories about Him presented in the philosophies and theologies. Who is to manifest Him? Those who realize Him. Who are to unfold Him? Those who are filled, even unto the body, with the power of His glorious Love and Light.

Children of the Father-Mother, if ye have dreamed that there were no great heights for you to climb, behold them, and let such a dream give place to true vision. If in the lowliness of your heart, ye have imagined you could never rise to such transcendent things as those of which we have often spoken to you, know this, that they are all in you, all in you as truly as the full glory of the rose, its glorious colour, its wonderful form, its rich fragrance, are all in the bud. It is a question of unfoldment, of growth. The mystery is in the rose, even the hidden mystery of its life, long before it makes manifest its mystery in its fulness of life, form, colour, fragrance. And this is a tiny expression of the Great Mystery that is in each one of you. These states are potentially and latently in all. They are greatly unfolded in some degrees in you.

See the nature of the life unto which ye are called, even to know the Mystery. For Christhood leads you into that consciousness. And the attainment of that consciousness was the meaning of the Manifestation known as Jesus Christ the Lord, to show souls the way into the realization of the Great Mystery, even the realization of God the Father-Mother. Ye are His children. Behold what manner of Love the Father-Mother hath bestowed upon you that ye should be called His children. Now are ye His children; and, though the mystery of the manner in which ye have become so is not yet fully unveiled to you, know ye this, that, *when He shall have become again in you through those holy estates, ye shall be in fashion* (that is in your attributes) *like unto Him, and ye shall know Him as He is.* That is, ye shall know the Mystery, understand the Mystery, the mystery of your own created life. The mystery of Being is found in Christhood. Unto that ye are called. Ye are called to make manifest the Divine Presence through the holy estates of Jesushood, the Love-Principle—Christhood, the radiance of the Love—the Lord consciousness, the summit of the way reached in oneness of Being, the Soul being one with the Lord of all Being.

345

The Mystery of Evil,

as set forth in

The Allegory of Cain and Abel.

In the Divine World all things are beautiful. In the Divine Creation all things are perfect.

In the manifestation of Life as fashioned by the Divine Love and manifested upon the spiritual world, all things are in perfect harmony. Though there are major notes and minor notes, the symphonic harmony in the Divine Creation is most complete.

There were no shadows upon the threshold of this world when God walked with man. There were great heights to climb, and the children of the Divine Love essayed to climb those heights, moving upward, ever upward, from crag to crag, from lower pinnacle to higher pinnacles of the Hills of God. There were no deep valleys in the sense of spiritual darkness, and pain begotten of the darkness, and sorrow issuing from the pain.

Though the limitations of childhood were necessarily imposed upon all the children according to their state, yet there was no hurt in the limitation. There was no wrong manifested because of the limitation. The direction of all things was true; and the manifestation through all things was beautiful.

Of the Divine Substance is man formulated and fashioned.

From and through the Eternal Spirit, man is quickened into a living Soul or Sanctuary, where all things scintillate, vibrate, radiate.

Man is, in his true state, a manifest expression of the Eternal Mystery of the Father-Mother. If man had remained in the consciousness of that state, the tragedy represented in the story of Cain and Abel would never have been known, and, consequently, could have found no repetition from age to age in all the children.

*   *   *   *

The Garden of Eden was a perfect garden. It was full

347

of Life, and the Life was clothed in the beauty of perfect bloom. The whole garden was aromatic with the perfumes of the graces of the Spirit.

The Garden of Eden was a holy place. It was the inner state of the Being. The waters of its rivers were living waters; and they not only refreshed, but nourished wheresoever they flowed. As a place of divine manifestation, the Garden of Eden was a glorious reality, for in it God walked with man. Within man's own consciousness the Eternal Mystery was known. Man communed with the angels, and rose into the vision of the Presence, and heard that Voice which speaketh as no man speaketh.

The world then was young. The term 'young' is generally used in relation to limitation of years and form, attributes and experience; but that is not the spiritual significance of it. To be young is to be buoyant. It is to be full of Life, to radiate Joy, to pour forth Love. For, in the Divine World there is no age, except the hoary radiance of Eternal Wisdom when the Being attains.

In those unfallen days, the whole world was young. It was buoyant. It was glad. It was full of spiritual exhilaration. The breaths of the Heavens wafted through its planes unto the children dwelling upon them. It was the Golden Age.

The unfallen world was a glorious reality. Few today seem to believe that it was so. So many are the voices calling, and the messages of the voices are so contrary, that it is difficult for the human mind to grasp the significance of Divine Things, until the vision be healed again. It is one thing to believe the traditional stories and interpretations of them concerning an unfallen world; it is another thing to know that it was unfallen, and to see it in its unfallen glory.

*   *   *   *

Yet it has to be recorded that the change did take place, and that it brought about such a tragedy as is set forth in the story of Cain and Abel. For that is not a personal story. It is mystical. As the terms Adam and Eve represent the Substance and the Spirit of the Eternal Father-Mother in man, and the realization of Yahweh; so Cain and Abel represent two states in manifestation of the Being.

It is a story embodying the resultant of planetary tragedy.

It is a parable illustrating the conflict which grew up in the lives of all the children.

It is also an allegory setting forth the direction of the real spiritual Being, and the attitude of the Mind in its fallen state. For Cain and Abel represent the Mind and the Intuition.

Cain is said to have been the elder. And it is true that, in the order of manifestation, the Mind is the elder; for the Intuition, whilst present in the very mystery of Being itself, comes into manifestation later in point of time, as the outcome of upgathered experience.

Yet Abel represents even more than the Intuition understood as a faculty, or as a realm of ministry. He represents the very Being! Yet in outer ministries, the Mind is the elder. That means, that it is the more outward in manifestation.

*   *   *   *

The tragedy is set forth in the story as the resultant of partaking of the Tree of Knowledge of good and evil. In the midst of the garden was the Tree of Life, the central Mystery of God within the individuated Being. Of that Tree man could eat. It was meant that he should eat of it, even unto the realization of the Divine Mystery. He was to nourish himself upon the Eternal Mystery of the Love and Wisdom of the Father-Mother.

The Tree of Knowledge of Good and Evil which also was of the very nature of the Tree of Life, and related to it, but which might bring evil, was the power in man to choose. The power to choose is given to all created Beings. If all life for the Soul were fixed as to the path it must pursue, the methods it must seek, the circles it must perform, there would be no individualizations. There could be no individuality, free, spontaneous, glorious, and most blessed in its giving in ministry.

It is of the nature of Love that it does not contain within itself any spirit of bondage. Divine Love knows no bondage. When the Great Love creates systems or fashions worlds, there is at the heart of each the Tree of Life in the midst of the Garden. It is the Tree of Power to know, to act, to realize. It may become the knowledge of evil as well as good. That depends upon the uses to which the Soul puts its power. It is the Will in its power to choose. Great laws are set in operation, and these have to be followed to find the perfect realization of Life; but it is given to the individual system and world, and, consequently, to the individual Soul, to choose from time to time in his and her experience, the path to be pursued.

It is out of this very liberty that divinity is made manifest through a Soul. Man is not a machine set in motion and compelled by the exigencies of his creation, to go in that one way. He is a living Soul. He is vibrant. He has deep consciousness. He is divine in his attributes. He has power to choose.

It was this very power resident at the heart of the planetary life that led to the moving of the Planet away from the Divine Kingdom, and the tragic change wrought in the state of her mind. It is this very power in you that gives you freedom of choice.

It was after man partook of the Tree of the Knowledge of evil as well as the good, that it was said the gates of Eden were closed, and the Angel with the flaming sword guarded its gates. And it was after that act in the drama that it is recorded that Elohim said, Lest man partake of the Tree of Life in the midst of the Garden in this state, it must be guarded.

And thus, that which is the very heart of the Great Mystery of Being itself, became veiled. It was veiled from man's vision in order to defend the Heavens. Aye, it was veiled to defend man himself. What would not fallen humanity do with a knowledge of the Eternal Mystery, when you know what humanity does with the knowledge it acquires of a physical and mental and magical occult order? So there is a wisdom even in that monogram of the driving of man out of Eden, which is entirely hidden from those who cannot understand the Divine Mystery of man's Being.

*   *   *   *

But ever since the great Descent was accomplished, the struggle to return has been as the surging of the great Deep, in all the beautiful ones who knew something of the Mystery. The Soul is said to have offered up again to the Eternal Love, its best sacrifice. It has sought that One with whom it walked in Eden. The Being in its yearnings has sought to consecrate all its powers unto the Father-Mother. But the darkness has been great, in many ages, aye, through countless ages, though in some ages worse than in others, with the result that many tragedies have taken place.

The writer of the story of Cain and Abel understood the

mystery. It is reminiscent not only of individual history, but also of planetary. It is always to be understood as entirely soulic. If shadows are cast by it athwart the threshold of our vision, there is nevertheless a light breaking from the very heart of it, revealing the divinity of the human unit.

*   *   *   *

Now, Cain and Abel represent the two degrees of manifestation in sacrifice which express the Being's best desire, and the fallen Mind's way. Abel was a keeper of sheep. That is, he was a shepherd. Cain was a tiller of the ground. That implies that he was as a gardener. Abel represents the shepherdhood of the Soul. His ministry is shepherdhood over the flocks—the thoughts, the feelings, the desires. Cain represents the Mind tilling the earth, seeking for the fruits of the substance on the outer planes, a tiller of the astral and occult, or super-physical and mental worlds.

Now, there was nothing wrong surely in Cain's offering. In itself it should have been as beautiful as that of Abel. If Abel offered the firstling of his flock with the fat thereof, he only offered that which was most natural to him as a shepherd. And if Cain offered the fruits of the ground, surely as a tiller of the ground, he offered that which was most natural and beautiful in sacrifice. Indeed, if the story were a literal record, Cain's offering excelled Abel's offering unspeakably, for he offered the beautiful fruits of the earth, whereas Abel is said to have caused a beautiful creature to involuntarily lay down its life in order to make a sacrifice for him.

Mystically, however, the sacrifice of Abel is the sacrifice of the Lamb of God. The Firstling of the Flock is the first fruit of the Lamb of God. The Lamb of God is the Sacrificial Spirit of the Eternal Love within the Being.

352

When a Soul offers its Love, it offers all. When it offers the Lamb of God, it sacrifices its Being.

Abel represents the prophet, the seer, the sacrificer who is a priest after the order of Melchisedek. He embodies the Soul's oblation. To offer the firstling of the flock, with the fat thereof, was to offer the first fruits of his Soul's love, his very Being, with all the enrichment thereof. Abel offers his inner Being to the Divine. And, when that is offered, all the rest of the Being is shepherded, and becomes ministrant in shepherdhood.

Cain offered of the fruits of the ground.

The Mind is not the shepherd; it has to be shepherded.

The Mind is not the prophet; it has to be illumined.

The Mind is not the seer; it has to be taught and unveiled.

The Mind is not the priest after the order of Melchisedek, though it can render priestly office in sweet and gracious ministry.

When the Mind brings the fruits of its tilling, the resultants of its service, and lays these on the altar, it must bring them in lowly spirit, with sweet and pure purpose, without heart of envy or earthliness. To offer the fruits of the Mind's service to God, is surely as sacred as to offer the fruits of the shepherdhood! But they must be offered sacredly.

How must they be offered as the ultimate? They must not be offered in the sense of taking the place of the inner, but only as the love-gifts of the Mind, and the outworking of the Divine from the Innermost. They are to be the expressions of love, the revealings of our Soul's deepest yearning, the testimonies that all our ministry is for God,

353

begotten of Him, sustained by Him, inspired through His Holy Spirit in us, and wrought for His glory alone.

Abel is the prophet: Cain is the mental teacher.

Abel is the realizer: Cain is the reflector.

They are brothers, and should ever be in harmony.

If Abel appear to be the younger, it is only in point of manifestation; for, in nature he is of the very Substance and Spirit of God.

Cain is also of that Substance. But the plane of his manifestation is of lower degree. For the Mind is a luminary to accompany the innermost Being, reflecting back the glory of the Heavens. It has its function to perform, and its office to fill.

In the unfallen days Abel and Cain were brothers. They were at one. They worshipped the same Lord. They served the same glorious Love.

In the fallen state the Mind is turned earthward. This came to pass through the Mind of the Planet undergoing change.

As with the Mind of the Planet, so is it with the Mind of all the children. The Mind tills the ground. All its thoughts are centred on the earth. It values the outwardness of things. It measures Life by the phenomenal. Its judgment concerning the mass or sum of a Soul, is by the resultant upon the outermost planes, or super-planes, or the occult plane of intellectual knowledges and powers.

In the fallen state the Intuition and the Mind have been, as it were, at war. Cain has slain Abel. The Mind has oppressed the Intuition. This has taken place in the individual system as well as in the planetary world. Men have valued Mind, and looked askance at the Intuition.

Men have exalted Mind, and brought low the Intuition. Men have set up the resultants of their tilling of the ground, and worshipped those as God; whilst they have laid low, even unto death, that power within them by which heavenly secrets are discerned, true spiritual vision is come at, and the glorious realization of the Overshadowing and Encompassing Presence becomes the heritage within the consciousness of the Being.

The works of Cain are manifest throughout the planetary history, since the Descent. Through all the races, through all the ages, aye, through all the religious manifestations, they have been wrought. In the embodiments of the mystery in man and woman, the woman as representing the Intuition has known oppression and humiliating subjection, even unto the death of her true womanhood. That is an illustration of the outworking of this very principle of the wrong choice, the wrong direction, the false vision, the mirage, the Maya, the illusion, the vain imaginings, from the intermediary realm to the outermost plane of life.

*   *   *   *

In the allegory we see the inversion of the all-important part of the Divine Mystery in Man. The tragedy of evil in the world is too real to our consciousness, to be blotted out by any affirmations that there is no evil in the world. And the evil that is in the world will continue until the Mind, Cain, be healed, and the Prophet, Abel, be again triumphant.

And the healing of Cain can only be through the Prophet. That means, that the Mind can be healed only from the Divine Centre of the Being. And it can be accomplished only through the sacrifice of the Being in the offering up of the Firstling of the Flock with the enrichment thereof— the beautiful Love-principle, and all that it has gathered unto itself. It will bring back Eden, the holy state, the state of Peace in which is found true harmony; the state of Joy wherein the symphony is heaven-born; the state of Radiance because the veil will be taken away, and the Cloud of His Presence be once more upon the Sanctuary.

This is the day of the healing of Cain.

It is the day of the resurrection of Abel.

It is the day of the restoration of Eden.

The flaming sword that is said to have guarded the way of the Angel of His Presence, is once more the Sacred Flame of His Spirit illumining the Being, throwing wide open the gates leading into the state of Eden, that the Being may enter in to the great Realization, and find there again the Tree of Life amid the Rivers of Living Waters, whose leaves, fruits, and manifestations of service, are for the healing of the nations.

For the nations can only be healed through the Light of the Presence interpreted in the Love of the Indwelling One, manifested in our attributes as the graces of His Spirit, re-interpreted in our ministries as the leaves full of balm. The world can only be healed through the communities of nations; the communities of nations through the communities that compose them; the communities through the families that build them up; and the families through the individual lives coming into the consciousness of the Great and Holy Love.

The day is coming when the blood of Abel shall no longer cry from the ground unto Cain. By that is meant, when the beautiful powers of the Soul shall no more be so impoverished as to be as dead, but be again filled with Life from on high to help Cain to till the ground, and bring him once more into beautiful fellowship, and sweet brotherhood. Then the Mind shall be in tune with the Inner Being, and

356

in harmony with the Divine Centre. For, when the Mind is chastened, healed and illumined, all its trouble will be changed into the great and holy calm; and the waters that were tempestuous will once more be beautiful with Divine Peace.

This is the day of the healing of the sin brought upon the world through its wrong choice. It is the day of the healing of the Mind of the world; for the Oblation has accomplished that healing in all the reaches where the Angelic Heavens are now able to minister to the children there. And it is the day when the lower reaches are also being healed through the outpouring of Heaven's Light and Life into them, and the ministry of Heaven's Love unto the perfect healing of them.

And if the Mind of the world be perfectly healed, what a radiant world it will become again! And everyone who is healed is contributing to the sum of that healing. For, if the Cain in every life is healed, and the whole Being grows to be one with the Divine, that one becomes a medium through which the divine ministry is given to the world.

*   *   *   *

The mystery of evil is the mystery of Cain. The healing of Cain is the healing of evil. The day is hastening when that mystery shall be understood, and the perfect healing through the understanding, be fully accomplished. For the mystery of the Immanence of the Father-Mother in all His children, shall yet be apprehended. And it shall be known how that Love never forgot His children throughout all the ages, and how that Love has been able to find Cain in the land of Nod, and to heal him. For Nod is the state of the wanderer and wayfarer.

*   *   *   *

Now, in this unveiling there is much meaning for all.

And for you reader most specially there is the call to sacrifice in the fulness of your days, the Firstling of your Flock—the first things begotten of Divine Love in you, with all the enrichment thereof, as Prophet-children of the Father-Mother, Seers seeking the vision of Him, Priests in sacred office desiring only to mediate for Him.

Let Cain's influence in you find the perfect healing now; and the Abel principle in you ascend from the ground of all earthliness, into triumphant power, to make manifest that which is most glorious, even the Mystery of the Father-Mother in you as His child.

It is thus alone Souls can come to see once more in manifested form, the nature, the attributes, the wisdom and the radiance of the Love of God.

It is thus alone that Souls can be permanently won and healed, restored and transformed, and find for themselves that glorious realization wherein they will become partakers of the transcendent mystery of transfiguration, when the whole Being becomes clothed with the Radiance of the Love of the Father-Mother.

Unto this end may ye live. For this sacred purpose are ye here, even that the Father-Mother may be glorified.

Unto Him who has ever loved us with the Love immeasurable, the Eternal and Ever Most Blessed Holy Father-Mother, King of all Heaven's Kings and Lord of All, our Lord, our Radiance, we would ascribe the praise and the honour and the power and the glory; for the Kingdom within us is His, and He hath given it unto us as our Inheritance from Him, that we may possess the consciousness for evermore of His Indwelling Glory.

The Festival of Easter.

A Planetary and Soulic Event.

EASTER DAY. The Festival of Easter is one associated with the historical setting given to the resurrection of the Master known as Jesus. It is the morning on which He is supposed to have risen from the dead, three days after His crucifixion. It was the morning on which the angels once more visited these planes to liberate Him and to wait for those who came to His tomb in order to proclaim unto them that He had risen. It should, therefore, be a day of true spiritual Soul rejoicing, because it is not only commemorative of that supposed event, but it is also the testimony to the Soul's triumph over the world-powers represented by those who crucify, and the elemental powers represented by the grave, and the darkest powers which oppress the Soul, implied in Spiritual death. It is celebrated, not only in commemoration of that great event, but as the perpetual prophecy of the triumph of all who follow Jesus Christ. For it is viewed supremely as the one outstanding event in religious history, which demonstrates to the believer that death and the grave can no longer have any terrors, or any power to retain the Soul.

*   *   *   *

There is something significant in the Easter Festival being placed in Spring. Though it is a movable feast in the Church's calendar, it nevertheless moves within the months of Spring in this hemisphere. For Easter Day is one prophetic of glorious triumph over all elemental limitations, all adverse conditions, all the contracting and preventive influences and all the breaths of Winter, in the Soul's experience. It is the triumph within the Being of the divine potencies, the ascendency of the manifest Life of the Father-Mother contained in the Heavenly Principle of the Soul's Being, by which the elemental soils are penetrated, and the life rises into the clear atmosphere where is found the Radiant Presence, to drink in of the glory of that Radiance, and to become clothed with the glory that Radiance gives; to be stimulated by the magnetic flow from that glorious Sun, until every attribute inherent in the Being unfolds unto perfect manifestation.

Thus, Easter Morning is like Spring when all nature is awakening in this hemisphere, quickened anew in its hidden life for manifestation, rejuvenated through the glorious magnetic Life-stream flowing from the Divine Kingdom entering the atmosphere of the planet. For the advent of Spring is a divine advent, though it would not be so spoken of in the Church's calendar. It is a divine advent of the most momentous nature for this planet and all her children. Yearly and æonially, Spring has come, and the children of this world have looked upon it as one of the natural events begotten of the planet's motion round the sun. And it has received explanations which are perfectly logical and beautiful and reasonable, from the scientific standpoint, whose office it is to observe and correlate phenomena within the manifest world. To science, Spring comes as one of the seasons, and is supposed to be the outcome of the inclination of the polar axis towards the ecliptic, which brings this hemisphere more directly under the sun's rays. And this seems quite a feasible explanation, because in our autumn the tilt of the polar axes causes the southern hemisphere to be inclined twenty-three and a half degrees towards the ecliptic, with the result that, in our autumn, Spring comes at the antipodes.

But surely there is something more in it than merely the inclination of the poles of the earth toward the imaginary plane known as the ecliptic? Oft-times, notwithstanding this new direction given to the planet's motion, in our hemisphere, for many weeks Spring will be retarded. Of course, that can be explained atmospherically. But the atmospheric problem must needs be solved.

With the coming of Spring in this hemisphere, as with its return in the southern hemisphere, great magnetic changes take place. Tremendous storm-winds blow about the period of the vernal and the autumnal seasons. These are called the equinoctial gales. Oft-times these storm-winds seem most devastating; and they are always, more or less, disturbing. Yet, after they have passed, the atmosphere of the planet seems remarkably purified, re-charged with some exhilarating power which even the human children feel. In a sense everything has within itself the feeling of some strange mystery. In the young, it is manifest in joy. In the aged, it becomes renewal of strength and the consciousness of rehabilitation. In nature, it is revealed in the outpouring of song, of form, of colour and of fragrance.

When the sun is highest, speaking in common language, during our midsummer, and its power to give not only greater light, but greater heat, all the consciousness of the mystery of Spring seems to have passed, though fruits are ripening unto harvest. It is, therefore, not when the sun is highest and greatest in power upon the manifest world in this hemisphere that Spring breaks forth. It is actually halfway between mid-winter and mid-summer. Nor is it when the planet is nearest the sun, as it is in our mid-winter, nor furthest from the sun, as it is in our mid-summer, but at a point in its orbit in which its distance is its mean distance from the sun.

Here we are face to face with a sublime mystery. We have called it a divine advent; and so it is. It is the advent, or the coming into the planetary heavens, with mighty rushing wind, of the Eternal Spirit expressed in the life-giving stream of magnetic nature which flows out from the sun parallel to its equator and which forms the Divine Plane or Ecliptic. In that stream the planet does not always move, though once it did. It only touches it, passing through it for a brief period twice in its yearly round. Those periods are what have been termed the vernal and autumnal equinoxes. The orbit of the planet, which forms its own ecliptic, is so arranged that during the third to fourth weeks in March and the third to fourth weeks in September, the planet moves through that Stream, its orbit intersecting at those points, called the node, the Divine Plane which we have termed the Divine Ecliptic. That magnetic stream contains many elements which stimulate life, re-quickening, reviving, re-clothing and filling the world with beauty and hope and joy; for Spring surely is of all seasons the time of joy. As the planet moves in its orbit towards the point of intersection of that divine stream with its orbit, it becomes magnetically disturbed, strangely attracted, made to vibrate in ways profoundly mysterious even to the scientist; its motion being accelerated as if it must needs hasten through that stream. And, having passed through it, a process of retardation takes place in its motion until its action becomes normal. It is the approach to this stream that brings the influences of the new life into the planet, quickening and preparing for the reception of the inrush of that stream for one full week. It is the coming into the atmosphere of the magnetic elements of that divine flow, which sets up the conditions in the atmosphere of the planet resulting in great magnetic changes. The planet in this hemisphere is rejuvenated, and even the hemisphere turned away from the direct rays

363

of the sun, is also rejuvenated, receiving that which will enable it to go on nourishing in the secret and the silence. Even Souls are nourished by the outpouring of that Stream, for it passes through all the planes of the planet. It goes right through the planet, finding its centre, nourishing that Mystery of Being contained there which no human eye could look upon, and which none understand unless it be given to them to understand from the Divine Kingdom.

*   *   *   *

It has often been questioned how it was that the Church did not fix the date of Easter, instead of having it a movable feast. Little do they understand that the true date for Easter is the beginning of the fourth week in March. Of course, the Church associates it with the resurrection of the Master, and not with anything planetary. Therefore, when we say it should be in that week, we mean that there is a great relationship in a planetary sense between the Soul's rejuvenation and triumph, and the rejuvenation which comes to the planet when it is passing through the Stream. And never was it more so than in these days. For the great changes effected in the circuli of the planetary heavens wherein its atmosphere is contained, by the great work known as the Oblation or Sin-offering, have prepared the way for the transmuting and life-giving power of the Divine Life-Stream flowing through the Divine Ecliptic, to accomplish the redemption of this world and all its children by changing the Elemental Kingdoms into the true spiritual status in which originally they were fashioned, and bringing to bear upon the children of this world a more direct spiritual ministry to influence them to walk in the beautiful ways of life, seeking only joys that are unalloyed, and love that is Angelic.

Easter Day is, therefore, beautifully prophetic. It is

the day of the Soul's awakening, when God anew calls forth His Son into glorious manifestation as one coming forth from the dead. It is Esther's day, for Esther is the Soul. The story of Esther is the story of a divine Soul. It is a drama in allegorical setting of the Soul's deposition, or descent through the inimical influences that came upon it, the overthrow of those elemental influences, and the restoration of the Soul to the Right Hand of her Lord. Easter Day, though held as a festival to celebrate the supposed resurrection of the Master, is none other than the day of Esther, when the angels are once more met in the way, the grave of material things is forsaken, the grave-clothes are laid aside, the sepulchre stone is rolled away, all hindrance to divine liberty overcome, and the Lord of Being beheld once more.

The Way of Divine Healing.

THE MINISTRY OF HEALING. Healing is one of the most beautiful ministries committed to the care of man. It is an office which should ever be held sacred, never thought lightly of, nor used for personal ends. The power to heal is a gift bestowed by the Eternal Love alone; and if it seem to belong to the individual healer, it is only because the Divine Love is able to make use of some special faculty with which that one has been endowed.

There is much that passes for spiritual and divine healing which we could not possibly bring under the cover of so sacred a science. Of these things we will write later. But true divine healing is ever soulic. It is of God through the healer and in the healed. It is never personal, though the personal touch may be used. It is never merely individual, though the individual is the vehicle of its expression. It is always, and must ever be so regarded, of that most glorious One from whom all Being proceeds, and in whom and from whom alone power is realized for the healing of souls.

That man of himself cannot truly heal, is manifest upon various planes of experience. We would not deny for a moment that comfort and apparent healing of superficial diseases, come at times to patients under medical treatment, and even where organic trouble has manifested itself; for many in the medical profession are by nature true physicians, and would be most successful healers if they were liberated from the bondage in which *materia medica* holds them. Were they able to understand, not simply the bodies of men and women in a physiological sense, and the pathology by which physiologists pursue their diagnosing of disease, but also the other vehicles of the Being, the nature and constitution of the human Ego or Soul, and the true pathology by which alone a Soul can be understood, and the inner

367

cause or causes of the outer manifestations in what is termed disease, they could accomplish much.

To heal is not to patch up. To heal is not simply to suspend pain or the outer manifestation of some trouble in the organism. To heal truly is to get at the cause, which is usually deep seated in the mind or in the emotion of the individual, and by a true spiritual pathology, to proceed from there outward, driving the trouble out of the vehicle through healing the cause of it in the mind, or in the emotion, or, it may be, in the love-principle, or even in the higher will. In most of the healing imparted through the medical faculty, and through certain forms of mental science which oft-times is misnamed spiritual healing, all that is accomplished is the temporary comforting of the mind or body of the individual. And indeed in many instances the means used to give that comfort, which is mistaken for true healing, sow the seeds of other tribulations which make themselves manifest by and bye.

The whole world cries out for healing. Some are sick in their bodies. Some are sick in their astral or super-sensuous bodies. Some are sick in their mental bodies. Some are sick in their etheric bodies, and others in the stream of the emotion. Upon one or more of these planes of consciousness will most men and women be found to be suffering. And there are those who suffer still more inwardly, some even to the very centre of their Being. All organic trouble proceeds from within. In this it must be distinguished from superficial troubles imposed from and by the conditions around the life. Organic trouble is the expression in the vehicle of astral disturbance, or misdirection in the life-stream of the astral body produced through wrong desire. Some organic troubles are the issues of the inversion of the polarity of the mind. Some mental and astral, as well as physical troubles, are the direct outcome of hurt in the etheric body. The etheric body is the real spiritual vehicle, through which the Being, when perfectly healed and in a state of perfect love, would manifest on the true spiritual world called the Angelic Kingdom. When that body is hurt, the other vehicles which are necessary to the Being for expression upon the realms of outer manifestation, suffer and, as a result, oft-times most serious organic and functional troubles ensue. Some of the functional troubles are the direct outcome of the wrong direction of the magnetic currents of the emotional stream which flows through the etheric body.

*   *   *   *

Now, superficial troubles may be helped through purification of the body from without; others through changing the direction of the thought; and others through helping the mind to desire beautifully. But these things, though they are beautiful in themselves and must be applied by the sufferer to the body, the mind, and the desire body, cannot heal the etheric body when it is deeply wounded. That body can be touched unto healing only from the very innermost. By no outward processes can it be healed unto restoration, but only from the Divine Centre. THE EMOTION IS A MAGNETIC STREAM THAT CIRCULATES THROUGH THE ETHERIC BODY, JUST AS THE BLOOD CIRCULATES THROUGH THE PHYSICAL BODY, AND THE MAGNETIC STREAMS THROUGH THE ASTRAL BODY. THE EMOTION, WHICH IN APPEARANCE TO THOSE WHO CAN DISCERN FROM THE INNERMOST WOULD RESEMBLE AN ATMOSPHERE, MAY BE COMPARED TO A STREAM OF BEAUTIFUL WATER BECOMING CHARGED WITH MAGNETIC CURRENTS GREATER THAN THOSE BELONGING TO THE NATURAL

STATE OF THE ELEMENTS COMPOSING THE STREAM. THOSE MAGNETIC CURRENTS ARE THE DIRECT OUTCOME OF THE POLAR ACTION OF THE LOVE-PRINCIPLE. WHEN THAT OUTFLOW FROM THE LOVE-PRINCIPLE IS NOT TRULY DIRECTED, OR IS IN ITSELF NOT TRULY PURE AND BEAUTIFUL, IT AFFECTS THE EMOTION, AND THE EMOTION AFFECTS THE ETHERIC BODY, JUST AS WRONG MAGNETIC INFLUENCES AFFECT THE LIFE-STREAM OF THE BODY, THE BLOOD, AND AS A RESULT THE BODY ITSELF THROUGH WHICH IT COURSES TO NOURISH AND VITALIZE. WHEN THE ETHERIC BODY IS HURT, THE WHOLE LIFE IS WOUNDED. IF THE HURT BE GRIEVOUS, THE WHOLE LIFE DEEPLY SUFFERS. IF THE WOUNDING BE THE RESULT OF AGES OF MISDIRECTION, THEN LIFE AFTER LIFE WILL HAVE BEEN LIVED MORE OR LESS IN A STATE OF ACUTE BURDEN-BEARING.

It is this which lies at the heart of many organic troubles. The Soul's history for ages is expressed in the very troubles themselves. To understand these is to get to the within of the Being. No one can get there unless they be full of lowliness begotten of pure and beautiful love and reverence. But the true healer will get there, for he will be full of love and lowliness and reverence. Such an one will understand through divine illumination, the history expressed in the organic trouble. In so doing, the healer can direct the Being to be healed, unveiling just so much of the afflicted one's history as may be wise and necessary to reveal, and showing to that one how again to find the Divine Centre of his or her own Being.

It is from that Centre alone that the healing can come. It is God within that Being who alone can accomplish the healing. By means of the Blessed Presence Overshadowing the magnetic pole of the sufferer, stimulating it into direct spiritual activity, and giving to it power of equipoise that it may be celestially sustained, perfect healing of the whole

Being may be accomplished. For those things impossible to man of himself, are always possible where the Eternal Soul reigns.

*   *   *   *

It might be of service here to show by illustration the supreme inwardness of divine healing. Many indeed seem to think that all disease is simply physical, and produced only by outward conditions or mental states, and that no such thing as disease ever touches the life beyond the physical and mental realms. There are many who strenuously deny that any hurt can come to the inner Being of man, because he has within him, in an individuated form, the Divine Principle of Life. That man can be hurt from the outermost realm of his life through his various vehicles to the very innermost realm of his Being, we do know. Nay more! We also know that, although man is of the Divine Substance in his Being, and all his vehicles were originally formed out of most glorious spiritual substances in varying degree of density, yet it is not an impossible thing for disaster to come to his vehicles, and even to the substances out of which they have been fashioned. It is even possible amid certain well-known conditions in this world in its fallen state, for man, through his vehicles, to be so injured in his inner life, that spiritual atrophy takes place. And when such a state is entered upon, there is a gradual weakening of all spiritual desire, of all yearning for beautiful divine realization, of the crying out for the Light whose radiance is our Life. Atrophy is the beginning of death. Death is the deadening of the substances, and the cessation of the flow of the magnetic stream. The process may be slow, but it is actual. The atrophication of all the powers of the Being, means the gradual weakening of the Soul's attributes, the changing of its very substance until its state

371

is such that it cannot be regarded as Divine Substance, any more than the substances which in these outer planes of this world now designated matter truly represent the divine substances which once they were, or even their spiritual state during the unfallen days of the planet.

True, the Divine Spirit never dies. It is ever full of quickening power, illumining power, glorifying power, transfiguring power, transmuting power. But the Divine Spirit can only operate truly through a vehicle in a true state of polarity. It can manifest only within substances which are responsive to its operation. And if the feminine properties of a Being, which are the substances out from which that Being takes fashion, become so changed through wrong desire, wrong direction, wrong purpose, that the Spirit cannot operate, *then the Spirit is withdrawn*; and it may be that that beautiful ego which became in its consciousness an individuation of the Divine Consciousness, ceases to be such an individuation, its consciousness being withdrawn because contained in the Spirit.

Nothing is lost in the universe in the ultimate as to Substance and Spirit. But it is sometimes necessary in the evolution of manifest worlds and the life manifested through individuated beings such as humanity represents, to make the earth, so to speak, "melt with fervent heat" and resolve all the elements back into their original states of incandescency that they may be purified and separated and regathered for purposes of new manifestation. In the case of a human Soul this does not often happen, blessed be that Love who never leaves any individuated life, however far away it may have gone in desire, whilst there is the possibility of healing it and bringing it back into a state of beautiful love and the consciousness of the Presence within it.

Though there is nothing in the ultimate lost as to

Substance and Spirit, it is thus possible for a human Soul to lose its identity. Such an event, though rare, has been passed through. This experience is the eternal loss. No Soul ever knows that loss except by choice. It can come to a Soul only through persistent refusal of the Divine Love in its ministry. And, of course, this does not cover simply one life, but thousands of incarnations.

The healing given by the Great Love to souls is so wonderful that such an experience as we have described is almost outside the range of the Soul's evolution. The beauty of the ministry of that Love has oft-times been illustrated, shown forth in lives, in story and in allegory. It has been proclaimed by the true prophets and seers and priests of the Kingdom of God.

*　　*　　*　　*

As an illustration of these things we might take a notable case recorded in the Old Testament. It is that of Naaman the Syrian. This story is presented in narrative form as an actual event in the history of the healing given by the prophet Elisha. In the story Naaman is represented as a great man, but a leper. Captain of the hosts of the King of Syria, he was able to seek and have the best treatment that could be vouchsafed to him for the healing of his tribulation. But it is recorded that he could not be healed. The story opens beautifully when it is understood in its mystic significance, for it must not be for one moment imagined that it could have been literal. The terms which are used are full of meaning in themselves, and, when understood, reveal how the story, whilst presented as the history of a man, is soulic. There are five leading actors in the story—Naaman, the Hebrew maid, Naaman's servant, the prophet and the prophet's servant.

Now, Naaman represents a state of the mind. The mind

has great power for ruling, for overcoming, for conquering, for acquisition. Naaman was a great man. He had great wealth. He had large retinue. He had great thoughts about himself, about his powers and his conquests. He stood in high countenance with the king of Syria; but he was a leper.

The land of Syria speaks of beautiful things. In it are the Galilean hills. Those hills are high states of spiritual consciousness where glorious vision is beheld. The king of Syria, when that land is a pleasant and beautiful land in its spiritual atmosphere, is the Divine. The mind stands in high countenance or beautiful estate before the Divine Presence who is within us. And this is even so through the Love of the Eternal and Ever Most Blessed One, though the mind, like Naaman, be touched with leprosy. Naaman was great in his conquests. He had gathered much treasure to himself. He had manifested his prowess and in so doing had, by his powers, carried away much out of the land of Israel. But he was a leper. No one could heal him in the state of mind in which he was. Though he tried the means placed at his disposal through his conquests, all failed. Naaman, therefore, represents the mind in a state of wrong polarity, resulting in spiritual darkness, and issuing in what is termed leprosy, or spiritual atrophy.

Amongst his conquests there is said to have been a little Hebrew maid whom he carried back into the land of Syria. She heard of his deep seated trouble; for she waited upon Naaman's wife. Naaman's wife represented the Soul itself in its negative or passive mode. In that mode or state, it was possible for the maid of Israel to communicate a message and get it conveyed to Naaman. The little Israel-itish maid made captive, and who serves Naaman's wife, is none other than the intuition; for the intuition is of the innermost faculties of the Being. It may only be in the state of a little maid, that is, limited vision, and captive; but, nevertheless, it can discern things that are vitally important to the well-being of the Soul. It is she who says to her mistress—"Would that Naaman my master were with the prophet of God, for he would cure him of his leprosy." And the message of the Intuition reaches Naaman the mind. And he, being in a state of despair concerning his condition, notwithstanding his conquests, sets out to find the prophet. But he makes his journey after the fashion of the great man he believed himself to be, taking with him his treasures which he had accumulated, believing that that was the way to greet the prophet and acquire healing.

In the story it is said that when he reached the abode where the prophet was, having driven up in great state, the prophet did not even open the door to him, let alone come out. He just sent his message by his servant. In the story the prophet is represented as having been Elisha. Elisha was a prophet of God on whom the divine mantle rested. He was a vehicle of most marvellous ministry in the midst of Israel, for Elisha is the Sacred Fire of God. Here the prophet is also to be understood mystically; for in every Soul there is not only the Mind which can be great, and the Intuition which can be illumined and full of discernment, but there is also the Prophet. The prophetic voice is the Divine Voice within. The prophet's servant is his message, the message which the Voice gives.

Now the message given to Naaman was, to go and wash in the river Jordan seven times. And the promise was given that, if he did so, his flesh would come upon him again as that of a little child. That the message brought great disappointment to Naaman, is scarcely surprising. He did not believe in it. He said he would not obey it. That method of healing was not his idea of how things should have been done for him. He was filled with anger, and went away in that state crying out—"Behold! I thought he will surely come out to me, and strike with his hand the part that is leprous, and make me whole. Are not the rivers of Damascus, Abana and Pharpar, better than all the waters of Jordan? May I not wash in them and be clean?" So his latter state was even worse than his former, and the leprosy cleaved to him.

HERE IS A REPRESENTATION OF THE METHODS WHICH A MIND, HELD IN THE BONDAGE OF MATERIALITY AND PRIDE, BELIEVES TO BE THE TRUE PATH OF HEALING. HERE IS AN UNVEILING OF THE PRIDE OF HEART AND THE AWFUL MATERIALIZATIONS OF THE THINGS THAT ARE MOST SACRED, PRODUCING WHAT IS KNOWN AS SPIRITUAL LEPROSY WHICH MAY EVEN FIND, AND DOES AT TIMES FIND, ITS MANIFESTATION IN THE OUTER VEHICLE. HERE IS AN UNVEILING OF THE DIVINE METHOD OF PURIFICATION EVEN UNTO THE HEALING OF THAT WHICH IS TERMED LEPROSY. HERE IS A LIVING TESTIMONY OF THE GREATNESS OF THAT LOVE WHICH FINDS A WAY TO HEAL UNTO THE UTTERMOST.

*   *   *   *

It is recorded that in the midst of Naaman's wrath his servant spoke to him, reasoned with him, and showed him it was a mistake to refuse to carry out the message of the prophet. "My master," he said, "if the prophet had asked thee to do a great thing, thou wouldst have done it; but when he asked thee to wash in the Jordan seven times (a little thing and apparently needless), why not do it?"

The servant was beautiful in his ministry and influenced Naaman. So he set out for the waters of Jordan where he dipped seven times, and after the seventh time his flesh came to him again as the flesh of a little child.

Who was this servant that accompanied Naaman? Surely that remarkable pole of magnetic influence called the conscience. The conscience reasons. The conscience indicates. What is the conscience? It is the pole star of the Being whose light or power is the sum of all that Being's consciousness, so that the conscience is, in its degree of manifestation, the revelation of the sum or fulness of the consciousness which obtains in that Being. Many things pass under the name of conscience which are only opinions of the lower or higher mind. It is thus people have done things unto the injury of many, for what they called conscience sake, when it was only for their opinions. It was thus the religious institutions sought to crush new aspiration and vision and life in the name of conscience, when it was nothing more than vanity of mind, and pride in their own particular ways of thinking. The conscience counsels the mind. It may well say to a mind full of its own pride and greatness in an outward sense: "If the prophet asked thee to do some great thing, to seek some outer conquest, even to bestow of the wealth thou hast accumulated there, thou wouldst gladly do that. Why not do that which the message contains, and wash the seven times in the Jordan?"

Now the servant knew that the waters of Abana and Pharpar, rivers of the land of the Damascene, were not equal to the waters of Jordan. The servant understood the message of the prophet. Abana represents stony elements, or materialized states and conditions of life. The water or elements and influences, the streams of such a state, could not possibly heal leprosy. The river Abana thus represents the outermost things in a most fallen state. The waters of Pharpar are mental. The river is swift. It represents the onrush of mental states, the restless emotions of the Being who functions continually upon the lower mind. There is no healing for leprosy contained in those waters, not even though they flow from the higher mental, or occult springs. But the servant knew that the waters of Jordan ought to heal, for Jordan means the waters which flow from above, which come down from the heights.

*　　　*　　　*　　　*

The river Jordan is the path of the waters of divine knowledges given for the purification, the healing, the invigoration of the Being of man. Those waters represent the truths that come from above, truths which are ever sure, truths which are beautiful in their healing power, in their cleansing ministries, in their preserving and nourishing processes. To be baptised in the waters of the Jordan is essential to the initiation of the Soul into the mysteries of divine experience by which it comes to know the most blessed life represented in Jesushood, the life of love, of purity, of goodness, of compassion and pity. For only through the baptism of John, or the waters which flow down from above and are vitalized by the love which brings healing to the life and purity to the mind, can any Soul find Jesus. Not the man, but the state. Not the human messenger, but the inner love. Not the message in its outer form, but that message in its glorious salving and glorifying power.

It was into such waters Naaman, the Mind, was recommended to go. Amid such waters was he recommended to bathe himself seven times. And it was only when he fulfilled the prophetic command, that he was healed, and his flesh became to him again as that of a little child. It was then that he knew there was a God in Israel. By this

378

must be understood the mystical significance of the states implied in the three roots of which the term Israel is built up:—Issa-Ra-El, the Holy Spirit, the Radiant Presence, the Reigning Lord. In such states, God was realized and made manifest.

There is also a profound meaning under-lying the washing in the Jordan seven times. It represents the purification of the seven planes of the Being. For the human Soul has seven planes of consciousness. These are not to be confounded with the seven planes of the planet, nor the seven planes of the Celestial Hierarchy, nor the seven planes of the Divine Kingdom, though they are the correspondences in man of all these. It is by means of these that he is able to reach unto the others, even unto the Divine Kingdom, to function there, and to find perfect fulness of Being before the Divine and from the Divine and in the Divine Presence.

To wash seven times implies that there is hurt even to the innermost Being. We know that many would deny that this was possible. But the denial of it does not affect the sad reality. And if those who deny such an interpretation, only knew from the innermost what leprosy stands for, they would also understand the necessity for the washing seven times in the waters of Jordan.

For what is leprosy? A terrible disease from which all people by something within them shrink. It is a disease incurable by physiologists or any known process of *materia medica*. All that can be done from without is to mitigate the conditions of the sufferer. Usually it is taken for granted that when once a life is smitten with leprosy there is no possible healing. So lepers have always been separated from others, lest, through contact, others should be affected. *What is this leprosy, this disease looked upon as loathsome? It is the outer expression of the atrophication of the very substances*

379

out of which the beautiful vehicles are built up, through the
atrophication of the very substances out of which the Being
was fashioned.

There are some diseases which can be healed by dipping
once in the Jordan—purifying the body and making the life
true and pure on the outermost. There are some that require
to bathe twice, the body and the desire body—the purification
of the physical organism through right dieting and right ways,
and the purification of the desire. There are some afflictions which demand that the waters should be bathed in
three times—that means, that the vehicle of the mind which
cognises in the phenomenal world, should also be made
pure and beautiful and truthful. There are some tribulations
which require dipping in the waters of the Jordan four
times, for the emotions can then be made beautiful in their
action and manifestation, and be made to feel truly, purely
and beautifully always. There are afflictions which require
that the waters be entered unto the fifth time. Thus the
mind in its reflective power and ambition may be cleansed
and fashioned as the mind of a little child, lowly and pure.
There are spiritual diseases which necessitate the waters to
be applied unto the sixth time—this is unto the healing of
the intuition, the purification of its vision, and the restoration of its power to discern.

Thus all the outer vehicles have to be cleansed. They
have to be made magnetically beautiful. The inner attributes
have to be made consecrate. Even the intuition must be
healed, till it is unfailing in its vision and judgment. But in
the case of leprosy, all these have not only to be gone
through, but for the seventh time the waters must be entered.
The will has to be changed from a state of self-regard,

380

and earthly ambition, and love of domination, and from all things which hurt.

When the will is healed, it is full of willinghood to be even as the will of the Father-Mother. Then the glorious substances, which have been hurt unto atrophication, are revitalized. There is a renewal of polar action produced through the Overshadowing of the Presence, and the resultant effect of that Presence upon the Being's divine magnetic pole. In the outer plane the body can be helped. It can be comforted. Healing can be prepared for through the changing of the desire body, and the true polarizing of the mind's vehicle that its ambitions be beautiful and true. The direction of the emotion unto purity of feeling, and change in the attitude of the mind itself, both in its outward look and in its inward look, are great contributions. So is the attitude of the mind towards the Divine, and bringing the intuition to have faith, or heavenly discernment that the divine way is the true way, and that there is no other way unto the most blessed healing. And then the will, healing its love, healing its desire, healing its action. New and more blessed conditions obtain as the result. The substances that were once glorious, but which became weakened in the way and changed through the action of the will as it was influenced by the conditions through which it manifested, become again vitalized with the Divine Life-stream. They are quickened into newness of Being, so that atrophication is suspended, and new power flows once more through the attributes, changing them back again into most beautiful powers for service, even unto the body. For the substances of the etheric body become like those of a little child again—that is, like the Soul in its childhood. The resultant is true mentality, a true desire body manifesting into and through the outermost body, re-vitalizing it, changing its substances through the change effected in its life-stream by means of the new magnetic currents. Thus alone can leprosy be healed.

Though comparatively few suffer from extreme leprosy on the outer planes of manifestation, yet many are in a state of spiritual atrophy which would ultimately, if not healed, find manifestation. But it is glorious to know that all leprosy can be healed; that there is no tribulation that cannot be made whole. The divine streams, whose truths of living waters flow from the heights, can make the whole Being pure and beautiful. The Divine Love can accomplish all things. It can change the will and make the Soul as radiant as a child of the Radiant Heavens. It can heal the mind of its pride, and enable it to express that sublime lowliness which ever characterizes true childhood to the Great Love. It can make the intuition so clear in its perception that it misunderstands not, but cometh to know all things. It can transfuse the etheric body and make of it a body of glorious radiance, which inwardly pours itself in adoration before the Divine, and outwardly creates the atmosphere by which the child of God should ever be encompassed. It makes the vehicle of the mind, through which the mind cognizes the phenomenal world and correlates it, true, pure and lowly. It re-fashions the astral body till its defects are made good, all its woundings healed, its attributes made whole, and its desire become sweet and wholesome. It can even touch the body of the outermost and transform its substances, purifying and revivifying its life-stream, until even the transfiguration of the Being in the innermost pours its radiance through the outermost.

*   *   *   *

Oh, ye who read these words, and find yourselves sick in body, or in your finer body, or in your mind, or in your emotion, or in your ambitions, or in your visions of life which may be without understanding, or in your will, desiring your own will rather than the Divine, know ye this, that if ye be sick, Love can heal you. If ye wash in the waters of His Jordan, ye will be healed. If ye cleanse every plane of your Being, ye shall be made perfectly whole. And should these words fall into the hands of one who is a leper, turn ye your face Godward and be of good comfort, and know that that Love can heal unto the uttermost, even your sad affliction.

And ye who are healers, called of God to serve Him thus, know ye this—that, whilst the prophetic office is yours in the sense that the message has to be given to the afflicted ones, and the way of true healing shown them, that in yourselves ye are nothing, and that all is of and from the Divine. The healer must be humble and lowly, of humble heart and lowly mind. Glory not in yourselves or in your powers, even though the devils seem subject unto you. Glory only in The Lord of Love and Power. For devils are subject only unto God who is in the healer working for the healing of the obsessed and the afflicted. The healer should ever be in his or her own thought and desire and will and love, only the servant of the Most High One. Let the healers glory in God only, and not in any powers they may think they possess. Let him who glorieth, glory in the Lord alone. And whilst as healers ye may rejoice that ye are the divine vehicles for healing, your rejoicing should ever be begotten of the thought, that your names are written in the Heavens, and that within you is written large in the book of your Life the Lamb of God, even the mystery of the Divine Love in His burden-bearing for the healing of His children.

The Twelve Labours of
the Soul.

THE TWELVE
LABOURS OF
THE SOUL.

THE
TWELVE
LABOURS OF
THE SOUL.

In the unfallen days when no discordant elements had to be met with upon any of the planes of life, or within any of the Kingdoms of the planet, the Labours of the Soul were travail without pain such as is known to-day, burden-bearing without the sorrow which now becomes the portion of so many. The Soul's journey was one of joy.

It is difficult to unveil the history of a Soul from its inception to the consummation of its Being in the consciousness of the Divine Indwelling, so inward is it, and so much does it partake of the Divine Mystery. Indeed, it is the Divine Mystery in action in an individuated miniature form. We can, therefore, only touch upon some features of the Soul's growth, and the way by which that growth was reached.

When there were no adverse conditions to contend with and overcome, the Soul performed its Labours amid beautiful, harmonious conditions around it and within it. For the term Labour does not mean travailing in the sense in which the term came to be interpreted in later ages. It was the Law of the Soul's growth as it passed along the Human Kingdom, from lower degree to higher degree of spiritual consciousness.

There is a divine mystery in the very purpose of manifestation such as is expressed through the history of a human Soul; in the order of its evolution; in the syntheses found in the order of its experiences; in the travail from stage to stage of its journey; in the ever-deepening feeling expressed in its consciousness, its emotion, its love; in its power and flight of thought, apprehension and comprehension; in its desire and its yearning, which is like a sacred flame with breath blowing upon it, full of that strange element, which, on the outer planes is named oxygen, causing the flame to become greater, and still greater, and yet greater, making the Being one with the Sacred Flame of the Indwelling Mystery of the Spirit; in its yearning and seeking for the Great Realization in consciousness of the Mystery within, essaying to find the interpretation of that Mystery through contact with that greater Mystery which the Soul comes to recognise, the Over-Soul of all, the Divine Mystery we speak of as the Father-Mother.

*   *   *   *

The Labours of the Soul were like twelve great stages of realization. In the profoundest, mystical sense, but separated entirely from all thought of a fallen world, and the need for the redemption of the planetary heavens, such as was accomplished by means of the Oblation, and, consequently, separated from all painful, sad, sorrowful, anguishing thoughts associated with the burden-bearing of the Cross; the Twelve Stations of the Cross in the High Ritualistic churches and Roman Catholic churches represent the Twelve Degrees or Labours of the Soul, the meaning of which is hidden beneath the symbol, and utterly lost.

In those Labours the Soul passed through the Twelve Houses of Jacob:—astrologically, the Twelve Houses in a horoscope; celestially, the Twelve Houses represented by the zodiacal signs, each sign signifying a divine attribute, manifold in its manifestation. But the Divine Principle is that which is represented in the name of the sign.

Those Labours were accomplished, we said, without pain. But there had to be endeavour. The Hills had to be ascended. The Mountains must needs be climbed. For there were no other paths by which the vision splendid could be seen in its manifold degrees from the Hills, and the Eternal Splendour of that sublimest of visions beheld

386

upon the exceeding High Mountains, could break upon the Soul.

But the travail did not mean pain and sorrow, struggle amidst dense spiritual darkness, heart anguish begotten of contention and oppression. The elements had to be overcome. But these were not in states inimical to progress. They had only to be transcended.

To see the movement of Souls away back in those days is to witness that which was exquisitely beautiful on all the Kingdoms where Souls were functioning. Indeed, it is beautiful to look into a human Soul today, its marred visage notwithstanding, and see the wealth of sacred story gathered by it in its journeyings, and treasured within its treasure-house. It is a Sacred Office to witness a Soul amid its travails today, when you separate from its motions and experiences, the pain, the sorrow, and the anguish of those far away days.

Now, usually it is thought that the Labours of the Soul represent the travail that implies pain and sorrow and anguish. That is because those Labours are referred to the fallen state, and are written of, and spoken of, because thought of, in relation to the *Return journey of the Soul*, its labour to bring forth into manifestation redeemed attributes; its travail to obtain, and accomplish, and realize. All of which things are true in this sense, that those who are travailing today in the greatness of their strength, whose very garments are red-dyed in their travail, are those who travailed long, long ages ago in the unfallen world states, who laboured, attained and entered into the fruits of their labours. They acquired their attributes in great fulness, offered them for, and sacrificed them in, beautiful ministry. They gave themselves that they might become the helpers of those who were performing their Labours.

387

For such Souls the Labours, in these days, imply the passing through again of the Houses of experience which represent each attribute, for the purification of the attributes and the liberation of each from the elements which have gathered around it, and have held it captive. They Labour or Travail, unto the healing of all the woundings that have been imposed upon the attributes during their sojourn in the midst of a fallen world. The Labours of such Souls represent the Via Crucis and Via Dolorosa through which they come back into the Kingdom of most blessed Realization.

*   *   *   *

Now, it is remarkable that the twelve names given to those disciples who were specially chosen to become apostles, represent those states. They embody the attributes. They signify the powers acquired by the Soul in its Labours. These attributes all gather around, and emanate from, and are nourished by, and are the reflectors of, the Divine Mystery Presence within us, known as the Eternal Love.

We have in the innermost realm, John, James and Peter, the trinity of Love and Life and Light.

Then we have Andrew, Simon Peter's brother, and Philip of the same city, and Thomas Didymus. These form the trinity of the Higher Mind Realm, the Celestial.

Following these come Bartholomew (who is really the twin of Thomas Didymus—the one representing the Celestial power, and the other that power revealed on the Kingdom beneath), James the Less, called James Alphaeus, and Matthew, who is also Thaddeus. These represent the Angelic realm and powers.

And after these there are Jude, and Simon who was said to have been Canaanite and Zelotes, and then Nathanael. These are the powers for the expression of all the others upon the true Human Kingdom.

388

And you will understand that, though we begin at the
centre and work outward, when we reach the twelfth we
touch again that which unites all to the centre. They make a
circle, like the zodiacal signs. Nathanael comes next to
John, the Love-Principle manifested. None are outward.
None are to be thought of in an earthly sense. They are all
inward. They are all most beautiful. They all represent
degrees of Divine Power, states of Divine Realization,
scope of Divine Regnancy, and offices of ministry. The
manifestation proceeds from the centre through John,
James, Peter; Andrew, Philip, Thomas; Bartholomew, James
Alphaeus, Matthew Thaddeus; Jude, Simon and Nathanael.
The reader will find in referring to what we said on the
Training of the Twelve[1], that there was a trinity in each of
the four Kingdoms—the Divine, the Celestial, Angelic and
true Human, each trinity manifesting on the Kingdom
which they represent. In the full-grown man they are all
present. They are all essential. The Divine Man has all
those attributes.

In the return of the Soul through its Labours, it passes
from without, inward. The travailing may also go on in the
very innermost. There may be travail in the Soul's Return
through every House. Yes, there may even be travail, for
the very, very few, in all the Houses together and at the
same time.

We would not have you ignorant of this Divine Mystery,
though many things have been said by others which are
contrary to that which we have stated, namely, that it is
possible to travail in the very innermost Kingdom of the
Being. The travail that is most anguishing is there. The
travail that is most redemptive for the healing of the world

[1] See page 201

has had to be there. And, therefore, it is not true to say that a Soul in its own Divine Kingdom, cannot travail in sorrow. Within that Kingdom anguish is most poignant and sorrow most profound.[2]

But the ministry of the Divine Love is so beautiful unto His children, that few indeed travail in all the Houses at once. Indeed, in these days now at hand, no one has so travailed, except that One who had to celebrate within his Sanctuary the way of the Oblation. But you may travail in several Houses at once. And yet, the Divine ministry is so beautiful, that it is accommodated to you in the Return. Oh, ye whose atmosphere is not yet rarified, and whose vision is partial, never doubt the Divine Love amid all your travail! Never falter in your devotion to that Love's sublimest vision in you, and transcendent Life for you.

*   *   *   *

And now we will look for a few moments at the path of the travail of the Labours of the Soul unto the Return. For each word to you is something more than a philosophical statement of what is thought historically and philosophically of the Twelve Labours of the Soul, called the Twelve Labours of Hercules, which statement really belongs to an unfallen state, and not to the Return in the fallen days.

THE GATE OF   Nathanael seems to be the outermost.
THE INTENTION.   There is no outermost. In the circle Nathanael comes next to the Love-Principle. Nathanael is the guilelessness of love, the guileless spirit, the spirit in which there is no subtlety—(though, originally the old word subtlety meant wisdom, but not as we use it); the spirit that is open and frank; the spirit whose Sanctuary door is

---

[2] The section on Sorrow should be read to apprehend the full meaning here.

not closed against a vision that is apparently beyond accep- THE
tance in the first gleams of it; the spirit which, in its lowliness, TWELVE
says, How can Christ come out of the Nazareth state, since the LABOURS OF
Nazareth state is a despised one, a lowly one, a separate one? THE SOUL.

Yet, the diffident lowly spirit has to learn the Divine
Wisdom. And it is Philip who speaks. Come and see, says
Philip. Now Philip is of the city of Andrew and Simon Peter.
Peter is the Radiance, the Light, the Understanding illumined.
Andrew is the embodiment of the Love-Principle in burden-
bearing. Philip is the Life on the Celestial planes reflecting
the Glory of it through the mind. That reflected Glory is in
the language of "Come and see!" And the guileless spirit
discerns; it recognises; it apprehends; and it is full of love
in its adoration. Though seeming of the outer, Nathanael is
of the very elect. The guileless spirit, though expressed in
the outermost as the Twelfth Attribute, is that attitude of
Heart that is adjacent to, and which partakes of the nature
of, the very central Principle of the Being, the Love-Principle.

The first great realization in life is to have the guileless
spirit, to be pure and beautiful in love. Purify the love of
all subtlety, of all that is unlike itself. Make it child-like,
lowly, gentle, beautiful, having only the desire to be that
which love should ever be. Let it be ever responsive to the
call of the Light of the Divine Love, that is, the Christ-
Light, the Radiance of the Presence. Train it to acquire
power, that it may have the property of aiding all the
Labours, and thus accomplish the healing of all the other
attributes.

In the measure in which we love beautifully, all our
attributes will be healed.

In the measure in which Nathanael is our spirit, or represents our spirit, shall all our attributes be made beautiful.

*   *   *   *

*THE GATE OF
THE DESIRE.* Through the Gate of Nathanael, Simon, who was Canaanite, or one in a state of the inversion of the Love-Principle, becomes healed. He who was Zelote captivated by outer things, becomes one zealous for the purified Life. Love purifies the mind, makes beautiful its thought, fills it with zeal for good things, and changes the manifestation into all that is beautiful.

*   *   *   *

*THE GATE OF
GENTLENESS.* Jude represents the attribute of great gentleness, which is the corollary of the inheritance of a guileless love and a purified mind. For, love exalted and the mind healed, the very desire-nature expresses itself in the yearning to be beautiful, gentle. Jude is said to have been related to the Master. Jude is related, as all were related, to the central Principle. The Lord Himself is represented in that Principle.

Here you have a triune, the three Houses, a trinity representing the manifestations of the very innermost Love and Light and Life, in Nathanael, Simon and Jude. For the Holy Trinity has to be manifested on the outer Human Kingdom, the true Kingdom of Manifestation, as well as in the Divine Kingdom of Realization. For there is manifestation in the Great Realization. If you saw a Soul realizing in the innermost, you would see the manifestation of its realization. And there are manifestations upon all the Kingdoms .

*   *   *   *

*THE GATE
OF POWER.* Then comes the next three-fold unveiling of the Soul's Being in Matthew Thaddeus, James Alphaeus and Bartholomew. Matthew Thaddeus is said to have been a publican. He is thought of as a Roman tax-gatherer. He embodies the realm of the Mind

392

in the office of ingathering. He sits at the receipt of custom.
Does he criticise? No, but he examines. Always distinguish
between criticism, discernment and separation. The critical
faculty is a divine power in man. When divinely used it is
beautiful; when otherwise used it is hurtful. It hurts Souls.
It hurts them in their thought. It hurts them in their love. It
hurts them in their endeavour. It may become cynical, and
wound a Soul so deeply that it may take that one long ages
to recover from the hurt.

Matthew gathers the wealth of the Roman tribute. The
Roman represents power. Power comes through knowledge.
Knowledge when transmuted, becomes power for ministry.
He represents the Mind; who, having gathered sufficient
knowledge to transmute into power for ministry, is called to
arise and follow yet further on the way to the Christ
Realization. No longer is he to be simply seeking and
gathering; he is to arise and transmute that which has been
gathered as the result of the seeking, into power for beautiful
ministry. Matthew is the attribute of the service to which
true knowledge can be put. Knowledge of divine things,
knowledge of life's experiences, knowledge even of Souls,
is gathered in the way as these unburden their sorrow and
their travail, and that knowledge has to be transmuted into
power, and used to minister unto them. It is thus seen to be
a most beautiful attribute.

Matthew also is the scribe. It is said he wrote the first
life, or brief outline which was concerned with the ministry
of the Master. But the name indicates, through the transmutation of the knowledge, the writing of the Life which is
seen and sought for as Divine Realization, the writing of that
history which will culminate in the sublime Attainment. It
is the faculty by which transmutation on the Middle Kingdom
takes place.

THE GATE OF SACRIFICE. James Alphaeus represents the Life-Principle of the innermost brought into the intermediary realm for manifestation. Through the Gate of Nathanael the guileless spirit is acquired. Love in the Desire-body is healed, and Simon is no more Canaanite, but the Gate of Love's conquest. Through the Gate of Jude the Will in its outward desires is once more made beautiful. The mind with its powers so glorified and strengthened that it is able to transmute its receipts of knowledge into blessed dynamic force for ministry to Souls, and be full of understanding, is the gift gained as the Gate of Matthew is passed through.

And how beautiful it is to understand Souls in their travail! It is true that power can only fully be given from the very innermost. But each one who is travailing to-day, bearing the burden of the Labours in the Return, understands in the Innermost. And the power will be brought through as the attributes are purified.

James the Less is the embodiment of the Inner Life on the outer realm, which embodiment is less than the realization of it in the inner; for the manifestation is always less in degree, than the realization of that which is manifested. When you loved with all your Being even, you never loved to that extent, nor could you love to that extent, in which the manifestation became greater than that which you manifested from, or even equal to it. So is it with the Life realized through the Gate or Labour of James Alphaeus. It represents the Angelic Life, the life of sweet and gracious ministry embodied in Jesushood.

*   *   *   *

THE GATE OF EMOTION. The Labour of Bartholomew comes next. That disciple is the Gate for the Angelic Manifestation of which Thomas Didymus is the Celestial embodiment. Bartholomew is the deep emotion whose waters rise and flow full of Angelic Life and sweet ministry. It is the radiation of Love through the true etheric body, the outflow of Divine Power in Healing. To pass through this Gate is to accomplish the Labour of Desire as it affects the intermediary bodies. When that Labour is attained, Desire is selfless. It is not negatived by repression. It is active, and great with longing to find fulfilment. But it is selfless. It seeketh not its own. Its giving is for the blessing of others.

* * * *

THE GATE OF THE WILL. The twin of Bartholomew is Thomas. He is the Desire on the Celestial realm, whose manifestation is through the Will. The Gate, therefore, has relation to the travail of the Will. To pass through that Gate is the path of the Labour by which the Will is made selfless. To accomplish so much is a Labour of great Travail. It is the House wherein perfect lowliness must needs be learnt. For, though Thomas signifies the attribute of Celestial Vision, with the power to ascend, yet the acquisition of the power to ascend to the realm of Innermost Vision, is accomplished only in the measure in which the Will is filled with the lowly desire that only the Divine Purpose should be fulfilled in the Being, and through the ministry Thomas has to render.

* * * *

THE GATE OF THE UNDERSTANDING. But even Thomas derives his vision through Philip. For Philip is the Higher Mind whose true balance is found within the Celestial Kingdom. He is like a great reflector, mirroring the Heavens, catching the points of light from the glorious galaxy of Divine radiating Centres. It is in that realm he gathers his inner knowledge, as the Mystery of Being is reflected unto him.

The Labour of Philip is, therefore, the process by which the Higher Mind is purified and balanced in the Celestial Heavens. And he represents the Gate or degree of Soul Initiation within the Celestial Kingdom. He is the Mind healed through the Labours of all the other attributes, and purified so beautifully that now its function is uninterrupted and most sublime, and its power to reflect the Divine Glory within the Celestial estate is fully restored. And this may be true of its estate, though Philip still makes request, "Show us the Father-Mother, that we may be sufficed." For even the Divine Vision that comes to Thomas Didymus, must needs come through a redeemed Philip; for only in the Redeemed state can the full glory be received upon the Higher Mind, and then only by reflection.

*　　*　　*　　*

THE GATE OF THE CROSS. But the crown of the Celestial Attributes is won through the Cross. The Labour of the Being to reach that state of Realization is through the Gate of Andrew. He is the House of the cross-bearing. It is not the Cross of self-denial, which is the mere negation of Desire. It is the Cross of true Soul-giving, named Self-sacrifice. Andrew is the Being travailing for high attainment. It is the Soul in Celestial ministry, enduring unto the realization of the Life and Light of the Divine Kingdom. For he is the manifestation of the Divine Love upon the Celestial Realm, as the Cross-bearer. In this fallen world he represents the suffering saint; and in this Labour he becomes in fashion like unto The Divine Cross, and is henceforth one with it.

The ninth Labour of the Soul is the journey by which the Being attains to the threshold of the Cross of Christ. For the Cross of Christ is Celestial—the cross of a Son of God. It is the Labour which completes the Third Round of

attainment. It is the Gate through which the Celestial
Kingdom becomes fully the Soul's inheritance. It is, in
attainment, the House of great Realization which heralds the
ascent of the Being on to the threshold of the Divine Kingdom.
For Andrew is brother to Simon Peter, who is the outermost
of the Trinity of attributes within the Divine Kingdom.

*   *   *   *

THE GATE OF   At last the threshold of the Divine Kingdom
APPREHENSION.   is reached. There the Vision glorious becomes
the crown of all previous Labours. The power by which the
Vision splendid is beheld, is the attribute embodied in Peter.
He is the Mind in the Divine World. He is the illumined
Understanding. He, therefore, stands for Divine Intelligence
within the Being.

It is by this faculty the Soul catches the Light of Love,
as that Light is radiated by the Love-Principle when this latter
is affected by Divine Magnetic action. And the Labour of
the Petrine attribute, is the process by which the Mind
becomes truly balanced in the Divine Realm, attuned to the
vibrations flowing from the Divine Centre, acquiring the
power to look upon the Ineffable Light. Peter is the Gate into
the Innermost Realm of consciousness. The Soul, through
that Gate, fully stands within the Tenth House. Within that
state of consciousness, the Being may behold the Glory of
Divine Transfiguration; and also witness within the Garden
of Gethsemane, the Divine Sorrow of Love in crucifixion.

*   *   *   *

THE GATE OF   Then doth the Being come to the James
COMPREHENSION.   state. He is the Life of which Peter is
the Light. He represents the eleventh attribute of the
Being. In the full realization of that attribute, the Being

397

is in the second degree of high Christhood. That attribute enables the one who has attained it, to share the Glory of the Mount and the mystery of the Sorrow in the Garden. It is the power by which the Eternal Life is realized, which is to *Know God*.

The Labour through the Gate into the House of James, is accomplished through partaking of the contents of the Sacred Chalice, the Divine Mystery; and being baptized with the Divine Fire. It is the travail of the Being into the consciousness of the Great Realization of the Vision Splendid, which Peter glimpses and then fully beholds as the splendour of God. To attain to the Innermost Realm of Being in realization, means great travail even in an unfallen world. It is the Gift of God unto all who endure unto the end.

In the Return in these days of the Regeneration, the Labour represented by James, is one that demands great sacrifice. The Peter state is found only after the great Renunciation, or giving up of the Will; the James state is the resultant of sublime self-abandonment to the Divine Will. It is the Gate into the yet sublimer state of realization, to know the Divine Mystery.

*　　*　　*　　*

THE GATE OF REALIZATION. The Twelfth Labour of the Soul is represented by John. He is in the third degree of Christhood. The Love-Principle is expressed by him as the Life-Principle is by James, and the Light-Principle by Peter.

The Labour is the process by which the Being realizes the fulness of the Mystery of Divine Love. It is through Love that God is known. It is through Love that the Mystery of the Father-Mother is realized. It is through the attribute of perfect Love that the Eternal Love can be truly manifested.

In the Labour, the Soul drinks of the Cup. John shares this privilege with James. Together they are the sons of Boanerges. They are of the Divine Fire. Both drink of the same cup, and receive of the same baptism. For what the Love knows and endures, the Life must needs share.

It is Divine Love that bears the burden of the cross. John is that attribute within us. He is the Gate through which we pass into the high consciousness of the sublimest mystery of life, and the Realization of our absolute oneness with the Divine Mystery. The Labour that carries us through that Gate, is the service of Love, through which the Being acquires the power of laying down the Life attained, that it may be outpoured for redeeming ministry. For the full Christhood of the Soul is then reached. God is known through Realization. The Soul's Atonement (AT-ONE-MENT) is complete.

It is alone in this state of Love that one can fully behold the Glory of God, enter into the Christ-Glory, realize that Glory as the Radiant Presence within, and also have the power to pass from that transcendent state to be the Divine Burden-bearer, travail amid the Garden of Sorrow, full of anguish as one heavily laden and crushed through the attitude of a loveless people or the state of a fallen world.

Through the Labours of the Soul, the Being gets there. There is no crown without the Cross. There is no attainment but by Labour. There is no perfect fulness of Divine Realization, until the Being passes through all the Gates. Glints and gleamings come on the way as the Labours proceed; and these call the Being ever upward and onward, yet higher and still higher towards the perfect Day. And as the progressive steps are made, there breaks upon the vision an ever deepening consciousness of the sublimity of that Life Eternal which is the inheritance of the Being, and gives power for inward and upward attainment, and to descend for blessed ministry.

Well may all Souls inquire—"What is man? Thou art so mindful of him? Who is this Son of Man in whom Thou dost visit him?"

The Divine Mystery is within him. He is the replica of the Heavens. The embodiment of the Angelic is his; for the Mystery of that world is within him. The Celestial Mystery expressed in the Zodiacal Signs, is written within him; their story is repeated in miniature in him. He is a microcosm of the Divine World. Thus within is latent the power to apprehend the Life Mystery of these worlds, and even to comprehend in vast degree the very Mystery of God.

Nathanael, Simon and Jude, are most beautiful Jesushood attributes. To accomplish the Labours they represent, and pass through the Gates, is to become children of Pity, Compassion and Love, and inherit the guileless Heart.

Matthew, James Alphaeus and Bartholomew, are more advanced Jesushood attributes, leading the Being into the first degrees of Christhood. To accomplish their Labours and pass through the Gates, is to acquire the power to transmute the elements of knowledge into power, and to attain a planetary cosmic consciousness.

Thomas, Philip and Andrew, are Gates of high initiation, full of transcendent vision and ministry. They represent Labours of profound moment, the accomplishment of which makes them Knights of the Temple.

Peter, James and John, comprise the three Eastern Gates whose Labours lift the Being on to the very threshold of the Divine Realm, giving the vision and the great Realization of the Radiant One. On passing through these Gates, the Innermost Sanctuary is again found.

Children of the Kingdom! It is the day of your return, and all these Gates are yours. It is the day of your coming back into the realization, and all these Celestial Houses are homes for you. You have passed through them in other days many a time; and again you are realizing through them, coming upward, ascending the Hill of God. Your ascension is commensurate with the realization of the guileless love of Nathanael, the beautiful mind of Simon, the gentle spirit of Jude; the consecrated power of Matthew Thaddeus, the sweet and gracious love expressed through the James Alphaeus ministry, the power for catching the reflections of the Celestial World in Bartholomew; the keen vision to look into the Celestial Realm and the potency to descend for ministry as Thomas Didymus, the power to receive into the mind the reflection of the Celestial Heavens like Philip of Bethsaida, the strength to take up the Divine Cross and bear it as a Celestial Being for the Divine Healing of Souls, as in Andrew. In Peter and James and John, you will find the qualities of the Transfiguration—the Divine Trinity of the Radiance, the Life Eternal, and the Great Love Mystery.

We have seen you travailing. How greatly some of you have done so of late days! We have beheld the opening of your Gates, each Gate becoming redeemed, crowned with a precious pearl. For in the accomplishment of your Labours, this gift is yours. The Celestial city has twelve Gates, each one a pearl. The Gate crowned with the pearl, represents the Attribute healed, redeemed, perfected again. And the Gates of the City shall be no more shut in that day. There shall be no more night. The power of the attribute will henceforth be no more under limitation, no longer in a state of helplessness. Each attribute will have the power

401

to bring of its own ministry into the Holy City, and of the wealth which it has gathered.

How beautiful all this is! We have tried to show you yourselves. For is not that the purpose of all our ministry unto you, to show you something of your own glorious Being? For is not that why we have travailed, and do travail, that ye may enter into the joy of the holy ones of God?

Let the Divine Thought touch you now wherein you are travailing, and transmute your sorrow into joy, your trouble into peace, and all your anguishing into perfect healing. Go forward in the consciousness of your childhood to that Love who understands you in your down-sitting and your up-rising, in all your states and in all your needs. That Love will give you the Crown of Life that fadeth not away. It is the crown of your own attributes, healed and restored, His gift to you at the beginning, His gift to you again in the Regeneration.

Most Ever Blessed Father-Mother! We Thy children adore Thee. Help us that our adoration may be without shadow.

Ever Blessed be Thy Glorious Name! We adore Thee for all Thou art to us, all we are to Thee; for Thou hast fashioned us, and we are Thy children.

That we might bear Thine image most beautifully, Thou didst fashion us; that we may bear that image most perfectly, we do pray.

Unto this end cause Thy Holy One to fill the Sanctuary of each with the power of Thy Love, and the Radiance of Thy Glory. And in our lives and in our ministry, we would ever more and more adore Thee!

402

The Work of Transmutation

through

the Alembic and the Crucible.

403

THE DIVINE ALEMBIC AND CRUCIBLE.

An alembic is a vessel used for distillation. It was used by those who distilled alcoholic spirits. The Chemists of old time used it. They called its use, distillation. Our thoughts radiating around that term, are far away from anything associated with the alembic processes in distilleries and chemistry. True, it is possible to pervert anything by inverting the order of its use, which is the case in the distillation of alcoholic spirits; for, like all the high and holy things, whether as to their nature, their substance, or their uses, this also has been brought down.

An alembic is a vessel within which volatile elements are changed and separated. A crucible is a vessel within which substances are reduced and separated. In the alembic the volatile elements undergo a process of transmutation. In the crucible the substances undergo a process by which they are reduced, then purified, and also transmuted.

In spiritual alchemy, you cast the gold into the crucible, but the waters into the alembic. It is through the fire of searching trial in the crucible that love manifests its triumphant nature. It is within the alembic that the knowledges of the mind express their true value. The waters which are unto the healing of the life become at last the Waters of Life when they have been distilled. It is in the alembic that the waters of the mind's knowledges are placed; and through evaporation and change and transformation, transmutation is accomplished. God's Alembic goes hand in hand in life's mystery, amid its travail, with God's Crucible. Cast the gold into the furnace, into the crucible, that it may be fully refined. Cast the elements of your knowledge into the alembic, purifying them, distilling from them those Waters of Life which are as the very attar of roses, even all the ingathered knowledges transmuted until they themselves

404

become of the very nature of the gold of Divine Love that is purified from all alloy and made triumphant.

In the way of a soul's going in these days of the Return, not to speak of the long ages of the soul's tragic history, the Being knows the meaning of God's Alembic and God's Crucible. The children of this world seek joy, the younger children especially seek it and must have it. From the little children, in the earthly sense, you would not take a moment's joy, real joy, pure unalloyed joy; joy that hallows their dreams, joy that surrounds their life with a halo which, if somewhat unreal, is real enough to them, and afterwards becomes fragrant in sacred memories of the childhood days. The younger souls of this world also seek joy. They once had it, free from accompaniment of the burden-bearing such as they know today. And they seek that joy today. In all the ways of their going and their coming, their down-sitting and their uprising, their eating and their drinking, their toiling and their pleasure-seeking, they desire to find joy. It is inherent in their nature. You might as well ask the rose not to bloom and shed its fragrance, as ask them not to seek joy, for joy is inherent in an unfallen state. But such children seeking joy, when they come to it, find it, even in these days of the return and the redemption, without knowing anything of the great travail of those souls who have borne the burden of the ages in ministry for these children. They never were in the great heights. And although they have been in the depths in their spiritual state, they have never known the anguish begotten of the depths. They could not. For anguish is not begotten of physical pain, though you may have also a kind of anguish from that pain, as we know even the creatures have when they are tortured. But that which stands before our vision and is ever present to our consciousness, is the anguish of a soul

405

who has known the Radiance, the glory of the heights, the transcendent vision, the perfect fellowship of Angels, the Overshadowing Presence, and, in some degree, the Great Realization, and who has always the inner consciousness of these things as having once been strangely familiar to them, and who, in the deep valley where the dark shadows have been cast, and still lie athwart the life, cry out again for the realization. That soul can know anguish, indeed. But the children of this world could not possibly know. They could know anguish of physical pain begotten of hurt to the outer form. Or they might touch its threshold through certain mental states. But they could not know that anguish which is begotten of the very Being yearning to be back in divine consciousness, to be up on those heights of the beatific glory, to be beholding the Radiant Vision, to be hearing anew the Hallelujah without discordant note, to be conscious once more of the Overshadowing of His Glorious Presence, to feel from day to day and hour to hour, aye, continually, the encompassing of that Love that never wearies and never fails, and to have perfect trust in that Love, knowing it could not weary and it could not fail; crying out for that trust, that the Being's cup might be filled again with that Love.

In the process of a soul's arising again to return to such an inheritance, that soul comes to know in a very real sense the Alembic of God, and the Crucible of God. Its love is tried in the fire until it is absolutely pure and selfless. Its knowledges are touched, acted upon, taken, poured into the alembic and distilled. All that is not right is separated, and all that is beautiful and abiding is brought forth out of the knowledges as the Waters of Life. The resultant is as the attar of roses, the very essences of the Love of Truth, Love as Truth and Good. For there is the Truth of Love and the Good of Love. Truth is not Love as it has often been affirmed. Love is Truth. Good is not Love in the sense in which it also has been affirmed. But Love is ever Good. The Good of Love is Love's compassion and pity. The Truth of Love is the Wisdom of Love as knowledge transmuted, waters distilled for service. Truth and Good are qualities of Love. And there is no Love without them. For Love is ever compassionate and beautiful. Love is ever sweet and pure and true. Love is of the very essence of the Spirit.

The children of the Kingdom of the Heavens in whom that Kingdom is not only potentially present (for the Kingdom is in all souls potentially), but in whom the Kingdom is latently unveiled, aye, who knew that Kingdom with the power and the glory of it—that Kingdom which is the consciousness of the living God in us, the overshadowing and the encompassing Presence and is the Divine Principle of our Being—those children in their return bring with them out of their vast history, their gold and their knowledges. They are on the way back to the heights of the Radiant Vision, to the glorious Realization, to hearing again the Hallelujahs within their Being. They are coming back again as the children of Zion, marching to that Holy City in Blessed state, with songs of everlasting joy upon their heads—that is, within their thoughts. Though they have been coming up out of a land filled with sorrow and sighing and mourning, yet in the day of their return, the sighing and the mourning arising out of their sorrow are all to pass away.

But as they return they come through those states of consciousness represented by the Divine Alembic and the Divine Crucible. The law of transmutation operates within them. Their redemption differs in some respects from the redemption of the world-children. Their redemption is the healing of the wounding they have received whilst sojourning in this world, and ministering to its children. It is the bringing of them back again to a salved or found state, "finding the children of Israel," for that is the meaning of it. It is the finding of those souls individually who came out from the glory of the Kingdom, full of its power; who spent its power within them in ministry, but whose glory became veiled as they went down. Their redemption is the healing of all their wounding. In the process of the healing and the restoration, they pass through the Alembic and the Crucible. It is there the gold of their life is all brought out and made pure once more, without anything of this world's alloy in it, separated from all that is of the self in a self-regarding way, purified from all mere earthliness in desire, in outlook, or in purpose, that may have been acquired though serving in very beautiful ministry on the earth. Parted from everything that would debar the Being from rising up to the heights again, to the Vision of the Radiance, to hearing the Voice within, to the consciousness of the Overshadowing and Encompassing Presence, and on to the Indwelling, their love is thus made beautiful. It is as Gold refined seven times upon every plane of consciousness, the Soul's Love upon every plane of its manifestation, from the outermost to the innermost, purified seven times in the Crucible of God. Love is there so purified that it can be beaten out into the most exquisitely formed expressions in life, in ministry, inwoven into the very garments. For the King's daughters have their garments (mystically) inwoven with gold, even with finest gold, even with the gold of Ophir, as you will read in the XLV psalm, a mystic poem. The Gold of Ophir signifies Love as it is known on the Divine Kingdom.

408

When Love is thus exalted, transmutation has again taken place. Even in love, in the gold of love as it rises from degree to degree, from plane to plane, from one kingdom to another kingdom of experience, there is the process of the transmutation; from the outer personal to the inner personal; from the inner personal to the higher realm of the mind; from the mind to the emotion in its inward stream; from the higher emotion to the very centre of the Being where nought can change it. For even though all the world should change, and all souls upon it be changed, and all in whom your hopes were placed were to be changed, the Love knows no change. That is Divine Love. It is Divine Love once again realized. It is difficult to express in human speech the things of the innermost. For love, true love, beautiful love, is ever Divine, though the manifestation may be in the outer, or within the limitation of the personal. For the limitation put upon love for its ministry to the one or the few, or the many, does not change the love in its nature. It is always Divine Love; and when it becomes the Divine Love fully realized, that Love knows no change. It never lessens the love for the one, or the two, or the three. Nor does it interfere with the beautiful ministry to the one, or the two, or the three, or the few, in the personal ministry. It exalts the Being. It lifts it to the realm where love has larger vision. And then the whole Being seeks in the one, the two, the three, the few, the coming of the realization. All the ministry of the love is unto this end.

The path of your own travail is also the way of God's Alembic. The knowledges you have gathered on the way, many of them influenced by elements foreign to the Spirit, many of them not truths in their purity from the Divine Realm, but truths from the Divine Realm wrongly reflected, those knowledges have to pass through the Divine

Alembic. Water is the symbol of knowledge:—"Except ye be baptised of water and the Spirit"—except the life be baptised into the Jordan, the waters which are vitalized by the Spirit, the waters that make life pure and sweet and beautiful, the waters that make all the ways of life fragrant. Those waters of life are the outcome of distillation. Distillation is the process by which the very essences of those waters of knowledge are gathered out for your abiding inheritance, something permanent, something beautiful, even to turn them into the Waters of Life. In them Life becomes. In them the great fish are found, the Divine Mysteries. You can understand through them. In them are the vital force of the Breath of the Spirit, the magnetic flow from the Divine Realm. When your knowledges are transmuted as they pass through the Alembic of God, all that is not of them must be put away, evaporated, so to speak. All foreign elements have to be separated. Separation of these elements leaves the very essence. The result of distillation is this, that naught but the essences remain. The truths of knowledge are purified, and transmuted into realizations. When they come out of the Alembic they are of the Being.

When the soul has passed through the Crucible it is the embodiment of Love. It does not know Love as a knowledge; it has Love as its life. When it passes through the Alembic it does not know things as knowledges; when it has come forth it knows them as realizations. And it is never conscious for a moment that it is burdened with great knowledge, that it has vast resources within itself, that it is great in any degree whatsoever in the world. It simply knows itself to be a child in the Infinite and Eternal Love, whose gracious Spirit doth reveal. There is no burden or weight in carrying that knowledge; it never so appears, it is never so felt. That one is a little child. That one

410

could not be other than a little child, knowing nothing, having nothing, of himself or herself, though having all things in that Love that never fails, and whose ministry never knows weariness.

Do you question these things? We ask, not because we sense that you do, but because ye might do in your daily toil and ministry. When confronted with your difficulties, and you are able to see only the outer aspect because the inner is hidden from you, when you realize little segments of the great circle of your Being nearest where you are operating, and forget the vastness of that part of the circle which you cannot see at all, do you doubt that you have been placed in the Crucible of God, and still are in that Crucible, being made glorious for service? Or, that He has put you with your knowledges into His Alembic to distil from you for your permanent use, the glorious essences of Being? Read your own history in this life, apart from the age-long history! Read your own history in this life, its ups and downs, its shadows and its sunshine, its sorrows and its gleams of joy, its minor and pathetic hours when the soul has been burdened as those who sat by the streams of Babylon and whose harps hung on the willow, songless, and its times of real major song when it could not do other than praise the Lord, and you will see how the Great Love has been working through the Crucible to make your gold, the Love in your Being, glorious again, and also how ye have been passing in your experience, in your mental states, through the Alembic.

It is the heart that goes through the Crucible: it is the mind that goes through the Alembic. It is the heart whose gold is made beautiful by the searching fire of the energy of the Eternal Love: it is the mind that is made lowly and sweet and beautiful through the distillation of its elements and all its upgathered conscious history. It is through the heart, life is beautifully

411

fashioned: it is through the mind, the glory of that life is reflected. It is in the heart the Love Principle abides in its motion: it is through the mind its magnetic stream is to flow, through the thoughts, through the ministries, even unto the body.

The glory of earthly things is a beautiful glory, when it is the reflection of the glory of the heavens. The children who reflected the heavenly things upon this world are the children who are to reflect them again. They were able to reflect them, not simply as specula receiving upon themselves the glory thrown from outside. They had the power of the speculum when acted upon from the Radiant Presence, to throw that glory down upon the children who needed to behold it. Those are the children who are again to reveal the glory of that Love—that Love that knows no self, that knows no weariness, that knows no bitterness; that Love that is just Love, perfect Love. It is God in the very heart of the Being as the Great Love.

Children of the Father-Mother, for whom our very Being travails unto the day of the perfect realization in yourselves of that Love, and the complete distillation of all the essences of your Being through these being gathered up out of the flowers of your experience, and the fruits begotten through you from the Divine, that ye may make manifest what is that good, that true, that acceptable way of God; may ye now reveal the Love transcendent, and be the vehicles of the sweet breaths of Being poured forth upon the world. Having come through the Crucible yourselves, and out from the Alembic, and in your experiences, having been made radiant, gracious, hallowed, sweet and beautiful, in your life-service, let all your garments drop myrrh, fragrant, preserving power; all your raiment radiate the Glory of the Lord, being iridescent in nature, expressing the Radiance of the Eternal Light of the Eternal Love. Be once more the

412

world's healers, the world's conquerors. Comfort those who mourn with the divine thought, the divine knowledge, the divine consciousness. Speaking of the things ye now know, though ye know them only in Him and from Him. Speak with the full assurance of children who have realized, not as those who have learned from books—though learning from books has to be a part of the education. Speak as those who have gone through the Crucible and know, and the Alembic and understand. Yet never speak of yourselves as speaking from yourselves. No! Never even think of such a thing. The mind having accomplished its passage through the Alembic, surely has found the lowly state? And the love that has passed through the Crucible triumphantly as gold refined, surely knows that of itself it is nothing, and that all the power it has is of God? All is of Him—His Love in us; His Presence with us, and His Power in us. Without Him, we are nothing worth being at all; and apart from what He gives, we have nothing worth the holding.

We have spoken most directly to you; the hour has come. Embody in every way of your going, that Love; and in every service, the essences begotten of the distillation. Whilst being lowly in your consciousness, and selfless in your love, be great in the strength of His abiding with you and in you; majestic in your love, revealing of its sweetness, its graciousness, its lowliness, and its gentleness. So shall ye verily be the distilled Life-waters of the Eternal Love, the exponents and embodiments of that Love, the radiant children of the Kingdom once more, the living embodiments of His glory and His power.

413

The Two Arks of God.

The Ark upon the Great Deep.
The Ark within the Sanctuary.

In the Old Testament story two Arks are spoken of. One is said to have been built by Noah, and the other under the administration of Moses. The building of the Ark by Noah is associated with what is known as the Deluge. The building of the Ark under Moses is associated with the journeyings of Israel. The one was an Ark built to float upon the flood: the other was fashioned to go before the people and abide with them as a symbol of the Divine Presence.

THE ARK UPON THE DEEP which was said to have been built by Noah to preserve himself and his family and representatives of all the creatures from the destruction of the Deluge, had no relation as such to that unspeakable catastrophe which overtook this world. It was a mystical story representing the building of the Soul or the Sanctuary of man's Being. Noah represents a divine manifestation. It is a term embodying the Divine Principle that is in all Being, and is, therefore, to be understood as the Divine Principle within the constitution of man. It expresses the great Mystery whose operations fashion man, raising him up from lowly childhood into high degrees of spiritual consciousness, and even divine consciousness. In the process of divine outworking in the mystery of man's own Being, he has grown from lowly childhood to the high degree of consciousness obtaining on the human kingdom, and that yet higher degree realized by those who have come to know the Great Mystery. And in this path of spiritual evolution, the creatures represent degrees of life, of consciousness, and of manifestation. They are all gathered up into man's Being. For Noah's Ark is a story of the evolution of man.

When the Eternal and Ever Most Blessed One creates a

human Soul, or planetary world, or a celestial system, the beginning is lowly. From the Heavenly Arche from which he becomes, man has within himself all the latent potentialities which, when fully expressed, crown him as "Son of God." A planetary world is also, from its inception as a generating system, Divine. The celestial realms are the transcendent expression of the Majesty of that Love whose magnetic power holds all things within itself, and draws them to itself.

The going of the creatures into the Ark in pairs represents the processes by which man has grown into the high altitudes of consciousness and vision, desire and love, that he may occupy today. For he has within himself all that is beneath him—the true mineral world, the true vegetable world, the true creature world, along with the true human attributes. And he has all these in their two modes of manifestation called the masculine and the feminine, or the centrifugal outgoing creative force and the centripetal converging, returning, indrawing, nourishing, perfecting power. These things, so to speak, are in the basement of his Ark.

But the Ark is three storeyed, and he himself, when truly floating upon the bosom of the Great Deep, is in the upper storey, looking out from it into that vast Mystery by which he is overshadowed, even the mystery of God the Father-Mother. Man ascends from the basement of things, or the world of objective manifestation which first he enters when functioning upon a world like this, to the next storey where all his mental attributes learn to correlate in some degree the things he has observed in the world of manifestation, finding out their apparent meanings, and their relationship to each other. For he passes through the occult realm with its manifold mental states, ere he reaches that higher consciousness which we speak of as divine.

In an unfallen world the whole of this evolutionary process is spiritual. The path is spiritual. The outlook is spiritual. The manifestation is spiritual. The things observed have spiritual quantities and qualities. All the relationships are spiritual. There is nothing in the vision that has not its spiritual significance. For, in an unfallen world, all is in perfect harmony. All is beautiful manifestation. All is interpretive of high and holy things. Even the denser planes of manifestation are pure and beautiful. They are volatile as to motion, being wholly responsive to the divine attraction; and so there is harmony. The true evolution of man's Being is spiritual. It was always spiritual. And all the doctrines propounded by the evolutionary philosophies concerning the ascent of man from lower forms of manifest life are simply endeavours to interpret from observable phenomena, as well as uncertain hypotheses, the mystery of man's dwelling upon this world. There is evolution. It is ever spiritual. Its principle of action is divine. God is at the heart of all Being, whether it be in the perfect realization, or in the Principle just beginning to manifest.

Thus, from the very inception of the human Soul, the Divine Mystery of the Father-Mother was inherent in man. And it was always that Divine Mystery working up through him for individuated manifestation. Though the path of the ascent was from lowly states and through lowly forms, it was ever upward, still upward, and yet still upward through countless ages. And it was ever beautiful in manifestation until the crown was reached in the form known as the human. And then upward, still upward, and yet still upward the Being rose in its thought, in its desire, in its love, in its power, in its vision; its outlook ever

417

widening, its light ever increasing, the splendour of the Divine Mystery growing more and more wonderful within the Being, until the Soul was a perfect Sanctuary, an Ark capable of floating in its consciousness upon the great sea of the Divine Mystery, without disaster, without hurt of any kind, and at last resting in that divine consciousness known as the state of Ararat. For Noah's Ark was indeed God's Ark or Sanctuary of man's Being, the story being a mystical embodiment of the fashioning of man.

It is that Ark which is borne upon the Great Deep. The Great Deep is the Divine Mystery of Being. The Mystery of Being comes to the Soul as it realizes. Its realizations become as the result of the opening of the fountains of the Great Deep within it. All its springs are unlocked to pour forth the waters of their desire and energy, and through the outflow, to find that which they must needs find. The opening of the fountains of the heavens and the windows of the heavens, and the outpouring of the Divine elements into the consciousness, enable him to ascend into the realization of the great and glorious radiance of the Presence. The descent into his consciousness of the powers of the eternal world, powers which in man have their correspondence so that he is able to respond to them, gives him power to launch upon the Great Deep. The waters of experience form the Great Deep. And they become more and more so unto him. They bear up above the outer things, the denser planes, the Ark of his own Being, carrying it upon the bosom of the Great Mystery, bearing it thither to that lofty altitude known as Divine consciousness within the Soul, in which consciousness the Ark of Being rests upon Mount Ararat, or the summit of that state known as the Son of God.

Amid the vast mystery it is said that Noah sent out a dove,

418

and the dove returned. The word Noah implies that for which the dove stands. It is the symbol of the Spirit's descent. It is said that again Noah sent forth the dove, and the dove returned with an olive branch. The Divine Spirit in man is as a dove, which, sent forth, heralds peace, and returning, still as the Spirit, bears, into the consciousness of that Being, that which is symbolized by the olive branch— peace, the healing of peace, the ministry of peace upon the earth. But the olive branch is the symbol of that which gives forth the oil of gladness, the oil of anointing, and, therefore, speaks of that divine anointing of the Being through the Spirit by which it comes to rest upon Ararat and knows itself Son of God, one in the glorious consciousness of the Father-Mother.

*   *   *   *

THE ARK OF THE COVENANT. The Ark of the Covenant or Testimony is said to have been fashioned as a memorial of divine promise to go before Israel into the land that had been promised. It was said to have been built of Shittim wood and overlaid within and without with pure gold, gold well beaten out. Its dimensions were limited, being two and a half cubits long and one and a half thick. It has been represented as a portable symbol which could be carried hither and thither according to the journeys of the children of Israel. Upon the Ark there was built up another symbol called the Mercy Seat, made from pure gold, and upon the Mercy Seat there stood two forms representing Cherubim, facing one another, and with wings outstretched, but looking towards the Mercy Seat. This sacred Ark was not a house to dwell in. But it was to be the symbol of the dwelling of God with Israel. Consequently it was regarded as most sacred.

419

This Ark is said to have been carried before Israel as they essayed to cross the waters of Jordan, and when they entered the Promised Land. It had the power within itself to cause the waters of the Jordan to divide and make a passage possible for all Israel from the one side to the other side. It is said to have been carried by the priests of Israel around Jericho seven times, whilst the silver trumpets proclaimed the coming of the Lord, and that during the process of the seventh round the walls of Jericho fell. It is likewise recorded that in one of their conflicts with the Philistine powers, Israel were defeated, and that their Sacred Ark was carried off by the enemy; and also that Israel mourned because of all that they had lost in the sacred symbol of God's Presence with them, for they regarded that Ark as the most precious inheritance. It is further stated that the Divine Power came again upon Israel, and that they were able to recover the Ark from the Philistine hands which had taken it away. It is recorded also that the recovery of it brought back to them great joy, great honour, and great power. It is said that the Ark was treasured and guarded even until Solomon's temple was fully built, and that it found a resting place within the most holy place of that most sacred house. When that Ark was built it is narrated that there were placed within it to be preserved forever, Aaron's Rod, the Tables of Testimony, and the Manna.

That Ark of Covenant, which was also a Testimony, and which was the special inheritance of Israel, was and is none other than the Sacred Ark of the Divine Presence in the innermost sanctuary of the Being. It is the irradiation in the conscious life of the Divine Principle in man, and the overshadowing of that Principle by the macrocosmic mystery known as the Father-Mother. God's Covenant with man

420

is God's Testimony to him that he, man, as an individuated Being, shall know the Lord and adoringly rejoice in Him. God's Covenant with man is the Testimony of the Father-Mother that His child shall know that high estate named Son of God when the Great Mystery is realized, and man knows himself to be the sacred Ark of God's Covenant wherein is the Rod of the eternal power of Love, the inherent knowledge or wisdom of the Laws of Being operative in all things, and that Mystery Bread, the food or strength of God, the flesh and the blood of the Son of God in us, that Manna which is the Wisdom of the Love.

It is that Presence who goes before Israel, for Israel once knew that Presence. It is that Presence who divides the waters of Jordan as Israel once more passes in consciousness from bondage, and travail in the outer planes of ministry, into the land of new vision (or the old vision come anew), the land flowing with the milk and the honey of a great glad hope, and the efflorescence of all the flowers of love; a land to be once more possessed in high consciousness in manifold states. It is that Sacred Presence who brings to Israel once more the possession of the city of Jericho, the city of roses, the city of Angelic Love, with all the beautiful wealth which Angelic Love holds within its mystery. It is that beautiful Presence Israel lost through many ages, but had restored from time to time during their ministry in this world; the Sacred Ark which the Philistines took—those enemies to spiritual thought and desire and ministry, who took away the consciousness of the Presence on many occasions from the midst of Israel.

That Sacred Presence is again coming back to Israel. Each one hears the call to arise and shake himself free from all the humiliating conditions amid which he has had to lie down in this fallen world. Through the Day-spring from on high once more visiting Israel, that Holy Ark of the Testimony of the Lord is being restored. The Presence today goeth before Israel. The Presence has to speak once more from out the cloud until the Temple of the Christhood is again restored unto each of the children of Israel, and the Sacred Ark can rest again within the Soul's consciousness in the Most Holy Place, to be no longer as a sojourner and a wayfarer in a strange and weary land, or as a spiritual nomadic, moving from place to place and state to state, but to abide forever in this consciousness of all Israel within the Holy Place. The Ark of the Covenant with its Divine Rod of power—the Rod of the power of the Eternal Love; the Sacred Manna—the flesh and the blood or Life-substance of God realized as Son of God in the Being; with high illumination within the consciousness through the knowledge of the Laws of the Testimony in which the mystery of Being manifest and unmanifest becomes known: that Ark of the Mercy-Seat is now with Israel once more.

And how sacred that Ark is! That Holy Presence! That most glorious One! That transcendent vision! That Eternal Radiance within our sanctuary! That Ark of His Testimony from whose Presence we shall go out no more! That Ark of His Covenant where He doth speak face to face with us from between the Cherubim!

It is God in us. Let holy reverence fill us. It is the Lord of Love within each Soul. Let all love and revere that Glorious Mystery Presence.

The Theosophia

or

Divine Love and Wisdom.

LIFE'S
MYSTERIES
UNVEILED.

*THE
DIVINE
WISDOM.*

The Divine Wisdom expresses the Divine Love, for Wisdom is the Radiance or Light of Love.

The Divine Love is greatly dwelt upon, for the very Being feels the need for the realization of that Love, and craves more and more as it ascends, to be touched from that Love, healed, uplifted, gathered up into the Cloud of His Presence to find the Great Realization. The Divine Love expresses the potency in the Mystery of God, which draws the Being towards realization.

The Divine Wisdom is that quality in the Divine Love manifest in all true created things, whose marvellous Radiance attracts the mind, calls it to behold and enquire and search out, that it may discover something of the Mystery of Love itself, as the Mystery is revealed in all created and manifest life.

The Divine Wisdom is, therefore, the expression of the Divine Thought made concrete, for the setting forth of the purpose of Love, the nature of Love itself in its glorious purpose, and the ultimate for which all things have been created, even the purpose for which Being was individuated and expressed as Human Soul, child of the great Mystery of the Father-Mother.

You will thus observe, that the real nature of the Divine Sophia, is the Radiance of Love made manifest in manifold forms, in different realms, upon the several Kingdoms, and upon each plane and sphere within each Kingdom.

The Divine Mystery of Love is inseparable from the Divine Mystery of the Sophia; for Love is ever radiant; it is always beautiful; its manifestations have a glory of their own; in garments of purity are they manifested; and in states of perfect equilibrium, according to the Kingdom and Plane and Degree of their manifestation, are they to be found.

"ALL THY WORKS PRAISE THEE, O LORD! THEY MAKE MANIFEST THE GLORY OF THY LOVE."

Wherever you find true beauty expressed through form and colour and radiance and rhythm and fragrance and purpose of ministry, there, you may be assured, you meet with the Sophia of God, according to the Kingdom and the Plane and the Degree of the manifestation. There are no discordant elements in the Divine Wisdom. It casts no shadows by wrong thoughts. There are no hurtful vibrations sent forth from it through wrong feelings. The Divine Wisdom is the perfect expression of the Divine Love; and the Divine Love is absolutely perfect.

Such is the nature of the Wisdom or Sophia of God. The Theosophia means the perfect unveiling of His Wisdom.

The manifestation of that Wisdom is obvious. It is obvious upon all the Kingdoms where the Soul may function, except where the shadows dark and terrible have been thrown, and where the works of God are obscured or defaced. If the flowers are exquisite in their beauty of form, and multiple colour, and distinctive fragrance, and in that more inward and hidden quality named rhythm, or the motion of the Lifestream out of which they become; what shall we say of the Realms where the dark and terrible shadows have not fallen, where the Wisdom of God is not veiled, where His handiwork is not marred, but His Glory is beautifully reflected, where the Love lying behind all the manifestation is felt, and the Glory of the Love is most obvious as the sublime Radiance shining through the manifested Wisdom?

The Wisdom of God is the accompaniment of the Love of God in manifestation. It is manifest in the human estate. There is nothing more beautiful than the perfect human form. There is nothing more wonderful than a Human Soul, the Being who animates all the vehicles, even unto the outer form which expresses the grace, the majesty, the Mystery of Life. Most wonderful is the Wisdom of God revealed in the human estate, in the way the Human Being grows and unfolds, learns, realizes, evolves, becomes crowned from stage to stage, passing through state unto state, and rising from glory to glory. There is nothing more wonderfully beautiful than a Human Soul clad in Angelic garments. These are the garments of pure beautiful Love, made radiant by the Love, and reflecting the glory of The Divine Sophia, the Wisdom of God.

The complexity of the Being of a Human Soul is, in miniature, the complexity of a world. Its constitution, though it be only a microcosm, is potentially so marvellous, that a world is expressed in it and through it. So great are the potencies within its constitution, that the Ego or Being can realize the Mystery of Love itself, and know it; not only can touch its Realm, but realize it, and know it, and be of it as a part of the Great Mystery. And this "lot" or inheritance in the Great Mystery, is not found through mere affirmation or intellectual concepts and beliefs, but through and in manifested Being within the Sanctuary, where the Mystery of God the Father-Mother is found and realized. And through this realization of the Divine Mystery of Love, man has the power to apprehend unto the full comprehension and understanding, of the Wisdom of God, even the Divine Sophia. Only through Love is God realized. Only through such realization is God known. Only through such knowing of Him is the Wisdom of God unveiled.

Yet the Sophia is manifest everywhere. At every turn we see it. We breathe its atmosphere. We feel its vibrations

426

notwithstanding contrary vibrations coming from those elements which have been marred and shadowed and brought down. To *know* the Love of God is a triumphant state, betokening the victory over all things, and proclaiming the Being the inheritor of the Divine Sophia, one who understands the Mystery of the Wisdom and the Love of the Father-Mother. It is not of man. Nor is it begotten of any human system. It is potentially within everyone; but the Realization is of God alone. It is from Him; it is by Him; and it is in Him. It is from Him, because the gift is within us to be realized. It is by Him, for it is through His action and Overshadowing that our aspirations ascend, and our Being attains. It is in Him, for all realization is in the measure in which we touch Him and He abides in us. He Himself gives the gift of God which is Eternal Life—the Realization of Himself in His Love and His beautiful Wisdom.

*   *   *   *

In the unfallen days, that is, before what is known as the great Descent took place, life upon these planes was radiant. The children flung joy from them and about them. Their hearts were full of gladness. They sang and they danced in gladness, and their dancing truly expressed the rhythmic motion of soul. They had to grow, however, into the knowledge of the Wisdom of the Father-Mother. They had to grow into that knowledge, through the realization of His Love. But on the way, they were taught concerning the manifestations of that Wisdom and Love—the Love that created and the Wisdom that revealed—through the flowers, through the elements of the planet, through the motions of the stars, all the realms being touched by the wand of Love, which interpreted and transfigured them. *Science was a living art in those days.* Those who taught

427

knew. They did not merely search out and speculate; they came to give knowledge of the Divine Love and Wisdom. They were physicists and chemists and geologists. They were true astronomers, though the true term for them is astrologists. All the sciences were gathered up into the knowledge which they possessed. But their knowledge was not their possession through having gained from any material aspects taught in the schools. They were children of the Kingdom of the Heavens, the Sons of God. They were those who had, upon other Worlds realized something of the Divine Mystery of the Agapê and the Sophia, the Divine Love and the Divine Wisdom. They were of the Christs of God. During their settlement away up amid the sources of the Nile they were the Israel who, later, came down into Egypt and founded the great Egyptian religion, and passed into other lands as well, and came ultimately into Syria and were known in the Hebraic Scripture days as the Children of Zion and the Children of Israel. But in the Heavens they have always been known as of the Christhood of God. They were illumined souls who had realized the Love with its Radiance in great degree, apprehending unto vast comprehension of the Mystery of God, in nature, in the elements, in the flowers, in life, in the human estate, in the planetary world, in the Angelic Realms, and even in the Celestial and Divine Realms. They taught the supremeness of Love, and the glory of the Love of the Father-Mother. They gave it forth that that Love was the Life-Principle of every Soul, the magnetic centre of every Being. In a divine sense, it was the Pole Star towards which every Being's pole must point, the magnetic centre of all Life, holding all things, containing all Being, and setting all true Being in motion. And they taught that everything was the expression of Love. The flowers were

428

gifts of Love. They were concrete embodiments of Angelic thoughts. Their very substances were so transformed that the process of interior transformation and transmutation, was to become the expression of Angelic thoughts in the form, the substance, the colour, the fragrance, the uses. The Wisdom of God was interpreted through them, and the interpretation was in harmony with the Divine Wisdom given. The very elements, which were then perfectly beautiful, and obeyed the law of their own Kingdom, and the realm and sphere of their ministry on the earth, were understood by these Souls. They were, as we have said, true chemists and physicists, true botanists and physiologists, knowing interiorly the Wisdom of God, and able to see through all the objective manifestations, the inner significance of things. Their knowledge came from within. In their interpretations they proceeded from the without, inward, so that the children of the world were educated concerning the true expressions of the Wisdom of the Father-Mother. The motions of the planet were understood. Its relation and inter-relationships were well known. And the whole Celestial Hierarchy became unto them as a language of signs and wonders for expressing the Wisdom of the Father-Mother.

*   *   *   *

Owing to the great changes which took place, even those who taught the Love and Wisdom of the Father-Mother, found their vision becoming gradually veiled. From time to time they were taken away to inward states and Upper Realms where they were re-illumined and sent back. It was thus they came in different ages as Messengers and great Teachers and segregated communities of great Souls —not great in an earthly sense, but in an inward sense; Souls filled from the Divine. It was they who founded the

429

language of symbols, to preserve some outer expression of the inner Mysteries. It was they who founded the true Schools of the Prophets wherein the prophets taught the Mysteries. The Schools of the Prophets were not for the training of prophets, but for the teaching of the Mysteries by the Prophets or Illumined ones. They were of the communities who were gathered together in the different ages for the founding of the great religions. For they alone could understand the message of the Messengers. The Messengers were of themselves. Though at the time of their appearing upon the earth they came direct from the Heavens, yet they were of their order.

It was thus that they became segregated communities, able to receive from the Messengers the aspects of the Divine Love and Wisdom to be presented. It was thus there grew up in different ages what are known to-day as the seven Great Religions. There are many offshoots, and there are many systems which are purely ethical philosophies. We do not speak of those latter, but of the Great Religions, such as the two great religions of India, those of Egypt, of Persia, of Greece, of Israel, and that which has been received in the western world under the nomenclature of Christianity. In all of these the Wisdom of God was brought to the very threshold of the children of this world.

True, there were departments; and the elder children were taught in higher schools. But the Wisdom was reflected right down to the children. Those Teachers knew, as we said, the language of flowers, the language of symbolism, the language of the elements, the language of planetary motions, the language of Celestial motion and state, the language of Angelic life and ministry, the language of Divine realization in some degree.

Thus, upon every plane of consciousness they were able

to minister. Unto everyone who desired help, they were able to give of their oil, of their substance, of their light; for the Divine Light and Life and Love were in them. Yet they knew, and they taught, that the Wisdom of God, though shadowed forth in that way, could not be known through merely learning about it; and that all the language of symbolism, and that of nature in the flowers, and the elements, and planetary motion, and that of the Celestial Hierarchy, and also of Angelic life and ministry, and even of the Divine Kingdom, must be used as power by which the Soul would express itself in its onwardness and upwardness, applying the language it had learned, gathering up of the fulness poured forth upon its threshold, marching from state to state of spiritual consciousness, learning more and more, becoming more inward in desire, more intense in apprehension and perception, having the horizon ever enlarging as the Being rose, so that the comprehension became greater and still greater. For the Wisdom of God, like His Love, could only be known through realization, though it may be shadowed forth in beautiful form, in wonderful colour, in exquisite rhythm, in the sweetest of fragrance, in motion that is perfect harmony, in the glory of motion that speaks of Mysteries, in the language of Life that embodies itself in ministry, in the transcendency of Being that finds the goal. From state to state the Soul had to rise, recognizing, cognizing, relating and correlating, apprehending and comprehending, partaking more and more of the Wisdom of God as revealed and made bread—bread of the outward expression, bread of mental knowledge, bread for the desire, bread for the mind and the heart, until the Being, having transmuted all gathered on the way, became participator of the very Ambrosia of the Gods, which is the Manna that is the Substance or Flesh of the

Son of God. Thus did the Soul enter into a consciousness of all the vital forces of Being from the Divine Mystery, and know Him as the Eternal Love and the Eternal Wisdom.

*   *   *   *

The Coming again of that Wisdom unto this world, is the testimony of the Great Love. Its coming is manifest all around us. The return of the Children of the Kingdom who knew the glory of His Love in the Mystery of His Wisdom, is again made manifest. As they return they travail through their emotion, and they seek through their mind. They travail in their desire, and they essay to again apprehend fully, that they may comprehend with all the saints, the height and the depth, the length and the breadth of the Love of God the Father-Mother, and His Sophia. It is this travail of desire, this feeling after what was once a possession, this yearning again for the realization, which reveals the Return of Israel, the Children of Zion, the inheritors of the Divine Love and Wisdom. The travail of souls towards the Realization, is the testimony of the coming unto each one of the day of the Realization. The endeavour to find out and recover the Divine Wisdom again, is the sure testimony to the coming of the day of the Lord.

There are those who still search from without, to discover the Mysteries. And they do come at most wonderful things. But they view them all, with rare exceptions, from a standpoint that is altogether material. Although they may have wonderful spectacular through kaleidoscoping the elements in their interpretations of them, yet the secret cannot be come at in that way, nor the Wisdom of God discovered. Its adumbrations may be observed, or its shadowing forth be beheld. But there is only one royal road to the Heavens, and though there are many paths which may lead on to that road, yet all the paths must

432

converge upon that road. It is the Royal Road of Love— His Love, His beautiful, unfallen, immeasurable Love.

The Divine Sophia is a glorious reality, and may become the inheritance of the seeker; yet only through finding the goal of the Divine Love. The goal may be beheld, and its radiance apprehended through its marvellous scintillations; but the Vision is within the goal, and not outside. Even those who were of ancient Israel have to return to the goal of Love, to come at the full realization of the Mystery of the Divine Sophia.

True theosophy is to know God in His Wisdom, through having realized His Love. All that points towards that realization is the Path of the Theosophia. All the knowledge from the objective world's manifestations and motions, all the knowledge concerning nature's secrets, all the knowledge gathered concerning the wonderful manifestations in ancient times, must needs be transmuted on the way; for these things are not the Wisdom of God, but only the reflections of it through different Kingdoms, and upon different planes, into distinctive spheres of action and knowledge. The Wisdom of God remains up in the exalted heights of the Divine Realms, awaiting those who realize the Mystery of Love, to be their inheritance.

Love descends into the lowly estate of the individuated Being; the Wisdom of God remains transcendent to be discovered through the unfolding of the individuated Being, in the upwardness of its Life from state to state and from glory to glory, even until the Son of God be found within it, and it knows as a Son of God the glory of the Father-Mother in His Love and His Wisdom.

It is the Age of the Return, the Age that is prophetic, the Age that is burdened with glorious history to be manifested bye and bye. It is the age of the re-manifestation of Christ through the Christhood; it is the age in which the Love of God is to become a reality, and the Wisdom of God made manifest. It is the age and the time when the Lord Himself should come with a mighty trumpet, the heraldic message of the Heavens proclaiming His coming in the lives of Israel. It is the time when He should appear in the lives of all His children, the lives of those who knew Him, proclaiming His coming in the manifestation of Jesus Christ in their life, in their love, in the ministry of their love, in the radiance of their love. It is the time when He should come and bring all things to their remembrance, bring back the heavenly Wisdom to them, give them again the heritage of the Kingdom of the Heavens, restore to their consciousness the regnancy of the Kingdom of God through the Presence reigning within them. It is the day in which He would lift them up from their bowed down estates, and exalt them again in their consciousness, in their love, in their vision, and in their ministry, and cause them again to reflect the glory of the Inner Worlds. It is the day of the return of the Lord to make manifest His Love and His Wisdom—the most Sacred Agapê and the Divine Sophia. The glory of that Love and Wisdom will be displayed everywhere in a world healed, in life redeemed, in exalted ministry, in self-less and beautiful service, in Life clothed in the very garments of the Heavens and vibrant with the Love that knows no measure in its giving, Love begotten of God within the Sanctuary, Love that is the glorious realization of Himself.

*   *   *   *

Be children of the Theosophia. Wisdom is of Love. The more nobly you love, the more will the Radiance of the Love bring back to your vision the glory of the Lord of Love. And if for one moment you say to yourself, "I may have been there long, long ages ago, and I fain would dream so, believe so, yet when I look at my environment and behold the marring of mine attributes, and see how my visage must be heavily shadowed; when I remember how conscious I am of my limitations, of the very heaviness of my thought and my feelings, so that I seem unable to rise as I would; when I remember that though I know Love is the triumphant power, and is the very Mystery of God in me, and should be without measure and ever glorious, yet when I see how limited the output from my Sanctuary seems to be, how other than selfless my love appears to be in service, I grow hopeless, and think such heights could never be mine again, that such realizations are outside of the possibility of my finding, or, if it be that I am again to be the inheritor of such transcendent Love and Glory, it must be in ages hence after sore travail and great sorrow."

Such thoughts and feelings are worthy of the Children of the Kingdom, in the sense of being of lowly mind and gentle love and tender affection. But we have to repeat to you, it is the day of the Return, and even such shadowed thoughts and feelings are begotten of the past, and are part of your travail towards that Kingdom whose glory ye once knew, and which shall again be yours, with its power and its radiance. For they are the gifts of the Great Love unto His children. The Theosophia is expressed in the Mystery of your own consciousness of Being, and your desire to be like that Love. The Spirit maketh intercession within us in our unutterable groaning amid our travail. The Divine Spirit in us, our Sacred Flame, maketh intercession in language unutterable, and hasteneth the coming of the perfect realization. He who knoweth the mind of the Lord, understandeth our spirit, and doth read the language of its

435

motion, its desire, its purpose and its travail. So, come along. Come up higher, and fear not. Be once more embodiments of that Theosophia which is begotten of Love, and is Love's Radiance, first, within the Being, illumining it; through the Being, transmitting it; around the Being, transmuting by it the conditions which it finds, and live henceforth your child-hood to the Father-Mother Whose Mystery of Godliness is in you, the Mystery of Godlikeness, the Love and the Wisdom, the Agapê and the Sophia, with all the attributes of God miniatured in the world of your Being. Be of good heart. It is the Father-Mother's good pleasure to give you the Kingdom. Be great of heart. Press onward and upward. The Heavens are encompassing you. The great Cloud of Witnesses surrounds you. The Divine Presence is Overshadowing you.

"To Him who overcometh," saith the Lord, "will I grant to sit with me in my Kingdom" (that is, to reign in state, in consciousness).

"To him who attaineth, shall I give the White Stone"— the Glowing Stone or Sacred Flame of Love, whose Radiance filleth the Being with the consciousness of the Divine Sophia.

"To him who overcometh, shall I give the power to be a pillar in the Temple of God."

"To him who overcometh, shall it be given that Sacred Mystery Name which I shall write within him, even the Mystery of the Great Realization."

"To him who overcometh it shall be given that he hath right to the Tree of Life" the secret or Mystery of Being, of which none but the Gods may eat.

"He who overcometh shall be my Son. His light shall no more go down; and he shall no more go out from My Presence."

436

The Seven Golden Candlesticks.

*THE FASHION
OF THE
ADONAI.* In all Innermost Vision, there is always experienced the motion of that Breath which is of the Divine Mystery. When such visions are read, as in the Apocalypse, the Breath moves, through the vibrations set in motion by the very terms in which the vision is expressed.

That which is of the Innermost Realm ever touches the innermost. Its call is to the Being. Through its call, the Being's planes feel the action of the Breath of the Divine Mystery.

In the Presence of such a vision there is no room for superstition or idolatry. Upon the threshold of such a Sanctuary as that wherein such a vision may be beheld, there is no room for doubt or the shadow of fear, or any uncertainty as to the reality of it. As the Being bows before the Altar of the Sanctuary where such a vision is beheld, it knows itself to be a little child indeed, though verily in nature divine.

*   *   *   *

Here, in this Vision of the Seven Golden Candlesticks, we are at the threshold, aye, across the threshold, of the Great Sanctuary of His Divine Indwelling Whose children we are.

We will look first at the Presence. He was in fashion as the Son of Man, the divine formulated manifestation unto the soul of the Mystery of Being. The human form has more in it than seems obvious from the outer expression and interpretation, expressing as it does the transcendency of Life over all things, and the realization within the form through divine involution, the glory of the Lord of Being, through having the high consciousness of His Indwelling, the Mystery of His Presence realized in sublime fulness.

The Word of God is the Logos. The Lord of Life is not

438

the Logos individuated, like the Logos of the Celestial Hierarchies, He is the Lord of Love Who is the Alpha and the Omega, the Arche and the Sevenfold Amen. He is the First, out from whose bosom all manifest things become, and the Last, in whose Presence all Being is realized. Of course there is no first and last, or beginning and end, in the sense in which we have to make use of the terms in our human speech. For, to begin on the Divine Realm, is for a Manifestation to come out from the Mystery that ever is; and to consummate or end, is for the Manifestation to find its fulness of expression from out that Mystery, returning unto it again, as all Being must return, and even all substance in its manifestations called Things.

The Presence is the Logos Who is not simply Planetary Angel, but the very Mystery, the very Divine Being, the Father-Mother, Who is as truly in the individuated human unit as in the individuated human world, and as in the individuated Celestial System. The Mystery of our Life is the Mystery of God in us. The Mystery of God in us is the Mystery of a Presence. The Mystery of that Presence is the Mystery of consciousness in us; for our consciousness is the resultant of the motion of that Presence within our system. It is the Mystery of His Presence which gives conscious Being. It is the resultant of the motion of His Presence, when we are crowned with the glory of the Sevenfold Amen, even with that glory in its Onefoldness, Twofoldness, Threefoldness, up to Sevenfoldness. For all spiritual realization is begotten of the Indwelling of that Presence, and the fulness is the ultimate of spiritual experience, of soul expansion, of the Being's motion from, in, for, and with the Divine Mystery, the Presence within.

*   *   *   *

Now look at the Motion of that Presence. He walked

amid the Seven Golden Candlesticks. His motion was spiral. In Himself, as His fashion is described, He revealed the Glory of the Divine Mystery. His Radiance, called His hair, was white light, white as snow. His eyes were flames of fire like the Sardius stone. His raiment was marvellous to behold. The Word of His mouth was as that which consumeth, energizeth and divideth, like a flame of fire. His feet were iridescent with the radiance of His countenance. The ways of His motion were as beautiful as His Radiance.

The ways of the Lord are ever beautiful. The paths of His walking are always glorious. His footprints leave no shadows; they leave impressions of a radiant love. His motion consumeth in the sense of purifying. It divideth the elements, bringing each element into its true place. It energizeth, giving power to the elements, more potency to the Being, and to all the attributes increased strength for manifestation.

The motion of the Presence through our Being is the motion of One Whose ways are ever beautiful; Whose footsteps, so to speak, to carry out the metaphor, are more gracious than the footfalls of the angels; Who in His walking doth make the streams of Life magnetic, and flow and divide and become energized, exalted and radiant with the Light of His countenance.

When He moveth through a soul's thought, He doth touch it to the exaltation and the illumination of it. When He moveth through the emotion of a Being, He doth make it a stream of magnetic love, whose power is ever affluent unto healing, blessing and realization. That motion of His Presence is one that is felt when the soul doth stand upon that threshold where the vision is beheld. The motion of His Presence is felt within the Being before the threshold

440

is reached; for what may be considered strange disturbing elements, feelings, desires, emotions within the Being, are most direct evidences of His motion through the planes, testifying of His Dwelling within, and His moving unto the regeneration of the Being.

It is thus you may understand your innermost feelings when you cannot correlate them; the deep movements of your emotion, though unable to fully interpret them. Thus you may be somehow conscious that the movement is from the innermost Divine Realm, even when all the outer life seems, in its power and its glory, to be melting away. You may thus have a deep feeling that your Being is being drawn inward and upward, not to lose anything it ever held, but to be enriched from His Presence through the consciousness of His abiding with you. For He moveth amid all the planes that they may be enriched, and all the spheres of activity be made consecrate, even unto the outermost.

The motion of the Presence is as mysterious as the Presence Himself. But it is ever as beautiful as the very nature of that Love and Wisdom Whose children we are.

*　　*　　*　　*

And now look at the Seven Candlesticks. What were they? Who and what do they represent? It is said they were Churches which once were in Asia. In that respect they would represent the ministry of the Christhood community who came to this world. That would be the Celestial interpretation of them. The Seven Churches that once were in Asia, were the seven great communities of Beings sent from the Divine World for a ministry representing the Divine Love and the Divine Wisdom in most glorious embodiments, interpreting the Divine Love and the Wisdom in the inner realms of consciousness and vision, manifesting the Divine Love in the life of service upon the

441

intermediary planes and spheres of service, even unto the outermost where the objective realm had to be touched and interpreted in relation to the Divine Love and the Divine Wisdom.

That the Presence walked amid those Churches we can well understand. None could know the Divine Love except through realization; nor what the Divine Sophia stood for, except through that vision which is begotten of the Great Love in realization. They alone could be the interpreters of such a Love; of the Mystery of that Love. And they alone could be the revealers of the glory of that Love. Only such souls could be the true interpreters of the Divine Wisdom and manifestors of the Divine Love. Only they who had known it in the innermost could interpret it truly in the outermost, correlating through all the planes.

The Seven Churches of Asia were the churches or communities of souls who were the inheritors in consciousness of the Divine Presence in varying degrees for manifestation. The Ecclesia of God is an inheritance. For God's Church is not anything outward. It is an inward state of most blessed experience; the lot or inheritance of the soul; the Kingdom of God as a living consciousness within the Being. It was only through the motion of the Presence amid the planes represented by those Seven Churches that they were able to catch the radiance and receive the glory and the power of His Kingdom which was within them, and reveal unto all the children of this world that glory in its ministry. The Presence moved through the planes represented; each community having its distinctive ministry, but all correlated in the one; none greater than the other; none higher than the other; but all lowly servants of the Most Blessed One, and glorious venues through which His Presence could be revealed and power manifested. That message was given again for the churches who once were in Asia, to bring back to them the real vision of the Presence within, to awaken every one of them to the consciousness of their childhood to the Great Mystery, to recall them to the threshold where the Presence maketh His dwelling unto the recognition of His motion through the planes of the Being.

The land of Asia is the country or state of the Spirit. It is not the Sacred Flame, but it is the land of the ministry of the Sacred Flame. It is the realm of the service of those in whom is found the Sacred Flame. That message is for such souls and communities to-day. Behold He cometh! Every eye shall behold Him and see Him. And even they who have pierced that Love shall know of His piercing, and mourn for having caused such sorrow. But the sorrow will be unto healing. Behold He cometh! and all the children who formed those churches shall again behold Him. They shall again be conscious of His becoming within them. The motion of their planes shall testify to His becoming. His motion through the planes of their Being will heal them, and equilibrate them, and glorify them again, giving to them the abiding consciousness of His Love and His Wisdom. For them the abiding consciousness of the Divine Love and the Divine Wisdom is to be in that soul state where the Vision Splendid is gloriously realized, and from which glorious state the Being goes out no more. For them there is no more any night.

*　　*　　*　　*

That message is for you, children of the Hills and the soul's Uplands, who once knew the glory of that Love in its great Mystery, and the Radiance of it in the consciousness of the Divine Sophia or Wisdom of God, through functioning upon those planes that enabled you to touch the Divine

Realm of consciousness even until the attribute of Omniscience from the Divine lay upon your attribute so that you understood Innermost Things, in which there were given to you great vistas of the Eternal Mystery. The vision is for you today that once more ye may behold the glory of your Lord, even that Love that has been so pierced, and that ye may give forth the testimony of that Love in the states of Jesus Christ. The vision is for you, that again ye may know the glory of the Divine Love and the Divine Wisdom, and regain the power to embody the Love and interpret the Wisdom. The Vision is for you that ye may have such intensification of realization of the Presence as will enable you to manifest Jesus Christ as the children who walk clad in white, who love the brethren, and who are real meritorious workers; children whose very deeds are vibrant with the Love of God, whose every ministry is the expression in some degree of His Love and His Wisdom, in the fashioning of things of beauty from the desire, through the thought, into the action, and thus becoming His real mediators, manifestors, and interpreters unto the children of men.

With such a regained power the very elements will become transformed, and all earthly ministries will bear the transfigured light.

Of the Planet itself shall it be spoken again, that its Angels are as the Stars carried in the right hand of that Most Glorious One—the right hand signifying the Divine Power, creative where necessary, redemptive, exalting, glorifying through renewing.

For the Seven Stars are the Seven Angels of the Seven Spheres. They are the Angels of the planetary spheres in the planetary manifestation. In the Divine Realm they are Elohim, the Seven Stars or Sacred Spirits, whose Light is

444

our Radiance, and whose motion is through all the spheres of Being, creating, fashioning, enriching, perfecting, exalting, transfiguring.

In the planetary life the Angel shall again rejoice, even Lucifer, one time Star of the Morning, whose fall was even unto the hells. He shall arise again, and his crest shall be restored within the planetary spheres, through the blessed manifestation of the Seven Churches that once were in Asia. For these will be in Asia again.

And the Planet will be healed. Its streams of sorrow will be dried up. Its woundings will all be made whole. Its passion will be purified, and again made beautiful and divine. Its power will be altogether gloriously spiritual, and its radiance once more the perfect reflex of the glory of the Lord.

For the coming of the Presence into the consciousness of the children of the Kingdom, and its manifestation through their life and ministry, will bring about the restoration of all things, the healing of Judah, the making whole of her rent Kingdom.

For all Israel shall be fully found and restored, and the Kingdom of the Father-Mother be once more regnant in them.

What an *outlook!* What an *inlook!* What an *uplook!* What depth of significance lies within the vision given on the Isle of Patmos!

Behold ye His becoming, Who is your Lord and your King!

Behold ye the Life unto which He calleth you back, the glory He would have you share, the divine nature of the work He would accomplish through you, the beauty of the ministry unto which He would appoint you! And let your response be in full measure.

445

The Divine Science of Numbers:
Showing how the Mystery of God
and the Soul is expressed in
manifold Degrees through
and in the Numbers,
One to Twelve and
Thirteen.

Numbers are associated chiefly with commercial calculations, or historical or scientific research, or with the numbering of a people. Few dream of the great mystery that lies within numbers as signs. The universe itself is expressed in numbers. The art of creation embodies the most glorious expression of the use of numbers. All the celestial hosts are numbered. All worlds have their number, and none is overlooked. All souls are numbered and not one is forgotten. The stars of the heavens are not only numbered as systems and members, but they each have their number. This system, of whose great household we are members, has its number, and each member of the system also has its number. Even every child of the Father-Mother upon each of the members or planets, has its number.

As it is in the Above, so is it in the Beneath. As is the Overshadowing, so is it in that which is overshadowed. As it is in the Heavens, so is it in the Realm which reflects the Heavens. As it is in the Macrocosmic or universal manifestation, so is it in the Microcosmic or individuated miniature manifestation. There is harmony in all the works of God, from the Divine Realm unto the outermost Kingdom of manifestation.

This great truth lies at the heart of much to be found in the sacred writings. When reading those writings, the numbers that are used are often taken by the reader to express that which is numerical; but to the seer the numbers would express that which was of the state and quality of Being. This will be clearer to your vision as we endeavour to unfold a few aspects of this vast theme.

In the sacred writings we meet with quite a number of terms which would seem to indicate numerical value, but whose real value is found in the mystic sense. It is thus

447

with the numbers which proceed from 1 to 13. Beyond that number there are others which are of great value, but they are multiples of the numbers which lead up to 10.

The Divine Mystery of Being is expressed in the 1. God the Lord of Love, Life and Light, is One. He is the I AM. Our language very inadequately expresses what is meant by that saying. It means *The Sublime Mystery*. I AM THAT I AM is the language used in the old-world story associated with the vision of Moses called the Burning Bush. And how marvellously it expresses that which cannot be comprehended by the mind, though it can be in some degree apprehended as to its significance by the mind. I AM THAT I AM! The Mystery of Being, which no man of himself knoweth. The Divine Mystery which nevertheless, can be known. Yet only through Realization.

All numbers are evolved from the 1. All numbers converge to the 1. All numbers are summed up in the 1. He is the I AM THAT I AM. He is the Sum of all Being, of all that is expressed in the Divine Realm, of all that is manifest in the Celestial Realms, of all that is revealed and interpreted in the Angelic Realms, of all life manifested on the Kingdom beneath the Angelic, named the Human. The Kingdom of Man is the outer expression of the glory of Being, man being in himself the embodiment in miniature of the Mystery of Him who is the I AM THAT I AM. There is no other who may be spoken of in the absolute sense as being the One, but that One who is the Sublime Mystery of all Being. We are all but little children of that most glorious Mystery.

We said that all numbers were evolved from that 1, and that all found their full expression in that 1: hence we take 2. And in the number 2 we have the expression of perfect combination, unification, harmony; the two-fold power, the two-fold mode, the two-fold harmonious action; positive and negative, the Fatherhood and Motherhood of Being in the I AM THAT I AM.

And even as we have the Divine Mystery of the 1 in us, so have we of the 2; for from that 1 there is evolved within us that which is expressed in the 2, the Fatherhood-Motherhood in the centrifugal and centripetal powers of our Being, the outgoing and the incoming, the creative force, the return of that which is created Being, fashioned and perfected. The modes of function are two—the positive, or the willing and the acting; the negative, or the reception of that which is willed, to express it in beautiful fashion. On the outer planes these are expressed in the masculine and the feminine. Neither is greater than the other, though the one expresses the out-going, and the other the incoming. The one is the positive expression of the will; the other is the negative or indrawing and nourishing power. They are the two modes of manifestation, the Fatherhood-Motherhood revealed in perfect oneness of life and purpose on the outer even as in the inner realms.

From the one, the two are manifested. I + I. From the one and the two, three become. I+II=III. For the embodiment is in the third, and hence we speak of the Trinity.

The Trinity is spoken of after the fashion of the Father, the Son, and the Holy Ghost. That is the orthodox traditional school interpretation of the Trinity. But the Mystery is expressed in the Father-Mother—the Divine Spirit and Substance—manifested in His Son who in the Divine World is Adonai. He is the concrete embodiment (if we may use such an expression of the Eternal Mystery in relation to the Divine World, for it is not concrete as understood in the outer) of the Mystery of Elohim in the Divine Realm. In the Celestial World, in the Angelic Kingdom, in the Human

449

Estate, He is Son of God. He makes of the Soul in the human estate, a Son of God. In the Divine Absolute Realm, He is the Son of God. Each child of the Father-Mother is, in its Divine Principle, created a Son of God. Being evolved from that Divine Mystery, each has that One, in miniature, who is the I AM. In each one is the two-foldness of that One who is the I AM THAT I AM—Fatherhood-Motherhood; centrifugal, centripetal; positive, negative; masculine creative, feminine upholding, endearing, nourishing, perfecting.

The Trinity is in us. We have the One, and we have the Two, and we have the Three. We are of God. We are of His very Substance, and of the very Spirit. Of the Son of God we partake, of His Flesh and His Blood, the Substance of His Being, and the Lifestream of His Being.

What a mystery is here! In yourself there is that One who is no person or mere individual, but who is the Eternal Being whose Mystery, in miniature, you are to express, embody, reveal, interpret, showing forth the splendid Reality. And in doing so, the Being acquires that property in the Holy Trinity that is expressed by the term Holy Ghost, which is also Holy Ghaist or Guest. And that most precious inheritance means the indwelling conscious-ness of the Presence of God, the realization of the Divine Mystery in that degree which enables the Being to be conscious of Divine Overshadowing, and the Presence within the Sanctuary. For the Holy Guest is, in principle, within each one. The Trinity is the inheritance of each soul. In the outer world even for purposes of manifestation, there is the expression of triune life in fatherhood, mother-hood and childhood. And where these are pure and beautiful, and the very Radiance of God encompasses the home and the lives, there is nothing more heavenly. It is truly Angelic, though the Angelic properties are manifested in the outer Human Kingdom, as the Angelic World is the inner Human Kingdom.

*   *   *   *

Having broken the mystery thus far to you, we will now find in some of the other numbers, more profound things than we have been wont to see in them.

Four is used as a sacred number. The Holy City is foursquare. Three signifies a cube, four a square. But foursquare is even more than a cube. Four is a symbol of the Four-fold Kingdom of the Soul. It expresses the Being of man. It is the measurement of his Temple, the Mystery of Being in him. He has the Divine Kingdom, the Celestial Kingdom, the Angelic Kingdom and the Human Kingdom. The Human Kingdom is perfected. It realizes the Angelic, and is clothed upon with it. The Angelic state, or the state of beautiful love, realizes the Son of God in Sonship to God, the state that is named Celestial state. There the Being arrives even at the Divine estate, the highest, the most inward, the most glorious, the most blessed realization of the Sublimest Mystery, the Mystery of God within.

Four represents the four dimensions. What are the four dimensions? Length and breadth. Those are accounted one and two dimensions, because they are superficial. Their measurement is by what is called superficial feet or inches. But there is height, and there is depth. There is a length and a breadth. And there is a circumference. And there is a transcendency or power of ascension, and a descendency or power of fathoming. And there is also a realization that takes them all in, and realizes from the innermost centre.

There are even more than four dimensions when a soul stands in the innermost and can look through all the planes of

451

consciousness, Elohim illumining every plane of the Being. The Elohim are Seven. The Divine Man sees through the seven dimensions.

Four is a sacred number. The Temple was four-square; and it had four courts. The Holy City is four-square. Man has his four courts also, being the correspondence of the Holy Temple of the Lord. Four also expresses the cross. Four is a most beautiful number. In the full ministry for which it stands, all numbers are gathered up; for its ministry is four-fold. It ministers within each of the Kingdoms; and it ministers through all of the Kingdoms. In itself it contains the Divine Mystery, for the cross is in God, and God is in the cross. And the bearing of the cross is the sharing of the Divine Mystery of Being in blessed ministry unto souls. The carrying of the cross, and even the crucifixion which the cross sometimes brings to the bearer, is part of the travail of that Mystery who is the I AM THAT I AM, in the creating, fashioning, transfiguring, glorifying of worlds, systems, children; and, where systems or members of them have missed their way, finding them again and bearing them back in the Bosom of the Love which the cross expresses, unto perfect healing, motion, ministry; transforming, redeeming, healing, transfiguring them once more.

Thus number 1 is the Mystery, 2 the Divine Duality, 3 its Trinity of manifestation, and 4 its Motion through the Kingdoms of the Being of man, expressing his travail, even in an unfallen world, up through those Kingdoms to the great Realization.

Five, in a very human way, is taken to represent the senses. There are five senses. But there are also five fingers on each hand, for the thumb is a finger, though it is otherwise expressed. There are five toes on each foot.

So that man has qualities that are expressed by five fives. He has twice five in toes, and twice five in fingers, and he has five senses. If we were taking this in progressional numbers, and dealing with them in a lower degree than we are at present, we would say this to you, that the five fives represent twenty-five.

Now twenty-five represent seven. Such evolution of the numbers makes the sacred number 7, revealing man to be an expression of Elohim. And it is remarkable how this should come to pass, since 5 is the symbol of the Star. There are stars with five points, and stars with six points; and those who pursue occult studies accept five, the pentagram, as symbolizing the Divine Man, and the six as Solomon's Seal.

Those of you who have been through Masonry will know a little about the occult historical significance of Solomon's Seal. But in the pentagram, five as the symbol of the Divine Man, is the real Seal of Solomon. Solomon means the Divine Man. The Solomon of ancient story is the Divine Christ. The Temple of Solomon is the Temple of the Christhood, reared by Solomon the Divine Christ within us. Five, as the pentagram, expresses Adonai in the five-pointed star, the symbol of Christhood; the symbol adopted by the Order of the Star and worn by the members indicating that they are looking for a world teacher to come who shall be as Christ to the world. The Divine Man is a soul who has realized the Four-fold Kingdom, one in whom Adonai has found realization, one who has come to know the depth of the Mystery of the Four-square Temple which is within man,— the Divine, Celestial, Angelic expressed in the Human,— and whose Sonship to the Divine is become a reality, who knows the Mystery of the Fatherhood - Motherhood

453

sufficiently within, to know it is The Reality, and to be conscious of being equipoised or polarized in that great Mystery.

Now, five is the Seal of Solomon; it is the mystery of the Divine Man realized.

Six is also the Seal of Solomon. It is the Seal of creation.

The wisdom of Solomon is the knowledge of the Divine Laws of creation. The intertwined triangles represent the outgoing manifestation, and the return unto perfect Being. It is the mystery of the creative outgoing and return realized in the Divine Man, who is symbolized in the pentagram. The Triangle is a symbol of the Divine. And the combination of the upright and the inverted interlinked Triangles representing centrifugal and centripetal powers, forms the seal of the Wisdom of Solomon.

And if five and six be so marvellously sacred in relation to the human life, that they express in the Being, first, the Realization within of the Presence, and secondly, the understanding of the Divine Mystery in its creative outgoing and manifest Wisdom, what shall we say of that number which is spoken of as the most sacred, the number seven? As 1 is the Eternal Mystery, and 4 the Four-fold dimension, and 5 the realization through those dimensions of the Mystery in Adonai, so 7 is the revealing of the Divine Mystery of Adonai as Elohim.

Elohim are the Seven Spirits of God.

Elohim are found in the Seven glorious Principles of Creation.

Elohim are expressed in the Seven glorious Radiations called the Seven Thunders.

Elohim are revealed in the Amen, which, when seven-fold, completes the whole motion of our Being, through the planes of our Spiral, which are Seven.

454

The Seven most sacred Fires, are the activities and revealings of Elohim.

The Seven Sacred Altars, are the Altars upon each of the divine planes of Elohim.

The Seven Sacred Censers, are the ministries rendered by Elohim.

The Seven Angels who take from the Sacred Fire within the Censer, and pour out upon the earth unto its healing, are the ministrants for Elohim.

The Mystery of Creation is so great and yet so beautiful in unity, so mysterious and yet so obvious when the veil is drawn, that Seven may be seen to play a great part in all the realms. There are seven planes within the Divine Kingdom. There are seven planes in the Celestial Realm. There are seven in the Angelic Kingdom. There are seven in the Human Kingdom. And there are seven in our human life. They express themselves on the outermost realms of mani-festation in the human estate in wonderful ways, and right through the whole of the Human Kingdom. There are seven great Races: all other races are sub-races or offshoots from them. There are seven orders of manifest life in nature, in its fruits, from the lowest to the highest degrees. There are seven orders even of the Creatures, not counting, of course, the orders which are strangers, being departures from the true races, and ought not to have been. Our own life is seven-fold. From the outermost to the innermost, it is expressed in seven. The Sabbath of the Lord, the most exalted realization, is said to be the seventh day. In colour and in tone the seven appears. In music in the seven tones with the semi-tones: in the full score in the seven octaves. From the White Light are the seven true colours; and these have their seven sub-divisions. For there are seven sub-divisions or expressions of each colour,

455

thus making the perfect number run right through all things, and in their action, perfect all things, evoluting in seven times seven, forty-nine, in colour, ultimating in the white; in tone, in the fiftieth note that makes the seven octaves complete; in a soul's Being, that gives to it the Jubilee, so that it can sing its Jubilate Deo.

The mystery of the seven is therefore great; and it is within us. It speaks of the pentagram as the Divine within us realized, and as the mystery of Solomon's Seal, the Wisdom of God as an inheritance, the Love and the Wisdom of the Infinite One expressed in us. Even our senses, symbolized in the number five, are soul powers given to us to sense through all the Kingdoms. For these do not belong to the body. Though it is quite possible, and does happen often, that men and women through habit can build up senses in the body which are not true senses at all, and which may veil the true senses, and even prevent them from sensing.

The mystery of seven, how great it is in its ever-deepening and far reaching revelations! In the vision in the Apocalypse, One walked amid the Seven Golden Candlesticks. The Candlesticks represented the Light-bearer. The Candle symbolizes that which gives the Light. The Light is the Sacred Flame of the Spirit of Elohim upon each plane. And He Who walked amongst them was none other than the Lord of Being. He walks amidst the planes of our Being, amidst the Candlesticks of our Sanctuary.

The seven works out in many other ways, such as in the Seven Churches in Asia and in the Seven Baskets of Fragments.

Now we come to a very interesting number—8, and you will understand that all these numbers are sacred and that you are not to fear any of them. There are those who speak of numbers as being bad, and as having an evil influence. Do not believe it. Nothing is bad if you do not make it so. The number 8 is really formed by two circles laid on top of each other. That is the perfect form of the number.

Eight symbolizes two Realms, the Angelic and the Celestial. When men sought to build sanctuaries in the form of an octagon, they were sensing something. Some parts of a few of the beautiful sanctuaries in this country are built in the form of an octagon. Eight is not only the note that completes the octave and begins the next, but it is the number which symbolizes the mystery of Knighthood for ministry, that most sacred seal, that beautiful symbol of ministry which the Knights Templar used, and which has come down to us as the Maltese Cross. The real Maltese Cross was formed like a four-fold radius vector, a central radiating point, and each vector grading and culminating in the fish's tail, giving to each two points or apexes, so that the four made eight points, and symbolized the sublime mystery of Knighthood. The real Knights Templar were not such as those historically written and spoken of, but the Knights of the Mysteries. They were men, and women too, who, having overcome the elemental realms, realized great things within themselves, and were consecrated to the Life of the Divine Mystery in the Cross. The Cross symbolized sacrifice. It signified Realization. It expressed the outpouring of the Divine Life. It testified of the call of the Soul to blessed ministries. And it spoke of the Four-fold Kingdom; of the Divine Mystery of each Kingdom; of the Human realm as being as full of the Divine Mystery after its order, as the Angelic is as full after its order as the Celestial, and the Celestial as full as the Divine. It symbolized the most glorious heritage of Knighthood for the Being. It was also the symbol, at one time,

457

of the Gift of the Spirit. The symbol of the Divine Spirit was not unlike our capital S. And the Knight had the Spirit; for the Spirit was his sword, and by the sword he conquered. So his was a most sacred number. He was of the eight—8, the Angelic and Celestial.

And now we will look at some numbers which are associated very specially with states of consciousness symbolized in the Christian churches.

The number 9 is the square of 3: cubed it makes 9. Three times three make nine, and three times nine make twenty-seven, and two and seven in progressional numbers make nine. Nine is the number of the Jesushood. It expresses Knighthood in manifestation, even as the mystery of the Seal of Solomon is interpreted in the seven, and the ministry of the Knighthood expressed in the number 8, and the mystery of the pentagram revealed through the Knighthood as the Eternal Love—Adonai. Jesushood is the beautiful manifestation of the Divine compassion and pity in the healing ministry of the Knighthood of Love.

And after that number you come back to the One. There is no higher number till you return to the One. You cannot get beyond Jesushood, till you return to the One. The One is the Divine Mystery. That Mystery is in 10, although in the Divine Science of numbers, ciphers usually do not count. They are sometimes used to express terms, states, quantities and qualities. When you pass beyond nine, you are in the first house of the Divine Mystery of the Christhood. In Jesushood, love is known and manifested, but it is the love of the child, the love which is child-like in its joy. It is the love of Being, the love of serving, the love that has power to rejoice.

In the Christhood, that state is transcended. There is still joy; but the cup may be filled with other than joy.

458

There is still gladness; for the soul sees beyond the lower state. But the life may be called to give up all its joy. There is vision, and the vision is transcendent; but in the outer planes, the light may be veiled because of some ministry. It is the Mystery of man's Being, coming back to the consciousness of the Divine Mystery realized in the Houses of the Christhood. And there is nothing that confronts the soul so greatly as that Mystery, when it awakes to find that it is all about it; that the Mystery runs through all things, and is within itself.

Nor is the Realization of that Mystery found in ten. There were two disciples who enquired of John the Baptizer where Christ dwelt, and he said "Come and see!" and they went with him, it being about the tenth hour. They entered in with him. Now, that means that they were in Jesushood, and were approaching the threshold of the Christhood state and ministry. Hence the enquiry. It was about the tenth hour, the first House of the Christhood realization. They went in to learn the first degree of the Divine Mystery. But the full realization comes later.

The number eleven is but the square of one. You know how the number is used in Christian teaching. The eleventh hour is viewed as the last opportunity. It is said that there is still hope, even to the eleventh hour.

But this is not its mystic meaning. The eleventh hour is one that is most sacred. It is an hour of tremendous realization. It is the symbol of that which is beautifully sacred, even as thirteen is most profoundly sacred in its meaning. Eleven is the hour when the Mystery is becoming manifest—not only being sought for and learned about, but becoming manifest as the two-fold Divine Power realized within the Being, that of the outgoing sacrificial power, and that of the indrawing force. These are represented

459

in the Cancerian, Arian powers, a desire to possess and to hold, but only to possess of God, and to hold from God, in order to minister.

The eleventh hour is the hour of the second degree, the initiation into the middle court of the Christ-Temple, as the tenth hour is the initiation into the first court. The past degrees of Jesushood are found in the outer court of that Temple. The Divine Mystery is coming to the soul in that House of the Fatherhood. The Duality of God is being realized in the manifest positive and negative marvellous creative potencies within the Being. To the Soul, it is the house of the manifestation of a Mystery that touches every Kingdom, and every plane of every Kingdom of Being, revealing itself even in the lowest degrees. It is thus of high Christhood. The eleventh hour is, therefore, the hour when your very travail after the realization is about to find fulfilment in a measure of understanding of the Mystery of God within yourself as the Father Principle and the Mother Principle, the glorious Love and Wisdom of the Eternal Lord of Being.

And then you come to the third degree. The third degree is expressed in the sacred numbers of One and Two, making Twelve. The number ten often occurs in sacred writings, so does the number twelve. There were Twelve Sons of Jacob, there were Twelve Tribes of Israel, there were Twelve Parcels of Land. In the Celestial Heavens there are Twelve Zodiacal Signs. In the Christian Scriptures there are Twelve Disciples who become Apostles. There is also the Sacred City whose foundations are Twelve; whose life is expressed by Twelve Precious Stones; whose Gates are Twelve; and whose Gates are crowned with Twelve Pearls. Likewise there flows from out that City the River of Life upon whose banks there grows the Tree

460

of Life whose leaves are for the healing of the nations: that Tree bears twelve manner of fruits.

As seven is the compound of the three which represent the Trinity, and the four which signify the Four Dimensions and Four Kingdoms, so Twelve is the compound in multiple of three and four. Three and four make the seven; three times four make twelve. When each dimension is added to the life, and multiplied into the life, the City lieth Four-square. Its length and breadth, its height and depth are equal. It has Twelve Foundations built in discipleship expressing apostolic ministry, and prophetic realization of the perfect vision of the Son of God, the Lord of Being who is the Temple thereof. It has Twelve Gates in its Walls, the Walls being built upon the Twelve Foundations. The Gates are three-fold power upon each Kingdom by which the soul cognizes, receives and realizes in the Human estate, the Angelic Life, the Celestial consciousness, and the Divine world. Three lie Eastward. They are of the innermost. They are the Love-Principle, the Life-Principle and the Light-Principle—the Trinity of Being in us. Three lie towards the West. These are the outer gates of the Human Kingdom made beautiful until each gate is as a pearl, meaning a glorious conquest, a victory, an attainment, an overcoming, a realization. There are three in the South. These are the Gates of the Angelic World of our Being when the emotion is beautiful, its passion purified, and its gates become as precious pearls. Three Gates are in the North. These represent the Celestial Realm of the mind when its powers are all redeemed. These Gates give the power to receive Divine Intelligence, to understand its import, and to reflect its glory.

Twelve is the number of the City of Zion, the Holy City It is the number of the Christ realization. And the square

461

of twelve is the expression of its ministry. The square of twelve makes one hundred and forty-four, the number of the Household of Israel. Ciphers are added on to make the Sum of the Square 144,000. But these do not count. In progressional numbers, 144 represents the manifestation of the Christ ministry in Jesushood. 144 make 9. The Christ Light is manifest through Jesushood. When a Soul divinely ministers upon these planes, the ministry must be through Jesushood. Whatever the Christ ministry may mean in its transcendent realizations, it must be given through Jesushood. Jesushood represents Love. Love is full of compassion. Love is ever beautiful and full of pity. There is no other way of effective soul ministry. Thus it may be understood that the perfect ministry of the Household of Israel, or those souls who realize the Divine, is through Jesushood.

Thus we have the most glorious evolution of numbers from the One, the return to it as you enter Christhood where the Mystery is first apprehended within, in the tenth and eleventh Houses, and in the Twelfth House, realized as the Son of God. For twelve makes three (1+2 =3), and three is the Trinity, the Divine Mystery, the Divine Unity of that Mystery, and the Realization of it in our childhood and our Sonship to the Father-Mother.

Now we come to another number that we could not leave without unveiling its secret to you, because it is related to the twelve. It is the number Thirteen. What sad things have been said about it! How often it has been blamed for disasters. The superstitious amongst the people, have regarded it as tragical in its influences. Yet Thirteen is most beautiful. If there were twelve disciples and the Master, they made Thirteen. If there were twelve knights around the table of King Arthur, with King

Arthur they made Thirteen. Thirteen symbolizes the Divine Christhood. It is the number of ministry. Twelve is the Christ realization. Thirteen is a Divine Christhood manifestation. It is the Mystery in the One, the Realization of it in the Three, the revealing of it in the Four (1 and 3 make 4)—the four-fold dimension. It symbolizes a soul in perfect realization of the Presence with the twelve degrees or powers of Being represented in the Twelve. As we have said elsewhere in writing upon the Labours of the Soul and the Training of the Twelve, the Twelve Disciples represent the attributes of the Being, and the Twelve Labours of the Soul, the path by which the attributes become beautiful. Twelve, therefore, signifies the powers of the Being expressed on the four-fold Kingdom, three on each, like the Three Gates; and Thirteen is the Being with the powers in the centre, the Holy City with its Twelve Gates and Pearls or Degrees of Attainment, the Being and the Twelve foundations, the Apostolic discipleship, the Apostolic ministry, the Prophetic illumination. So great is the Realization, that the City hath no need of any earthly sun; for the Lord is its illumination. The Divine Radiance is its luminary. No more any outward light is needed by the Being; for the Indwelling Presence reveals all things unto the Soul.

Numbers will thus be seen to be most sacred. The Divine Mystery of your own life is expressed in numbers. Ye are numbered. Nay more! The very state of your life is expressed in numbers. When you read occult books about numbers being unholy, fateful, disastrous, bear this thought in remembrance, that He Who created all things, the Eternal Mystery of Being, brought into manifest expression all numbers, and gave them their mystic significance. In His creation there is nought that is lacking in beauty, or true form, or exquisite harmony. There are no discordant elements in the Divine World. Every tone is perfect. There are no false colours there. All radiations are exquisitely beautiful. Numbers have their power of tone and radiation. All numbers should therefore be beautiful. They may be beautiful. Aye, they will be beautiful, if we be beautiful in our thought, in our purpose, in our love, in our giving of ourselves in blessing in our sweet ministries one to another, and in our consecration to the Great and Holy Love. May ye see more and yet more in it of the ever-deepening Mystery that may not be unveiled just now. May you find in it an ever enriching sense of the value of your own Being as a child of the Father-Mother, and of the glory of the Life unto which He hath called you. For unto this end are ye all numbered as the stones of that Sacred Temple which will contain within itself evoluted numbers. For ye are to be as living members of the Temple of Christhood, every one of whom is numbered, that ye may know more and yet more of the length and breadth, the height and the depth, of the Love of God and the Wisdom of God expressed in Nine and Ten, Eleven and Twelve. Aye, that ye may find the fulness of that Life expressed in Thirteen—even Jesus, Christ, and the Lord.

Unto Him be the power, and the glory, and all the hon - our; for the Kingdom within us is His, with its Mystery of Apprehension, Comprehension and Realization. Him we would adore. Him alone would we ever seek to serve. To embody Him in all our attributes and ministry, would be our chiefest and holiest yearning and endeavour, and thus to reveal the Divine Mystery through His Love, and the Radiance of His Love, finding beautiful expression in our own manifestations in all Life and Service.

464

INDEX

TO

"LIFE'S MYSTERIES UNVEILED"

ASTERISKS DENOTE PRINCIPAL REFERENCES
MAINARTICLES INDICATED BY BLOCK LETTERS.

466

468

The Order of the Cross
FOUNDED OCTOBER 1904

AIMS AND IDEALS
(FOUNDATION STATEMENT)

TO ATTAIN, by mutual helpfulness, the realization of the Christ-life, by the path of self-denial, self-sacrifice, and absolute self-abandonment to the Divine will and service:

It is of these things that the Cross as a symbol speaks. It stands for the Sign of the Order of the Cross, because its three steps are those which have to be taken in order to arrive at that Estate which it symbolizes. It speaks of the quest after the humble spirit and the pure heart. It speaks also of that further state of realization when the Soul gives itself in absolute abandonment for the Divine Service. The Three Steps are:-

PURITY OF LIVING
PURITY OF THE MIND
PURITY OF THE SOUL

Thus to endeavour by example and teaching to win all men to the love of Truth, Purity and Right-doing.

To proclaim the Brotherhood of Man, the essential one-ness of all religious aspirations, and the unity of all living creatures in the Divine.

To teach the moral necessity for humaneness towards all men and all creatures.

To protest against, and to work for the abolition of, all national and social customs which violate the teachings of the Christ, especially such as involve bloodshed, the oppression of the weak and defenceless, the perpetuation of the brutal mind, and the infliction of cruelty upon animals, *viz.*: war, vivisection, the slaughter of animals for food, fashion and sport, and kindred evils.

To advocate the universal adoption of a bloodless diet, and the return to simple and natural foods.

To proclaim a message of peace and happiness, health and purity, spirituality and Divine Love.

SYNOPSIS OF MAIN PUBLICATIONS

THE MASTER sets forth the Inner Meanings of the Master's Teachings and gives a true picture of Him as He was in His Life, public and private. The Birth Stories and the Allegories of the Soul are revealed in their true setting; with the Teachings on the profound Mystery of the Sin-offering, and the Allegories of the Soul's Awakening. ISBN 0-900235-05-5

THE LOGIA contains the chief utterances of the Master, in the form in which they were spoken by Him. Here they are restored, including the real Mystic Sayings, found in the Synoptic Records, the Gnostic Record, the Pauline Letters, and the Apocalypse, containing remarkable histories of the Soul, the Planet, the Ancient Christhood Order, and the Oblation or Sin-offering. ISBN 0-900235-06-3

LIFE'S MYSTERIES UNVEILED gives the Path of Discipleship and Aids to the Path of the Realization. It includes definitions of terms in their relation to these Teachings and many answers to questions asked at Healing and other Meetings. The principal theme of the volume is Initiations of the Soul. ISBN 0-900235-07-1

THE DIVINE RENAISSANCE, Vol. 1. i. The Message. The Divine Adept. The Superstructure of Man. ii. The Eternal Mystery. A Divine Apologia. The Seat of Authority. iii. The Path of the Recovery. The Redemption. The Divine Purpose of the Oblation. The Mass and the Oblation. Altars and Sacrifices. The Flame before the Altar. ISBN 0-900235-08-x

THE DIVINE RENAISSANCE, Vol. 11. i. Unto the Great Silence, Science and Religion. The Angelic Realms. Corpus Christi. The Sabbath of the Lord. ii. Beginnings of Historical Christianity. Pentecost. The Advent of Paul. The Stone the Builders Rejected. The Church of the Living Christ. The Seven Sacraments. iii. A Renascent Redemption. The Seven Thunders. The Healer, Manifestor, Redeemer. The Obedience of Christ. Our Lord and Our Lady. The Three Altars. iv. A Divine Oratorio. The Ministry of the Gods. The Divine Government. The Cosmic Consciousness. The Regnancy of Christ. ISBN 0-900235-09-8

THE MESSAGE OF EZEKIEL. *A COSMIC DRAMA*. The Office of a Prophet. The Purport of the Book. The Divine World Unveiled. The Distinction given to Israel. The Mystery of Tyre and Zidon. The Pharaoh of Egypt. The Arising of Israel. The Logia of the Prophet Ezekiel: with extensive Notes to the *Logia*. *The Logia of Israel*. Vol. 1. ISBN 0-900235-10-1

THE MYSTERY OF THE LIGHT WITHIN US. *With 17 coloured plates by Amy Wright Todd Ferrier*. i. The Luminous Cross and the Cross of the Elohim. ii. The Spectra of Souls and Stars. iii. The Solar Fashion. iii. Auric Glimpses of the Master. iv. Celestial and Divine Estates. v. A Holy Convocation. Jacob's Ladder. The Adamic Race. The Secrets of God. The Girdle. The Blessing of Israel. A Divine Rhapsody. ISBN 0-900235-12-8

ISAIAH. *A COSMIC AND MESSIANIC DRAMA*. i. The Unity of Divine Revelation. ii. The Prophecy. iii. The Word of the Lord. iv. A Divine Drama. v. The Mystery of the Sin-offering. vi. A Momentous Promise. vii. The Triumph of Adonai. viii. The Drama of Israel. ix. The Sign of the Cross. x. The Daysman of Israel. xi. The Appointed Redeemer. xii. The Five Cities of Egypt. xiii. The City of the Sun. xiv. The *Logia* of the Prophet Isaiah: with extensive Notes. *The Logia of Israel*. Vol. 11. ISBN 0-900235-11-x

PITY   COMPASSION   LOVE

SELF-ABANDONMENT

REDEMPTION

The Order of the Cross

SPIRITUAL
AIMS AND IDEALS

The Order is an informal Brotherhood and Fellowship, having for
its service in life the cultivation of
the Spirit of Love towards all Souls:
Helping the weak and defending the
defenceless and oppressed; Abstaining
from hurting the creatures, eschewing
bloodshed and flesh eating, and living
upon the pure foods so abundantly
provided by nature; Walking in the
Mystic Way of Life, whose Path leads
to the realization of the Christhood;
And sending forth the Mystic Teachings
unto all who may be able to receive
them — those sacred interpretations
of the Soul, the Christhood, and
the Divine Love and Wisdom, for
which the Order of the Cross stands.

SELF-SACRIFICE

REGENERATION

SELF-DENIAL

ILLUMINATION

SERVICE   DEVOTION   PURITY

LIFE'S
MYSTERIES
UNVEILED.

478

0790607294 7.